W9-BZY-584

ABC's
OF THE
BIBLE

READER'S DIGEST

ABC's OF THE BIBLE

**Intriguing
Questions and Answers
About the Greatest Book
Ever Written**

The Reader's Digest Association, Inc.   Pleasantville, New York / Montreal

ABC's OF THE BIBLE

Staff

Editor: Kaari Ward
Art Editor: Robert M. Grant
Senior Staff Editor: Edmund H. Harvey, Jr.
Senior Editors: James Cassidy, David Rattray,
    Suzanne E. Weiss
Research Editors: Diane Zito (Chief), Sandra
    Streepey Burgheim, Mary Jane Hodges
Senior Associate Editor: Thomas A. Ranieri
Associate Editor: Donna Campbell
Art Associates: Judith Carmel, Colin Joh,
    Nancy Mace
Editorial Assistant: Jason L. Peterson

Contributors

Editor: Joseph L. Gardner
Research Editor: Josephine Reidy
Picture Editor: Marion Bodine
Copy Editor: Harriet Bachman
Indexer: Sydney Wolfe Cohen
Writers: Robert M. Brown, Charles Flowers,
    Robert Kiener, Claudia McDonnell,
    Donald Pfarrer, Thomas L. Robinson,
    Anne Shepherd, Deborah Shepherd,
    Bryce Walker

Reader's Digest General Books

Editor in Chief: John A. Pope, Jr.
Managing Editor: Jane Polley
Executive Editor: Susan J. Wernert
Art Director: David Trooper
Group Editors: Will Bradbury,
    Norman B. Mack, Kaari Ward
Group Art Editors: Evelyn Bauer, Joel Musler
Chief of Research: Monica Borrowman
Copy Chief: Edward W. Atkinson
Picture Editor: Richard Pasqual
Rights and Permissions: Pat Colomban
Head Librarian: Jo Manning

BOARD OF CONSULTANTS

Principal Consultants

David Noel Freedman
Professor of Biblical Studies
The University of Michigan
Professor of Hebrew Biblical Studies
University of California, San Diego

Thomas L. Robinson
Former Professor of Biblical Studies
Union Theological Seminary (New York)

Contributing Consultants and Writers

David Graf
Professor of History
University of Miami

Lawrence Grossman
Director of Publications
The American Jewish
    Committee

Ronald S. Hendel
Professor of Religious Studies
Southern Methodist University

Nahum M. Sarna
Professor Emeritus
Department of Near Eastern
    and Judaic Studies
Brandeis University

Gerald T. Sheppard
Professor of Old Testament
    Literature and Exegesis
Emmanuel College of
    Victoria University in the
    University of Toronto

Dennis E. Smith
Associate Professor of
    New Testament
Phillips Graduate Seminary

The Scripture quotations contained herein are from the
Revised Standard Version of the Bible, copyright 1946, 1952,
1971 by the Division of Christian Education of the National
Council of the Churches of Christ in the U.S.A.
Used by permission.

The credits and acknowledgments that appear on pages 320
and 321 are hereby made a part of this copyright page.

Copyright © 1991 The Reader's Digest Association, Inc.
Copyright © 1991 The Reader's Digest Association (Canada) Ltd.
Copyright © 1991 Reader's Digest Association Far East Ltd.
Philippine Copyright 1991 Reader's Digest Association
    Far East Ltd.

All rights reserved. Unauthorized reproduction, in any
manner, is prohibited.

READER'S DIGEST and the Pegasus logo are registered trademarks
of The Reader's Digest Association, Inc.

Library of Congress Cataloging in Publication Data
ABC's of the Bible
    p. cm.
    Includes index.
    ISBN 0-89577-375-9
    1. Bible—Miscellanea.   I. Reader's Digest Association.
BS612.A25   1991
220—dc20   90-45962

Reader's Digest Fund for the Blind is publisher of the Large-
Type Edition of *Reader's Digest.* For subscription information about
this magazine, please contact Reader's Digest Fund for the
Blind, Inc., Dept. 250, Pleasantville, N.Y. 10570.

Printed in the United States of America

About This Book

In setting before us the magnificent story of God and his people, the Bible does not always pause to fill in details, specify the relationships among individuals and families, or describe what happened before and after an event. Even experienced Bible readers are sometimes puzzled by the significance of an action, the meaning of a phrase, the context of an idea. ABC'S OF THE BIBLE is for the person who wants to explore such things.

A Bible scribe at work, page 296.

Its more than 400 questions have been carefully formulated to bring to light the kind of information that will give readers new insights, wider perspectives for appreciating the Scriptures. The questions are arranged in eight topical chapters, starting with "The Beginnings," which considers the foundations laid in Genesis, and ending with "The Bible Through the Ages," which relates the still unfolding drama of the Bible as a book, the most far-reaching and influential one of all time.

Throughout ABC'S OF THE BIBLE more than 100 informational features supplement the question-and-answer text. Background boxes illuminate traditions and customs of biblical times and examine the turbulent social and political currents that swirled around the people of the Bible. Story boxes retell many best-loved moments, such as David's humbling of Goliath and Jesus' walking on the storm-tossed Sea of Galilee. Short, incisive word boxes track words like *shibboleth* from their biblical origins and explore the various scriptural meanings of words like *love* and *call*. Most of the more than 300 illustrations in ABC'S OF THE BIBLE are the creation of artists inspired by the Scripture to transform biblical stories into enduring works of art. Finally, in using ABC'S OF THE BIBLE, the reader is never more than a glance away from the Bible itself, for alongside each of the hundreds of quoted biblical passages is the precise source of the quotation: book, chapter, and verse.

—*The Editors*

Contents

Led by David, a procession enters Jerusalem with the ark of the covenant: 14th-century painting, page 53.

Chronology of Bible Times

2000 **AGE OF PATRIARCHS**
Abraham leaves Mesopotamia for Canaan.
Sodom and Gomorrah destroyed.
Hebrew patriarchs in Canaan: Isaac, Jacob, Joseph, and his brothers. Joseph is sold into slavery in Egypt.

1700 **SOJOURN IN EGYPT**
Joseph interprets Pharaoh's dream and rises to power in Egypt.
Jacob's family settles in Goshen.
Hebrews enslaved.

1400 **EXODUS AND CONQUEST**
Ten plagues occur.
Hebrews, led by Moses, escape from Egypt.
Moses receives Ten Commandments at Mount Sinai.
Hebrews wander for 40 years in the Sinai Desert.
Joshua leads invasion of Canaan, the Promised Land; fall of Jericho and Ai.

1200 **PERIOD OF THE JUDGES**
Twelve tribes settle areas of Canaan; local wars ensue.
Judges rule Israel during periods of war. Samson is betrayed by Delilah; conquers Philistines.
Israelites ask the prophet Samuel to name a king.

EARLY MONARCHY
*1020–Saul is designated first king of Israel.
Young David defeats Goliath.
1000 *1000–David becomes king of Judah, captures Jerusalem, and rules united kingdom.
*961–Solomon inherits throne; builds temple; unpopular tax policies lead to division of kingdom
at his death in about 922.

DIVIDED KINGDOM (see also page 191)

Judah (southern kingdom)	**Israel** (northern kingdom)
*922–Rehoboam becomes king of Judah.	*922–Jeroboam I sets up sanctuaries at Bethel and Dan.
*917–Egypt invades and weakens Judah.	*876–Omri builds new capital at Samaria.
	*869–Elijah denounces worship of foreign deities.
*842–Athaliah seizes throne, introduces Baal cult.	*842–Jehu destroys Omri's dynasty; weakened kingdom subdued by Syria.
*837–Joash repairs temple, pays tribute to Syria.	
*783–Uzziah reestablishes peace and prosperity.	*786–Jeroboam II regains lost territory; Amos and Hosea deplore social injustice and moral laxity.
	*746–Anarchy after Jeroboam's death.
*735–Under Ahaz, Judah becomes vassal of Assyria.	

900 *(appears to left of the timeline, near the 917/876 entries)*

Judah (southern kingdom)

*715–Hezekiah attempts rebellion.

*701–Hezekiah is forced to strip temple to pay tribute to victorious Sennacherib.

*687–Under Manasseh, Judah continues as Assyrian vassal; foreign altars allowed in temple.

*640–With Assyria's power waning, Josiah establishes sweeping religious reforms.

597–Jehoiachin surrenders to Babylonia; Jews deported.

*597–587–Under Zedekiah, Solomon's temple is destroyed and Jerusalem falls.

RETURN TO THE HOLY LAND
539–Cyrus the Great crushes Babylonia.

538–Jews return to Jerusalem and rebuild temple under Zerubbabel.

*458–Ezra outlaws mixed marriages and reinstates covenant between God and Jews.

*445–Nehemiah rebuilds walls of Jerusalem.

INTERTESTAMENTAL PERIOD
332–Alexander the Great conquers Holy Land.

*330–Samaritans build their own temple, confirming religious schism.

301–Holy Land under control of Alexander's successor, Ptolemy I of Egypt.

*300–200–Judea is staging ground for several battles between Seleucids of Syria and Ptolemies.

*198–Judea comes under Syrian rule.

*167–Maccabean revolt against Syrian desecration of temple.

*164–Rededication of temple.

*142–63–Hasmoneans, descendants of Maccabees, rule Judea.

63–Roman general Pompey captures Jerusalem, extends Roman rule to Holy Land.

40–Parthians invade, put Antigonus II on throne; Herod flees to Rome.

37–King Herod the Great rules Judea as puppet of Rome.

BIRTH OF CHRISTIANITY
*7–John the Baptist is born; Jesus is born.

4–At his death, Herod's kingdom is divided among his three sons.

26–36–Pontius Pilate governs Judea; Herod Antipas controls Galilee.

*28–Jesus begins his ministry in Galilee.

*30–Jesus' crucifixion and resurrection.

*35–Followers of Jesus begin to spread the word outside Palestine; Paul converted.

*47–Paul begins missionary journeys.

*50–62–Paul writes letters to churches.

*65–Christians persecuted in Rome; Apostles Paul and Peter executed.

66–Jewish revolt against Rome.

70–Romans destroy temple in Jerusalem.

*70–95–Gospels and Acts of Apostles are written.

Israel (northern kingdom)

*721–Israel falls to Assyria, and a number of inhabitants are deported; deportees from other provinces settle there.

A model of the "molten sea," an enormous bowl that stood outside Solomon's temple in Jerusalem.

* Dates are approximate.

Timeline markers:
700
600
400
200
A.D.1

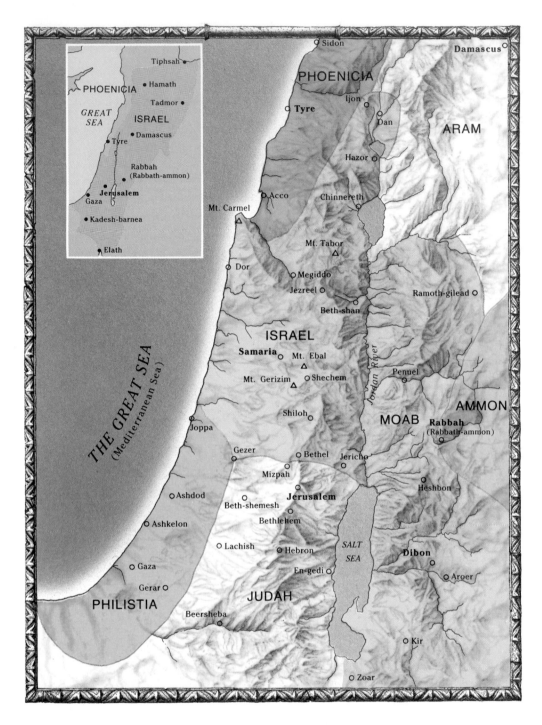

THE LAND OF THE OLD TESTAMENT

The Israelite monarchy reached its greatest extent in the empire of David and Solomon in the 10th century B.C. (inset). But after Solomon's death the vassal states that David had conquered regained their independence and the kingdom split in two: Judah in the south and Israel in the north (above). The northern kingdom was destroyed in 721 B.C., and the region gradually evolved into the territories of Samaria and Galilee. Judah was overthrown by Babylonia in 587 B.C. and reduced to a minor province. In the second century B.C., Galilee, Samaria, and Judah, called Judea, were reunited by the Hasmonean kings.

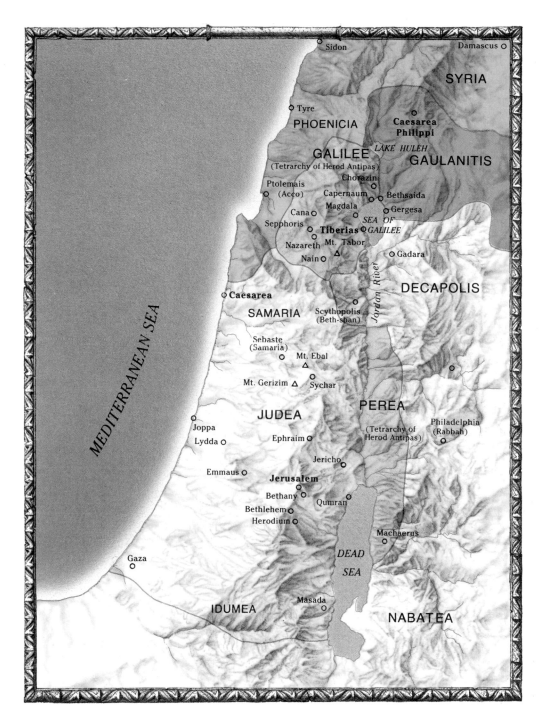

THE LAND OF THE NEW TESTAMENT

In 65 B.C. the Roman general Pompey marched on Judea and overturned the Hasmonean dynasty. When Jesus was born, the Romans were in power. They had installed their own governors or relied on loyal allies like Herod the Great. After Herod's death his kingdom was divided among three of his sons, Philip, Antipas, and Archelaus. In A.D. 6 the Romans deposed Archelaus and took direct control of Judea, Samaria, and Idumea, creating a minor Roman province administered from Caesarea. Galilee, where Jesus lived, remained under Antipas.

THE BEGINNINGS

Like a cherished family tale that is told again and again, the Book of Genesis grows richer each time we read it. Its very name, from the Greek word for origin, implies a perpetual fascination with our beginnings, for it addresses, in the simplest of terms, the most profound and enduring human questions: Who are we? Where did we come from? How did it all begin?

Every civilization has asked such questions and suggested answers—from the ancient Babylonians, who traced mankind's origins to the victory of the gods over the powers of chaos, to certain New World Indian tribes, who believed that the universe took shape when their ancestral deities leapt into a fire. Modern science takes a view that is as sweepingly dramatic as any primitive myth. Everything we know, from the smallest atom to the most distant star, physicists say, began some 15 billion years ago as an infinitesimal point of energy, which burst suddenly into being and has been expanding ever since. But of the mechanism that set this process in motion, science can offer no answer.

The most satisfying answer still comes from one of the world's oldest living documents of human faith, the Bible. The universe, it is written in Genesis, began with God. In the opening chapter of this first book of the Old Testament, God calls forth his creation through a simple yet supreme act of divine will. Day and night, continent and ocean, a landscape burgeoning with life—all these emerge in rapid succession. God's final creative gesture, of course, is man himself, a creature fashioned in God's own image and thus endowed with a spark of divine spirit.

The dream of a perfect world, like the one in Genesis, pervades virtually every human culture. Yet invariably the reality falls short, often because the dream is corrupted by man himself. And so the familiar story unfolds—Eve's temptation by the serpent, Adam's partnership with her in disobedience, the expulsion of both from Eden, and the destiny of toil and sorrow that ensues. Cain's murder of Abel is only the beginning. Adam's descendants grow so heedless and unruly that God is forced to express his anger and sorrow in a massive rebuke, the universal flood.

All the great biblical themes take initial shape in the early chapters of Genesis. The conflict between good and evil, faith and apostasy, courage and moral cowardice, appears here in purest form. Man's primary place in God's divine plan, and his consequent responsibilities, are firmly established. And permeating every verse is the life-giving presence of God himself. Though never described in full, the deity of Genesis is presented as a real person—paternal, accessible, and profoundly concerned with mankind's spiritual welfare. Like a stern but loving father, he punishes man's transgressions; but ultimately, like a devoted and selfless parent, he forgives.

Often the instrument of man's redemption is a single individual—like Noah before the flood—who is chosen because of his unquestioning faith. And in the process, as man becomes reconciled once again with his maker, a new and deeper bond of trust is established between them. As a sign of his covenant, God places his bow in the heavens, thereby transforming a weapon of war into a symbol of peace and hope. If only people will live up to their part of the bargain and subordinate their wayward impulses to God's sacred commandments, they may return in spirit to the Eden of Genesis.

Much of the appeal of Genesis derives from the easy, direct manner in which the story is told. The language of its verses is dignified yet vivid, and each familiar episode moves swiftly from one to the next, like scenes in a play. The men and women who walk through its pages typify the many aspects of human nature—heroic or villainous, wise or foolish as the case may be—and the roles they play are clearly defined. Supernatural elements keep stealing in, in the form of talking serpents, sword-wielding cherubim, and the like. This is the stuff of folk legend, of simple tales that reveal deep moral truths.

By long tradition, the Bible's first five books—Genesis, Exodus, Leviticus, Numbers, and Deuteronomy—are the words of God as set down by the patriarch Moses, but modern scholars suggest that the authorship is more complex. Most of these early stories derive from ancient Hebrew folk tales, which themselves were often adapted from even older Semitic legends. In some instances, two versions of the same tale have been woven together, as in the creation and flood accounts, with the result that minor conflicts of detail occur from verse to verse. But the overall dramatic thrust is always consistent.

Starting in Chapter 11, after the story of the tower of Babel, Genesis undergoes a significant transformation. Until this point the Bible has recounted the saga of mankind as a whole, from its primordial beginnings through its troubled early years. But now the focus narrows to concentrate on one specific people, the ancient Hebrews, and their special relationship with God. From here on the events in Genesis move into the spotlight of verifiable history.

Top left: God enthroned, from a 13th-century manuscript.

Days of Creation

GEN. 1:1

GEN. 1:31

HEB. 11:3

Did anything exist before creation?

With the opening words of Genesis—"In the beginning God created the heavens and the earth"—the curtain rises on the Bible's great drama. Out of a formless void, a watery abyss churning in darkness, God made a world that was bright, beautiful, and teeming with life. It was a world in which everything was "very good," as the Bible says at the end of the first chapter of Genesis.

Later generations of thinkers and teachers who pondered the story of creation after the ancient traditions were first written down (sometime between the 10th and 6th centuries B.C.) concluded that God had created the universe out of nothing—*creatio ex nihilo*—by the divine word. This idea was expressed in the New Testament: "By faith we understand that the world was created by the word of God, so that what is seen was made out of things which do not appear."

Yet the Genesis account does not offer explicit support for the later doctrine. It focuses far less on what existed before creation than on how the world began. Every bit of illumination, order, and purpose that separated the creation from chaos was the work of God.

In striking contrast to the Genesis creation story, other ancient, non-biblical creation stories from the Near East typically involve titanic battles of a god against chaos, personified by a sea monster. The most famous of these tales is a Babylonian epic called *Enuma elish,* which sees the world created out of killing and mutilation. Composed before 1000 B.C., the story tells how the god Marduk slays the monster Tiamat and forms earth and sky from the halves of her broken body. In the Genesis account, however, there are no battles or conflicts of any kind. Though chaos gives way to God's creation, it is neither an enemy nor a rival.

The six days of creation can be arranged in three sets of related events. On the first day (top left) God created light; on the fourth day (top right) he made lights for the day and night. On the second day he made the dome of sky to divide waters above and below it;

How long were the days of creation?

GEN. 1:5,8,13

"And there was evening and there was morning, one day . . . a second day . . . a third day." In stately procession, the days marched by as God brought order and beauty to primal chaos.

14

on the fifth he created all creatures of the waters and birds of the sky. On the third day he made dry land and its plants; on the sixth he created animals and humans to inhabit the lands. This illumination appears in a 17th-century Armenian Bible.

dawn to dawn. As for the length of the days, the Bible is evidently describing 24-hour periods—a notion reinforced in Exodus, where the seventh day of the week is consecrated to rest because on the seventh day of creation God rested.

Some scholars have attempted to reconcile the days in Genesis with the vast ages of the earth, as suggested by geological discoveries. But lengthening the days of creation into eons seems futile, since it still fails to bring the biblical accounts of creation into agreement with scientific evidence. Perhaps that's because the days of Genesis 1 follow a literary pattern and are not intended to provide an exact chronology.

What is a firmament, and what are the waters above and below it?

On the second day of creation God placed a "firmament in the midst of GEN. 1:6 the waters" and called this vast divider heaven. The waters below it became the seas; those above, the heavenly ocean that men could not see but knew existed by observing the rains that fell from it. The deluge later loosed on an evil world was an unprecedented catastrophe in which the heavens opened and the fountains of the deep burst forth, causing a torrential downpour and a rising sea level.

The word *firmament* is derived from a Hebrew word suggesting beaten metal. In the ancient world the vault of the skies was perceived as something akin to an upside-down bowl over the earth into which God had fixed the sun, moon, and stars—a striking example of his handiwork. The image of a solid dome is echoed in the Book of Job, where God is said to have "spread out the skies, hard as a molten mirror." JOB 37:18 And both Isaiah 40:22 and Psalm 104:2 liken the heavens to a vast tent erected by God, under which his people could dwell.

GEN. 1:5   The phrase "and there was evening and there was morning, one day" suggests that Genesis is following the Hebrew tradition of reckoning the day from sunset to sunset. But since Genesis also says that the first day began when God made light, it can be argued that this reflects the earlier Hebrew practice of counting days from ✳

15

LORD GOD. *In the Genesis 1 creation story God is simply called God, but in the parallel creation story that begins in Genesis 2:4 he is referred to as Lord God. The word Lord stands for Yahweh, the Hebrew name of God, which was represented by the four consonants of his name, YHWH.*

Because devout Jews thought Yahweh was too sacred to pronounce, they substituted the word Adonai (my Lord) when reading aloud from the Bible. Nevertheless, in giving God a personal name, the Bible conveys the idea that he is a living presence.

Why were the sun and the moon not named?

GEN. 1:14 To shed light upon the earth and "to separate the day from the night," God made two lights, a greater light and a lesser light. We call these heavenly bodies the sun and the moon, but Genesis never mentions those names. Though this may seem like an error or oversight, it is in fact an affirmation that there is only one biblical God.

Many of ancient Israel's neighbors worshiped the sun and moon as their deities. By not naming them, Genesis plays down their importance. As mere lamps in the dome of the heavens, they are signs for days, seasons, and

On the fourth day of creation, God placed the sun and the moon in the firmament, as shown in this 14th-century English psalter.

years, but little more. Thus God's supremacy is established at the outset of the biblical narrative, and no rival gods are permitted to challenge him.

Does Genesis say that humans resemble God?

Before undertaking his supreme creation, God announced his intention to make man in his image and likeness. The Hebrew word for image usually refers to a statue (often used in the Old Testament for pagan idols), while a different word for likeness suggests a physical resemblance. Later generations interpreted the terms more generally, however. They thought of themselves as resembling God not in a physical sense, but in a spiritual sense by possessing a soul, intelligence, and the capacity to make moral distinctions.

The New Testament added to the notion that man was created in the image of God by proposing that Jesus was the sole embodiment of divine perfection.

What does it mean for man to have dominion over the earth?

Having created man and woman, God blessed them and told them to "be fruitful and multi- GEN. 1:28 ply" so as to "fill the earth and subdue it." Then GEN. 1:28 he gave them dominion over fish, birds, and "every living thing that moves upon the earth." GEN. 1:28 There were limits to this power, however.

By giving Adam mastery over creation, God was sharing his sovereignty over the earth with humans. Above all, God's gift implied a measure of responsibility. He placed man in the Garden of Eden "to till it and keep it," but man's GEN. 2:15 obligation went beyond merely tending the earth. He was also expected not to exploit or destroy what had been entrusted to him.

Another restriction on mankind was a dietary one whereby the only food people could eat was fruits and vegetables. Animals, too, were allowed to eat only plants, perhaps so that they could enjoy the ideal state that Isaiah predicted would be regained when "the wolf shall dwell IS. 11:6 with the lamb." After the flood, however, the ban on eating animals was lifted.

The phrase "Let us make man" in Genesis 1:26 suggests that the hosts of heaven, depicted in this detail from a 15th-century painting, joined God in creating humanity.

BIBLICAL TALES OF CREATION

Genesis contains two creation stories—alike in fundamentals but so different in style and content that one might wonder if the same tale is being told. The two accounts agree that God is the only creator, and that mankind is at the center of creation. But while the first story emphasizes God's grandeur and power, the second reveals his tender care.

In the first creation story, God created the world in precisely six days, followed by a day of rest. In contrast, the second account contains no such pattern. It opens, "In the day that the Lord God made the earth and the heavens [Gen. 2:4]," but does not say how much time passes.

The sequence of events also differs in the two accounts. In Genesis 1 the creation of man and woman comes at the end of the story, after God has created all the plants and animals. But in Genesis 2, God first creates man. Then, since "no plant of the field was yet in the earth [Gen. 2:5]," he plants a garden for man to till and makes

animals for him to name. In the climax of the story, he creates a helper, woman.

The two stories also describe God's actions differently. In the first account God creates by command, and the recurring phrase that expresses his authority is "And God said. . . ." In Genesis 2, the Lord God (which means Yahweh God) works with his hands, taking pride in his creations. Like a potter, he shapes man from dust. Like a gardener, he plants trees. With a surgeon's skill, he removes a rib from the sleeping man.

Proverbs tells us a third tale of creation. Wisdom, a celestial being, relates her own story: "The Lord created me at the beginning of his work . . . before the beginning of the earth [Pv. 8:22]." Wisdom says that she assisted God in each step of creation "like a master workman; and I was daily his delight [Pv. 8:30]."

In the New Testament, the role of Wisdom is filled by the pre-existing Word, Jesus. "In the beginning was the Word," reads the opening verse of the Gospel

of John; ". . . all things were made through him." In Colossians 1:15, Christ is called "the first-born of all creation; for in him all things were created, in heaven and on earth." In Hebrews 1:2, God appoints Jesus "heir of all things, through whom also he created the world."

Various poetic passages alluding to a primordial struggle between God and a great sea monster reveal yet another biblical creation story—echoing, perhaps, the cosmic battle that appears in earlier Mesopotamian creation myths. Before he can begin the orderly act of creation, God must first tame this monster, also known as Leviathan, Rahab, or the dragon, which represents the watery chaos. "Thou didst divide the sea by thy might," Psalm 74:13 affirms. "Thou didst break the heads of the dragons on the waters. Thou didst crush the heads of Leviathan." And Psalm 104:24 is a resounding hymn of praise to God the creator: "O Lord, how manifold are thy works! In wisdom hast thou made them all; the earth is full of thy creatures."

Family of Man

What does the Bible reveal about man's relationship to the earth?

The name God gave the first man provides a key insight into mankind's relationship to the earth. *Adam* is the common Hebrew word for a human being and humanity. It also bears a resemblance to *adamah,* the Hebrew word for ground, from which God "formed man." The similarity of *adam* and *adamah* suggests an intimate link between man and the earth from which he was created. GEN. 2:7

The word *formed*—commonly applied to the handiwork of potters and other craftsmen—conveys the love and care God put into the creation of man. After shaping him from the dust of the earth, God breathed into his nostrils; and "man became a living being." It was "the breath of the Almighty," we later learn from the Book of Job, that gave man both life and understanding. GEN. 2:7
JOB 33:4; 32:8

Finding no fit helper for man among living creatures, God created Eve, as shown in this 15th-century Dutch illustration.

Why did God make a helper for man?

The one shadow that fell over Eden was loneliness; so God resolved to make "a helper fit" for his solitary creature, man. GEN. 2:18

As he had done with man, God formed the beasts of the field and the birds of the air, and brought them to Adam, who was asked to name each one. But when none of the creatures proved to be a suitable helper, God put Adam into a deep sleep and fashioned from one of his ribs the first woman. Seeing her, Adam exclaimed: "This at last is bone of my bones and flesh of my flesh." There, for the first time, the Bible makes a distinction between man and woman: "She shall be called Woman, because she was taken out of Man." GEN. 2:23 GEN. 2:23

The word *helper,* though, has sometimes been taken to imply that God wished to create a subordinate or an assistant to man. But the Hebrew text does not support this notion. In the Bible the word for helper (*ezer*) can also mean partner; indeed, it is most often used to refer to God as Israel's ally. Rather than being a subordinate to his chosen people, God is portrayed as Israel's partner and protector.

Where was the Garden of Eden?

The principal geographical clue to the location of the Garden of Eden is the river that flowed out of it and divided to become four rivers. The third and fourth rivers—the Tigris and Euphrates—still exist, but the first two—the Pishon and Gihon—are unknown, as is the exact location of the lands around which they flowed, Havilah and Cush. Theories range widely as to which bodies of water these rivers may have been. Some people speculate that one was the Nile and the other the Ganges. Others suggest that they may be dried-up tributaries of the Tigris and Euphrates.

Regardless of its location, the garden has come to symbolize an earthly paradise. In Hebrew *Eden* means delight, pleasure, or luxuriance, conveying a sense of abundance and contentment. When the Hebrew Bible was translated into Greek in the second century B.C., the word *garden* was translated as *paradeisos,* meaning a park or formal garden, which came into English as *paradise.* And so we have the familiar

*Amid the idyllic beauty of Eden, portrayed by a 19th-century American folk artist, Eve yields
to temptation as Adam looks on and the serpent slithers away.*

image of a lush garden, its trees pleasing to the
eye and heavy with delicious fruit, and its landscape teeming with wildlife for which Adam was
also appointed caretaker.

**What is the difference
between the tree of life and
the tree of the knowledge
of good and evil?**

GEN. 2:9   In the Garden of Eden, God "made to grow every
tree that is pleasant to the sight and good for
food," but only two are named: the tree of life
and the tree of the knowledge of good and evil. ❋

The tree of life, whose fruit conferred eternal
life, grew "in the midst of the garden." At the end   GEN. 2:9
of the Eden story, God drives man from the gar-
den and places the cherubim and a flaming
sword "to guard the way to the tree of life." It is   GEN. 3:24
seldom mentioned again until the Book of Revelation, which describes a version of "the para-   REV. 2:7
dise of God," where grows "the tree of life with   REV. 22:2
its twelve kinds of fruit, yielding its fruit each
month; and the leaves of the tree were for the
healing of the nations."

Unlike the tree of life, which appears in the
literature of other ancient Near Eastern religions
and in the literature of other religions throughout

Eve plucking the forbidden fruit, from Autun cathedral, France.

not cool enough to produce good apples. Others have proposed that the fruit was a citron, orange, or quince, or even a golden apricot.

Why did Eve eat the fruit?

Looking at the tree of the knowledge of good and evil, the woman saw that it was beautiful and that its fruit was good, but God had said that eating the fruit would bring death. The serpent, however, told her otherwise: it would not bring death but instead would make her "like God, know- GEN. 3:5 ing good and evil."

Yearning for wisdom and assured by the serpent that disobedience would not result in punishment from God, the woman made a choice that would change mankind forever. She ate the fruit, "and she also gave some to her husband, GEN. 3:6 and he ate." Suddenly, they saw that they were naked and they felt afraid. They covered themselves with fig leaves and tried to hide from God among the trees.

The forbidden fruit did indeed impart knowledge, as the serpent had said. As soon as Adam and Eve had eaten it, they knew the difference between good and evil. But the knowledge did not bestow divinity; on the contrary, it reaffirmed their humanity—their distinction from God.

What was Adam and Eve's sin?

In making their fateful choice to eat forbidden fruit, the man and woman ignored the only restriction that God had imposed on their life in Eden. Thus their sin was disobedience to their creator.

Some have suggested that the sin was carnal knowledge between man and woman, but there is no evidence in the Bible to support such a notion. The relationship between man and woman was already sanctified by God when he created woman and brought her to man. In the Old Testament nakedness often symbolizes weakness

the world, the tree of the knowledge of good and evil has no known parallel. It is the only tree in the entire Garden of Eden whose fruit God expressly forbade man to eat.

Though the terms *good* and *evil* are not defined in these passages, they seem to be used in a broad sense to include values of morality and justice. The Bible sometimes equates an ignorance of good and evil with childhood. By implying that the man and woman lacked what the tree offered, Genesis portrays them in a state of innocent ignorance.

What was the forbidden fruit?

Though Genesis does not name the fruit that the serpent used to tempt Eve, it is commonly depicted as an apple. This identification can perhaps be traced to a misunderstanding of the fifth-century A.D. translation of the Bible into Latin. The word for evil in Latin is *malum*, which can also mean apple.

The Hebrew word *tappuach*, usually translated as apple, appears in the Books of Proverbs, Song of Solomon, and Joel, where it refers to a sweet, golden fruit that grows on a shade tree. However, some botanists have challenged the identification of *tappuach* as an apple, believing that apples did not grow in the ancient Near East, where the climate throughout much of the region is ✳

THE EVIL SERPENT

The first animal named in the Bible, the serpent, is cast as a villain—though a clever one. The serpent who beguiles Eve into eating the forbidden fruit is described as "more subtle than any other wild creature [Gen. 3:1]," a characterization confirmed by Jesus, who charged his disciples to be "wise as serpents and innocent as doves [Mt. 10:16]." For its role as tempter, God condemned the serpent to crawl on its belly, eat dust, and be the enemy of man. Although the serpent is often portrayed as being venomous and repulsive, there are exceptions. When Aaron cast down his rod before the pharaoh, it turned into a serpent. Even when the pharaoh's magicians did the same, Aaron's rod devoured theirs.

Later, during their wanderings in the wilderness, the Israelites railed against God for the hardships they were forced to endure, and were punished with a plague of fiery serpents. When they repented, God offered a remedy: he commanded Moses to raise a bronze serpent on a pole. When the bronze serpent became an object of worship, King Hezekiah had to destroy it. Nonetheless, the Gospel of John tells that it was the image of Moses' bronze serpent that Jesus cited to confirm that man's salvation depends on Jesus being raised on the cross.

Yet the prevailing image of the serpent is a negative one. Israel's enemies and wicked men are likened to serpents. Micah warned that Israel's enemies "shall lick the dust like a serpent [Mic. 7:17]," and Jesus denounced certain scribes and Pharisees as "You serpents, you brood of vipers [Mt. 23:33]."

The image of the serpent as the embodiment of evil reached a climax in Revelation, the last book of the Bible. Here it is called a dragon (derived from the Greek word for serpent, *drakon*). In one of his visions John beholds a heavenly war between good and evil, represented by "a woman clothed with the sun [Rev. 12:1]" and a red dragon.

When angelic armies prevail, John declares that "the great dragon was thrown down, that ancient serpent, who is called the Devil and Satan [Rev. 12:9]." Later, John sees the dragon bound for a thousand years and cast into a bottomless pit. Loosed from imprisonment for the final conflict, the Devil will once more be defeated and "thrown into the lake of fire and sulphur" to be "tormented day and night for ever and ever [Rev. 20:10]." The serpent who deceived Eve will have received its final punishment.

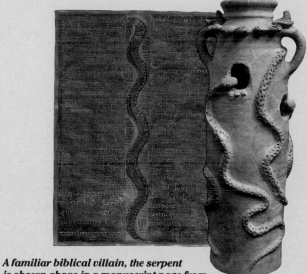

A familiar biblical villain, the serpent is shown above in a manuscript page from a 10th-century German Gospel. Snakes also decorate the ancient pottery stand at right, used in ceremonies in a Canaanite temple.

or helplessness. The fear that the man and woman felt in their nakedness arose not so much from their modesty as from an anxious realization that they were powerless and, because of their disobedience, could no longer be confident that they would be favored by their creator.

What was Adam and Eve's punishment?

Cringing among the trees in shame and dread, Adam and Eve heard the terrible pronouncement of God's punishment: a lifetime of toil and pain.

Man would no longer till effortlessly and keep the luxuriant garden for God. Instead, God condemned Adam to earn his bread by the sweat of his face. On Eve and all women after her, God imposed the pain of childbirth, and from this time on, husband would rule wife, giving rise to a patriarchal society. God reserved the most bitter punishment, a sentence of banishment and death, for last. Out of dust man was taken, God GEN. 3:19 reminded him, and "to dust you shall return." To prevent Adam and Eve from eating fruit from the tree of life and living forever, God drove them out of the garden.

How did God prevent Adam and Eve from returning to the garden?

When God expelled Adam and Eve from the Garden of Eden, he blocked forever their access to the tree of life. On the east side—perhaps at a gateway to the enclosed paradise—he stationed the cherubim and "a flaming sword which GEN. 3:24 turned every way."

Cherubim were celestial beings, usually portrayed as winged animals with human faces. In addition, according to the Bible, the cherubim supported the throne of God, their golden wings shielded the ark of the covenant, and their carved images covered a wall of the holy of holies in Solomon's temple in Jerusalem.

The flaming, turning sword that also guarded Eden is possibly an early attempt to describe lightning. Though artists have often portrayed the sword as an actual weapon held by the cherubim, the wording in Genesis does not confirm this idea.

Obviously, no mere mortal could elude such terrifying guardians to regain Eden. The message was clear: human beings had lost their chance to be immortal and would never be able to overcome death by eating the fruit of the tree of life.

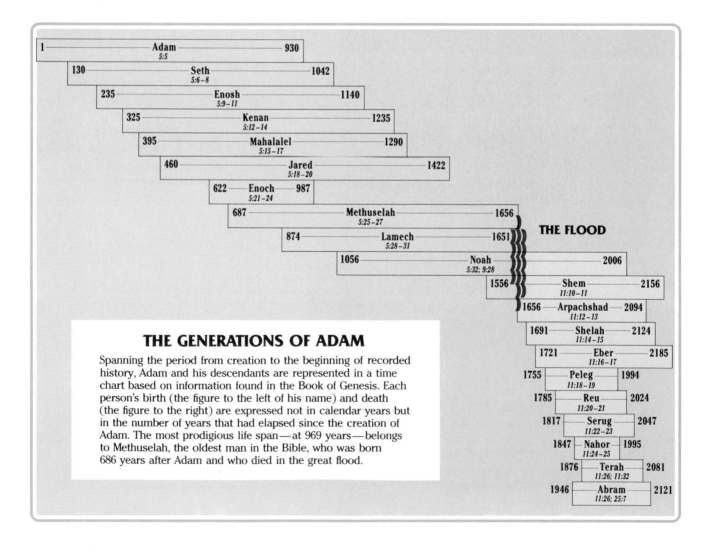

THE GENERATIONS OF ADAM

Spanning the period from creation to the beginning of recorded history, Adam and his descendants are represented in a time chart based on information found in the Book of Genesis. Each person's birth (the figure to the left of his name) and death (the figure to the right) are expressed not in calendar years but in the number of years that had elapsed since the creation of Adam. The most prodigious life span—at 969 years—belongs to Methuselah, the oldest man in the Bible, who was born 686 years after Adam and who died in the great flood.

Henceforth, they must live with the thorns, thistles, pain, and ultimate death in a world outside the gates of paradise.

What do the names in Genesis signify?

Only three offspring of Adam and Eve are named: Cain, Eve's firstborn; his brother Abel; and Seth, a replacement for Abel, who was slain by Cain. Genesis says that after the birth of Seth, Adam lived GEN. 5:4 another 800 years and "had other sons and daughters." Neither the names nor the number of the other offspring are specified.

The names at the beginning of Genesis have special significance, either by derivation or as a play on words. *Adam*, as mentioned earlier, is the Hebrew word for human and, by extension, humanity. Adam named the woman Eve, which resembles the Hebrew word for living, because she was "the mother of all GEN. 3:20 living."

GEN. 4:1 Of Cain, Eve said, "I have gotten a man with the help of the Lord." The name Cain means spear or metalworker, but it can also be associated with the Hebrew word *qanah* (acquired), a reminder to Eve that Cain was a gift from God.

There is an ominous ring to the name Abel, for it is a Hebrew word that can be translated as vapor, breath, or futility—appropriate, since his life was cut short. Eve called her third son Seth GEN. 4:25 (or Sheth) because "God has appointed [*shath*] for me another child instead of Abel."

Why did God look favorably upon Abel's offering but not Cain's?

Cain and Abel brought different offerings to God, GEN. 4:4 who "had regard for Abel and his offering, but for Cain and his offering he had no regard." Genesis ✳

Adam and Eve are expelled from the Garden of Eden by an angel of the Lord in this 15th-century Italian painting.

gives no word of explanation for God's preference. It does not reveal whether there was any difference between the brothers' motives, or whether one gift was somehow superior to the other. Facts that would seem crucial to understanding the story are not provided.

Many have sought a reason for God's decision. New Testament writers credited the faith of Abel or blamed the depravity of Cain. Others have argued that the text shows God's preference for animal sacrifice or that it endorses Israel's pastoral roots (represented by Abel the shepherd) over a settled life of agriculture (symbolized by Cain the farmer). Or God's choice may reflect a pattern found often in Genesis: the preference for a younger brother over an older one.

What was the mark of Cain?

GEN. 4:14

Condemned to live as a fugitive for having murdered his brother in a fit of rage, Cain called out in despair: "Whoever finds me will slay me." But God put a mark on Cain and promised that vengeance would be sevenfold for anyone who killed him. The Hebrew word translated as mark is also frequently translated as token or sign. In many biblical passages the word refers to a miraculous event, and some interpreters have thought that Cain's sign was a miracle—perhaps a flash of lightning—that God used to assure the wanderer's protection from retribution.

But when the Bible does not explain, interpretations often vary widely. One ancient commentator suggested that the token of God's protection was a dog that accompanied Cain. Others have speculated that the sign was a tattoo (forbidden in the Bible), horns, leprosy, or even a letter of the divine name inscribed on his forehead—all of which would have warned or frightened off would-be attackers.

Some have even proposed that the Cain and Abel story is a parable of tribal rivalry. Cain's mark, they suggest, identified him as a member of a tribe or clan that would exact a terrible toll on the tribe of anyone who killed Cain. Thus the mark warned hostile tribes to let Cain alone.

Where did Cain get his wife?

After Cain went to dwell in the land of Nod, he married and had a family. But Genesis does not name his wife or tell where she came from. One explanation that has been proposed since ancient times is that Adam and Eve had other children who grew up with Cain and Abel, and that Cain married one of his sisters. For example, some nonbiblical writings supply information

Subjects of the world's first—and most infamous—case of sibling rivalry, Abel (left) and Cain (right) make their offerings to God in these Italian mosaics from the Middle Ages.

that seems to be missing from Genesis. A work called the Book of Jubilees—an early Jewish commentary on the Torah that is sometimes referred to as "little Genesis"—mentions two daughters of Adam and Eve, Awan and Azura. Third-born after Cain and Abel, Awan is taken by Cain as his wife; Azura, born after Seth, becomes Seth's wife.

Why does the Bible not identify Cain's wife? The answer lies in the nature of Genesis itself, for this first book of the Bible combines traditions from a variety of sources. As these traditions were joined, the irregularities between them were never smoothed out to make a seamless narrative.

The stories about Cain, for example, assume the presence of other people who would threaten his life as he wandered in exile. It was evidently among such unidentified people that Cain found his wife, but these people are not included in the tradition that tells of Adam and Eve's children. It is the message of the story that is important, not its apparent inconsistencies.

Who were Cain's descendants?

It is perhaps surprising that the Bible has anything positive to say about Cain's descendants. As the progeny of a fugitive murderer, they might be expected to have shared his exile from God and to have vanished from history. Instead, Genesis attributes momentous achievements to Cain and his line.

No longer the frightened and marked wanderer, Cain was the founder of the first city—a settled man with a family and considerable resources. The Bible lists six more generations of descendants, ending with three brothers. One of them is described as the ancestor of tent-dwelling nomadic herders; another, as the father of all musicians of the lyre and pipe; and a third, the first forger of instruments in bronze and iron.

Perhaps the most colorful of Cain's heirs was Lamech, the father of the three brothers. He is the first man in the Bible said to have had more than one wife. His proud and vengeful personality comes through in a verse known as the song of Lamech, in which he celebrates himself for killing a young man who had merely struck him GEN. 4:24 and boasts: "If Cain is avenged sevenfold, truly Lamech seventy-sevenfold." Thus Genesis links ✳

CAIN AND ABEL

Adam's two sons—Cain and Abel—grew up together, but they grew apart. Cain followed in his father's footsteps as a farmer; Abel became a wandering shepherd. The seasons passed and the young men prospered, so each decided to offer God a gift. Cain brought a portion of the crop he had labored to harvest among thistles and weeds. Abel brought some of the firstborn of the flock he had grazed on plains and hills.

As the offerings were ascending in smoke, it became apparent that God took notice of Abel's gift but ignored Cain's. Angered and hurt, Cain burned with wounded pride. He, a firstborn son, had been outstripped by his younger brother. Though God warned Cain to master his rage, Cain turned it against his brother, and one day while out in the field killed Abel.

When God asked Cain, "Where is Abel your brother?" Cain's resentment turned to sarcasm: "I do not know; am I my brother's keeper [Gen. 4:9]?" Cain's haunting question has made his story a symbol of the failure of human responsibility and affection.

As punishment for spilling his brother's blood and polluting the earth, Cain was to live in the land of Nod, east of Eden—cut off from God and the fertile earth, which would no longer yield him crops.

facets of later society, such as nomadic life and city life, music and metallurgy, polygamy and blood vengeance, to Cain and his descendants.

What was special about Methuselah's father, Enoch?

"Enoch walked with God; and he was not, for GEN. 5:24 God took him." This short sentence—a mere nine words in Hebrew—makes Enoch one of the most enigmatic figures of the Bible. Evidently it means that Enoch was spared death because of his righteousness, a reward confirmed by the anonymous author of the New Testament HEB. 11:5 Letter to the Hebrews: "By faith Enoch was taken up so that he should not see death." Only Enoch and the prophet Elijah (in the chariot of fire) were taken by God without having to die.

The Book of Jubilees, a second-century B.C. commentary on the Torah, tells of angels bearing Enoch to the Garden of Eden, where he remained to record the condemnation and judgment of the world. Because of Enoch's presence, the story goes, God spared Eden from the waters of the flood.

According to Jubilees, Enoch acquired knowledge and wisdom; another Jewish tradition makes him a teacher of astronomy and mathematics and the one to whom an angel revealed the true

calendar. In Islamic literature Enoch is the first man to practice the art of writing. Major Jewish works of prophecy and religious instruction are attributed to Enoch. The most important of these is a complex work of 108 chapters, compiled sometime between the third century B.C. and the first century A.D., known as 1 Enoch. It includes a history of the world from the time of Adam. Once widely read and highly influential, 1 Enoch is quoted by Jude: "Behold, the Lord came with his JUDE 1:14 holy myriads, to execute judgment on all."

Who were "the sons of God" who married "the daughters of men"?

Amidst the growing wickedness of humanity, depicted in Genesis 6, "the sons of God saw that GEN. 6:2 the daughters of men were fair; and they took to

A chilling and mysterious portrait of evil personified, William Blake's 19th-century painting shows Satan calling up his legions from a fiery underworld.

SIN: MASTER AND ENSLAVER

The word *sin* occurs in the Bible for the first time not in the story of Adam and Eve, but in the dramatic story of Cain and Abel. When Cain

could not overcome his rage at God's rejection of his offering, the Lord warned him: "Sin is couching at the door; its desire is for you, but you must master

it [Gen. 4:7]." Sin is portrayed as a living force that lies in ambush and must be mastered to keep it from becoming the master. Such personification of sin is rare in the Old Testament.

Centuries later, Paul used a similar image in the New Testament. He developed at some length a portrayal of sin as a living power that becomes master over people. Paul personifies sin as an enslaver and a killer. Its force is such that even good things, even God's commandments, become weapons of destruction. As Paul observed: "If it had not been for the law, I should not have known sin [Rom. 7:7]." For him sin is an evil that always "lies close at hand [Rom. 7:21]"— like the sin couching at Cain's door.

wife such of them as they chose." To many readers this verse sounds like Greek mythology and seems curiously out of place in the Bible. But does the Bible speak of such beings elsewhere? Could they be angels or other divine beings, or perhaps righteous humans?

GEN. 6:2 Old Testament passages outside Genesis suggest that "sons of God" refers to members of God's heavenly court. The Book of Job tells how JOB 1:6 "the sons of God" presented themselves before the Lord, and hymns in the Psalms call upon PS. 29:1;89:6 "heavenly beings" (in Hebrew, sons of gods) to praise the Lord.

Perhaps Genesis is describing the reverse of what happened in the Garden of Eden. There, humans were tempted to eat the fruit and become like God; here, godlike beings mingle with humans. In both cases, blurring the distinction between human and divine brings disaster.

In an attempt to explain these puzzling verses, some scholars suggest that the sons of God were the descendants of Seth corrupted by marriage to GEN. 6:2 "the daughters of men," who are identified with the line of Cain.

Who were "the giants in the earth"?

The King James Version of Genesis 6:4 speaks of "giants in the earth," while the Revised Standard Version uses the enigmatic name Nephilim for the remarkable offspring of the sons of God and the daughters of men—or possibly for a separate race of beings. The text adds another puzzle when it says that these Nephilim were on earth GEN. 6:4 "in those days, and also afterward." In other words, the Nephilim were a race of giants who appeared both before and after the flood.

The Nephilim are also mentioned when the Lord commands Moses to send spies into the land of Canaan to see whether the land is good and whether it can be conquered by the people NUM. 13:32 of Israel. "All the people that we saw in it are NUM. 13:33 men of great stature," the spies reported. "And there we saw the Nephilim [the sons of Anak, who come from the Nephilim]; and we seemed to ourselves like grasshoppers, and so we seemed to them." The Bible often depicts Israel's enemies as awesome opponents who can be overcome only with God's help. Perhaps even the Philistine champion Goliath was a descendant of the Nephilim.

Though the Bible mentions no murder weapon, Cain bludgeons Abel with the jawbone of an ass in this 14th-century German painting.

RAISING CAIN. *As the world's first murderer, Cain was said in the New Testament to be "of the evil one [1Jn. 3:12]," and his name came to be associated with the devil. To describe acts that stirred up a commotion or caused trouble, people used the expression "raising the devil." Those who wanted to avoid using the word* devil *substituted such phrases as "raising hell," "raising dickens," and "raising Cain"—the last being a popular expression in the American West that was used by Harriet Beecher Stowe in* Uncle Tom's Cabin.

The Great Flood

Two workmen building Noah's ark, from a medieval frieze in the cathedral at Gerona, Spain.

Why did God choose Noah to save mankind?

By the tenth generation of mankind the world was filled with corruption and violence, causing God great sorrow and grief and even making him GEN. 6:8 regret the creation. Only Noah "found favor in GEN. 6:9 the eyes of the Lord," for he was "a righteous man, blameless in his generation." Like his an- GEN 5:24 cestor Enoch, Noah "walked with God."

To punish the evildoers, God decided to destroy all living creatures, including mankind. But his terrible judgment was tempered with mercy, and he singled out Noah and his family for survival. With them and the animals they would save, there would be a new beginning.

What was the ark?

Angered by mankind's wickedness, God told the GEN. 6:13 righteous Noah that he was "determined to make an end of all flesh" and commanded him to GEN. 6:14 make "an ark of gopher wood" to save him and his family from the coming deluge.

In the midst of death and destruction, the ark was a repository of life. Since it was intended to ride out the flood, the ark has often been visualized as a great ship, the largest vessel before modern times; but, more likely, it was shaped like a sturdy, rectangular houseboat. Colossal in size, it was approximately 450 feet ✳ long, 75 feet wide, and 45 feet high. Its three decks were divided into rooms, and the hull was covered with pitch, or bitumen, to make it watertight. The entrance to the ark was through a door in its side.

The Genesis description of the ark is filled with rare Hebrew words that give the account an antique and poetic ring, as if drawn from an ancient story. Genesis never calls the ark a boat or a ship. The Hebrew word that is translated as ark can mean chest or box. The Bible uses this word in only two instances: the story of the deluge and the description of the basket of bulrushes in which the infant Moses was hidden. The *ark of the covenant* comes from a different Hebrew word.

On top the ark had something called in Hebrew a *tsohar*. The word occurs only in this Bible story, and no one is sure whether it refers to a roof, a window, or simply an open space between the walls and roof. One ancient tradition even described the *tsohar* as a precious jewel, so brilliant that it lit up the inside of the ark.

A final puzzle is the material used to build the ark: gopher wood. The word *gopher* appears only here in the Bible, and it is uncertain what kind of tree or plant would be the source of such wood. Some, however, believe that gopher wood was cypress wood, which was used in ancient times for shipbuilding.

Which animals did Noah take with him into the ark?

The ark was huge, but so was its passenger list. Genesis twice gives God's instructions to Noah for preserving the earth's animal life. First, God tells him to take "two of every sort" of bird, ani- GEN. 6:20 mal, and creeping thing. A few verses later, the command is modified to seven pairs of clean animals and birds and a pair each of unclean animals "to keep their kind alive upon the face of GEN. 7:3

all the earth." Fish, presumably, would survive in the waters without Noah's help.

Only much later, in Leviticus, does the Bible specify the differences between clean and unclean animals. There, clean animals refer to those that one may eat; unclean animals must not be eaten. In Genesis, however, clean animals seem to be those that can be offered in sacrifice. GEN. 8:20 After the flood, Noah made a sacrifice "of every clean animal and of every clean bird," but God placed no restriction on what Noah and his fam- GEN. 9:3 ily could eat. "Every moving thing that lives shall be food for you," he promised.

Even with deck space totaling 100,000 square feet, the ark would have burst with two each of even a fraction of the species now known. And how could Noah and his family have fed them all? To get around such difficulties, some have suggested that the animals were put into hibernation during the period of confinement.

In later centuries many stories arose about Noah's troubles with his vast menagerie, and some artists even invented detailed floor plans of the ark's compartments.

Where did the floodwaters come from, and where did they go?

The ancient Israelites saw God's hand in the flood because nothing else could explain where the vast amounts of water came from. Normally, as the Preacher in Ecclesiastes says, "All streams EC. 1:7 run to the sea, but the sea is not full." Yet Genesis describes a deluge in which "all the high GEN. 7:19 mountains under the whole heaven" were covered by 15 cubits (about 22 feet) of water.

The very word translated as flood (*mabbul*)

In this Sistine Chapel fresco, Michelangelo portrays the doomed unrighteous as they swarm toward the ark, trying desperately to escape God's wrath.

*Bearing proof that the waters have subsided,
a dove brings a fresh green olive leaf
to Noah in this stained glass window from
the cathedral at Ulm in Germany.*

Genesis is clear about the universal scope of the flood, and flood stories from other cultures in the Near East support the stories of widespread inundations in the ancient past.

How long did the flood last?

Genesis 7 gives precise information about the chronology of the flood. It began when Noah was 600 years old, on the 17th day of the second month, though it does not say what time of year. (By matching the modern calendar to the biblical calendar, some say the flood began in February.) The waters rose for 40 days and remained high for 110 more days—a total of five months.

The ark then landed in the mountains of Ararat, but remarkably, the tops of the mountains could not be seen until 2½ months later. After 40 more days Noah began to send out birds at weekly intervals to determine whether dry land had appeared. On the first day of a new year, the earth was finally dry, and Noah could remove the covering of the ark and look out. Still, he remained in the ark for nearly two more months, until God commanded him to take his family and all the animals from the ark—a year and 10 days after they had entered it.

How did Noah learn that the flood was over?

Cut off from the outside world for many months, Noah could only imagine what surprises awaited him. With characteristic patience and hope, he sent birds to gather information about the post-flood world. His first two attempts ended in disappointment: neither a raven nor a dove was able to find a resting place.

Sent a second time, seven days later, the dove returned with a sign of the earth's renewed vitality and its readiness to support the ark's inhabitants: "a freshly plucked olive leaf." Dispatched GEN. 8:11 again after another seven days, the dove presumably found a nesting place and did not return, signaling to Noah and his family that they too could leave the ark after a year of confinement.

One of the most powerful images to emerge from the story of the flood is that of the dove bearing an olive leaf in its beak—a symbol of peace and hope. In the New Testament, too, the dove is a symbol of hope and rebirth. This is

is used in the Bible only for this deluge. This unique superstorm, according to Genesis, swept across the earth from above and below. During the creation, described in Genesis 1, God placed a firmament in the midst of the watery chaos, keeping some waters above the dome of heaven. Then God gathered the waters under the heavens into one place and called it the Seas. From these GEN. 7:11 two sources came the floodwaters; when "all the fountains of the great deep burst forth, and the windows of the heavens were opened."

The fury that Noah had to endure was not just a heavy storm; it was a return to the primeval state. When the flood's destruction was complete, God closed the fountains of the deep and the windows of the heavens, the rain stopped, and the waters receded. Earth has no reservoirs to hold the amount of water described in Genesis, but the wind God sent and the 150 days it took for the waters to abate may indicate natural processes of evaporation and subsidence.

clearest at Jesus' baptism, when the heavens open, the Holy Spirit appears as a dove, and the voice of God says: "This is my beloved Son, with whom I am well pleased."

MT. 3:17

How did Noah fulfill his father's prophecy?

GEN. 9:20 After the flood Noah became "the first tiller of the soil" and planted a vineyard. His success as a farmer and vintner fulfilled the prophecy his fa-

ther Lamech made at his birth: "Out of the ground which the Lord has cursed this one shall bring us relief from our work and from the toil of our hands."

GEN. 5:29

The relief Lamech predicted was wine, as the psalmist later wrote, "to gladden the heart of man." Along with grain, grapes were an important crop in Bible times, and several biblical passages describe how carefully the Hebrews tended their vineyards. To sit under your own vine and fig tree was a symbol of peace and prosperi-

PS. 104:15

A BABYLONIAN FLOOD STORY

Tales of great floods are found among the legends of many of the world's peoples. Several accounts come from Mesopotamia, the homeland of the patriarch Abraham. They were told and retold for centuries before Genesis was written and contain striking parallels to the story of Noah.

One version, dating to at least the second millennium B.C., is an ancient flood narrative that appears in a Babylonian epic about a handsome hero named Gilgamesh and his quest for eternal life. Visiting a far-off land, Gilgamesh talks to Utnapishtim, who—like Noah—has survived a great flood.

When the Babylonian gods decided to destroy mankind, one of them whispered a warning to Utnapishtim. He was told to build a ship in the form of a giant cube, made watertight—like Noah's ark—with pitch. Into this vessel Utnapishtim brought his family, his wealth in gold and silver, craftsmen, domestic animals, and wild creatures. As an awesome storm approached, he battened down the hatch and commanded

Utnapishtim, a character in the Babylonian flood story, watches Gilgamesh slay a bull in this scene from a cylinder seal created during the second millennium B.C.

his boatman to set out.

For six days and nights a storm raged, frightening even the gods, but on the seventh day the vessel came to rest on a mountaintop. Outside, "all of mankind had returned to clay." Like Noah, Utnapishtim sent out birds to see if the waters had receded—a dove, a swallow, and finally a raven, which did not return. Also like Noah, he offered a sacrifice, which pleased the gods so much that they bestowed immortality on him.

The discovery and publication of this part of the Gilgamesh epic in 1872 caused a furor because of its striking similarities to Genesis. Close study of the Babylonian text, however, has revealed that although Utnapishtim's story may be related to Noah's, it is clearly different. Genesis shows one God reaching a painful moral judgment on corruption and violence, and contains nothing of the intrigue among dueling deities that underlies the Babylonian flood story.

Free to roam the earth again, a magnificent menagerie emerges from the ark in this 19th-century Italian painting. Spanning the sky is a rainbow—the sign of God's covenant with all living creatures.

ty. Typically, wine was served at every meal—in fact, the Hebrew word for banquet, *mishteh*, translates as drinking. Yet too much wine could rob a man of his dignity and bring disgrace. Writing to the Ephesians, Paul instructs them not to EPH. 5:18 get drunk on wine, "for that is debauchery," and PR. 23:21 Proverbs warns that "the drunkard and the glutton will come to poverty."

Apparently the first to overindulge, Noah lay naked in his tent as he slept off the wine's effect. By seeing his father naked and telling his brothers, Ham so angered Noah that the patriarch laid a curse upon Canaan, one of Ham's sons.

What is the table of nations?

Genesis 10 is an imposing list of names not especially easy to read. But this chapter, containGEN. 10:1 ing "the generations of the sons of Noah," ex-

presses the idea of humanity as a single family.

The peoples and places named are spread out from the eastern Mediterranean across the Near East and into Africa. The divisions are along geographical and political rather than racial or linguistic lines—though the families of Noah's three sons are all said to have had their own languages, families, lands, and nations.

The descendants of Japheth were identified with the peoples of Asia Minor, Greece, and some Mediterranean islands. Ham's descendants were associated with Egypt and Mesopotamia, and included the legendary founders of Ethiopia, Babylon, Nineveh, and all the Canaanite peoples.

The last person on the list of nations is Shem, the eldest son of Noah. His descendants, the Semites, include Eber, the father of the Hebrews. Eber is fourth in the line of ten that leads to the ✳ patriarch Abraham.

THE QUEST FOR THE ARK

As the centerpiece of one of the Bible's most famous and beloved stories, Noah's ark has been the object of intense searches for centuries. Genesis reports that "the ark came to rest upon the mountains of Ararat [Gen. 8:4]"—but where are they?

Ararat was the Hebrew name for the kingdom of Urartu, which was located in the mountainous region north of Assyria, today known as Armenia. The name has now been given to a twin-peaked mountain in northeastern Turkey near the border of Iran.

In the third century B.C. a Babylonian priest named Berosus wrote that the people of Armenia claimed to know the site of the ship that was described in the Babylonian flood story and that these people broke off pieces of its bitumen for talismans. In the Christian Era, monks at a monastery near Mount Ararat displayed what they said were relics of the ark.

Explorers in recent times still seek proof that the ark rests on the mountain, encouraged by claims during the last century—often reported second or third hand—from people who say they have actually seen and touched Noah's legendary vessel.

One such report came from Archdeacon Nouri, episcopal head of the Nestorian Church of Malabar, South India. He claimed to have scaled Mount Ararat in 1887 and come upon a ship measuring 900 feet long and 100 feet high, half

In this 12th-century relief from a Sicilian cathedral, Noah's ark is depicted straddling the twin peaks of Mount Ararat.

filled with snow. Nouri promised investors that he could retrieve the great hulk and have it delivered to the 1893 Columbian Exposition in Chicago, but

the Turkish authorities blocked his efforts.

In 1955 a retired French industrialist, Fernand Navarra, returned from the mountain with pieces of hand-worked timber recovered from a glacier at 13,000 feet. The particular color and density of the wood persuaded some experts that the fragments could be 5,000 years old, which fits the biblical chronology. Elated by his discovery, Navarra published his findings in a book. The English version was called *Forbidden Mountain*. But when scientists employed the carbon 14 method to test the age of the wood, they found that it dated only to the early Middle Ages—old, but not old enough to be Noah's ark.

Still the quest continues. Year after year, explorers examine rock formations and search for wood, ever hopeful that they will find the elusive ark.

An extinct volcano, Mount Ararat, located in present-day Turkey, is the site where some believe Noah's ark came to rest. At nearly 17,000 feet, it is the highest mountain in the region.

The Tower of Babel

Why did the people build a tower?

The table of nations in Genesis 10 shows that after the flood Noah's descendants multiplied rapidly and spread across the earth.

The story of the tower of Babel is set, perhaps, in the fifth generation after Noah, in the time of GEN. 10:25 Peleg, when "the earth was divided." As people migrated from the east, they came to a plain in the land of Shinar, where the mighty hunter Nimrod established the cities of his kingdom. Shinar has been identified as the part of Mesopotamia called Babylonia, an ancient region of the Tigris-Euphrates basin in what is present-day Iraq.

After their arrival in Mesopotamia, the people learned to manufacture not only sun-baked bricks, such as those used in the construction of common dwellings, but also kiln-fired bricks that were strong enough to support massive structures. For mortar they used bitumen, a substance easily scooped from tar pits in this oil-rich region—a technique of masonry that was common only in Mesopotamia. Archeology confirms the detailed account in Genesis of this technological breakthrough.

With this technical know-how, the people undertook a great project: the building of a city and GEN. 11:4 "a tower with its top in the heavens." Such a grand accomplishment, they reasoned, would keep them strong and make them famous.

BABEL. *The word* Babel *was well known in ancient times. It was the name of the great Mesopotamian city-state of Babylon.*

The Genesis writer plays on the similar sounds of Babel *and* balal, *a Hebrew word for confuse: "Therefore its name was called Babel, because there the Lord confused [balal] the language of all the earth [Gen.11:9]."*

Despite their similarity in sound, and despite what many believe, there is no link between Babel *and the English word* babble—*though God's act of stopping the building no doubt raised an unintelligible babble of tongues among the people of the world.*

Some students of the Bible have suggested that mankind wanted to storm the heavens with this ancient skyscraper, but the biblical text does not support such a notion.

What was wrong with building a tower?

Genesis offers no explanation for God's displeasure, but a common interpretation is that by deciding to build a tower that would unify and strengthen them, the people had put themselves

The tower of Babel probably resembled the ziggurat at Ur, shown in the reconstruction below. Among the ruins of the original, dating from about 2100 B.C., is the central staircase (left), whose steps seem to ascend into heaven.

The tower of Babel dominates the barren landscape, looming over tiny sailing vessels and an army of human workers in this 16th-century painting by Flemish artist Jan Bruegel.

in direct opposition to God's command to Noah: GEN. 9:1 "Be fruitful and multiply, and fill the earth." If the project had been successful, the speculation goes, the people would have remained clustered in Mesopotamia and would never have spread out around the world, as God had prescribed.

According to Genesis, God also knew that the fame the tower would bring would only serve to GEN. 11:6 fire their ambition. Since they were "one people" GEN. 11:6 with "one language," God reasoned, "nothing that they propose to do will now be impossible for them."

The tower of Babel marks the end of God's relationship to humanity as a whole. After Babel, Genesis shows, God makes himself known principally, if not exclusively, to a single family and nation, the descendants of Abraham.

How did God stop work on the tower?

"Come, let us go down, and there confuse their GEN. 11:7 language," the Lord proposed to the divine council after seeing the city and tower that men had built. God decided to stop the construction and restrain the ambition of humanity by letting men experience division and disorder. Without a common language to unite them, the people would not be able to maintain a common purpose, and would scatter across the earth as God had commanded. Once God confused their language, concerted effort ceased, and the descendants of Noah were separated, as Genesis had already noted, "by their families, their languages, GEN. 10:31 their lands, and their nations."

THE WORSHIP OF GOD

The people of the Bible knew of only one great power that was responsible for all aspects of life from the most ordinary to the most exalted. That power was God—not a crowd of divinities such as those served in neighboring nations, but one all-seeing God, who was gracious, demanding, loving. Not only religious experiences but also physical existence, moral responsibilities, family ties and social interactions, past history and future hopes—all these were expressions of the will of God.

But how could one know such a God, majestic beyond all imagination? It was only possible, they believed, because in his own good time and in his own distinct ways God had chosen to make himself known to man. The ways were sometimes overwhelming or mysterious, as when God descended in fire on Mount Sinai. But far more often God made his presence known in ways readily recognizable by humans. He appeared to Abraham as a man, to Elijah in a still small voice, to Isaiah in a vision of a royal throne, and ultimately, as Christians proclaimed, through Jesus the Messiah. Hundreds, even thousands, of times the Bible describes the one God, whom no human image can ever capture, revealing his will to humanity. He makes covenants with his creatures, guides them by his laws, helps them in their struggles, turns them away from injustice and corruption, blesses them with freedom and prosperity, punishes them for faithlessness and oppression, and always calls them to become better than they are.

Since the most fundamental theme of the Bible is the relationship between God and human beings, it is not surprising to find its pages filled with insights into how men and women through the ages expressed their faith in God. Indeed, from the first sacrifice of Cain and Abel in Genesis to the last ringing "Amen" of Revelation, the Bible resounds with the worship of God. God reached out to mortals by making himself known, and mortals reached up to God in worship.

In the laws and traditions of ancient Israel, an elaborate mosaic of sacred places, objects, people, and rites represented the meeting between the holy God and his often sinful people. Some holy places were simple spots where ancient patriarchs had set up rude altars of stones. Others, like Solomon's temple, were embellished with the most sumptuous decoration that Israel's richest king could muster. Both kinds of places, however, carried for the Israelites a tangible quality of holiness that set them apart. Here, in sacrifice, prayer, and praise, men met God. The Bible describes how God prescribed a particularly holy object, the ark of the covenant, as the symbolic center of worship. It focused the worshipers' attention not on an image of God that could become an idol but on their covenant with God, which emphasized his mercy toward the people and their obligation to be faithful to him. The ark was always to be kept in the most holy place, the dark inner sanctum of the temple sanctuary, to be approached only once each year by the high priest when he made atonement for the sins of the people.

Worship always involved prayer and song, often expressed in poetry like that in the Book of Psalms, but the central act of worship was the sacrifice administered by the specially ordained priests. Every morning and evening, day by day over the centuries, the priests sacrificed the offerings prescribed by God's law—as automatic and necessary as breathing. Alongside these the smoke of countless other offerings ascended to the sky: sacrifices that expressed repentance for sin, thanksgiving for blessings, the cleansing of impurity, or perhaps the fulfillment of a vow to God. Many such sacrifices were the occasion of joyous banquets with family and friends. The daily rhythm of sacrifice was modulated by the weekly rhythm of rest on the Sabbath and by the annual recurrence of festivals celebrating Israel's history and God's blessings of prosperity and freedom. In all, Israel's life of worship was marked by moments of intense solemnity within an overall spirit of thanksgiving and celebration.

Among early Christians, the new faith transformed the ancient traditions into new patterns of worship. Gone was the grand spectacle of the great temple; the new faith was celebrated in the homes of believers. Anyplace where "two or three are gathered in my name [Mt. 18:20]," Jesus said, became a holy place. The ancient rites and festivals were viewed through the prism of the story of Jesus and were transformed as they became linked to Jesus' life, death, and resurrection.

Still, the spirit of solemnity and celebration in worship remained. And the same deep root of faith continued to guide the new communities—the belief that the one loving and demanding God had made himself known in his own unique way and that his people could respond by reaching out to him with their whole hearts, worshiping, as Jesus said, "in spirit and truth [Jn. 4:24]."

Top left: A carving from a fifth-century A.D. synagogue.

Knowing God

Can God be seen?

According to the Bible, people only rarely have an opportunity to see God directly—and even then he is cloaked in an impenetrable radiance, or glory. When the Hebrews were camped in the wilderness of Sinai, God warned Moses not to let his followers come too close to Mount Sinai, EX. 19:21 "lest they break through to the Lord to gaze and many of them perish." So important was God's veil of invisibility that even when Moses asked the Lord to show him his glory, the Lord an-EX. 33:20 swered: "You cannot see my face; for man shall not see me and live."

The New Testament reaffirms the notion that people are not allowed to see God. Paul tells his 1 TIM. 6:16 traveling companion, Timothy: "No man has ever seen or can see" God.

Yet there are apparent exceptions to that prohibition—when, for example, Moses, Aaron, Na-EX. 24:10 dab, Abihu, and 70 Israelite elders "saw the God of Israel"; or when the envious Miriam and Aaron NUM. 12:8 were told that Moses "beholds the form of the IS. 6:1 Lord." Also, the prophet Isaiah "saw the Lord sit-

ting upon a throne, high and lifted up." In addition, another prophet, Ezekiel, heard "a voice EZEK. 1:25 from above the firmament" and then saw God, whom he describes as "a likeness as it were of a EZEK. 1:26 human form." All survived the experience.

In the New Testament, God has been made visible in the person of Jesus. At the Last Supper, Jesus declared that God was manifested in him when he said to the Apostles, "He who has JN. 14:9 seen me has seen the Father." And the missionary Paul in his Letter to the Colossians wrote that Jesus was "the image of the invisible COL. 1:15 God."

What does God look like?

There is no complete physical description of God in the Bible, but in order to describe God's actions, biblical writers gave him eyes, ears, and a mouth so that he sees, hears, and speaks. He walks in the Garden of Eden, smells Noah's offering, comes down to Earth to investigate the tower of Babel, and writes the Ten Commandments. The New Testament continues to use such an-

In a painting by Raphael, God's spiritual presence in the burning bush is represented by a human figure, but Moses does not dare to look toward the divine voice.

The Hebrew letters for God's sacred and unutterable name, Yahweh, shown above a menorah, appear between hands extended in heavenly blessing in this 19th-century papercut from Morocco.

IN THE NAME OF GOD

When God called to Moses out of the burning bush, telling him to free the Israelites from bondage in Egypt, Moses asked: "If I come to the people of Israel and say to them, 'The God of your fathers has sent me to you,' and they ask me, 'What is his name?' what shall I say to them [Ex. 3:13]?"

God answered Moses enigmatically, "I am who I am [Ex. 3:14]," which can also be translated as "I shall be what I shall be." The name God actually spoke to Moses was *Yahweh* (often translated in English as the Lord), the Hebrew verb to be. Spelled with the four Hebrew consonants *YHWH*, it is called the Tetragrammaton. "Say this to the people of Israel, 'The Lord,

YHWH, framed by the star of David, in Winchester Cathedral.

the God of your fathers . . . has sent me to you': this is my name for ever [Ex. 3:15]."

In order not to break the commandment against taking

God's name in vain, the Hebrews avoided saying *Yahweh* altogether and instead referred to God as *Adonai* or my Lord. About the 13th century A.D. the vowels of *Adonai* were combined with *YHWH* to form a new name, *Jehovah*, which appears a few times in the King James Bible.

The simplest Hebrew name for God is *El*; it was a popular term for any deity and one widely used by the Israelites and their neighbors. In the Hebrew Bible, *El* is often modified by a second word. *El Shaddai*, for example, means God Almighty, and *El Elyon* means God Most High. The most common name for God, however, is the plural term *Elohim*, suggesting that God in his majesty represents all aspects of divinity.

God the creator, "ancient of days [Dan. 7:9]"
though he may be, is still a supremely masterful
figure in this 16th-century illumination.

What roles does God assume in the Bible?

In sharp contrast to ancient polytheistic religions, in which each member of the pantheon was assigned a particular role—such as a god of war or a goddess of fertility—the God of the Bible controls all things and fills a multitude of roles.

First and foremost, God is the creator and life-giver: "In the beginning, God created the heavens and the earth." But he is also the destroyer: "The Lord saw that the wickedness of man was great in the earth . . . and it grieved him to his heart. So the Lord said, 'I will blot out man whom I have created from the face of the ground, man and beast and creeping things and birds of the air, for I am sorry that I have made them.'" The result of this ominous vow was the flood—which only Noah, his family, and specimens of all lesser creatures survived. GEN. 1:1 GEN. 6:5

The Old Testament God is also a king, who reacts angrily when the elders of Israel ask Samuel to appoint an earthly king to govern them; he is a judge, weighing the rights and wrongs of human behavior; a shepherd, caring for his flock; a husband who will never abandon his wife even

RIGHTEOUS. *In the Bible, a righteous person is one who fulfills his or her responsibilities to God and to society. The first time the Bible uses the term is in reference to Noah, who is described as "a righteous man, blameless in his generation; Noah walked with God [Gen. 6:9]." While all others plunged into wickedness, Noah remained faithful to his obligations and was saved from the great flood.*

In the Old Testament, righteousness was understood in terms of God's covenant with the Israelites. Those who obeyed the covenant were righteous; those who broke it were not. God himself was righteous, showing mercy and justice in fulfilling his part of the covenant with the people.

According to New Testament teaching, man cannot attain righteousness on his own; it is God's gift to those who accept Jesus Christ as their Lord.

thropomorphisms with references to God's finger, face, hand, and bosom.

One description that has influenced countless illustrations of the deity comes from the Book of Daniel, where God is described as "ancient of days . . . his raiment was white as snow, and the hair of his head like pure wool." DAN. 7:9

❋

God reaches down from heaven in this wall painting of Ezekiel's famous encounter with the deity, a third-century work in the synagogue at Dura-Europos, Syria. Lost in a trance, the prophet avoids gazing directly at the sight.

when she strays; a warrior who defeats his people's enemies; a lawgiver who promulgates the Ten Commandments; and a father to all his people. The same metaphors appear in the New Testament, where they are often applied to Jesus Christ: he is the lawgiver whose law is love; the husband of his bride, the church; the good shepherd; and the final judge of the earth.

Why are images of God forbidden in the Bible?

EX. 20:4 "You shall not make for yourself a graven image . . . you shall not bow down to them or serve them." This ringing denunciation of idolatry that is so prominent in the Ten Commandments reverberates throughout the Bible. Not only is the worship of other gods prohibited but so are representations of the one God: "Since you saw no

DT. 4:15 form on the day that the Lord spoke to you . . . beware lest you act corruptly by making a graven image for yourselves."

Isaiah pointed out the impossibility of representing God: "To whom then will you liken God,

IS. 40:18 senting God: "To whom then will you liken God, or what likeness compare with him?" Jeremiah

JER. 10:5 ridiculed the gods of Israel's neighbors: "Their idols are like scarecrows in a cucumber field, ✳

and they cannot speak; they have to be carried, for they cannot walk."

Nonetheless, the temptation to worship other gods often proved irresistible. The Israelites repeatedly fell into idolatry from the time they made the golden calf until the Babylonian exile. Later, pagans saw Jews and Christians as atheists because they did not make images of God.

By the first century A.D. the continuing pervasiveness of Greek and Roman idols greatly troubled people who had once worshiped pagan images. Some would not eat meat for fear it had come from an animal sacrificed to an idol. To Paul this seemed like an excessive reaction, though he firmly forbade idol worship. In his First Letter to the Corinthians, he explained, "Food will not commend us to God. 1 COR. 8:8 We are no worse off if we do not eat [meat from animals sacrificed to idols], and no better off if we do." The reason, said Paul, is that "an idol has no 1 COR. 8:4 real existence . . . there is no God but one."

How does God communicate with his people?

In the Bible, God often spoke directly to individuals, including Adam and Eve, Abraham, Job, Joshua, Gideon, Solomon, the prophets, and Jesus. Sometimes, as in the case of Moses, God's

EX. 33:11 relationship to a person was so special that he spoke to him "face to face, as a man speaks to his friend."

God also manifested himself through signs linked to nature. At Mount Sinai he made his presence known amid thunder, lightning, smoke, and trumpet blasts. This proved to be a terrifying experience for the Israelites; they were EX. 20:19 so afraid that they pleaded with Moses: "You speak to us, and we will hear; but let not God speak to us, lest we die."

Another way God communicated was in dreams and visions. God sent messages to patriarchs, prophets, and even ordinary people while they slept. In Jacob's dream the Lord appeared at the top of the ladder that vanished into heaven and told Jacob, "I am with you and will keep you GEN. 28:15 wherever you go."

In this 15th-century altarpiece, God watches from above as the archangel Gabriel announces to Mary the conception of Jesus.

HEAVENLY MESSENGERS

"Angel" is the translation of a Hebrew word meaning messenger, and in the Bible, God uses angels to convey his word to man and carry out tasks for him on earth.

Though not gods themselves, angels are celestial beings who possess "wisdom . . . to know all things that are on the earth [2 Sam. 14:20]." They are countless in number because throughout the Old Testament God is referred to as the Lord of hosts. They take on a human form so as to conceal their true identity from those to whom they are sent. At the battle of Jericho, for instance, Joshua sees the commander of the Lord's army as a man with a drawn sword.

In a number of biblical narratives, God and his messenger-angel are referred to interchangeably, so that it is sometimes unclear who exactly is being designated. The expression angel of the Lord, then, may have been a synonym for God himself. Thus the angel who appears to Jacob in a dream suddenly announces, "I am the God of Bethel [Gen. 31:13]."

It is an angel as well as God who appears to Moses out of the burning bush, escorts the Israelites through the wilderness, feeds Elijah in the desert, and slays 185,000 Assyrian invaders. Angels announce future events, such as unexpected births, protect the righteous, and punish the wicked.

Living under Persian influence after the Babylonian exile, the Jews developed the idea of good versus bad angels; and Revelation contains a battle between the two forces, with Satan leading the bad angels. The New Testament supports the traditional role of angels as messengers of God sent to do his work on earth. The seven orders or "choirs" of angels—thrones, dominions, virtues, powers, principalities, archangels, and angels—are a post-biblical tradition of the early Christian church; they are sometimes linked to cherubim and seraphim, the enigmatic winged figures of the Old Testament.

How does God make things happen?

The Bible describes an all-powerful God, who works his will in a great variety of ways. God has only to speak, and his word becomes reality: GEN. 1:3 "And God said, 'Let there be light,' and there was IS. 55:11 light." "My word," God says through Isaiah, "shall not return to me empty, but it shall accomplish that which I purpose."

Often God intervenes directly in the affairs of men. For example, he saved the Israelites from EX. 14:25 the pursuing Egyptians by "clogging their chariot GEN. 19:24 wheels," and he "rained . . . fire" on the sinful GAL. 4:4 city of Sodom. In the New Testament, God "sent forth his Son," and after Jesus was crucified, ACTS 13:30 "raised him from the dead."

Sometimes God instills the divine spirit in humans, enabling them to carry out his will. The judges who ruled over Israel's early settlements and the prophets who spoke in God's name are often described as possessing the spirit of God. MIC. 3:8 Micah declares: "I am filled with power, with the Spirit of the Lord, and with justice and might." In LK. 4:14 the New Testament, Jesus was filled with "the power of the Spirit" at his baptism; following Jesus' death his disciples began their missionary ACTS 2:4 work only after they had been "filled with the Holy Spirit."

The Scriptures also show God using many agents to cause things to happen. Angels, for example, feed a prophet, bring a plague, and announce the birth of the Messiah. Even Satan served as God's intermediary to test the piety of Job. Similarly, God selects human agents to do his work. He uses the savage Assyrian invaders to punish the idolatry of Israel and the Persian king Cyrus to restore his people after their exile. The Bible asserts that when God wills it, anything, even "winds" and "fire and flame," can PS. 104:4 serve as his "messengers" and "ministers."

Which biblical figures argued with God?

The Bible teaches that God gave humans the power to think and act for themselves—even though their thoughts or actions might be in direct opposition to divine will. One of the most famous examples of this kind of conflict was the one between God and Abraham. Informed that God planned to punish Sodom, Abraham pro- ✳

CREATE. *The word* create *(in Hebrew, bara) takes on special significance in the Old Testament. As a verb used exclusively to express divine activity, it takes only God as its subject. In creating the world in Genesis 1, God needs only to say "Let there be" and his command is fulfilled.*

Apart from Genesis, the verb is particularly important in the Book of Isaiah. There the prophet envisions the renewal of the people of Israel after long years of exile in Babylon. The God who created the world also created his people by bringing them out of Egypt and would now create them anew by restoring their nation.

tested that there must be at least 50 good people in the evil city. "Wilt thou indeed destroy the GEN. 18:23 righteous with the wicked?" he asked. "Shall not GEN. 18:25 the Judge of all the earth do right?" Before the bargaining ended, the Lord had promised Abraham to spare the city for the sake of even 10 righteous persons.

The Book of Job is a sustained challenge to God's sense of justice. To test whether Job will remain faithful even under conditions of dire suffering, God let the adversary destroy Job's children and all his possessions and afflicted him with a painful skin disease. Against the suggestions of his friends that he must have done something terrible to deserve such a fate, Job proclaimed his innocence and accused God of being unjust.

In contrast to these direct challenges to God's wishes, Moses simply tried to evade the mission God had given him to lead the Israelites out of bondage in Egypt. "Who am I that I should go to EX. 3:11 Pharaoh?" he plaintively asked the Lord. But God insisted. Still Moses hesitated, fearful that the mighty ruler would not believe him. God then granted him miraculous powers to impress the Egyptians. When Moses protested, "I am not elo- EX. 4:10 quent . . . I am slow of speech," God promised to teach him what to say. "Send, I pray, some other EX. 4:13 person," Moses begged—at which point the Lord became angry, but nonetheless designated Moses' brother Aaron to be his spokesman.

In the Book of Jonah, these two types of arguments are blended together. After trying to evade

God's command to prophesy against the wicked city of Nineveh, Jonah eventually carried out his mission. When the Ninevites repented, Jonah was furious because they would escape punishment for their formerly sinful ways; God was too merciful. But God taught the prophet a lesson, making a large plant grow up overnight to provide Jonah with shade from the burning sun. Then God made the plant wither, causing Jonah JON. 4:10 great discomfort. God explained to Jonah: "You pity the plant, for which you did not labor, nor did you make it grow. . . . And should not I pity Nineveh, that great city, in which there are more than a hundred and twenty thousand persons?"

What does it mean for a person to "know" God?

In the Bible, the word *know* implies a personal experience involving two individuals. (Sexual relations are often referred to in this way, as in "Now Adam knew Eve his wife.") Thus to know GEN. 4:1 God was to have a sustained, intimate relationship with him. Indeed, the Lord's covenant with the Israelites was described as between husband and wife: "I will betroth you to me for ever; I will HOS. 2:19 betroth you to me in righteousness and in justice, in steadfast love, and in mercy."

In the New Testament, acceptance of Jesus

Kneeling with hands raised in supplication, Jesus assumes the posture of prayer in Mantegna's moving portrayal of the ordeal at Gethsemane.

THE POWER OF PRAYER

Although Adam, Eve, and Cain talked with God, it was not in the form of a prayer. The first mention of prayer in the Bible is after Seth named his son Enosh: "At that time men began to call upon the name of the Lord [Gen. 4:26]."

Since the God of the Bible related personally to individuals, they in turn felt free to attempt to converse with him in prayer. Throughout the Old Testament, people sought communion with the deity through different types of prayer, such as adoration or worship, praise, confession, intercession, petition (supplication on behalf of another), and thanksgiving. The same forms of prayer continued in early Christianity.

The Lord's Prayer, as spoken by Jesus, was not only a guide but the epitome of what a prayer should be. The first three of its six petitions attest to God's supremacy; the last three acknowledge people's need for sustenance, forgiveness, and deliverance from evil.

The most poignant prayer is Jesus' anguished utterance at Gethsemane: "Abba, Father, all things are possible to thee; remove this cup from me; yet not what I will, but what thou wilt [Mk. 14:36]."

Jesus and God the Father are enthroned beneath a dove, the traditional symbol of the Holy Spirit, the third person of the Trinity. This 15th-century Byzantine fresco from a Cyprus monastery was conceived as a teaching aid to help believers understand the nature of God.

brings knowledge of the divinity. The Gospel of John affirms that "this is eternal life, that they know thee the only true God, and Jesus Christ whom thou has sent." JN. 17:3

But when the Bible refers to someone as not knowing God, it is saying that that person has not experienced the reality of God. Young Samuel, for example, mistook the call of the Lord for a summons from the priest Eli, because Samuel "did not yet know the Lord, and the word of the Lord had not yet been revealed to him." Through Jeremiah, God condemned those who acted unjustly, who "proceed from evil to evil" because they do not know the Lord. And pagans were said to have no knowledge of God. In the New Testament, Paul reminds the Galatians: "When you did not know God, you were in bondage to beings that by nature are no gods." 1 SAM. 3:7 JER. 9:3 GAL. 4:8

What is the Trinity?

Although the word *Trinity* does not appear in the Bible, numerous New Testament passages can be seen as offering support for the doctrine of three persons in one God: Father, Son, and Holy Spirit. In announcing the birth of Jesus to Mary, the angel Gabriel mentions all three: "The Holy Spirit will come upon you, and the power of the Most High will overshadow you; therefore the ✳ LK. 1:35

child to be born will be called holy, the Son of God." At Jesus' baptism the Holy Spirit descends like a dove and the voice of God calls from heaven, "Thou art my beloved Son; with thee I am well pleased." In his farewell to his disciples, Jesus says, "Go therefore and make disciples of all nations, baptizing them in the name of the Father and of the Son and of the Holy Spirit." MK. 1:11 MT. 28:19

On Pentecost, Peter speaks of Jesus "exalted at the right hand of God, and having received from the Father the promise of the Holy Spirit." And Paul concludes his Second Letter to the Corinthians with the benediction: "The grace of the Lord Jesus Christ and the love of God and the fellowship of the Holy Spirit be with you all." ACTS 2:33 2 COR. 13:14

As the doctrine of the Trinity was gradually developed in the early centuries of Christianity, many Old Testament passages came to be regarded as references to the Trinity, even though such an idea was unknown to the Hebrews.

Which sin against God cannot be forgiven?

"You shall not revile God," the Lord commands in the Covenant Code given to Moses. When an Israelite woman's son quarreled in the camp and blasphemed the name of God, an awful punish- EX. 22:28

LEV. 24:16 ment was decreed by God: "He who blasphemes the name of the Lord shall be put to death; all the congregation shall stone him."

Speaking against God or showing contempt for him is a contentious issue in the New Testament. Jesus himself is accused of blasphemy for claiming to forgive sins and for asserting that he was MK. 14:61 "the Christ, the Son of the Blessed."

Paul confessed his original 1 TIM. 1:13 opposition to Jesus: "I formerly blasphemed and persecuted and insulted him; but I received mercy because I had acted ignorantly in unbelief." But after his conversion he taunted those Jews who boast of the law yet ROM. 2:24 break it: "The name of God is blasphemed among the Gentiles because of you."

Jesus turns the accusation of blasphemy against the Pharisees and proclaims the unfor- MK. 3:28 givable sin: "All sins will be forgiven the sons of men, and whatever blasphemies they utter; but whoever blasphemes against the Holy Spirit never has forgiveness, but is guilty of an eternal sin." He who denies the word and work of God and fails to distinguish between good and evil, Jesus is saying, is beyond pardoning because pardon can only be given to one who confesses error.

Where does God dwell?

IS. 6:3 "Holy, holy, holy is the Lord of hosts; the whole earth is full of his glory," proclaimed Isaiah. Since God is not a physical being, he cannot be said to reside in one particular location. Nevertheless the Bible contains numerous references to God's dwelling places. The first and foremost of these, of course, is heaven—suggested in EC. 5:2 Genesis and confirmed in Ecclesiastes: "God is in heaven, and you upon earth."

Following the Israelites' departure from Egypt, God wished to establish a presence among his ✳

"This is God Most Powerful,"
begins the Latin inscription
above the regal figure painted
by Jan and Hubert van Eyck.

chosen people. "Let them make EX. 25:8 me a sanctuary, that I may dwell in their midst," he commanded Moses. Seven chapters of Exodus are devoted to God's detailed instructions for building, furnishing, and worshiping in the tabernacle, the portable sanctuary that accompanied the Israelites during their 40 years of desert wandering. Another symbol of the Lord's presence was the ark of the covenant—the wooden chest overlaid with gold that contained the Ten Commandments. Later, the temple—and by extension the entire city of Jerusalem, where it stood—took the place of the tabernacle as the special dwelling place of God.

In the New Testament, Jesus speaks of God as "your Father MT. 6:1 who is in heaven," and early Christians believed that after his resurrection Jesus Christ was exalted "at the right hand of the HEB. 8:1 throne of the Majesty in heaven." They reiterated an Old Testament theme that God does not "dwell ACTS 7:48 in houses made with hands," and no temple could be his dwelling place; rather "in him we live . . . ACTS 17:28 and have our being." As Paul wrote to the Corinthians, "Do you 1 COR. 3:16 not know that you are God's temple and that God's Spirit dwells in you?"

Ultimately, according to the visions of Revelation, God will dwell directly with his people: "And I saw no temple in the city, for its temple is REV. 21:22 the Lord God the Almighty."

What is a covenant?

The people of the emerging Israelite nation would have been familiar with two kinds of covenants, or contracts, that were common in the ancient Near East. In one, a vassal pledged allegiance to a higher authority, such as a king, and took on the obligation of loyalty. In the other, the king made a grant to a subordinate ruler, perhaps as a reward, but there was no obligation on the part of the vassal in return for the grant.

Another word for covenant is testament, meaning a swearing to or witnessing of an agreement. Since the Hebrew Bible, essentially the story of God's covenant with the Israelites, was expanded in the first century A.D. to include God's new covenant with those who had faith in Christ, Christians call the former the Old Testament and the latter the New Testament.

What are the major covenants in the Old Testament?

The first covenant God made was with Noah and his descendants: never again to destroy the earth by flood. Since this was a covenant with all mankind, it differs from the three major biblical covenants involving Abraham, Moses, and David.

God's covenant with the patriarch Abraham was a grant of posterity, a homeland, and divine protection: "I will make you exceedingly fruitful. . . . And I will give to you, and to your descendants after you . . . all the land of Canaan, for an

GEN. 17:6

everlasting possession; and I will be their God."

Much later, God made a similar covenant with David—this time using the prophet Nathan as an intermediary. God granted David a permanent dynasty: "And your house and your kingdom shall be made sure for ever before me; your throne shall be established for ever."

2 SAM. 7:16

The covenant between God and the people of Israel is different from the other two because it is a covenant of obligation. Grateful for having been led out of bondage in Egypt, the Israelites at Mount Sinai pledged unconditional obedience to God: "All that the Lord has spoken we will do." God then set forth the obligations imposed on the Israelites: the Ten Commandments, which spell out the duties to God and their fellow men, and the Covenant Code, the laws that would later govern them in the Promised Land.

EX. 19:8

In addition to covenants between God and man, the Old Testament also contains numerous references to covenants between men, such as those between Isaac and Abimelech, Laban and Jacob, and Jonathan and David.

As a token of his promise never to flood the whole world again, God created the rainbow and made a covenant with Noah and his sons, as portrayed in this manuscript illumination.

Moses the Lawgiver

Alone atop Mount Sinai, Moses receives the stone tablets of the Ten Commandments from the hand of God, shown attended by an angelic host in this bronze relief on Ghiberti's baptistery doors in Florence.

What was Moses' role at Sinai?

As the central human figure in the drama that took place during the Hebrews' momentous sojourn at Sinai, Moses played several roles.

Above all, Moses was the lawgiver of Israel: he received the laws of the covenant on the holy mountain and transmitted them to the people. As intercessor on their behalf, he crossed the "holiness boundary" that separated them from the mountain where God revealed the law. As their moral advocate, he pleaded their case before God, urging forgiveness when the people lapsed into idol worship during his 40-day stay on the mountain. As a spokesman for God, he implemented sacrifice rituals, and after receiving God's blueprint for the tabernacle, he inaugurated daily worship and consecrated the clergy.

As the first and greatest of Israel's prophets—

DT. 34:10 "and there has not arisen a prophet since in Israel like Moses"—he was a model for all those ✳ who followed. As other prophets would do throughout Israel's history, Moses proclaimed the will of God to the people, promised blessings for their faithfulness, and warned of punishments for any disobedience.

Moses' face radiated light after he talked with God, but a mistranslation led artists to portray him with horns instead.

48

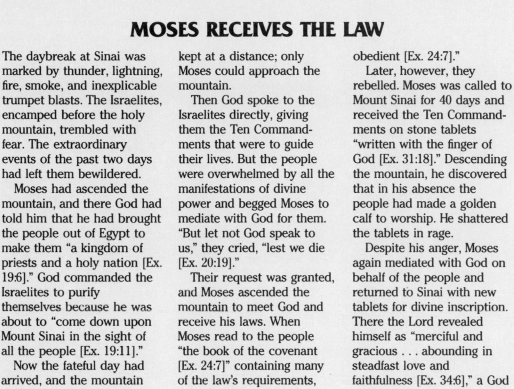

MOSES RECEIVES THE LAW

The daybreak at Sinai was marked by thunder, lightning, fire, smoke, and inexplicable trumpet blasts. The Israelites, encamped before the holy mountain, trembled with fear. The extraordinary events of the past two days had left them bewildered.

Moses had ascended the mountain, and there God had told him that he had brought the people out of Egypt to make them "a kingdom of priests and a holy nation [Ex. 19:6]." God commanded the Israelites to purify themselves because he was about to "come down upon Mount Sinai in the sight of all the people [Ex. 19:11]."

Now the fateful day had arrived, and the mountain quaked and smoked as "the Lord descended upon it [Ex. 19:18]." The multitude was kept at a distance; only Moses could approach the mountain.

Then God spoke to the Israelites directly, giving them the Ten Commandments that were to guide their lives. But the people were overwhelmed by all the manifestations of divine power and begged Moses to mediate with God for them. "But let not God speak to us," they cried, "lest we die [Ex. 20:19]."

Their request was granted, and Moses ascended the mountain to meet God and receive his laws. When Moses read to the people "the book of the covenant [Ex. 24:7]" containing many of the law's requirements, they affirmed them. "All that the Lord has spoken we will do, and we will be obedient [Ex. 24:7]."

Later, however, they rebelled. Moses was called to Mount Sinai for 40 days and received the Ten Commandments on stone tablets "written with the finger of God [Ex. 31:18]." Descending the mountain, he discovered that in his absence the people had made a golden calf to worship. He shattered the tablets in rage.

Despite his anger, Moses again mediated with God on behalf of the people and returned to Sinai with new tablets for divine inscription. There the Lord revealed himself as "merciful and gracious . . . abounding in steadfast love and faithfulness [Ex. 34:6]," a God who would forgive "iniquity and transgression and sin [Ex. 34:7]."

The Sinai story also portrays Moses in other roles—judge, miracle worker, sage—all central to the events that gave birth to the world's oldest monotheistic community.

How are the Ten Commandments different from other laws?

The laws that Moses brought down from Mount Sinai included the Ten Commandments—also called the Decalogue, or "Ten Words," spoken directly by God—and scores of other commandments, judgments, regulations, and ordinances meant to govern community life, personal behavior, and worship. Traditionally, the total number of commands given in the Pentateuch has been reckoned at 613, of which 365 were prohibitions and 248 positive commands.

The commands fall into two basic types: categorical law and case law. Most of them are ex- amples of case law, often dealing with very specific situations—"If a man steals an ox . . . he shall pay five oxen"—and are enforced by the judicial process. The Ten Commandments, however, belong to the smaller body of categorical law. They reflect neither specific cases nor specific penalties; rather, they serve as broad principles for a harmonious community life faithful to God's covenant. EX. 22:1

The first group of commands—no other gods, no idols, no blasphemy, and respect for the Sabbath—defines the basic relationship between God and his people. The remaining commands—honor for parents, no murder, no adultery, no theft, no fraud, and no envy—establish fundamental social values and set limits on human behavior. The Ten Commandments have had a profound influence on religious and social history. They are at the core of both Jewish and Christian moral teaching and are reflected in the civil law of many cultures and nations.

During Moses' absence, his people resorted to idolatrous worship of a golden calf, as shown at the top of this medieval psalter; below, an outraged Moses destroys the tablets.

in the fire, and made a "molten calf." EX. 32:4 In the ultimate perfidy, they exalted this work of their own hands: "These are your gods, O EX. 32:4 Israel, who brought you up out of the land of Egypt."

Moses knew about the Israelites' infidelity before he descended from Mount Sinai. His anger flared when he reached the foot of the mountain, where he saw them worshiping the idol. He hurled down the tablets and shattered them to show the people how their sin had shattered their covenant with the Lord. Then he burned the golden calf.

Ancient Near Eastern sources show that breaking tablets on which covenants were written was a common ritual for invalidating or repudiating agreements and contracts. Thus Moses' response was not only an angry reaction but a formal statement. There is symbolism as well in Moses' command to burn the golden calf, dissolve the gold powder in water, and make the people drink it. Such a practice is found in ancient trials by ordeal to test a person's innocence.

Where is Mount Sinai?

After the Israelites escaped from Egypt, they plunged into the hostile wilderness known today as the Sinai peninsula. They were heading for the Promised Land of Canaan, which lay to the northeast, but for reasons that are not clear they turned sharply south. The route they traveled likewise remains uncertain. Many of the place-names that Exodus associates with their journey are impossible to pinpoint, including the famous Mount Sinai, also called Mount Horeb or the "mountain of God." EX. 3:1

One commonly accepted site for Mount Sinai is the 7,500-foot-high peak known as Jebel Musa, meaning mountain of Moses, near the southern tip of the Sinai peninsula. Its link to Moses and Mount Sinai originated during the reign of the

Why did Moses break the tablets containing the Ten Commandments?

EX. 24:18 Moses had remained on the mountain for "forty days and forty nights"—a phrase often used in the Bible to indicate an indefinite but lengthy period of time. Impatient for Moses to return and resume their journey to the Promised Land, the people asked his brother, Aaron, to make them EX. 32:1 "gods, who shall go before us." Aaron collected the gold rings the people were wearing, put them ✳

Roman emperor Constantine in the fourth century A.D.—more than 1,500 years after the events described in Exodus. Helena, the emperor's mother, chose Jebel Musa as the place to build a chapel to commemorate the burning bush; since the sixth century a Christian monastery has occupied the site.

Because this identification of Mount Sinai was made so many centuries after events described in the Bible and because the location is so remote, many biblical geographers have argued that Mount Sinai is more likely a peak in the northern half of the peninsula, such as Jebel Halal, near one of the major caravan roads from Egypt to Canaan. But since the Bible does not provide enough information to confirm the location, many remain loyal to Jebel Musa as the traditional site of Mount Sinai.

The Ten Commandments are recorded on this fragment of an ancient scroll found at Qumran, Jordan, which is located near the Dead Sea.

THE FIRST COMMANDMENT

The words Moses brought down from Mount Sinai to the Israelites began with the supreme command: "I am the Lord your God. . . . You shall have no other gods before me [Ex. 20:2]." He was a jealous God who would tolerate no rivals; the devotion of his chosen people belonged exclusively to him.

The worship of one God is called monotheism, but not all scholars agree that the Israelites were monotheists from the time of Moses; rather, some suggest, they became so gradually over a period of centuries. Initially, they may have practiced monolatry—worshiping one god without denying the existence of others. All about them were people who recognized many deities, of which one or another might sometimes be elevated to a position of supremacy. To such people, the God of the Hebrews must have seemed just another tribal deity.

In the midst of such polytheistic cultures, God's call upon the Israelites to forsake other gods and acknowledge him alone was a revolutionary break with pagan religious custom. Many of the pagan gods were nature deities; they were presumed to control events like weather or endeavors like agriculture.

Israel's God was different; he was intimately involved with his people. "If you will obey my voice and keep my covenant," he promised, "you shall be my own possession among all peoples [Ex. 19:5]"; their obedience would be rewarded with his "steadfast love [Ex. 20:6]."

The prophets of Israel played an important role in shaping the people's faith and drawing them to the worship of one God. Beginning with Elijah, they spoke out against the belief that numerous gods controlled the forces of nature and taught that Israel's God was the Lord of creation. By the end of the Babylonian exile (c. 539 B.C.) the Jews were a monotheistic people: "I am the Lord, and there is no other, besides me there is no God [Is. 45:5]." Yet their faith was more than intellectual acceptance of belief in one God; it was adherence to the covenant that their God had made with them at Sinai. For the Jews, monotheism was a matter of the heart as well as the head.

Ark of the Covenant

What was the ark of the covenant?

In Hebrew, *aron*, or *aric*, means a box or casket. According to Exodus, the ark of the covenant was built of acacia wood and measured 45 by 27 inches. Whenever the Israelites were on the move, they carried it on gilded poles inserted through rings.

The ark was especially holy for two reasons. First, it contained the most precious relics of Israel's faith: the tablets of stone on which God had inscribed the Ten Commandments. Since these were at the heart of God's covenant with the people of Israel, the ark was known as the ark of the covenant, or the ark of the testimony. Second, the ark was a sign of the divine presence, symbolized by its lid of solid gold bearing the two golden cherubim. The cover, called the "mercy seat," represented the throne of God. EX. 25:17 1 SAM. 4:4 Thus this holy chest was called "the ark of the covenant of the Lord of hosts, who is enthroned on the cherubim."

Why was Uzzah punished for touching the ark?

Because the ark of the covenant symbolized God's presence, the Israelites believed that it was a source of potential danger to mere mortals. Members of the tribe of Levi were charged with carrying the ark when the Israelites traveled, but even the Levites were allowed neither to touch nor

This ancient Egyptian cedar chest recalls the biblical description of the ark of the covenant.

"to look upon the holy things even for a moment, NUM. 4:20 lest they die." They could lift the poles bearing the ark only after the high priest had draped the box with veils. When the Israelites were not marching, the high priest could approach the ark only once a year, on the Day of Atonement, and then only after careful purification and in a cloud of incense to hide the mercy seat from view.

When David wanted to make Jerusalem the religious center of Israel, he had the ark brought to the city in an oxcart led by a man named Uzzah and his brother. When the oxen stumbled, Uzzah put his hand on the ark to steady it, but his good intentions did not save him: "God smote him . . . 2 SAM. 6:7 and he died there beside the ark of God."

Why did the Philistines want to get rid of the ark?

The ark was prominent not only in worship but also in warfare. When the Israelites set out from Sinai with the ark, Moses said, "Arise, O Lord, NUM. 10:35 and let thy enemies be scattered."

In the time of Samuel, Israel's corrupt leaders hoped to force God to reverse a loss they had suffered at the hands of the Philistines by bringing the ark to the battlefront at Aphek. Though the Philistines recognized the ark and expected the worst, they captured the chest and took it to the temple of their chief god, Dagon, in Ashdod.

The loss of the ark was a tragedy to Israel but far from a blessing to the Philistines. The ark was blamed for causing the statue of Dagon to fall and shatter to pieces. Next, the people of Ashdod were afflicted with tumors, and they complained that the God of Israel's "hand is heavy 1 SAM. 5:7 upon us." They shuttled their fearsome booty from Ashdod to Gath to Ekron, but everywhere the sickness followed, setting off "a deathly 1 SAM. 5:11 panic." In desperation, the Philistines loaded the ark onto a driverless cart pulled by two milch cows and headed it back to Israel bearing "five golden tumors and five golden mice." 1 SAM. 6:4

It is possible that the tumors the Philistines suffered were the result of an outbreak of the bubonic plague, characterized by large, painful swellings. The Philistines were probably aware of a connection between this dread disease and rodents, which the Bible says were ravaging the land. It may explain the guilt offering of tumors and mice, which the Philistines hoped would please Israel's God and rid them of their troubles.

THE LOST ARK

King David triumphantly brings the revered chest into Jerusalem, as shown in this illuminated manuscript by an unknown 14th-century artist.

The ark was a portable shrine built for travel, well suited to the needs of the wandering Israelites. Its carrying poles were always kept in place so that it could quickly be readied for the march whenever the cloud representing the presence of God indicated that the people should break camp.

As the symbol of God's covenant, the ark led the way to the Promised Land. At the river Jordan, when "the feet of the priests bearing the ark were dipped in the brink of the water [Jos. 3:15]," the waters parted to allow the Israelites to cross on dry ground. Carried around the city of Jericho, the ark brought Israel its first victory in Canaan.

The ark was installed in the sanctuary of Gilgal near Jericho but was later moved to Shechem, between Mounts Ebal and Gerizim. There all the people gathered on opposite sides of the ark in front of the two mountains, listened to the reading of the law, and renewed the covenant represented by the ark.

The ark was also at Bethel for some time before it found a long-term home at Shiloh. From Shiloh it was taken to Israel's army at the battle of Aphek, where it was captured and held by the Philistines for seven months— shunted among the leading cities of Israel's enemy.

When the Philistines sent the ark back to Israel, it went briefly to Beth-shemesh. But 70 men died when they tried to look inside it, and the terrified populace dispatched it to Kiriath-jearim, where it remained in the care of a man named Eleazar for 20 years. Apparently it could not be returned to Shiloh, since the sanctuary there had been destroyed in the war with the Philistines. The text of 1 Samuel suggests that during this period the ark may customarily have been taken into battle to rally Israel's troops.

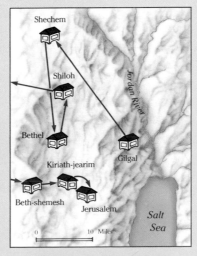

The journey of the ark from city to city ended in Jerusalem.

After David took Jerusalem for his capital, he tried to bring the ark there by oxcart but was stymied when Uzzah was struck dead for touching the chest; for three months it remained in the house of Obed-edom the Gittite. Finally, with great rejoicing, David had the ark brought into Jerusalem, where it was installed in a tent.

When Solomon built his temple, the ark was moved into the holy of holies, where it remained the focus of Israel's worship. But nothing more is told of it until a brief statement by the prophet Jeremiah seemed to indicate that it had been lost when the Babylonians destroyed the temple.

The fate of the ark is unknown, but many believed that so holy an object could not simply be carried off by the enemy. One tradition from the second century B.C. holds that Jeremiah, guided by God, took the ark to the mountain where Moses had died and sealed it in a cave. There it awaits the day when God gathers his people again, reveals the ark anew, and manifests his glory.

Holy Places

A stone sacred to Canaanites and later Israelites was discovered at an excavation site in the holy city of Shechem.

What made a place holy?

The Israelites, like many peoples in the ancient world, believed that certain places were holy. These were usually associated with aged trees, mountains, or man-made markers such as standing stones or altars.

When Abraham entered the land of Canaan, the Lord first appeared to him at a traditional Canaanite shrine at Shechem—a sacred tree called the oak of Moreh, meaning the oak of the soothsayer—and told the patriarch, "To your descendants I will give this land," whereupon Abraham built an altar to the Lord there. Later, when the Lord said to Abraham's son, Isaac, at Beersheba, "Fear not, for I am with you and will bless you and multiply your descendants," Isaac paused in his wanderings to build a shrine, pitch his tent, and dig a well there. GEN. 12:7 GEN. 26:24

Two mountains were deemed sacred to God: Sinai, where he had spoken to Moses, and Zion, where he was said to dwell. The exact location of Mount Sinai is uncertain, but Zion was the fortified hill in pre-Israelite Jerusalem that became the site of Solomon's temple.

In New Testament times any church or site of worship could be considered a holy place, in-

JACOB'S DREAM AT BETHEL

Jacob had succeeded in swindling his brother Esau out of both his inheritance and the patriarchal blessing of their father, Isaac. But all that his shrewdness had gained him was the mortal enmity of Esau.

Rebekah not only warned Jacob, her favored younger son, of Esau's vow to kill him, but devised a scheme to save him. Rather than let Jacob marry a Canaanite woman, she persuaded Isaac that Jacob should be sent to the land of her father to take as his wife a daughter of her

brother, Laban.

By nightfall of his flight, Jacob by chance had reached an ancient shrine, perhaps unused at that time. Exhausted, he put a stone under his head for a pillow and fell into a deep sleep, punctuated by a dream that was the turning point of his life. He saw a ladder reaching to heaven with angels ascending and descending. At the top stood God himself, who promised to give Jacob and his descendants the very land where he now lay and to be

with him and keep him wherever he went.

When Jacob awoke, he accepted the truth of the dream. "How awesome is this place!" he exclaimed. "This is none other than the house of God, and this is the gate of heaven [Gen. 28:17]." Jacob took the stone on which he had rested his head, raised it as a sacred pillar, anointed it with oil, and called the spot Bethel, or the house of God. If God blessed him, he vowed, he would return and make the place a true house of God.

MT. 18:20 fused with a holy presence—in the words of Jesus, "For where two or three are gathered in my name, there am I in the midst of them."

What was special about altars of unhewn stones?

After issuing the Ten Commandments, the Lord asked Moses to tell the people not to make gods of silver or gold but to make an altar of earth on which to offer sacrifices to God. Unlike the more elaborate worship of their pagan neighbors, the Israelites' homage to their God was to be simple. But if they chose to make an altar of stone, God EX. 20:25 added, "you shall not build it of hewn stones; for if you wield your tool upon it you profane it."

The Bible never explains why tools would desecrate an altar, and later interpreters suggested that iron tools were symbolically incompatible with an altar. "The altar is for forgiving," one rabbi wrote, "and iron is for punishing." Underlying the prohibition seems to have been the belief that anything as holy as an altar should be made of materials as they were created by God, unchanged by human hands.

A similar prohibition was enforced at the building of Solomon's temple. All stone for the 1 KG. 6:7 house of the Lord was dressed at the quarry, "so that neither hammer nor axe nor any tool of iron was heard in the temple."

What did horned altars symbolize?

The Bible contains numerous references to horned altars, beginning with God's precise instructions to Moses on how to construct and consecrate the tabernacle altar. The exact meaning of the horns is unclear, however. During certain sacrifices, priests took some of the victim's LEV. 4:25 blood and "put it on the horns of the altar." The horned altar also seems to signify sanctuary; a person would hold on to the horns in the hope of deterring capture and punishment.

What is the altar to the unknown god?

When Paul arrived in Athens, the cultural capital ACTS 17:16 of Greece, he found a city "full of idols" and a ACTS 17:21 people who "spent their time in nothing except telling or hearing something new." He took ad- ✳

Inspired by his dream, Jacob erected the pillar of Bethel to mark the site as sacred to God, as shown in a medieval parchment illumination.

vantage of the Athenians' fascination with philosophy and religion and their curiosity about "for- ACTS 17:18 eign divinities."

Paul began his preaching by recalling an altar dedicated "to an unknown god," a shrine erect- ACTS 17:23 ed by someone who did not know which deity to thank or to appease. This unknown divinity whom the Athenians worshiped, Paul proposed, was actually the "God who made the world and ACTS 17:24 everything in it; being Lord of heaven and earth, [God] does not live in shrines made by man, nor is he served by human hands, as though he needed anything, since he himself gives to all men life and breath and everything."

Though the altar referred to by Paul has never been found, other ancient authors also mention altars dedicated to "unknown gods."

Sacrifices

What kinds of sacrifices were made in Old Testament times?

The burnt offering, or holocaust, was at the core of Israel's religious life: each day began and ended with the sacrifice of an unblemished male yearling lamb in the sanctuary. It was called a holocaust because the animal was completely burned—and thus wholly given to God. The burning flesh produced a pungent fragrance that LEV. 1:9 was said to be "a pleasing odor to the Lord."

or in fulfillment of a vow that a person had made to God, or as an act of pure devotion that required no particular occasion.

A third type of sacrifice, the sin or guilt offering, was made in atonement for unintentional sin or impurity. In this case the fat portions of the animal were consumed by the fire, and the rest went to the priests. The offender received nothing. Some of the animal's blood was smeared on the horns of one of the altars and the rest poured out at the base of the altar of burnt offering. The blood was important because "without the shed- HEB. 9:22

A mosaic in St. Mark's Basilica in Venice portrays Noah at an altar, offering a sacrifice to God in gratitude for deliverance from the flood.

By such sacrifices, described in detail in Leviticus and also covered in Exodus and Numbers, the Israelites gave thanks to God and expressed their desire to maintain his favor.

Another type of sacrifice was the communion sacrifice, or shared offering. God's portion—much of the animal's fat, along with its kidneys and liver—was burned on the altar. The rest of the animal was divided between the priest, who received the breast and right thigh, and the worshiper, who prepared a banquet for his family and guests from the meat that remained. These sacrifices, also called peace offerings, were made in thanksgiving—when a person had survived some great ordeal or illness, for example, ✳

ding of blood there is no forgiveness. . . ." In these expiatory offerings the status of the sinner determined the value of the sacrifice. The sins of a high priest demanded the sacrifice of a bull; those of the poor, only two turtledoves.

Many of the animal sacrifices were also accompanied by cereal offerings of flour, parched grain, cakes, or loaves.

How were sacrifices performed?

Sacrifices were carefully ritualized acts. They involved both worshiper and priest and varied according to the type of offering.

If a man wished to make a burnt offering in the temple, he had to bathe to purify himself from any ritual uncleanness. Only then could he approach the temple court with his sacrificial animal and additional offerings of flour, oil, and wine.

When he reached the altar of burnt offering, he placed his hand upon the head of the animal so that LEV. 1:4 "it shall be accepted for him to make atonement for him." By this procedure he was not claiming to transfer his sins to the animal but was simply identifying himself as the one making the offering.

After leading his lamb to the north side of the altar, he killed the sacrificial animal by cutting its throat. A priest stood by with a basin to catch LEV. 17:11 the blood, "for the life of the flesh is in the blood; . . . it is the blood that makes atonement." The priest cast this lifeblood against the altar, signifying that the life belonged to God. The offerer next flayed the carcass and cut it into quarters, while the priest placed wood on the altar fire.

Then the priest took the butchered animal. As the worshiper looked on, the priest ritually washed the animal's entrails and legs and laid the entire carcass on the fire. At the same time he mingled with frankincense and oil a portion of the flour that had been brought, added the mixture to the fire, and poured out a libation of wine. As the powerful odor of the burning sacrifice filled the court, the worshiper could have confidence that his offering was pleasing to God.

How was the Passover sacrifice different from other sacrifices?

Passover—commemorating the night the Lord spared the Israelites from the slaughter of all the firstborn in Egypt—was one of the great pilgrimage feasts up until New Testament times. Worshipers came to Jerusalem from all over Israel and, in the time of Herod the Great, from all over the ancient world. Jerusalem was swollen with visitors—estimates range up to 200,000. From just such a multitude of people came those who ✳

The blood of a sacrificed lamb is saved for ritual use in this sculpture in the cathedral at Rheims.

welcomed Jesus on his entry into the city, calling out "Hosanna! Blessed is he who comes in the name of the Lord." MK. 11:9; JN. 12:13

The preparation of a great many paschal lambs was an assembly-line operation. Every priest in Israel was pressed into duty. The temple was purified of all leaven; the evening burnt offering was made early; and at 3 P.M. three trumpet blasts sounded, and the first worshipers were admitted to the altar court, where they faced lines of priests.

As each man with a lamb approached a priest, either he or a priest killed the animal. The priest caught the blood in a basin, which was passed along a line of priests and thrown against the altar—the life given to God. Then the priests burned the required portion of fat. Meanwhile, a Levite had flayed the carcass, careful not to break any bones; wrapped the lamb in its skin, ready for roasting; and delivered it back to the worshiper for the traditional feast before going on to the next sacrifice.

Each participant at the Passover meal had to eat a piece of the lamb at least as large as an

Two devout Jews sacrifice an unblemished lamb in this illumination from a Latin Bible produced in the 13th century.

In this mosaic from a floor in a synagogue built in the fifth or sixth century, Abraham is about to sacrifice his son Isaac on a fiery altar, as commanded by God, whose hand is at the top.

olive, and the entire offering had to be consumed that same evening. The Gospels of Matthew, Mark, and Luke call the Last Supper a Passover feast. Jesus took this occasion to announce the impending sacrifice of his own life, calling MT. 26:28 the wine "my blood of the covenant, which is poured out for many for the forgiveness of sins."

Did the Israelites ever practice human sacrifice?

When the Lord commanded Abraham to offer his GEN. 22:2 son Isaac "as a burnt offering upon one of the mountains of which I shall tell you," it was a test of the patriarch's fidelity and not a call for human sacrifice. Indeed, the law of Moses condemns child sacrifice, in recognition of the fact that such terrible offerings were made by Israel's neighbors to their gods. When the king of Moab 2 KG. 3:26 "saw that the battle was going against him," he proposed his eldest son as a burnt offering, to the horror of the Israelites, who gave up their cer- 2 KG. 3:27 tain victory and "withdrew from him and returned to their own land."

There is, however, an exceptional instance in the Bible of a child being sacrificed to the God of Israel. According to Judges 11:30, the judge Jephthah slew his only daughter in fulfillment of the reckless vow he had made to God in return for victory in battle. The story is told without ✳

explicit comment or condemnation. The prophets Jeremiah and Ezekiel condemned child sacrifice as widespread; yet in the Bible the practice is attributed to only two kings of Judah, Ahaz and Manasseh, who introduced pagan rites as the kingdom's official religion.

HELL. *A ravine south of Jerusalem gave hell its name. The word translated hell in the New Testament is the Greek word* gehenna, *which comes from a Hebrew phrase meaning valley of Hinnom. It refers to the valley near Jerusalem where there had been a pagan hearth used to burn the victims of child sacrifice. Although King Josiah (640 to 609 B.C.) destroyed the shrine, the prophet Jeremiah continued to condemn the abominations of the valley of Hinnom during the reign of his successor.*

As the site of horrible death by fire, the valley thus provides an appropriate metaphor for the place where God condemns the evil for eternity. The use of gehenna *for a place of punishment appears in the teaching of Jesus, who described it as a place that can "destroy both soul and body [Mt. 10:28]." The name also came to be used in later Jewish and Muslim writings.*

THE BINDING OF ISAAC

"Take your son," God commanded Abraham, "your only son Isaac, whom you love, and go to the land of Moriah, and offer him there as a burnt offering upon one of the mountains of which I shall tell you [Gen. 22:2]."

What could God possibly mean by so monstrous a command? Such a question must have echoed in Abraham's head as he looked at Isaac. The importance of this child was beyond reckoning. Here was the miraculous offspring of two aged parents, the son who bore all God's extravagant promises that Abraham's descendants would be as innumerable as the stars. Now God had stunned Abraham with a clear but inexplicable demand. The reader is informed that God's order was a test, but Abraham did not know this.

What would he do? With exquisite brevity Genesis describes how Abraham unflinchingly fulfilled God's command. The next dawn saw Abraham and Isaac with servants and provisions setting out for Moriah. Just as Abraham had left his family and followed God when God's promises seemed to be opening up the future, so did he follow when God seemed to be slamming shut all hope.

Three days of travel passed; Abraham and Isaac left the servants and approached the dread place of sacrifice. Isaac poignantly observed that all was not right: "Behold, the fire and the wood: but where is the lamb [Gen. 22:7]?" Abraham affirmed, "God will provide himself the lamb for a burnt offering, my son [Gen. 22:8]."

Still God gave no sign of a reprieve for Isaac. In silence Abraham arranged the altar, bound Isaac, and "took the knife to slay his son [Gen. 22:10]." Only at the last instant did God forestall the horror and save the child from his father's obedience. Abraham had passed the test, demonstrating his absolute trust in God, and God, in response, confirmed the very promises that he had seemed to shatter.

Though this harrowing story is never mentioned again in the Old Testament, it later became an important symbol in both Judaism and Christianity. In Judaism it became the model of sacrifice in obedience to God's will and the symbol of Jewish martyrdom. Christians, on the other hand, saw it as an example of true faith and a foreshadowing of the death of Christ.

Why did the prophets object to sacrifice?

Israel's prophets came to evaluate their nation's worship not by its purity of form—how well sacrifices were performed—but by how well worshipers met the ethical and moral responsibilities of Israel's covenant and laws. When they found that the form of worship had replaced the substance of obedience to God's law, they brought God's scorching judgment down on elaborate but empty rituals. "I hate, I despise your feasts. . . . Even though you offer me your burnt offerings. . . I will not accept them. . . . But let justice roll down like waters, and righteousness like an ever-flowing stream," Amos railed. AM. 5:21

The prophets in general assumed that the sacrifices would continue but warned that sacrifices alone were never enough. As Isaiah proclaimed, " 'What to me is the multitude of your sacrifices?' says the Lord; 'I have had enough of burnt offerings of rams . . . cease to do evil, learn to do good; seek justice, correct oppression.' " IS. 1:11 Only when a sacrifice was matched by faithful action outside the sanctuary, the prophets were saying, was it acceptable to God.

Could Gentiles perform sacrifices in the temple?

Gentiles, or non-Jews, could not enter the inner courts of the temple, but they could and did offer sacrifices, especially during the second temple period. The first-century A.D. historian Josephus records that kings of Egypt and Syria sacrificed in

Jerusalem, and in the time of Herod the Great a wealthy Roman, Marcus Agrippa, made an offering of 100 cattle. Also, during the first century, the future emperor Vitellius stopped in Jerusalem to make a sacrifice as an act of deference to what he considered a provincial deity.

Did early Christians continue sacrificing in the temple?

During the early days of Christianity, the Apostles and other believers continued to participate in temple worship, as described in the Book of Acts. "Attending the temple together and breaking bread in their homes" was a daily routine for the early Christian community in Jerusalem. Peter and John went to the temple "at the hour of prayer, the ninth hour," or 3 P.M., which was the time for the evening burnt offering to be made. Acts also relates that Paul "purified himself . . . and went into the temple" in preparation for

ACTS 2:46

ACTS 3:1

ACTS 21:26

Dressed in traditional garb, Samaritans perform a Passover sacrifice at Mount Gerizim. Most members of the sect live in two enclaves, one at Nablus, the other at Holon.

making a sacrifice; but his plans were interrupted when he was arrested.

In Christian theology the crucifixion of Christ supplanted all other sacrifices. In practice, however, there were occasions when Jewish Christians continued to offer temple sacrifices up until the destruction of the sanctuary in A.D. 70.

Are sacrifices still performed?

With the destruction of the temple, Jews stopped making animal sacrifices; Christians never included such sacrifices in their worship. However, a small community of Samaritans in present-day Israel practices at least one ancient sacrifice.

The Samaritans—best known, perhaps, for Jesus' parable of the Good Samaritan—claim to be descendants of ancient Israelites who intermarried with foreigners brought in by the Assyrians after the conquest of the northern kingdom in the eighth century B.C.. Today Samaritans preserve many of the tenets of ancient Judaism but have a separate religion, with the center of their worship at Mount Gerizim rather than Jerusalem. Every year at Passover they make a pilgrimage to the mountain, sacrifice the paschal lamb, and eat it, as is prescribed in the law of Moses.

How did church altars originate?

As early as the third century A.D., Christians began calling the table used for the Lord's Supper, or Eucharist, an altar. This usage arose because the Eucharist is a commemoration of Christ's death, which was regarded as a sacrifice. In early times, when private houses served as places of worship, altars were simple household tables. During the persecutions Christians began to venerate their martyrs and offer the Eucharist on their tombs. This led to the custom of depositing the bones of the martyrs in stone altars.

In the western half of the Roman Empire, the types of altars multiplied; there was not only the "high altar" but also several secondary altars dedicated to various saints. The altar was placed in the chancel, the area reserved for the clergy, which, starting in the Middle Ages, was separated from the main body of the church. It was covered with three cloths and two great candles, while seven candles burned alongside it.

Various aspects of the prescribed rite of sacrifice are shown in Michelangelo's depiction of a grand Jewish altar, part of a fresco in the Sistine Chapel.

ALTARS: TABLES FOR SLAUGHTER

Since sacrifice was the central act of worship for both Israel and its neighbors, altars are often mentioned when the Bible speaks of giving homage to the Lord. The first altar talked about in the Bible was built by Noah after the flood, though the story of Cain and Abel implies that they must have used an altar for their sacrifices.

Numerous altars have been uncovered among the ruins of the ancient Near East. The most typical kind was composed of a pile of rough stones: for example, the altar built by Elijah on Mount Carmel out of 12 stones representing the tribes of Israel. Anyone could build an altar, the Lord said, and "in every place where I cause my name to be remembered I will come to you and bless you [Ex. 20:24]."

Unlike these rough structures, the two altars—each with a specific function—used in the tabernacle were made of metal-covered wood. In front of the veil of the inner sanctum stood an incense altar (18 inches square and 36 inches high) of gold-plated wood with golden horns at its corners. Every morning and evening incense was burned there.

In the open court outside stood a larger altar (seven and a half feet square and four and a half feet high) made of wood covered with bronze and topped by a bronze grating, where animal sacrifices were burned daily. In Solomon's temple a far grander stone altar—30 feet square and 15 feet high—could accommodate larger sacrifices.

The word *altar* in Hebrew is derived from a verb meaning to slaughter; it calls to mind the time when Abraham "bound Isaac, his son, and laid him on the altar [Gen. 22:9]," prepared to do God's terrible bidding. For an altar was the place where life was given and atonement made.

Sacrificial animals were not actually slaughtered on the temple altar. They were first killed and butchered, and then only the blood and appropriate portions of the animal were placed on the altar. Wine, grain, and incense were also offered on altars.

Priests and Priesthood

One of the duties of a priest, described in Leviticus 13 and 14 and shown in this 18th-century woodcut, was to examine people for leprosy and other diseases affecting the skin.

men from the tribe of Levi priests. Before the temple in Jerusalem was built, Levites who were not from Aaron's clan occasionally served as priests in local sanctuaries. The Old Testament even records several instances when men from other tribes became priests. Samuel, who served as priest, judge, and prophet, belonged to the tribe of Ephraim. King David, from the tribe of Judah, had his own sons appointed priests as well as a man named Ira who came from the region of Gilead, east of the Jordan.

After Solomon built his temple, not all the descendants of Aaron were needed as priests in the central sanctuary. The right to priesthood was therefore limited to the successors of Zadok, a descendant of Eleazer, the third son of Aaron. The Zadokite chief priests became a wealthy elite that dominated the religious life in Jerusalem until the second century B.C.

Who could become a priest?

Across the 2,000 years of biblical history, the qualifications for becoming a priest changed dramatically. In the time of the patriarchs, there was no formal priesthood; the head of a clan acted as the local priest. Abraham, Isaac, and Jacob, for example, each built altars and offered sacrifices. Not until Israel became a nation, after the Exodus from Egypt, was the profession of priesthood assigned to a specific tribe, and to a specific clan within the tribe. After Moses and his brother Aaron—both from the tribe of Levi—led the people out of Egypt, the Lord commanded Moses to bring Aaron and his sons forward EX. 28:1 "to serve me as priests." Entering the priesthood thus became the exclusive privilege of Aaron's descendants rather than one of choice or calling. Furthermore, according to Leviticus, no descendant of Aaron who bore a blemish, or disfigurement, was permitted to LEV. 21:17 serve as a priest and "offer the bread of his God" in sacrifice.

However, elsewhere in the Bible it says that the priesthood was not strictly limited to Aaron's line. Deuteronomy, for example, calls all ✳

What was special about the tribe of Levi?

When Moses came down from the mountain and saw the Israelites worshiping an idol, the golden calf, rather than God, he called out, "Who is on EX. 32:26

An ancient Levite and his lyre, shown in a 14th-century miniature, reflect the importance of music in Hebrew worship.

the Lord's side? Come to me." The tribe of Levi immediately set itself apart from the rest of the tribes by exhibiting its loyalty to God. And Moses EX. 32:29 said to them: "Today you have ordained your-selves for the service of the Lord." So God chose the Levites for his own. In Israel's beliefs every firstborn animal and child belonged to God, but NUM. 8:18 God said, "I have taken the Levites instead of all the first-born among the people of Israel." In an elaborate ritual described in Numbers, the Le-vites were brought before the tabernacle and, as the people laid their hands on them, were given to God as a symbolic offering.

Unlike the other tribes of Israel, the Levites did not settle in one tribal territory when they entered Canaan; rather, they were assigned to 48 towns scattered throughout the other tribes' regions. The Levites lived on income from two sources: crops from the fields that surrounded their settle-ments and the tithes and offerings given to the sanctuaries by the people.

What were the duties of priests and Levites?

Taking care of the sanctuaries and serving those who came to worship were the main responsibil-ities of priests and Levites. During the Hebrews' wilderness wanderings the tribe of Levi acted as a buffer between the people and the holiness of the tabernacle: "The Levites shall encamp NUM. 1:53 around the tabernacle of the testimony, that there may be no wrath upon the congregation of the people of Israel; and the Levites shall keep charge of the tabernacle of the testimony." After the first Jerusalem temple was built, the tribe of Levi was charged with maintaining it as well as providing gatekeepers, choirs, musicians, and guardians of sacred vessels and other trea-sures. The Levites supplied men to collect tem-ple taxes, prepare cereal offerings, and butcher animals for sacrifice. The priests and Levites began their service when they were 25 to 30

PROPHECY AND DIVINATION

Throughout Israel's early history a major function of priests was to transmit oracles, or revelations, received from God. In seeking a solution to a problem, a person could "inquire of the Lord [Gen. 25:22]" through a priest, especially the high priest.

The inquiry was often made by means of two mysterious objects, called Urim and Thummim, that the high priest kept in a square pouch known as "the breastpiece of judgment [Ex. 28:29]" attached to a part of his vestments called the ephod. Apparently, the high priest cast lots, using Urim and Thummim, in order to choose between two options or give a yes or no answer to a question.

In 1 Samuel, when Saul wanted

When the high priest entered the holy of holies, he symbolically brought Israel's tribes with him on his breast-piece of judgment inset with 12 jewels.

to find out who had broken the fast he had decreed to ensure victory over the Philistines, he inquired of the Lord: "If this guilt is in me or in Jonathan my son,

O Lord, God of Israel, give Urim; but if this guilt is in thy people Israel, give Thummim [1 Sam. 14:41]." When the people were absolved, Saul asked for a second casting of the lots, and this determined his son's guilt. As a fugitive from Saul, David sometimes made decisions after consulting the priest Abiathar, who "came down with an ephod in his hand [1 Sam. 23:6]."

After David's time the prophets who rose to prominence in Israel largely replaced the priests as oracles, but even in Jesus' time people believed in the prophetic ability of the high priest. Caiaphas, John tells us, "being high priest . . . prophesied that Jesus should die for the nation [Jn. 11:51]."

Special vestments and a gem-studded breastpiece distinguish the high priest (second from right) from the other priests. Only bare feet could touch the temple's holy ground.

became one whose hands were filled with the offerings of the people, which he was to present at the altar and from which he now derived his livelihood.

Exodus and Leviticus describe in detail the splendid ceremony ordaining Aaron and his four sons as the first priests of the newly consecrated tabernacle. Before the congregation of Israel, assembled at the door of the tabernacle, the five men were bathed and clothed with new vestments. Each wore a long linen tunic with a distinctive checkered pattern, held in place by an embroidered belt. As chief priest, Aaron donned a blue robe fringed with golden bells that, with his every movement, rang throughout the sanctuary. Finally, he put on the multicolored sacred ephod, with its breastpiece of precious stones, and a turban bearing a golden plate inscribed "Holy to the Lord." EX. 28:36

Moses then anointed the tabernacle and altar and all their furnishings and "poured some of the anointing oil on LEV. 8:12 Aaron's head, and anointed him, to consecrate him." The anointing evoked such strong emotions among the Israelites that later, when one psalmist wanted to speak of something "good and pleasant," he PS. 133:1

years old and continued until they were 50.

While the first temple stood, priests were also responsible for educating people about the law—a role that often required them to act as judges in civil and criminal matters. After the exile this teaching role seems to have fallen more to the Levites and then, gradually, to lay scribes and rabbis from outside the tribe of Levi.

One duty, however, always remained central to the priesthood: service at the altar. In the temple only a priest could bring the lifeblood or body of a sacrificial animal to the altar. As other priestly duties diminished, the ministry of sacrifice remained the exclusive right of priests and the essential function of priesthood.

How were priests ordained?

LEV. 9:17 To make a man a priest the Israelites said that they "filled his hand"—a picturesque Hebrew phrase that is often translated into English as consecrated or ordained. The new priest literally ✳

PRIEST. *The Hebrew word for priest, kohen, has come down to us as the surname Cohen. Though the derivation of the word is uncertain, it may be related to a Hebrew word meaning to stand, for it was customary for a priest to stand before God in religious rites. While kohen appears over 700 times in the Old Testament, another Hebrew word for priest, komer, is used but three times, and only in reference to pagan priests.*

The English word priest is a shortening of the Greek title presbyter, which means elder. Beginning in the late second century A.D. the Lord's Supper came to be understood as a sacrifice, and presbyters came to be thought of as priests.

As with high priests of old, the elaborate attire of modern-day prelates conveys their authority.
Left to right: leaders of the Roman Catholic, Russian Orthodox, and Anglican churches.

PS. 133:2 — compared it to "the precious oil upon the head, running down upon the beard, upon the beard of Aaron, running down on the collar of his robes!"

Next Moses made three sacrifices—first, a bull as a sin offering to purify the altar; then a ram as a burnt offering; and finally a second ram for the ordination, a peace offering that reached its climax in a sacred meal held at the door of the tabernacle. Some of the sacrifices were repeated for seven days.

Why was the high priest so important?

The high priest performed the holiest and most crucial rites in the religious life of Israel. He alone entered the presence of God in the inner sanctum of the Jerusalem temple to make atonement for the people's sins. This unique function required that he be a man of special holiness.

First, he had to be born to his position, preferably in the line of firstborn descendants of Aaron and later of Zadok, who was high priest when the temple was first built. Like all priests, he had to be without physical blemish or injury, just as the animals he sacrificed had to be without blemish. His holiness required that he marry only a virgin from Israel—no one divorced, widowed, or of foreign birth. He was forbidden to go near a corpse or participate in mourning rites, even if the funeral services were for his own parents. Like a king, he was anointed and wore unique vestments.

During the period of Solomon's temple, the high priest was an important official accountable to the king. The Babylonian exile ended the monarchy; and when the temple was rebuilt following the return of the Hebrews, the high priest was recognized as head of the nation.

The Maccabean revolt in the second century B.C. produced the Hasmonean dynasty in Judea, who united the offices of king and high priest. Under King Herod, however, the high priest lost his royal status and became more like a political appointee, whose tenure was subject to the approval of the king or governor. It was just such an appointed high priest, Caiaphas, who headed the Sanhedrin court at the time of Jesus' trial.

Places of Worship

A grand portable shrine, the tabernacle is shown here set up in a desolate Sinai valley. Moving the shrine was the job of the sons of Levi, who packed tons of silver, bronze, and fabrics into four wagons.

Where did the Hebrews worship before the temple existed?

Until they settled in the Promised Land and built a temple, the wandering Hebrews worshiped God at a movable "tent of meeting," known as the tabernacle. At Sinai the Lord told Moses to gather from the people voluntary offerings of gold, silver, bronze, fine cloth, animal skins, wood, oil for lamps, spices, and gemstones; and with these, "let them make me a sanctuary, that I may dwell in their midst."

EX. 40:2

EX. 25:8

Elaborate enough to express the majesty of Israel's God, the tabernacle was erected at the center of the camp wherever the Israelites stopped. The outside measured 150 feet by 75 feet, and the entire space was enclosed by linen curtains hung from rods and poles set in bronze bases. Just inside the curtains was an ample courtyard area where sacrifices were made. For that purpose there was a bronze laver, or water basin, for priestly purification and a remarkable altar ✳ built of wood and covered with a bronze grating for burnt offerings.

Dominating the courtyard was the shrine itself, 45 feet long by 15 feet wide. Its walls were made of gilded wooden frames set in bases of silver, held together by gilded rods, and hung with curtains. The outer layer consisted of ram and goat skins; then came a curtain of goat hair; the innermost curtain was made of linen decorated with cherubim.

A blue, purple, and scarlet veil, also decorated with cherubim, divided this shrine into sections. Priests could enter the larger front room, sometimes called the holy place, which contained golden furniture—an incense altar, a table for holy bread, and a seven-branched lampstand, or menorah. Behind the veil was the cubical chamber called the most holy place or the holy of holies. There stood the ark of the covenant in isolation that could be broken only once each year, on the Day of Atonement, and even then only by the high priest.

THREE GREAT TEMPLES

FIRST TEMPLE
Solomon's Temple

Circa 957 B.C.–587 B.C.

Building of legendary splendor constructed by Solomon; symbol of national and religious unity; destroyed by Nebuchadnezzar, king of Babylon, on the 9th of Av (July-August), 587 B.C.

SECOND TEMPLE
(Stage 1)
Zerubbabel's Temple

520 B.C.–20 B.C.

Built by Zerubbabel, the Persian-appointed governor of Judah, after Jews' return from Babylonian exile; dismantled by Herod the Great in 20 B.C. in order to build a grander temple.

SECOND TEMPLE
(Stage 2)
Herod's Temple

20 B.C.– A.D. 70

As finally completed in A.D. 63, one of the largest and most magnificent building complexes in the ancient world; utterly demolished by Romans in crushing Jewish rebels, 9th of Av (July-August) in A.D. 70.

A symbol of faith, the menorah traces back to the golden candelabrum of the tabernacle.

For a recently enslaved people wandering in the desert, the tabernacle was surprisingly grand. Although some of the ornate details may have been incorporated after the Hebrews settled in Canaan, Exodus makes clear that the true splendor began when "the glory of the Lord filled the tabernacle." EX. 40:35

Why didn't David build a temple?

David's desire to build "a house" for the Lord 1 CHR. 22:7 began as soon as he brought the ark of the covenant to his new capital, Jerusalem. As recounted in 1 Chronicles, before his death David purchased the temple site, developed the plans for the building, had the stone quarried, gathered together all the necessary gold, silver, precious stones, bronze, iron, and timber, and organized all the priests and Levites to serve in the future temple.

However, the prophet Nathan rejected David's plan, saying that instead God had decided to build a house for David by establishing his descendants as a permanent dynasty over Israel. Later, God explained that because David was a warrior and had shed blood, it would be left to his son Solomon, whose very name meant peace (*shalom*), to "build a house for my name." It 1 CHR. 22:10 would seem that Solomon had little more to do than assemble the materials provided by David.

A passage in 2 Chronicles notes that the site where Solomon built the temple was called Mount Moriah, also the name of the spot where Abraham bound Isaac as a sacrifice.

How did the temple assume such great significance in Jewish life?

At the dedication of Solomon's temple in 957 B.C., when the priests placed the ark of the covenant in the inner sanctuary, they had to withdraw, we are told, "for the glory of the Lord filled 1 KG. 8:11 the house of the Lord." Though the Israelites never held that God dwelt only in the temple in Jerusalem, they believed that he was a constant presence there along with the tablets of testimony, the Ten Commandments, which represented the covenant that made them a nation.

In any time of trouble, even in a foreign land, a

Jew was to pray with hands outstretched toward the temple in Jerusalem—as Daniel did in Babylon under threat of being thrown into the lions' den. The temple was also the focus of pilgrimages three times a year.

From the first, the temple was more than just a religious center. For King Solomon, it was a royal sanctuary, and throughout a thousand years of history it served as a symbol of national unity and purpose—or of disunity and despair when it lay in ruins. When the kingdom of Israel was divided, the northern tribes marked their political break with the dynasty in Jerusalem by establishing new places of worship in their own territory. For the southern tribes, their possession of the temple gave them confidence—often misplaced confidence, according to the prophets—that God would always favor and defend them.

As long as the temple stood, no other institution—not the monarchy, not even the synagogues that played an ever larger role in Jewish life from the time of the Babylonian exile—could rival its importance for Israel.

Why did the people weep when work began on the second temple?

A few years after the Jews returned from five decades of exile in Babylonia, the foundations of a new temple in Jerusalem were laid. Priests in sacred vestments blew the haunting cry of the

No longer than a little finger, this ivory carving of a pomegranate may have topped a scepter used by priests in Solomon's temple. Inscribed below its petals in Hebrew are the words "holy to the priests."

68

shofar, the holy trumpet, and Levite choirs sang thanks to God. Many of the onlookers were moved to a great shout of praise and joy. The beginning of the reconstruction, which was finished in 515 B.C., meant that the exile was truly past and a new life was about to begin.

But to many elderly priests, Levites, and heads of houses—people who had seen the glory of Solomon's temple before it was destroyed—the new foundations evidently seemed so paltry that their feelings were overwhelmed by the realiza- EZRA 3:12 tion of how much had been lost, and they "wept with a loud voice." The confusion of emotions EZRA 3:13 became so great that witnesses "could not distinguish the sound of the joyful shout from the sound of the people's weeping." Yet prophets like Haggai and Zechariah, who supported the new structure, assured the emotional throngs that in the future God would once again "fill this HAG. 2:7 house with splendor."

How long did Herod's temple last?

Appointed by Rome to rule Jerusalem and the Jews, King Herod sought to ingratiate himself with his subjects by an ambitious rebuilding of the entire temple area, a project he began in 20 B.C. More than 80 years later, long after Herod's death, the construction was finally completed— only a few years before the Jewish revolt against Rome broke out in A.D. 66.

Left: Jerusalem in Solomon's time is re-created in this drawing based on biblical and archeological evidence. In the foreground is Gihon spring, source of the city's life-giving water; atop the hill at right is Solomon's grand temple.

Below: A model of the "molten sea," the huge copper bowl 15 feet wide and 7½ feet high that stood outside the temple, is based on the description in 1 Kings 7.

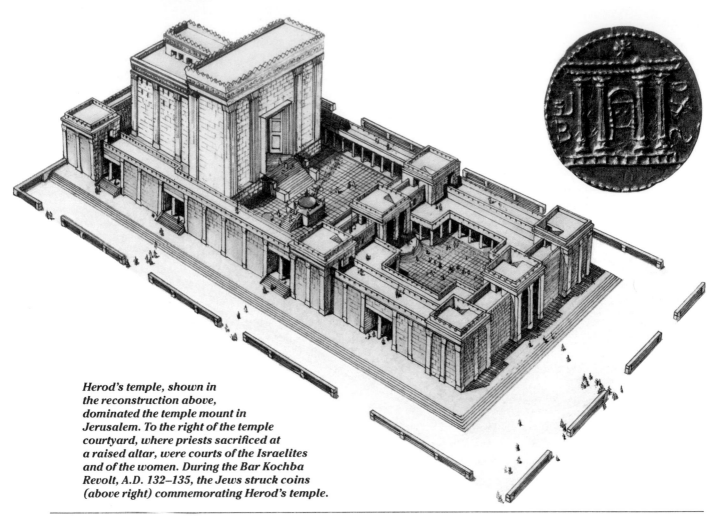

Herod's temple, shown in the reconstruction above, dominated the temple mount in Jerusalem. To the right of the temple courtyard, where priests sacrificed at a raised altar, were courts of the Israelites and of the women. During the Bar Kochba Revolt, A.D. 132–135, the Jews struck coins (above right) commemorating Herod's temple.

By the summer of A.D. 70, as the Roman counterattack gradually closed in on Jerusalem, the temple itself became the focus of the entire conflict. The Roman siege grew so intense that the daily burnt offering had to be stopped—either for lack of animals or for lack of priests—on the 17th of the month of Tammuz (June–July), still observed by a Jewish fast. Only three weeks after that last animal sacrifice was offered to the God of Israel, an unknown Roman soldier snatched a brand from a fire already burning in the temple court. "Hoisted up by one of his comrades," the Jewish historian Josephus wrote, the soldier "flung the fiery missile through a low golden door, which gave access on the north side to the chambers surrounding the sanctuary." The flames shot up, the conflagration grew, and the temple was consumed.

Ironically, the date was the same day of the same month that the Babylonians had destroyed the first temple, the great edifice of Solomon, ✳ more than 650 years earlier. The fateful day is still commemorated with the fast of the ninth of Av (or Ab) in the Jewish calendar.

Does anything remain of Herod's temple?

In the fury of their conquest of Jerusalem in A.D. 70, the Romans so thoroughly destroyed the city that visitors could scarcely believe that the site had ever been inhabited. Many Jewish survivors were executed immediately; others were sent to the mines to be worked to death or held to be killed in gladiatorial combat.

The only structure to survive the destruction was the temple mount built by Herod. It was a 1,000- by 1,500-foot rectangular rock platform on which the temple complex stood. Except for this massive elevated foundation, held in place by 100-foot-high retaining walls, not a single stone of any building remained in place.

After the Arab conquest of Jerusalem in 637, the Dome of the Rock—a Muslim shrine honoring the spot where the prophet Muhammad was said to have ascended to heaven—was built on the site of the temple. Until recent years only a short section of the temple mount's western retaining wall—the Wailing Wall, where pious Jews gather to mourn the temple's destruction—survived as a hint of its former magnificence. Beginning in 1968, however, excavations have uncovered traces of other structures around the ancient sanctuary.

People standing at the western wall today are actually above what was once a shop-lined thoroughfare along the base of the temple walls. Stones from the southwest tower have been uncovered, including one inscribed block that marked "the place of trumpeting" where a priest would blow the shofar over the city to announce the start of the Sabbath. Along the southern side of the temple, gates have been revealed that led through tunnels into the broad court around the structure. As more and more features such as steps, baths, and plazas are uncovered by archeologists, an ever clearer picture of Herod's temple mount emerges.

What was the significance of the holy of holies?

"The Lord has set the sun in the heavens," said Solomon, "but has said that he would dwell in thick darkness." That "darkness" was found in a cubical room 30 feet on a side, the holy of holies within the temple. It is called by various names in the Bible: inner sanctuary, most holy place, oracle, shrine, or in Hebrew, *debhir* or *devir*. It lay behind a thick veil in the ancient taber-

1 KG. 8:12

BAAL: RIVAL GOD

When the Israelites entered Canaan, they were invading a land devoted to Baal. The Semitic word *baal* means lord or master and was applied to the god believed to have dominion over the land and its people. In the Canaanite pantheon Baal was subordinate to the high god El, but in practice he was the chief deity of the land, the one who sent rain to water the crops on which survival depended.

From clay tablets found in the prehistoric city of Ugarit, archeologists have recovered the myths told of the great god Baal. One story recounts Baal's conflict with the powerful god Mot, or Death, who stood for drought and sterility. In a drama that the Canaanites saw played out regularly in nature, Mot demanded the surrender of the life-giving Baal, and the cry went up: "Baal is dead! What will

happen to the people?" A deadly drought hovered over the land until Baal's powerful sister Anath wrested Baal from Mot and returned him to life; whereupon all nature blossomed again and El proclaimed: "Baal the conqueror lives; the prince, the lord of the earth, has revived."

Baal was a dangerous opponent for the God of Israel and his prophets, especially in periods when the kings of Israel or Judah gave official support to the Canaanite cult. Jezebel, the Phoenician wife of King Ahab, installed 450 prophets of Baal as her court counselors. Their prominence led to Elijah's great contest with them on Mount Carmel. But though Israel's prophets denounced the corruption of Baal's fertility rites, the rival god remained a powerful attraction to the Israelites until the Babylonian exile.

Despite millennia of wear and a missing arm, this bronze figurine of Baal retains the haughty look given it by a Canaanite craftsman.

The temple interior followed the plan God gave Moses in Exodus. As shown in this 19th-century illustration, the holy room, adjoining the holy of holies, had an incense altar, a menorah, and a shewbread table.

nacle, behind olive-wood doors in Solomon's temple. Neither foreigner nor Israelite nor Levite nor ordinary priest could ever peer into this black room with its walls covered in gold. It was the resting place of the ark of the covenant, the spot where God's presence was most clearly centered. Only once each year, on the Day of Atonement, could one person, the high priest, enter the darkness to gain forgiveness for the people before God.

Its only furniture was the ark, though in Solomon's temple the cherubim of the ark were enlarged so that their wings spanned the entire room. When the temple was rebuilt after the ark was lost (probably in the Babylonian conquest), the holy of holies was left empty and dark.

What was kept in the temple treasury?

Around the inner court of the temple lay rooms that were used to safeguard the money and valuables that flowed in from worshipers. These rooms held national treasures as well, such as the spears and shield of King David, and gifts

and tribute from foreign nations. Thirteen receptacles shaped like trumpets stood in the temple courts to receive contributions to cover the costs of sacrifices and worship. At one of these Jesus saw a poor widow dropping in two copper coins and observed that she had given relatively far more than others who were much richer.

Each year every male Jew sent a half-shekel (about two days' pay for a laborer) to the temple; multiplied by thousands over the years, such contributions grew to vast sums. In addition, many wealthier people used the temple as a place of safe deposit. They hoped (not always wisely) that even conquerors would respect the temple's holiness and that God would protect the sanctuary. Thus the temple served some of the functions of a national treasury.

Why were there money changers at the temple?

In a society such as that of ancient Jerusalem, in which there were few financial institutions of any kind, money changers played some of the roles

SIGNS OF REVERENCE

In ancient Israel preparation for worship involved clothing, washing, and even postures of prayer, all of which were closely observed ways of expressing reverence for the Lord. The primary form of preparation for temple worship was a washing—not for hygiene but for ritual purity—before entering the sacred realm. Ritual baths, or *mikvehs,* from the time of the Herodian temple have been uncovered outside the southern entrances to the temple mount. Immersion in a *mikveh* was required to remove a variety of impurities, such as those caused by touching a corpse or giving birth. In contrast, Christian baptism is a rite that symbolizes forgiveness of sin and bestows moral purity on the recipient.

Distinctive clothing was also used by the Israelites to express reverence. Moses at the burning bush and Joshua at Jericho were both commanded to remove their shoes, since the place where they stood was holy ground. Later, priests would walk barefoot on the stone floors of the temple. However, they always kept their heads covered by a special cap—and over the centuries a head covering for both men and women became a symbol of reverence to Jews, especially when they were attending services or studying. The

This first-century A.D. phylactery, for holding scriptural writings, was found in a cave near the Dead Sea. Observant Jewish men wear phylacteries at weekday prayers.

practice continues today in the wearing of a skullcap called a yarmulke. Early Christians adopted different customs; although women were supposed to wear a hat or cover their heads with a veil, men had to remove their hats for praying.

To fulfill the command to bind God's laws on the hand and head, some Jewish men began wearing *tefillin* (phylacteries). These were small containers (today, black leather boxes) bound to the forehead and hand and containing passages of scripture. They also began to wear the *tallit,* a prayer shawl with tassels on the corners.

The various postures used in worship expressed both humility and devotion. Submission was indicated by a simple bowing of the head; in a more forceful gesture, the worshiper lay with his face toward the earth—a position held for an extended period of time to express deep penitence. Prayer was often offered with hands and eyes uplifted toward the heavens, God's abode. Both humility and expectation could be expressed by kneeling with arms stretched out to God.

At God's command Moses removes his sandals: a mosaic in San Vitale church, Ravenna, Italy.

All four Gospels relate Jesus' driving the money changers from the temple, seen here in a 13th-century fresco by Giotto.

centers for changing money were set up in Jewish areas outside Jerusalem immediately after Purim and 10 days later at the temple itself. The money changer typically was allowed a fee of 4 to 8 percent for each transaction.

When Jesus entered the temple precincts and overturned the tables of the money changers and of those who were selling animals, he was evidently not condemning the temple tax or the sacrifices in themselves. Rather, he was protesting the abuse of those transactions, such as excessive usury by some of the money changers. "It is written 'My house MT. 21:13 shall be called a house of prayer,' " he angrily reminded the offenders, "but you make it a den of robbers."

What part did music play in temple worship?

"Make a joyful noise to the Lord," ex- PS. 100:1 horts the 100th psalm. "Come into his PS. 100:2 presence with singing." Every day the temple courts were filled with the sound of Levite choirs singing the songs of praise and thanksgiving, repentance, and lament that make up the Book of Psalms. Songs accompanied the morning and evening sacrifices as well as other offerings of the people, processions, and assemblies. The First Book of Chronicles tells how David, to whom tradition has attributed many of the psalms, organized the Levite choirs, appointed a professional musician as their music director, and arranged for musicians playing cymbals, harps, lyres, and trumpets to accompany the choirs.

of modern bankers. They generally sat at tables in a major place of commerce to perform any sort of monetary exchange that people required. At the royal portico of Herod's temple, for example, they would change the foreign currency of a pilgrim so that he could purchase a sacrificial animal.

The money changers' most important function at the temple, however, was to facilitate the payment of the half-shekel temple tax due annually from every male Jew, as specified in the Torah. The tax was to be paid in native coin during the month between Purim and Passover. Since that coinage was not readily available to everyone, ✳

Although no musical notation has survived from Old Testament times, the great poetic range of the Book of Psalms suggests a richness and depth to Israel's music. One can only imagine the soaring strains that must have accompanied some of the psalms of devotion and thanksgiving, repentance and lament:

Create in me a clean heart, O God, PS. 51:10
and put a new and right spirit within me.

And one can almost hear the triumph and joy of the music that must have accompanied a procession entering the temple singing:

PS. 24:7
Lift up your heads, O gates!
and be lifted up, O ancient doors!
that the King of glory may come in. . . .

PS. 24:10
Who is this king of glory?
The Lord of hosts,
he is the King of glory.

Was anyone allowed to speak in the temple?

The broad temple courts were public plazas, and their proximity to the sanctuary made them ideal locations for religious teachers and prophets to propound their messages.

After the return from Babylon, when Ezra wanted to challenge the Jews to purify their commu-
EZRA 10:9 nity, he assembled them in "the open square before the house of God." When Jesus at age 12 wished to sit listening to the teachers and ask them questions, he remained in the temple courts, even after his parents had completed their pilgrimage and begun the journey home. Among the colonnaded spaces there was room for old and new. Traditional religious teachers could instruct disciples and scribes to interpret the law,

---

HOLINESS. *Holiness is the attribute that defines God; without it, he is not God. When Moses and the people praise the Lord, they ask: "Who is like thee, majestic in holiness [Ex. 15:11]?" In Isaiah's vision, a fiery being calls from above God's throne, "Holy, holy, holy is the Lord of hosts [Is. 6:3]"—a cry echoed in Revelation: "Holy, holy, holy, is the Lord God Almighty, who was and is and is to come [Rev. 4:8]!"*

Holiness is a translation of the Hebrew qodesh, whose root means separation. In the Old Testament, God's holiness is often represented by fire, which expresses purity and danger.

In the New Testament, holiness is used to define the Trinity. The angel informs Mary that "the Holy Spirit will come upon you . . . therefore the child to be born will be called holy [Lk. 1:35]." In his Letter to the Ephesians, Paul tells them that they are "members of the household of God," joined with Jesus "into a holy temple in the Lord [Eph. 2:19, 21]."

---

and members of fledgling reform movements, such as the first Christians, could also preach.

But there were limits. As a platform for his
JER. 7:2 scorching temple sermon, Jeremiah chose "the gate of the Lord's house," where he condemned allowing wrongdoers to use the temple as a kind
JER. 7:11 of safe haven, making it a "den of robbers." When Jeremiah prophesied that Solomon's temple would be destroyed like the sanctuary at Shi-
JER. 26:8 loh, "the priests and the prophets and all the people laid hold of him, saying, 'You shall die!' "

How did synagogues originate?

With the destruction of Solomon's temple and their exile to Babylonia, the Jews lost their central place of worship. Even after many returned and built the second temple in Jerusalem, others remained scattered throughout the Near East and Mediterranean. To preserve their faith they needed places to worship, study, and teach. The rise of new houses of religion, called synagogues, met this need. References to Jewish "places of prayer" occur on inscriptions in Egypt as early as the third century B.C., but evidence of synagogues is sparse until the Christian Era, when they were established in many parts of the Roman Empire, including Palestine and Jerusalem.

A synagogue of this period could either be a congregation of Jews who met to read the Scriptures and pray or the community building where they met. The term *synagogue* is derived directly from the Greek word *synagoge,* meaning a gathering or assembly, and is very close in meaning to the Greek word *ekklesia,* a translation of the Hebrew *kenesset,* "a gathering," which eventually became *church* in English.

In synagogue worship the Scriptures were read, probably first in Hebrew and then translated into Aramaic or Greek according to the needs of the audience, and this formed the basis for teaching and exhortation. The most emphasis was given to readings from the Torah, or Pentateuch, as copied on a scroll and housed in an ark, or chest, in the synagogue. But these readings were supplemented by selections from the prophets, such as the passage from Isaiah that Jesus read in the synagogue at Nazareth. In addition, prayers were offered and recited commu-
DT. 6:4 nally, including the traditional Shema, "Hear, O Israel . . . ," and a prayer of 18 benedictions.

How did the synagogue contribute to the spread of the Gospel?

Like Jesus himself, the entire first generation and most of the second generation of Jesus' followers were Jews. As they began to carry their belief in Jesus as the Messiah across the Roman Empire, the early Christians found many receptive listeners in the synagogues. In the Book of Acts, Christianity is described as virtually leaping from one synagogue to the next around the Mediterranean. Men like Paul, Barnabas, and Peter were at home in synagogue worship, and their first contact in any city was with the synagogue.

In the synagogues the early Christian missionaries found people who knew the Scriptures, a knowledge that helped them to understand the teachings of Jesus; and worshipers were already more or less familiar with the standards of morality and ethics that Christianity endorsed.

In addition, the Jewish synagogues had long encouraged Gentiles to renounce pagan polytheism and worship the one God. Many Gentiles did convert, but many others evidently became Godfearers. These were people who adhered to the worship and ethics of Judaism but were unwilling to undergo circumcision, to follow specific laws, such as those governing diet

GENTILES. *The word* Gentiles *simply means nations. In the ancient world many different peoples used some general term to identify all those who were outside their national group. The Greeks called non-Greeks* barboroi, *or barbarians. Romans called non-Romans* gentilis, *or nations. The Jews applied the Hebrew term* goyim, *nations, to non-Jews. Similarly, early Christians used* Gentiles *to describe those outside the church, and today Mormons refer to people outside their faith in the same manner.*

In the Bible, Gentiles *is used most often to mean people other than Jews. Many Jews opposed assimilation into non-Jewish society. The New Testament, however, ultimately extended God's covenant with his people to the Gentiles. Matthew presents Jesus as the fulfillment of Isaiah's prophecy: Jesus becomes the one to "proclaim justice to the Gentiles [Mt. 12:18]." In the new church, the God of the Jews will be the "God of Gentiles [Rom. 3:29]."*

and cleanliness, or to accept the social stigma that converts to Judaism faced. To these ambivalent converts, Christian teaching seems to have had a strong appeal.

Thus, synagogues provided both potential Jewish and Gentile converts to Christianity. It is not difficult to understand the tension that arose in synagogues as many of their own Jewish members and hard-won adherents to Judaism were drawn away into the new Christian communities.

What is a house church?

"Aquila and Prisca, together with the church in their house," Paul wrote from Ephesus to the Corinthians, "send you hearty greetings in the Lord." As Christian communities broke away from Jewish synagogues, converts to the new religion had no buildings of their own. Though Paul sometimes hired a lecture hall for teaching, the communities he established seem almost always to have met in the homes of the believers. The household setting was well suited to groups whose worship centered around a common meal consecrated as the Lord's Supper. It also

1 COR. 16:19

The beautiful limestone synagogue at Capernaum, Galilee, flourished in the third century A.D.

Jesus gives Peter the "keys of the kingdom of heaven [Mt. 16:19]" in a Sistine Chapel fresco painted in 1482 by the Italian artist Il Perugino. Roman Catholic tradition regards Peter as the first pope.

contributed to the way Christian communities
1 PET. 4:17 began to think of themselves as "the household of God," in which the family's love, mutual concern, and authority structure were paralleled.

For more than a century, Christian communities continued to meet and spread without using distinctive religious structures, and even when the earliest church buildings appeared, they were private houses converted to community purposes. The fact that Christians remained in house churches for so long had a considerable impact on the development of Christianity. It meant that in most large cities the whole church could not meet together. Diversity and even division were fostered, but so was a concern for unity that could keep the small groups together.

What did Jesus mean when he said, "On this rock I will build my church"?

MK. 8:27 When Jesus asked his disciples, "Who do men say that I am?" they told him John the Baptist,
MK. 8:29 Elijah, or another of the prophets. "But who do ✳

you say that I am?" he continued. Peter, according to the Gospel of Mark, answered simply, "You are the Christ." Luke's version of the event MK. 8:29 was much the same.

Matthew, however, expanded the story, giving Simon Peter's response as "You are the Christ, MT. 16:16 the Son of the Living God." Whereupon Jesus blessed him, because Peter had received his knowledge as a revelation from God. "And I tell MT. 16:18 you," Jesus continued, "You are Peter [in Greek, *Petros*], and on this rock [in Greek, *petra*] I will build my church." He added, "I will give you the MT. 16:19 keys of the kingdom of heaven."

Thus, Matthew portrayed Peter as spokesman for the Twelve and established him as the future leader of the Christian church. Peter, in fact, did become the spokesman and leader of the new faith in its early days, one of the so-called pillars of the Jerusalem church. After Peter left Jerusalem, he traveled to Antioch and finally to Rome, where he suffered martyrdom. According to tradition, he was crucified head downward when he told his executioners that he was not worthy to share Jesus' form of death.

Religious Parties

Who were the Pharisees and the Sadducees?

The late second century B.C. saw the rise of religious and political parties in Palestine, among them the Pharisees and the Sadducees. In their early days they contended for political influence, but by Jesus' time they were primarily concerned with religious issues. Somewhat like political parties today, each group had a core of several thousand and attracted the support of different segments of the wider society.

The Pharisees were lay teachers in the synagogues—rabbis whose authority derived not from the hereditary office of the priesthood but from the study of scripture and its interpretation. They strove to apply the ancient law of Moses to everyday life by developing an extensive body of traditions, handed down by word of mouth, specifying how the commands should be applied. The rigor with which they observed the laws of purity, for example, separated them from Jews who were not so observant—hence, perhaps, the name *Pharisees*, meaning separatists.

The Sadducees were drawn primarily from the priesthood and especially from the aristocratic families of Jerusalem's chief priests. The term *Sadducee* probably derives from *Zadok*, the name of the high priest of Solomon's temple. Zadok's descendants were considered the true heirs to the temple priesthood. By linking themselves to this ancient line, the Sadducees showed their close ties to the Jerusalem priesthood.

The Sadducees held to a strict interpretation of the law, without the traditions developed by the Pharisees. The Sadducees rejected any ideas of the resurrection of the dead, rewards and punishment after death, or angels and spirits—ideas that Christians came to share with the Pharisees. In Jesus' time, Pharisees and Sadducees had ongoing arguments about purity. The Pharisees preached that all Jews should observe the laws of ritual purity, even in such instances as ordinary meals, whereas the Sadducees believed that the highest standards of purity should be limited to priests performing temple rituals.

Who were the Zealots?

Jews who scrupulously observed the law of Moses as the sole basis for the political and religious life of Israel came to be known as Zealots.

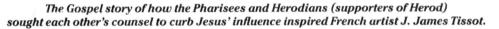

The Gospel story of how the Pharisees and Herodians (supporters of Herod) sought each other's counsel to curb Jesus' influence inspired French artist J. James Tissot.

In this painting attributed to Titian, Jesus tells the Pharisees, "Render . . . to God the things that are God's [Mt. 22:21]."

They fought any foreign attempts to impose other laws on the Jews. Often loosely applied to a variety of rebel groups who struggled against the Roman occupation, the name was adopted by a political party in the years just prior to the Jewish revolt of A.D. 66.

Resistance to Rome broke out immediately after Roman governors assumed direct control of Jerusalem in A.D. 6. A firebrand named Judas the Galilean upbraided his Jewish countrymen for consenting to pay tribute to the Romans and for tolerating human masters, when only God was their Lord. The Romans quashed his attempted rebellion, and resistance remained an underground guerrilla movement for the next half-century. One of Jesus' disciples, Simon the Zealot, had apparently been a member of this group.

Was John the Baptist an Essene?

Ever since the Dead Sea Scrolls were first discovered in 1947 at Qumran, southwest of where the Jordan River enters the Salt Sea, scholars have speculated about a connection between John the Baptist and the sect of Essenes revealed in the scrolls. For when John began preaching and baptizing in the area of the Jordan Valley, he was probably within a few miles of the Essene community at Qumran.

The Gospel of Luke seems to indicate that John, born to elderly parents, was reared in that region. Possibly John was raised by the Essenes, who would have instilled in him their desire for repentance in expectation of God's judgment. According to the first-century Jewish historian Josephus, the Essenes disdained marriage, but they would adopt other men's children "while yet pliable and docile . . . and mold them in accordance with their own principles."

If John was such an adopted child, he decided at some point to break with the Essenes. Like them, he wanted to fulfill the prophecy of Isaiah: "In the wilderness prepare the way of the Lord." IS. 40:3 But whereas the Essenes sought to prepare by forming a pure monastic community separate from the masses of Israel, John the Baptist chose to raise a lone voice in calling those masses to repentance and baptism in preparation for the coming judgment. His ministry was to the whole nation, and he became so influential that Herod Antipas, a son and successor of Herod the Great, had him arrested and executed.

Why did Jesus repeatedly criticize the Pharisees?

Disagreements arose between Jesus and the Pharisees over their different approaches to obedience to God. The Pharisees evidently sought to consecrate all of life by applying strict religious laws concerning purity to every aspect of living—for example, approaching every meal as if it were a temple sacrifice. Jesus went in the opposite direction. He did not require his disciples to be ritually pure for every meal and demonstrated that his mission was to all people by eating with "tax collectors and sinners," who made MK. 2:15 no attempt to keep ritual purity.

Jesus condemned certain Pharisees for the hypocrisy that marred their devotion to God; ironically, writings attributed to Pharisees also condemn hypocrisy. The New Testament acknowledges similar shortcomings among the early Christians, when Peter calls upon them to "put 1 PET. 2:1 away all malice and all guile and insincerity and envy and all slander."

Festivals

What calendar was used in Old Testament times?

The seminomadic early Israelites reckoned time by the waxing and waning of the moon. Each new moon signaled the beginning of a month. Two festivals—Succoth, or Tabernacles, and Passover—coincided with a full moon at midmonth. However, a problem with the lunar calendar is that it gets out of step with the solar year, which marks one complete revolution of the earth about the sun. And it is the solar year that measures the cycle of agricultural seasons: planting, ripening, harvesting.

As the Israelites settled into farming, they linked festivals to the harvesting of one crop or another. If not adjusted to the solar year, a lunar calendar soon would have harvest festivals falling in the wrong season. Therefore adjustments had to be made by adding a 13th month at two- or three-year intervals.

In the Old Testament months were first referred to by Canaanite names and later by their numbers—First, Second, Third, and so on. After the Babylonian captivity in the sixth century B.C., the numbers were replaced by Babylonian names, Nisan through Adar. The month added in Hebrew leap years was called Adar II.

When did the Hebrew year begin?

"This month shall be for you the beginning of months; it shall be the first month of the year for you," the Lord told Moses and Aaron. The month was Abib (March/April), later known as Nisan, during which the springtime festival, Passover, was celebrated. Elsewhere, however, God commands, "You shall keep the feast of ingathering at the end of the year, when you gather in from the field the fruit of your labor." And this suggests a new year beginning in the autumn, when the harvest feast of Succoth was celebrated in Tishri (September/October). EX. 12:2 ... EX. 23:16

Could there be two beginnings to the year? Some scholars have proposed that a secular year began in the spring, with kings counting the years of their reigns from Nisan, and a religious year began with Tishri after the harvest.

It is possible that in early times the Hebrews

This sixth-century mosaic from a synagogue at Beth Alpha, Israel, combines the 12 zodiacal signs with allegorical figures (in the corners) that represent the four seasons.

observed a spring New Year. But when they settled down to farming, they adopted an autumn New Year from the Canaanites and other agricultural neighbors. From Babylonia the Hebrews brought back not only new names for their months but also, once more, a spring New Year.

Rosh Hashanah, today's Jewish New Year, is not mentioned in the Bible. But it has been celebrated on the first and second days of Tishri (September/October) at least since A.D. 70, when Jewish rabbis were forced to reshape their religion after the Roman general Titus broke the Jews' resistance and destroyed their temple in Jerusalem. The rabbi Hillel II in the fourth century A.D. is credited with introducing the Jewish calendar still in use. Jewish years are numbered back to the creation; the year beginning September 9–10, 1991, is 5752.

Why was the seventh day a holy day?

GEN. 2:3 The consecration of the seventh day occurs in the second chapter of Genesis: "So God blessed the seventh day and hallowed it, because on it

As old as the Bible, the shofar, or ram's horn, sounds over Jerusalem's western wall, heralding the Jewish New Year.

SEVEN. *For Israelites the number seven and its multiples had sacred connotations. Certain religious festivals—Passover, the Feast of Weeks, and the Feast of Tabernacles—were celebrated for seven days; the Jewish New Year, the Day of Atonement, and Tabernacles all occur in the seventh Jewish month. The seventh day of the week was the Sabbath, a day of rest. The seventh (or Sabbath) year and the Jubilee year, which followed seven Sabbath years, were year-long festivals. Ordaining a priest and consecrating an altar took seven days.*

Both Old and New Testament writers linked seven with major events. God created the world in seven days. Accompanied by seven priests blowing trumpets, Joshua marched around Jericho; the seventh blast on the seventh day shattered the city walls. Joseph foretold seven years each of plenty and famine in Egypt. In Revelation, seven appears repeatedly in John's vision of the Apocalypse.

God rested from all his work which he had done in creation." The Lord reminded the Israelites of this in the commandment "Remember the sab- EX. 20:8 bath day, to keep it holy."

But this commandment is more than a reminder of God's rest at creation; it not only prohibits work but it extends a decree of rest to servants, transients, and cattle: "Six days you shall EX. 23:12 do your work, but on the seventh day you shall rest; that your ox and your ass may have rest, and the son of your bondmaid, and the alien, may be refreshed." The ban on labor is suggested in the very word *Sabbath,* which is derived from a Hebrew verb meaning cease or abstain and only secondarily meaning rest.

What activities were forbidden on the Sabbath?

The Pentateuch lists only a few specific Sabbath prohibitions. They concern activities typical of farming life: plowing and harvesting, cooking, gathering firewood, and kindling a fire. In addition, no one was permitted to light a lamp or candle. Later on fasting was forbidden on the eve of the Sabbath or on the Sabbath itself.

Although Moses proclaimed that anyone who worked on the Sabbath would be put to death, punishment for breaking Sabbath laws could be modified, depending on the motive for the infraction—for example, an effort to save a life.

Keeping the Sabbath became one of the hall-marks of Jewish identity, a protection against assimilation with the Gentiles. Many rabbis devoted themselves to evaluating and prescribing what might and might not constitute a Sabbath violation. The Mishnah, a second-century A.D. compilation of oral laws and interpretations, contains a list of 39 major categories, each of which contains more specific restrictions. For example, under the category of building and demolishing, the undoing of a woman's hair is restricted.

CALENDAR OF JEWISH HOLY DAYS

Occasion	Date	Origin	Traditional Customs
Passover Ex. 12:18, Lev. 23:5, Dt. 16:1, Jos. 5:10, Mk. 14:1	14th day of the first month, Nisan (March/April)	To force the release of the Hebrews, God sent a plague to slay every Egyptian firstborn, yet "passed over" the homes of Hebrews who sacrificed a lamb and sprinkled its blood on their doorposts.	Priests sacrificed a lamb to recall the first Passover, a tradition still observed symbolically.
Feast of Unleavened Bread Ex. 12:18, Lev. 23:6, Mk. 14:1	15th–21st days of Nisan	Recalls the haste in which the Israelites left Egypt—not even having time to allow their bread to rise. In New Testament times, a part of Passover.	Eating unleavened bread.
Feast of First Fruits Lev. 23:10 Dt. 26:10	16th day of Nisan	Marks the beginning of the barley and flax harvests following observances of Passover.	First half of the barley harvest presented to God.
Shavuot, Feast of Weeks, Pentecost Ex. 23:16, Lev. 23:16, Num. 28:26, Dt. 16:9	50 days after Passover; in the 3rd month, Sivan (May/June)	Celebrates the harvest of wheat, as well as the ripening and gathering of early figs and grapes.	Priests offered two loaves of bread made from new flour to God and made animal sacrifices.
Rosh Hashanah, Feast of Trumpets Lev. 23:24, Num. 29:1	1st day of 7th month, Tishri (September/October)	Marks the beginning of the most solemn month in the Jewish calendar. After the Exodus, it was celebrated as Jewish New Year.	Day of worship, rest, and sacrifices.
Yom Kippur, Day of Atonement Lev. 16:27; 23:27	10th day of Tishri	On this day, Israel confesses its sins and asks God's forgiveness and cleansing.	One animal, a scapegoat, sent into the wilderness to die for people's sins; another animal sacrificed in the temple; high priest enters the holy of holies.
Succoth, Feast of Booths, or Tabernacles, or Tents Ex. 34:22, Lev. 23:34, Dt. 16:13, Neh. 8:14, Jn. 7:2	15th–21st days of Tishri	Recalls the times when the Israelites had to live like nomads and celebrates the gathering of fruits and olives; year's final harvest celebration.	Thankfulness and merrymaking. People camp out in tents or huts.
Hanukkah, Feast of Lights, Dedication, or Maccabees 1 Macc. 4:36, Jn. 10:22	25th day of Chislev (December) and lasts 8 days	Commemorates cleansing and rededication of the temple in 164 B.C. by Judas Maccabeus.	Each evening, lamps are lit in the windows and doors of houses and synagogues. Gift-giving.
Purim Esther 9	14th or 15th of Adar (February/March)	Celebrates the deliverance of the Jews from death by the bravery of Queen Esther of Persia.	Pageantry; satires of biblical figures.

Having completed cooking, cleaning, and other traditional duties in preparation for the Sabbath, a devout wife finds a moment of peaceful rest in Isidor Kaufmann's oil painting "Friday Evening." Right: Ornate hanging lamps like this 300-year-old one from Frankfurt, Germany, were lit for Sabbaths and festivals.

Why was the Sabbath a source of friction in Jesus' time?

The Pharisees in the time of Jesus were one of several religious groups concerned with precisely defining Jewish law and how it should be followed in everyday living.

The Gospels describe a half-dozen instances of controversy between Jesus and the Pharisees on the issue of Sabbath observance. For instance, when the Pharisees objected to the disciples plucking and eating grain in violation of the ban on harvesting, Jesus reminded them that David was allowed to break a law to satisfy his hunger. In response to the Pharisees' objections to healings on the Sabbath, Jesus asked, "Which of you, having a son or an ox that has fallen into a well, will not immediately pull him out on a sabbath day?" How much more important, he implied, was it to free a person bound in infirmity.

LK. 14:5

But what most troubled the Pharisees was that Jesus seemed to equate himself with God, and this was blasphemous to them. Ultimately, they would seek his death, "because he not only broke the sabbath but also called God his own Father, making himself equal with God."

JN. 5:18

When did Christians begin observing Sunday as the Lord's Day?

It is likely that the early Christian community in Jerusalem and some Christians living outside Palestine, following the example of Jesus and the disciples, continued to observe the Jewish Sabbath on the last day of the week, Saturday. Paul himself kept the Jewish Sabbath, preaching on that day in the synagogue, but he did not insist that Christians uphold the tradition.

The Gospels report that Jesus rose from the dead on the first day of the week, Sunday. Probably for this reason, the first day of the week came to be known as the Lord's Day—a phrase that appears in Revelation 1:10. Some early Christians added observance of the Lord's Day on

Sunday to that of the Sabbath on Saturday. Compared to the Sabbath, the Lord's Day was not so much a day of rest as a celebration of Jesus' resurrection as fulfillment of the promised new age.

In the first two centuries after Jesus' death, Gentile Christians came to outnumber Jewish Christians, and Sunday became their accepted holy day. However, even though the Christian Sunday maintained the tradition of worship and rest, it differed from the Sabbath of Jews in significant ways. For instance, observance was not obligatory until A.D. 321, when the emperor Constantine declared it a weekly holiday on which certain types of work should not be performed. And not until 1234 was rest on Sunday mandated by church law. Later, Protestant reformers upheld the tradition of a day of rest, and some Protestant sects, such as the Puritans, became strict observers of the Lord's Day, or Puritan Sabbath, which they spent in "holy resting" and "public and private exercises of God's worship."

What was the purpose of the pilgrimages described in the Old Testament?

Three times a year the roads leading to Jerusalem were thronged with Jews making pilgrimages to their holy city. Following Moses' command- DT. 16:16 ment that "three times a year all your males shall appear before the Lord your God at the place which he will choose," these devout pilgrims came to celebrate the festivals of Passover (the Feast of Unleavened Bread), Shavuot (the Feast of Weeks, or Pentecost), and Succoth (the Feast of Booths, or Tabernacles, or Tents). These three pilgrimage festivals, detailed in Exodus, Leviticus, Numbers, and Deuteronomy, were celebrated in other parts of the Mediterranean world by Jews who could not make the trek to Jerusalem.

The week-long Passover festival commemorated the Jews' escape from the Egyptians—the Exodus—and also celebrated the early spring barley harvest. Shavuot marked the end of the grain harvest and the beginning of the fruit harvest in late spring. Succoth coincided with the fall harvest and commemorated the time the Hebrews lived in the wilderness before entering Canaan.

Before King Josiah (640–609 B.C.), Passover and Shavuot were largely neighborhood ceremonies involving local shrines, and Succoth was celebrated in the vineyards. But this king of Ju-

In a Reims Cathedral carving, a Jew in Egypt smears lamb's blood on the lintel so God will "pass over [Ex. 12:13]."

dah destroyed traditional shrines and centralized worship in the temple—thus institutionalizing the thrice-annual pilgrimages.

Why is Passover considered a feast of freedom?

The oldest annual festival of the Jewish liturgical calendar, Passover commemorates the beginning of the Israelites' escape from the clutches of the pharaoh, as related in Exodus. The Hebrew word for Passover, *Pesach,* is derived from a verb that can mean spare, save, or pass over; and the festival derives its name from God's instructions to Moses to lead the Hebrews out of bondage in Egypt.

To force the Egyptians to release the Israelites, God announced that he would strike dead all the firstborn in the land of Egypt. But the Israelites were instructed to mark the lintels and doorposts of their houses with lamb's blood so that God could identify and spare them: "The blood shall EX. 12:13

be a sign for you . . . ; and when I see the blood, I will pass over you, and no plague shall fall upon you to destroy you." Thus saved, the Israelites were led to freedom.

As a reminder of the role of lamb's blood in sparing the Hebrews, the sacrifice of a lamb became a part of Passover observance. A ritual supper, the Passover seder, commemorated the final meal in Egypt and included the retelling of the Passover story—traditions still maintained in Jewish homes.

The theme of freedom runs throughout the Passover celebrations. For example, the seder ritual dictates that every man must dine in a reclining position. This tradition reflects the participants' safety in freedom, in contrast to the first Passover, in which they were told to eat their roasted lamb in haste, "your loins girded, your sandals on your feet, and your staff in your hand." Throughout the week of celebration and prayer, Passover participants are reminded of God's words to Moses as he gave him the Ten

EX. 12:11

SABBATICALS AND JUBILEES

As the Lord rested on the seventh day of creation, so did he command his people to let the land rest every seventh year: "When you come into the land which I give you, the land shall keep a sabbath to the Lord. Six years you shall sow your field, and six years you shall prune your vineyard, and gather in its fruits; but in the seventh year there shall be a sabbath of solemn rest for the land, a sabbath to the Lord; you shall not sow your field or prune your vineyard [Lev. 25:2]."

Difficult as it might seem to comply with this commandment in a region where agriculture was precarious at best, there is evidence that the ancient Hebrews did observe this law during some historical periods. In the second-century B.C. Maccabean revolt, the Jewish defenders of Beth Zur were forced to yield to Syrian attackers for want of sufficient food, "since it was a sabbatical year for the land [1 Macc. 6:49]." And according to the historian Josephus, Julius Caesar granted a tax exemption to Palestine during the seventh year, "since they neither take fruit from the

Every seven years, according to God's command, the fields lay fallow. Whatever grew in the untilled ground was for the poor to take.

trees nor do they sow."

The sabbatical year probably had its origin in Hebrew traditions stretching back into prehistoric times, when land was held in common and was revered as belonging not to men but to God. The sabbatical year and the interwoven tradition of a Jubilee year—which fell after every

seventh sabbatical year—may have been a means of restoring the distribution of land and wealth ordained by God when the Jews conquered Canaan.

In sabbatical or Jubilee years Hebrew slaves were to be freed, encumbered land was to be restored to the original owners, debts were to be forgiven, and the spontaneous yield of fields and vineyards was to be given to the poor and to the beasts. Although such an outpouring of generosity may seem hard to imagine today, the spirit of open-heartedness remains a sturdy ideal. On the Liberty Bell, a symbol of American freedom and independence, are engraved the biblical words that describe the trumpet blast signaling the release of slaves at the start of ancient Jubilee years: "Proclaim liberty throughout all the land unto all the inhabitants thereof [Lev. 25:10 KJV]."

Taken together, the sabbatical and Jubilee years amounted to a pledge of brotherhood among the Jews, a placing of the welfare of the entire nation over that of a single family in fulfillment of the Lord's command, "You shall not wrong one another [Lev. 25:14]."

One of countless works of art inspired by the Last Supper's profound drama, this 14th-century Spanish altar painting shows Judas (no halo, hand outstretched) possessed by the devil at his shoulder.

EX. 20:2 Commandments: "I am the Lord your God, who brought you out of the land of Egypt, out of the house of bondage."

Why is Passover still associated with unleavened bread?

The rule against eating leavened bread during Passover reminded Jews that the Israelites, forced to leave Egypt in a hurry, had to eat unleavened bread (matzo) because they could not wait for the dough to rise. According to God's instructions to the Israelites, each house was to EX. 12:19 discard any leavened bread, "for if anyone eats what is leavened, that person shall be cut off from the congregation of Israel."

Unleavened bread later became a symbol of slavery, and eating it during Passover was a dietary reminder to Jews of their ancestors' long domination by the Egyptians. So strict did this custom become that any utensil in which leaven had been cooked, baked, or boiled had to be ✳

cleansed according to strict religious requirements. Today, similar laws govern the Passover celebration.

What importance did Passover have in the life and death of Jesus?

Luke tells us that Joseph and Mary went to Jerusalem every year to celebrate Passover and that Jesus joined them when he was 12 years old. It is uncertain whether this was Jesus' first Passover pilgrimage to Jerusalem, but there is no doubt that he was intimately familiar with the rituals of the week-long celebration. As a devout Jew, he would have participated in numerous Passover celebrations.

Scholars have long debated whether or not the Last Supper was a Passover meal. Matthew, Mark, and Luke indicate that it was a traditional seder, while John describes it as a meal held "before the feast of the Passover." JN. 13:1

Whatever the case, for Jesus' Jewish disciples

the significance of Passover was dramatically altered. For them, the Last Supper celebrated the future, with Jesus telling MT. 26: 29 his disciples, "I shall not drink again of this fruit of the vine until that day when I drink it new with you in my Father's 1 COR. 11:20 kingdom." This "Lord's Supper" would forever after symbolize for Christians redemption through Jesus' death.

The following afternoon, Jesus would die on a cross in Jerusalem, the same city he had visited as a Passover pilgrim some 20 years earlier. Some early church leaders suggested a parallel between his crucifixion and the temple sacrifice of the Passover lamb. Indeed, John the Baptist had referred to JN. 1:29 Jesus as "the Lamb of God, who takes away the sin of the world!" And Paul later wrote, 1 COR. 5:7 "Christ, our paschal lamb, has been sacrificed."

What was the meaning of the Feast of Pentecost?

On the sixth day of Sivan (May/June), Jews celebrated the festival of Shavuot, or the Feast of Weeks. This celebration marked the end of the grain harvest and the beginning of the fruit harvest. It took place 50 days after the first day of Passover. (Greek-speaking Jews called it Pentecost, meaning 50 days.) At Shavuot the Jewish farmer gave thanks to God for a plentiful harvest.

In contrast to Passover's somber reminder of deliverance from bondage, Shavuot was a joyful celebration of nature's abundance. The ritual required that celebrators offer to God two loaves of bread—baked from the finest new flour—as a sym-

A 15th-century artist evoked Succoth's spirit of thanks.

Succoth celebrators today make crude shelters like those of the Exodus wanderings.

bol of their gratitude for his great generosity.

Shavuot remained a mere harvest festival until the postbiblical period, when it took on an entirely new historical significance and spiritual dimension. By the second century A.D. it had been transformed into a festival commemorating the giving of the Ten Commandments and other laws to Moses on Mount Sinai.

The festival took on a special meaning for Christians when, at Pentecost, 50 days after the death of Jesus, the Apostles were gathered in Jerusalem. Suddenly "a sound came from ACTS 2:2 heaven like the rush of a mighty wind, and it filled all the house where they were sitting. . . . And they were all filled with the Holy Spirit and began to speak in other tongues."

At once the Apostles went out to preach the Gospel to the multitude of Shavuot pilgrims, an event that marked the beginning of the spread of Christianity. Today Pentecost ranks with Christmas and Easter as a major Christian holy day. It is often called the birthday of the Christian church.

What was the Festival of Succoth?

An agricultural festival that was somewhat similar to Canaanite celebrations that the Israelites encountered upon reaching the Promised Land, Succoth marked the end of the fruit, olive, and grape harvests. Over the years many historical and religious themes were incorporated into its various rituals.

Celebrators erected small booths or tabernacles (*succoth* in Hebrew) as a reminder of the

LEV. 23:42 dwellings in which the Israelites lived during their wanderings in the wilderness. "You shall dwell in booths for seven days," the Lord commands in Leviticus, " . . . that your generations may know that I made the people of Israel dwell in booths when I brought them out of the land of Egypt." Although it is likely that the Israelites slept in tents, not booths or huts, during their trek through the deserts, strict guidelines for the construction of the booths are set down in the Mishnah, the authoritative text of Jewish traditions. In Jerusalem pilgrims observed Succoth by living in booths erected for the occasion.

LEV. 23:40 In addition, the faithful performed special ceremonies as a sign of thanksgiving to God: "And you shall take on the first day the fruit of goodly trees, branches of palm trees, and boughs of leafy trees, and willows of the brook; and you

shall rejoice before the Lord your God seven days." During the festival celebrators carried clusters of branches, citron, and bits of myrtle and waved these as symbols of God's blessings and bounty. To ensure an abundant rainfall for the next growing season, priests poured a ceremonial pitcher of water over the altar each weekday of the festival. These libations were one of the few occasions when the people were permitted to approach the altar, and all adult males were invited to circle the altar seven times. Animal sacrifices took place daily.

Succoth stood in marked contrast to the solemn fast of Yom Kippur, the Day of Atonement, which fell only five days earlier. A later tradition is the holiday of Simhat Torah, two days after the last day of Succoth, which concludes the yearly cycle of reading the Torah.

ESTHER SAVES HER PEOPLE

The story of Esther is filled with palace intrigue, romance, and heroism. From among all the women in the kingdom, King Ahasuerus of Persia chose Esther to be queen, unaware that she was Jewish.

When Esther first became queen, the opulence of Ahasuerus's winter palace at Susa must have seemed decadent to the beautiful young woman who had grown up in the devout Jewish home of her cousin Mordecai.

In Ahasuerus's court was a high official named Haman, who bore a grudge against Mordecai because the Jew refused to bow down to him. To punish Esther's cousin for this disrespect, Haman talked King Ahasuerus into signing a decree that called for the execution of all Jews in Persia. Haman selected the

day for the massacre—the 13th day of the 12th month (March)— by casting lots, or pur.

Mordecai urged Esther to intercede with the king to save her people. Although she feared for her own life, Esther revealed her identity to Ahasuerus and begged him to prevent the massacre of the Jews.

Angered by Haman's self-serving plot, the king ordered that he be executed immediately on the very gallows Haman had built for Mordecai. The king appointed Mordecai grand vizier in Haman's stead.

Not even the king could rescind a royal decree, however. Mordecai issued a counterorder in the king's name, empowering the Jews to defend themselves against their persecutors. In Susa and across the Persian

Empire, Jews turned against their enemies.

To celebrate her people's deliverance, Queen Esther made the date of the intended massacre a holiday, calling it "Purim, after the term Pur. And therefore, because . . . of what had befallen them, the Jews ordained and took it upon themselves and their descendants and all who joined them, that without fail . . . these days of Purim should never fall into disuse among the Jews [Est. 9:26]."

Today the victory of the Jews and Esther's bravery are celebrated on the Feast of Purim. On the eve and morning of Purim, the rabbi reads the megillah, a parchment scroll containing the Book of Esther. Listeners stamp their feet and twirl noisemakers each time Haman's name is read.

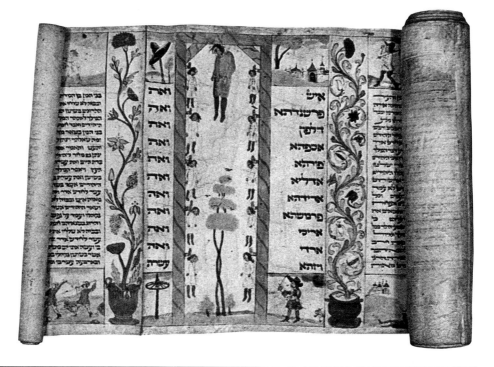

A parchment scroll of the Book of Esther is opened to the verses that tell how the treacherous Haman and his 10 sons were hanged on the orders of Mordecai. Other scenes show the Jews' victorious campaign against their would-be oppressors. The illuminated 17th-century scroll is from the Netherlands.

What happened to the scapegoat on the Day of Atonement?

The term *scapegoat* has come to mean one who bears the burden of guilt for the transgressions of another. It has its origins in the complex rituals of the Day of Atonement, or Yom Kippur—a day of confession, repentance, and prayers for the forgiveness of sins.

According to Leviticus, two goats were to be brought to the temple and lots cast to see which should be sacrificed to the Lord and which LEV. 16:10 should "be presented alive before the Lord to make atonement over it, that it may be sent away into the wilderness to Azazel." After the first goat was killed and its blood sprinkled on the mercy seat (the cover of the ark of the covenant) according to Moses' instructions, the high priest placed his hands upon the scapegoat and con- LEV. 16:21 fessed over it "all the iniquities of the people of Israel, and all their transgressions, all their sins." With the sins now transferred to the goat, the beast was led away to be abandoned in the wilderness. Scholars have disputed whether Azazel was a place or the name for a desert-dwelling evil spirit.

The scapegoat ritual, in which an animal was used to expiate the sins of an entire group of ✳

Part of Purim's tradition is dressing up as Esther, Haman, Mordecai, and the king.

people, was not limited to ancient Judaism. It was commonly practiced among ancient peoples, such as the Greeks and certain African and American Indian tribes.

What event does Hanukkah celebrate?

The eight-day festival of Hanukkah (Hebrew for dedication) commemorates one of Judaism's finest hours: Judas Maccabeus' rededication of the temple in Jerusalem in 164 B.C. The story is told in 1 and 2 Maccabees.

When Antiochus IV became king of Syria in 175 B.C., he set about persuading his Jewish subjects to accept a culture modeled on Greek lines. He appointed new high priests who supported his policy of Hellenization—that is, adopting Greek culture. Those Jews who refused to wear Greek clothes and follow Greek customs were denied citizens' rights. Not surprisingly, many Jews resented this challenge to Judaism and its laws. The event that precipitated armed rebel-

lion, however, was the conversion of the temple in 167 B.C. to the worship of Zeus. Swine's flesh, which Jewish laws declared unfit to eat, was offered on the temple altar.

First led by the aged priest Mattathias and then by his son Judas, the outnumbered Jews fought a cunning guerrilla war that culminated in the capture of Jerusalem. Just three years after the desecration, Judas Maccabeus (Judas the Hammer) removed the pagan altar, purified the temple, and led an eight-day celebration of the rededication in which "there was very great 1 MACC. 4:58 gladness among the people, and the reproach of the Gentiles was removed."

Today Hanukkah, also known as the Feast of Lights, Feast of Dedication, or Feast of the Maccabees, is one of the happiest festivals. To commemorate the original eight-day rededication of the temple, celebrators light a Hanukkah lamp— one candle a day until all eight are lit.

What Christian holidays can be traced to Old Testament times?

Easter and Pentecost, two of Christianity's most important holy days, have their origins in the Jewish festivals of Passover and Shavuot. Indeed, many early Jewish Christians continued not only to observe the Sabbath, or Saturday, as a holy day, they also continued to celebrate the Jewish festivals. In time, however, these festival observances were transformed into commemorations of New Testament events.

When the church began to celebrate Easter in the second century, there was disagreement over whether it should be kept on Passover or consistently on a Sunday. But the Council of Nicea in A.D. 325 fixed the date as the Sunday after the first full moon following the vernal, or spring, equinox. Thus the Jewish and Christian holy days were separated, though they continued to fall close together and occasionally on the same day. The link between Passover and Easter is preserved in such names for the Christian holy day as Pasqua (Italian), Pascua (Spanish), and Pâques (French).

The second of Christianity's movable feasts rooted in Jewish tradition is Pentecost (Greek for 50 days). Pentecost is now celebrated 50 days after Easter—whereas the Jewish Shavuot was a harvest festival coming 50 days after the first day

HOSANNA. *"Hosanna!" cried the crowds as Jesus entered Jerusalem on the day known as Palm Sunday. "Blessed is he who comes in the name of the Lord! . . . Hosanna in the highest [Mk. 11:9]!"*

The cry "Hosanna" comes from a Hebrew phrase hosha-na, *preserved in the Greek Gospels. It means "Save, we plead" and was drawn from Psalm 118:25, "Save us, we beseech thee, O Lord! . . . Blessed be he who enters in the name of the Lord!"*

This psalm was sung in the procession of worship for the Feast of Tabernacles. As the people waved branches of palm, myrtle, and willow (such a branch came to be called a hoshanah), they cried for God to save them by sending the Messiah, who would come "in the name of the Lord [Ps. 118:26]." Thus, as Mark says, the people shouted, "Blessed is the kingdom of our father David that is coming [Mk. 11:10]!" The cry of the psalm had been often repeated, but as Jesus entered Jerusalem, the crowd focused their hopes on him.

After crushing Jewish rebels in A.D. 70, the Romans took the menorah and other sacred booty from Herod's temple—a pillage commemorated in this relief on Rome's Arch of Titus.

THE TEMPLE DIES IN FLAMES

Thousands of Jews died trying to defend Jerusalem from the Roman legions in the summer of A.D. 70, and others were banished after its fall. The Sanhedrin, the Jews' supreme council and tribunal, was disbanded by the conquerors. But when the Romans put the torch to Herod's temple, they dealt the most severe blow to the religious life of the Jewish people. Without the temple there could be no sacrificial offerings, until then the primary form of Jewish worship; having no goal, pilgrimages ceased. "We have no prophet, no priest, no sacrifice, no sanctuary, no altar to help win forgiveness," a later Jewish commentator lamented; ". . . from the day the Temple was laid waste, nothing was left to us but prayer."

To ensure its survival, the Jews had to reshape their religion. Judaism's transformation is nowhere more strikingly revealed than in the celebration of Passover, the most popular of the pilgrim festivals. Since a sacrifice could take place only in the temple, the ritual slaughter of the paschal lamb disappeared. Yet Passover remained a major holy day and indeed grew in significance as it came not only to commemorate the Jews' deliverance from Egypt but also to symbolize their eventual return to Jerusalem. During the traditional seder meal, the recounting of the plagues inflicted upon the pharaoh became a fervent hope for the same punishment of Jerusalem's conquerors.

Observances of the Day of Atonement and Pentecost also changed. Sacrifice was no longer widely practiced on Yom Kippur, while the simple harvest festival of Pentecost was transformed into a commemoration of the Lord's giving the law to Moses at Mount Sinai.

Finally, the destruction of Jerusalem put an end to the Jewish Christian community there—its members were either killed or dispersed. Henceforth Christianity would be focused on Paul's teaching, and the gap between it and Judaism would widen. Central to Christian belief is the divinity of Jesus, which to Jews seemed to repudiate the distinction between God and man that was at the core of their form of monotheism.

Not with trumpets or the pomp of a princely welcome but to cries of hosanna and the rustle of palm fronds, Jesus entered Jerusalem astride a donkey, as depicted in a Russian icon.

of Passover. Since this was seven weeks later (49 days plus the 50th day for the festival itself), Shavuot was also referred to as the Feast of Weeks.

How are the days from Palm Sunday to Easter Sunday linked to Jesus' story?

JN. 12:13 Hearing that Jesus was coming to Jerusalem, Passover pilgrims "took branches of palm trees and went out to meet him," according to the Gospel of John. Mark relates that on Jesus' arriv-
MK. 11:8 al "many spread their garments on the road, and others spread leafy branches which they had cut
MK. 11:9 from the fields," and cries of "Hosanna!" filled the air. So began the first day of Jesus' last week, observed today as Palm Sunday.

Gradually, the commemoration of Jesus' death and resurrection expanded to an entire holy week that starts with Palm Sunday. Maundy, or Holy, Thursday marks the Last Supper; Good Friday, Jesus' death on the cross; Holy Saturday, a day of vigil; and Easter Sunday, his resurrection, the joyous confirmation of Christ's divinity.

Why is the Friday before Easter called Good Friday?

There is no single, widely accepted explanation of why the most solemn day of the Christian liturgical calendar—the commemoration of Jesus' ✳ death on the cross—came to be called Good Friday. Some claim that *good* is a corruption of *God* and that the name was actually God's Friday. Others hold that *good* refers to the belief that Christ died for the good of mankind, for human salvation from sin. A third theory states that *good* is an archaic term for *holy;* a fourth, that *good* was a euphemism for *bad.*

Not until the fourth century was Good Friday observed apart from Easter. Early names were the Festival of the Crucifixion and Day of Salvation. Today in France, Italy, and Spain, it is called Holy Friday; in Greece, Holy, or Great, Friday.

Why is Christmas celebrated on December 25?

Although the Gospels tell of Jesus' birth, there is no mention anywhere in the New Testament of the exact date. A clue found in Luke, who gives the fullest account of the Nativity, makes December 25 an unlikely possibility: "And in that region LK. 2:8 there were shepherds out in the field, keeping watch over their flock by night." Since sheep were usually kept indoors on winter nights and only taken out to graze on warm summer nights, a December date is highly questionable. Jesus' birth in summer or early fall is more probable.

Most early Christians were less concerned with the exact date of Christ's birthday than they were with the imminent Second Coming. Indeed, the early Christian father Origen wrote in A.D. 245 that it was a sin to celebrate Jesus' birth, "as though he were a king Pharaoh." Nevertheless, by the third century the birth of Jesus was being widely observed—though on various dates.

The first mention of December 25 as the date of Christ's birth is in a liturgical calendar for the year 336. Today it is generally accepted that December 25 was chosen to overshadow—and replace—the pagan merriment on *Natalis solis invicti* (birthday of the invincible sun), held to mark the lengthening of days following the winter solstice. Thus, Christ was worshiped as Light of the World or Sun of Righteousness.

The observance of December 25 as Christmas spread from Rome and was gradually accepted throughout the western world. In some eastern churches, however, January 6 commemorates both the birth and the baptism of Jesus.

What is the Epiphany?

MT. 2:10 "When they saw the star, they rejoiced exceedingly with great joy; and going into the house

XMAS. *This popular abbreviation is a combination of X, the first letter of the Greek name for Christ (transliterated into the Roman alphabet as Khristos), and mas, a shortened form of the word mass. Thus, Xmas literally means "the mass of Christ." While the word Christmas can be traced to 1038, the shortened version has been in use only since the 14th century. Some people object to the abbreviation because they feel Christ's full name should be attached to the holiday celebration of his birth.*

The first two Greek letters in Khristos (chi and rho) can be written as XP, and are often used as a symbol or emblem for Christ.

they saw the child with Mary his mother, and they fell down and worshiped him. Then, opening their treasures, they offered him gifts." The visit of the three Wise Men, or Magi, to the infant Jesus is one of the Bible's best-known stories. It is commemorated each January 6 by the Feast of the Epiphany.

From a Greek word meaning manifest, appear, or show, the Epiphany celebrates Christ's appearance to the Gentile world represented by the Wise Men. It occurs 12 days after December 25, now the widely observed date of Christ's birth and Christmas. As early as the second century, Christians in the East held a feast on January 6—but the manifestation they commemorated was not the visit of the Magi, but Christ's baptism by John or Christ's birth. Eastern Christians also included a third manifestation in their observance of the Epiphany: Jesus' first miracle, the turning of water into wine at the wedding feast in Cana.

In the sixth century European Christians began celebrating the period between Christmas and the Epiphany as the Twelve Days of Christmas, with the twelfth day also known as the Feast of Three Kings, Magi Day, or Day of Lights. The eve of the feast marked the end of a holiday season and was an occasion for gaiety and for entertainment not necessarily of a religious nature. Shakespeare wrote his play *Twelfth Night* for performance on the holiday eve—though his plot has little connection with the religious significance of the feast.

In Jerusalem modern-day Palm Sunday pilgrims retrace Jesus' steps on that fateful day.

HEROES OF FAITH

The Scriptures do not address the central issue of faith through discourses on abstract religious ideas, but through striking personalities who expressed their belief in and devotion to an almighty God by their deeds and words. These biblical heroes of faith were not heroes of their own making; they were imperfect human beings like everyone else. What set them apart was that they were called by God at a particular moment— usually when the future seemed very bleak indeed— and one by one they rose up to answer the call.

The story of the great people of the Bible begins with four generations of patriarchs— Abraham, Isaac, Jacob, and Jacob's 12 sons. From these impressive forebears the Israelites forged a sense of themselves more as a family than as a nation—a mighty clan descended from a single stock. But they were not united by blood alone. In each generation God intervened to shape their history. God chose Abraham over the people of his time as the father of the Hebrew nation and Isaac and Jacob, rather than their older brothers, as leaders of their people. And it was by God's will that Joseph became a ruler over Egypt in order to preserve the future of all Israel. But if the patriarchs could show heroic faith (Abraham's willingness to follow God's call into an unknown land), they could also be guilty of cowardly misdeeds (Jacob's cruel deception of the blind and elderly Isaac); and both of these human traits were woven into God's plans.

While the Hebrews were in Egypt, God raised up the greatest leader of their history, Moses: deliverer, law-giver, and prophet. Moses would probably have been content to remain a shepherd in the mountains of Midian, and indeed actively resisted God's summons to deliver Israel. But at God's insistence and with God's power, he met the challenge of the might of Egypt and a defiant pharaoh. Moses grew in moral stature to become what God had called him to be, and in that process he showed himself to be the model of a hero of faith. As God's chosen leader to deliver the Hebrews from Egypt, and as a prophet who conveyed God's will to the people, Moses transformed the Israelites into a nation living by a covenant with God—they had been delivered from slavery by God, and in return they vowed that they would obey God's law.

The centuries that followed the Exodus were tumultuous times for "the children of Israel [Ex. 10:20]." Religious, political, and military crises weakened the people's adherence to

God's covenant. During these difficult periods a variety of spiritual leaders arose to save the people from their enemies and to remind them of their commitment to God. There were the judges such as Deborah, Gideon, Jephthah, and Samson, who fought the Canaanites and Philistines in the Promised Land and won, with God's help. When foreign alliances and political divisions opened the door wide to pagan religions, prophets came forward to speak for God just as Moses had. But unlike Moses, who blended spiritual guidance and political leadership into a seamless whole, the new prophets challenged unjust and faithless rulers by the standard of God's law. Although the prophets were often persecuted by those in power, the wondrous stories of such dramatic figures as Elijah and Elisha and the passionate, courageous writings of men like Amos, Isaiah, and Jeremiah left to Israel and to the world a unique treasury of heroic faith.

After the traumatic period in the sixth century B.C. that saw the deportation of Jews to Babylonia and the return of the exiles to Judah, even the voices of the prophets seemed to fall silent. By the beginning of the Christian era, Rome had become the dominant power in the Mediterranean world and included Palestine among its dominions. The times brought new dangers and hopes; and John the Baptist, a prophet, appeared in the land, calling the people to repentance. But that moment in history belonged above all to young Jesus of Nazareth, whom John had baptized in the River Jordan, and to his prophetic words and work.

Jesus gathered around him a group of men and women from different walks of life, and he transformed them into a new generation of heroes of faith. Like the great figures of the Old Testament, the disciples and Apostles were ordinary people marked by weaknesses that the Gospel writers hold up prominently to view. The New Testament tells the story of their journey from doubt, denial, or self-glorification to self-knowledge and commitment to faith. Lifted by Jesus' call to become disciples and empowered by the Holy Spirit, Jesus' followers became a heroic community of faith in a hostile, largely pagan world. Their transformation was so powerful that even a vehement enemy such as Saul of Tarsus could find a new life as Paul, the tireless voice of the new Gospel—and another representative of the faith that permeates every book of the Bible.

Top left: A medieval illumination of St. John the Baptist.

Patriarchs of Old

Abraham and his family probably made the trek from Ur of the Chaldeans to Canaan on foot and by cart, as in this eighth-century B.C. relief showing soldiers and chariots on the move.

Who were the biblical patriarchs?

Genesis gives genealogies that explain the lines of descent from Adam down to the sons of Jacob, who were the founders of Israel's 12 tribes. The line from Adam to Noah has nine men (10 counting Noah), who are called antediluvian patriarchs because they lived before the great flood. They include Adam's son Seth, as well as Methuselah, the oldest person in the Bible, and Lamech, Noah's father. The patriarchs who lived after the flood, Noah's descendants, are called postdiluvian. The Bible does little more than list these patriarchs until the line reaches Abraham, who lived early in the second millennium B.C. But then Genesis gives fuller accounts of the lives of Abraham and his direct descendants: son Isaac, grandson Jacob, great-grandsons Joseph, Judah, and their 10 brothers.

GEN. 17:7 — It was Abraham whom the Lord chose for the covenant "to be God to you and to your descendants after you." God promised Abraham that he GEN. 17:4 would be "the father of a multitude of nations" GEN. 17:8 and granted to him and his line "all the land of Canaan, for an everlasting possession." To mark Abraham as the patriarch of his people, God changed his name from Abram to Abraham.

Why did God choose Abraham?

GEN. 12:1 — "Go from your country and your kindred and your father's house to the land that I will show GEN. 12:2 you," God commanded Abraham. "And I will ✳ make of you a great nation, and I will bless you." Abraham, a 75-year-old seminomadic shepherd living at Haran in northwestern Mesopotamia, obeyed without hesitation: "So Abram went, as GEN. 12:4 the Lord had told him."

Although the Bible does not specifically explain why God singled out Abraham to be the leader of the covenant people, the patriarch's immediate surrender to the Lord's will—giving up the known for the unknown—was perhaps the key. Abraham never questioned God's instructions. Although he and his wife were elderly and childless, he accepted God's promise that he would produce many descendants. Later, when God ordered him to sacrifice his only son, Isaac, Abraham again unquestioningly obeyed, but God intervened to spare Isaac. Given his remarkable faith in the Lord, it is not surprising that the Bible describes Abraham as "the friend of God." JAS. 2:23

Why isn't Lot considered one of the patriarchs?

In contrast to the life of his virtuous uncle, Abraham, who unwaveringly followed the commands of his Lord, Lot's story reveals the dangers of ignoring God's will. When the older man eventually became "very rich in cattle, in silver, and in GEN. 13:2 gold," Lot also grew prosperous. With their flocks quickly multiplying and threatening to overgraze their pastureland, Abraham and Lot decided to separate. The magnanimous Abraham offered Lot first choice of a new settlement. Instead of deferring to his uncle, Lot jumped at the chance GEN. 13:11 to take "for himself all the Jordan valley." He moved to Sodom, near the southern shores of GEN. 13:13 the Dead Sea. The residents of Sodom "were wicked, great sinners against the Lord."

Later, however, Lot bravely shielded two men who turned out to be angels from the lustful Sodomites; the angels in turn saved Lot and his family from death by telling them to flee before the GEN. 19:24 Lord "rained on Sodom and Gomorrah brimstone and fire." Only Lot's wife disobeyed the an-

gels' command not to look back, and she was turned into a pillar of salt. Lot and his two daughters took refuge in a remote cave in the hills. There, afraid they would remain childless (and possibly thinking they were the last people left on earth), Lot's daughters got their father drunk on wine, lay with him, and thus became pregnant by their father. The elder daughter bore a son called Moab, whose descendants were the Moabites; the younger daughter, a son named Benammi, whose heirs were the Ammonites. Since these people were considered Israel's enemies, Lot was not counted among the patriarchs.

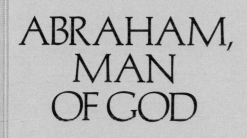

ABRAHAM, MAN OF GOD

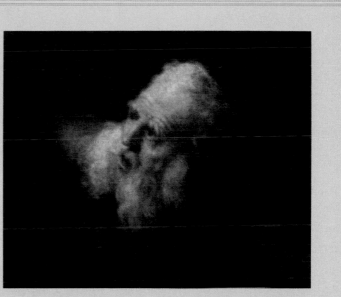

A startled Abraham, in a detail from a Rembrandt painting of the sacrifice of Isaac.

As the recipient of God's promise to make a great nation and to give the land of Canaan to that nation, Abraham was revered in the Old Testament as the forefather of the Israelites, who were called "the offspring of Abraham [Is. 41:8]."

The first sentence of the Gospel of Matthew declares that Jesus was descended from Abraham, and elsewhere in the New Testament the extraordinary faith of the patriarch was held up as an example to all. Abraham was seen as not only the progenitor of the Jews but the spiritual father of all the faithful, Gentile as well as Jew. Thus Paul wrote to the Galatians: "So you see that it is men of faith who are the sons of Abraham [Gal. 3:7]." In the parable of the rich man and Lazarus, Jesus described the envy of the rich man in Hades of

Lazarus, the poor man who is "carried by the angels to Abraham's bosom [Lk. 16:22]"— a phrase that gave Christians a metaphor for heaven.

Undeniably, the appeal of Abraham's unflinching faith largely accounted for his prominence in the New Testament. Quoting from Genesis, Paul wrote to the Romans: "For what does the scripture say? 'Abraham believed God, and it

was reckoned to him as righteousness.' . . . The promise to Abraham and his descendants, that they should inherit the world, did not come through the law but through the righteousness of faith [Rom. 4:3]."

Throughout the Bible (and in the Koran as well, for Muslims consider him a great prophet), Abraham appears as a man whose life was a shining example of faith in action.

Banished to the stark wilderness of Beersheba, Hagar bewails the death that she thinks awaits Ishmael, her son by Abraham; but God's angel comes to save both mother and son in this 19th-century painting by Jean-Baptiste Corot.

Why was Ishmael, Abraham's firstborn, banished?

In Abraham's time childlessness was viewed as a disgrace. So when Sarah failed to conceive, she offered her Egyptian maid Hagar to Abraham in the hope that she could give her husband a son—a common practice in the ancient Middle GEN. 16:4 East. "And he went in to Hagar," the Bible relates, "and she conceived." At 86, Abraham had finally been blessed with a son, Ishmael.

After Sarah miraculously gave birth to Isaac, she vented her jealousy of Abraham's firstborn. GEN. 21:10 "Cast out this slave woman with her son," Sarah told Abraham, "for the son of this slave woman shall not be heir with my son Isaac." Although Sarah's attitude toward Ishmael displeased him, Abraham granted his wife's wish after GEN. 21:12 ter God ordered him to do so, "for through Isaac ✳

shall your descendants be named." This meant that only Isaac could continue Abraham's line, but God assured Abraham that "I will make a na- GEN. 21:13 tion of the son of the slave woman also, because he is your offspring."

Thus Ishmael, whose name means God hears, was expelled and "lived in the wilderness, and GEN. 21:20 became an expert with the bow . . . and his mother took a wife for him from the land of Egypt." According to Muslim tradition, Bedouin tribes of the northern Arabian peninsula are descended from Ishmael.

How did Jacob's trickery fulfill God's purposes?

Jacob's twin brother, Esau, was the firstborn, which entitled him to family leadership and a double portion of his father Isaac's wealth.

Though it was prophesied before Jacob was born that God had chosen him to prevail over the elder Esau, that prophecy was fulfilled by Jacob's scheming and deception. First Jacob tricked Esau into selling his birthright for a bowl of lentil soup. Then, prodded by his mother, Rebekah, Jacob pretended to be Esau to win his blind old father's irrevocable blessing. "Let peoples serve you," the duped Isaac told Jacob, "and nations bow down to you." Warned by Rebekah that Esau planned to kill him to get even for what he had done, Jacob fled to his uncle, Laban, in Haran, where he met deceit as crafty as his own.

GEN. 27:29

Jacob fell in love with his cousin Rachel but was tricked into marrying her older sister, Leah, by their wily father, Laban, who employed a ruse much like the one Jacob and Rebekah had used on Isaac. (The heavily veiled bride Laban brought to Jacob was not the beautiful Rachel but her weak-eyed sister, Leah.) When Jacob realized that he had been deceived, he asked Laban for an explanation. "It is not so done in our country," Laban responded, "to give the younger before the firstborn."

GEN. 29:26

Beaten at his own game, Jacob had given Laban seven years of labor only to earn the hand of a woman he did not want, and then he had to promise seven more years in order to get Rachel as a wife. Tired of being exploited by his uncle, Jacob struck back by tricking Laban into giving him the best part of his herds.

But more misfortune awaited Jacob. His only daughter, Dinah, was raped; his beloved Rachel died in childbirth; and his favorite son, Joseph, was sold into slavery. Jacob's story, colorfully told in the Book of Genesis, was an account of one man's journey through the vicissitudes of life to fulfill God's prophecy, and it demonstrated how God made use of human shortcomings.

At times Jacob seemed to be the classic confidence man—an amoral underdog who cunningly outwitted those richer and more powerful than he. Genesis makes it clear, however, that Jacob's life was always under the direction of God. Through it all the Bible reveals a larger plan, represented by the prophecy that Jacob fulfilled as the noble patriarch whose final years were marked by humility and prayer.

THE IRREPROACHABLE JOSEPH RISES TO POWER

When the pharaoh appointed Joseph to rule "over all the land of Egypt [Gen. 41:41]," it was the culmination of an astonishing climb to power that began with a case of malevolent sibling rivalry. Provoked by their father's favoritism toward Joseph, his brothers kidnapped him and sold him to Ishmaelite traders, who took him to Egypt and sold him to Potiphar, captain of the pharaoh's guard. The handsome young Joseph resisted the advances of Potiphar's wife; angry at being spurned, she accused Joseph of trying to rape her,

and Potiphar imprisoned him.

Even a dungeon could not keep Joseph down for long. He became the prison keeper's trusted right-hand man and also attracted attention as an interpreter of dreams. His reputation reached the pharaoh, who was racked by disturbing, indecipherable visions.

Summoning Joseph, the pharaoh related a dream of seven fat cows consumed by seven thin cows and then seven thin heads of grain devouring seven plump, full ears. What it meant, Joseph said, was that Egypt would experience seven years of

plenty followed by seven years of famine. To prevent starvation, Joseph urged that one-fifth of the harvest during abundant years be stored in reserve.

When famine struck, just as Joseph had predicted, "all the earth came to Egypt to Joseph to buy grain [Gen. 41:57]." Among the suppliants were 10 of Joseph's brothers. Their appearance gave Joseph an opportunity to repay them in his own way for their cruelty to him and, more important, to assure the survival of his family, whom God had chosen for his covenant.

ISRAEL. *When God commanded Jacob to take the name Israel (Gen. 32:28; 35:10), it signified that Jacob had reached a turning point. He had been a clever, even deceitful usurper—implied by the name Jacob, which is similar to the Hebrew word for he supplants. But on his way home from Haran, where he had served his uncle, Laban, Jacob spent a remarkable night wrestling with a mysterious stranger who turned out to be a divine messenger. At daybreak the angel blessed him with the new name Israel, which is a compound of the Hebrew verb* sarah *(strive) and* El *(a name for God) and means either he who strives with God or God strives.*

When the kingdom of Israel was divided in 922 B.C., the name Israel was adopted by the tribes of the northern kingdom. Even after the fall of the northern kingdom and the deportation of its inhabitants, Israel remained the name for the Jewish people and is of course perpetuated in the modern state.

How did the evil acts of Joseph's brothers bring good in the end?

When 10 of Jacob's sons arrived from famine-stricken Canaan to buy grain in Egypt, they didn't recognize their long-lost brother, now a high Egyptian official. Joseph saw a perfect chance to test their character. First, he accused them of being spies and imprisoned them for three days. Then he made them an offer. He would sell them grain if they agreed to leave Simeon in prison while they went home and brought Benjamin, the youngest brother, back to Egypt. On their return, he would free Simeon. They agreed. (Secretly, Joseph put the money they had paid for the grain in their sacks, which they did not discover until well into their journey home.)

When the brothers returned with Benjamin (and, showing their honesty, with the money Joseph had secretly refunded them), Joseph freed Simeon and sold them more grain. But this time he had a silver dining goblet secreted in Benjamin's bag. Joseph ordered his steward to follow GEN. 44:4 the brothers, find the goblet, and say, "Why have you stolen my silver cup?" As the terrified broth-

ers were brought to him, Joseph continued his masquerade. "Only the man in whose hand the GEN. 44:17 cup was found shall be my slave," he told them. The fate of the youngest brother was now in their hands, just as Joseph's had been years earlier. But Judah, who had once conspired to sell Joseph into slavery, made an impassioned plea for Benjamin's freedom and offered to take his place. He had passed Joseph's test, and Joseph dismissed his courtiers and revealed, "I am your GEN. 45:4 brother, Joseph, whom you sold into Egypt."

Beyond Joseph's settling of personal scores lay a far greater purpose: saving his family from starvation in Canaan and bringing them to the land of Goshen. Their survival meant that the covenant God had made with Abraham and his descendants was secure.

Thus almost everything in Joseph's life, starting with the favoritism shown him by his father, indicated that God's will was being done. As recorded in the Book of Genesis, this was acknowledged by Joseph when he told his brothers: "You meant evil against me; but God meant GEN. 50:20 it for good, to bring it about that many people should be kept alive, as they are today."

After Jacob wrestled with the Lord's angel without succumbing, his name was changed to Israel to show he was a new man.

100

THE TWELVE TRIBES

When God appeared to Jacob for the second time at Bethel, he urged him, as he had Adam and Noah, to "be fruitful and multiply," and he added, "a nation and a company of nations shall come from you, and kings shall spring from you [Gen. 35:11]." Jacob had already multiplied, producing a dozen sons by his two wives, Leah and Rachel, and their two maids, Zilpah and Bilhah.

The traditional 12 tribes of Israel, which followed Moses in the desert and eventually won Canaan under the command of Joshua, are descendants of these 12 sons: Reuben, Simeon, Levi, Judah, Issachar, and Zebulun (born to Leah); Joseph and Benjamin (born to Rachel); Gad and Asher (born to Zilpah); and Dan and Naphtali (born to Bilhah).

Some scholars have suggested that the 12 tribes may not have actually represented direct descendants of Jacob's sons, but instead were a group of clans that in turn were made up of extended households, not necessarily all related to Jacob. In any case, each of the 12 tribes settled in a specific area within Canaan, according to the Book of Joshua. However, the priestly tribe of Levi was given no territory, and Joseph was awarded a double share of land, which was divided between his two sons, Ephraim and Manasseh.

Although commonly referred to as the 12 tribes of Israel, their number and their names vary in different books of the Bible. For example, the blessing of Moses in Deuteronomy 33 omits Simeon. And the Book of Judges

A 17th-century illustrator envisioned the tribes encamped around the tabernacle after the escape from Egypt.

does not mention Gad or Levi.

The tribes of the northern kingdom of Israel—the legendary 10 lost tribes—disappeared from history after the fall of Samaria to the Assyrians in 721 B.C., though some remnants may have merged with other conquered peoples in Samaria. The southern tribe of Judah, along with portions of Simeon, Benjamin, and Levi, continued as a kingdom for more than a century before being carried into exile in 587 B.C. under the Babylonian king Nebuchadnezzar. They survived the exile and returned a half-century later. Most Jews today trace their ancestry to the Jews of the southern kingdom.

Moses the Deliverer

Startled perhaps by the cries of the baby Moses, found among a thicket of bulrushes by the pharaoh's daughter, an ibis takes flight in this depiction by Frederick Dillon.

How did Moses become a hero of Israel?

The man who would become a towering national and spiritual leader began life as the son of Hebrew slaves, an infant marked for death. When Moses was born in Egypt, probably late in the 14th century B.C., the Hebrews had already lived there for about 350 years according to Exodus. At first their lot in Egypt had been tolerable, and they multiplied and even prospered as they tended their flocks in the land of Goshen.

EX. 1:8 But then "there arose a new king over Egypt, who did not know Joseph" (the patriarch who had once been Egypt's most powerful official). Launching an ambitious building campaign, the pharaoh forced the Hebrews into what was essentially slave labor. Still their numbers increased, and the obsessed tyrant decreed that all male Hebrew infants be thrown into the Nile.

Moses' mother, a woman of the house of Levi, contrived to save her infant son by placing him in a basket woven of bulrushes and setting it among reeds at the edge of the Nile. There the pharaoh's daughter found the baby and, taking ✳

pity, adopted him. She gave him the Egyptian name Moses, whose root appears in names such as Thutmose and Ahmose, in which the first syllable is a god's name and *-mose* means to beget a child or is born of. Used alone, Moses meant son. There is no other person in the Scriptures named Moses.

The pharaoh's plan to destroy the Israelites by drowning their sons resulted in Moses becoming an Egyptian prince. Later God used the pharaoh's evil against him by selecting the Israelites' liberator from the pharaoh's own household.

How were Moses' miracles different from the feats of the pharaoh's magicians?

Magic and sorcery played an important role in ancient Egyptian life and religion, as they also did throughout Mesopotamia. The pharaoh kept magicians on hand to try their magic for any purposes he desired. By giving Moses and his brother, Aaron, the power to perform miracles that exceeded the capabilities of the pharaoh's magicians, God not only made sure that the pha-

EX. 7:11 raoh and "the wise men and the sorcerers" would be humbled, but also that Moses and Aaron would be acknowledged by the Hebrews as respected and powerful leaders.

EX. 7:11 Though not denying that the "secret arts" of the pharaoh's magicians had a certain power, the Book of Exodus asserts the clear superiority of God the creator, who held absolute power over his creation and could not be used or controlled by human will. When Moses and Aaron challenged the pharaoh's magicians, the contest symbolized the dramatic clash between ancient polytheism and the monotheistic religion of Israel. The court magicians, who acted by their own power, failed, but Moses and Aaron, who acted through the power of God, triumphed.

In one demonstration of his supremacy, Exodus tells how God directed Aaron to throw his rod to the ground, and the rod became a serpent. The pharaoh arrogantly called upon his magicians to perform the same feat, which they did. God then caused Aaron's rod to swallow those of the Egyptian sorcerers. Later, Moses and Aaron turned the dust on the ground into swarms of

MIRIAM. *The name Miriam is the Hebrew form of Mary. In the Old Testament, Miriam is the name of Moses' sister; in the New Testament, Jesus' mother and several other women are named Mary. These holy associations help explain the enduring and widespread popularity of both names. Forms of* Mary *occur in Greek (Mariam or Mariamne); French (Marie); Italian, Spanish, and German (Maria); and other languages.*

The name Miriam may be derived from the Hebrew word marah, *meaning bitterness. It may also be related to the Hebrew* miryam *(rebellion) or to a Hebrew word for plump. Other possible roots are the Arabic* maram, *meaning the wished-for child, and the Egyptian* mer *(love).*

New Testament women named Mary include the sister of Martha and Lazarus; Mary of Magdala; the mother of James and Joseph; the mother of the evangelist Mark; and a woman greeted by Paul in his Letter to the Romans.

This colossal statue of Rameses II, ruler of Egypt for six decades, guards the Luxor temple, built in the 13th century B.C. Evidence suggests that Rameses the Great—Protector of Egypt, Chosen of Ra—was the pharaoh who refused to release Moses and the Hebrews from captivity.

gnats that afflicted people and beasts throughout the entire country. The pharaoh's magicians tried to raise their own swarms of gnats, but they could not. "This is the finger of God," they said, EX. 8:19 admitting that their power had reached its limit.

Why did the pharaoh stubbornly refuse to free the Hebrews?

While the God-directed plagues were ravaging Egypt, the pharaoh was repeatedly forced to negotiate with Moses, whose answer was "Let my EX. 5:1 people go." Several times the pharaoh agreed to let the Hebrews leave Egypt, and God stopped the prevailing plague; but each time the pharaoh reneged on his promise, stubbornly refusing to give up the Hebrew labor force he had come to depend upon.

Another of the pharaoh's ploys was to set conditions for the Hebrews' release that he knew Moses could not accept. For example, when Egypt was overrun with frogs, the pharaoh said he would let the people go if the plague ceased. ✳ Moses prayed and the frogs died. "But when Pha- EX. 8:15

raoh saw that there was a respite, he hardened his heart." When Moses foretold the plague of locusts, the pharaoh said he would allow the men of Israel to leave Egypt, but not the women or children—a condition that was unacceptable to Moses.

And when hail rained down on Egypt, the pharaoh seemed chastened. He admitted to Moses EX. 9:27 and Aaron, "I have sinned this time; the Lord is in the right, and I and my people are in the wrong." If the hail and thunder stopped, he said, he would let the Israelites go. Moses rebuked EX. 9:30 him, saying, "As for you and your servants, I know that you do not yet fear the Lord God." Moses was right; the plague ended but the Israelites' bondage continued.

The Lord had foretold the pharaoh's obstinacy, explaining to Moses at the outset of the EX. 7:3 plagues: "I will harden Pharaoh's heart, and though I multiply my signs and wonders in the land of Egypt, Pharaoh will not listen to you." The pharaoh's defiant but self-defeating attempts to negotiate fulfilled this prophecy and allowed God both to show his powerful support of the chosen people and to punish the Egyptian ruler.

After the Hebrews left Egypt, their route took them across the Sinai Desert; scholars have suggested four possible crossings.

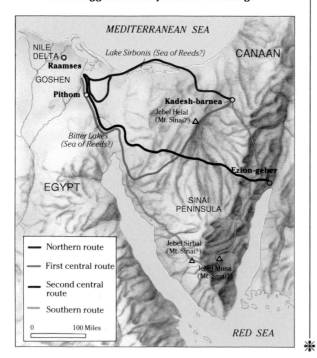

Were the plagues related to natural phenomena?

Exodus records 10 plagues: the Nile waters turning to blood; swarms of frogs, then gnats, then flies; a pestilence affecting cattle; boils "on man EX. 9:9 and beast"; hailstorms; locust swarms; darkness over the land; and finally, the death of the Egyptians' firstborn children and cattle. All but the final plague were similar to natural calamities that were known in Egypt. The 10th plague, the death of the Egyptians' firstborn, had no parallel as a natural occurrence.

One scholar has suggested that the plagues reflect certain seasonal events. Red earth from swollen tributaries upriver wash down the Nile from July to mid-September. As the river falls in September and October, frogs invade the land. Gnats or mosquitoes and other insects breed prolifically in stagnant pools of water through November. By January cattle are grazing in the open, where they are prey to disease-bearing organisms carried by the insects. February-March hailstorms imperil ripening crops. Locusts are blown in by Mediterranean winds from March to early May. And finally Sahara winds from March onward carry sand and dust that cause a darkness to fall over the land.

Yet at the core of the Exodus account is the belief that the plagues were acts of God, not merely natural events occurring by chance, and that God sent the plagues specifically to achieve the Hebrews' release from bondage. The Bible relates many incidents in which natural phenomena are used to serve a divine purpose. In the New Testament, for example, Jesus uses the storm on the Sea of Galilee to demonstrate his power; he orders the winds to be calm, and they obey. In the Book of Exodus, God's will can be seen in the severity of the plagues, in their rapid succession, and in the fact that they did not afflict the Israelites.

How did the Israelites survive in the desert?

After the Israelites had crossed the Red Sea, Moses led them into the wilderness of Shur, a desert where they wandered for three days without finding water. When they reached Marah (a name meaning bitterness), they found an oasis, but the water was bitter and they could not drink it.

104

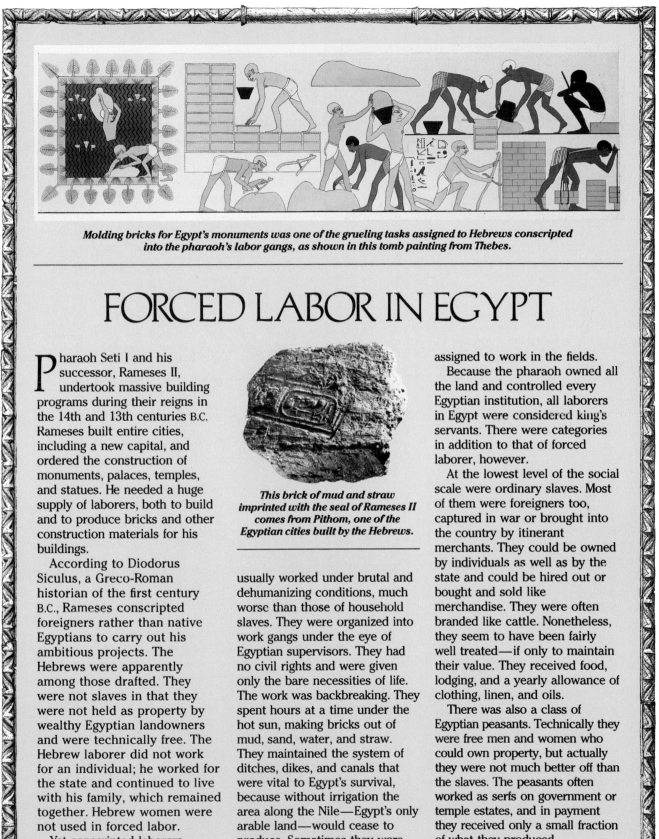

Molding bricks for Egypt's monuments was one of the grueling tasks assigned to Hebrews conscripted into the pharaoh's labor gangs, as shown in this tomb painting from Thebes.

FORCED LABOR IN EGYPT

Pharaoh Seti I and his successor, Rameses II, undertook massive building programs during their reigns in the 14th and 13th centuries B.C. Rameses built entire cities, including a new capital, and ordered the construction of monuments, palaces, temples, and statues. He needed a huge supply of laborers, both to build and to produce bricks and other construction materials for his buildings.

According to Diodorus Siculus, a Greco-Roman historian of the first century B.C., Rameses conscripted foreigners rather than native Egyptians to carry out his ambitious projects. The Hebrews were apparently among those drafted. They were not slaves in that they were not held as property by wealthy Egyptian landowners and were technically free. The Hebrew laborer did not work for an individual; he worked for the state and continued to live with his family, which remained together. Hebrew women were not used in forced labor.

Yet conscripted laborers

This brick of mud and straw imprinted with the seal of Rameses II comes from Pithom, one of the Egyptian cities built by the Hebrews.

usually worked under brutal and dehumanizing conditions, much worse than those of household slaves. They were organized into work gangs under the eye of Egyptian supervisors. They had no civil rights and were given only the bare necessities of life. The work was backbreaking. They spent hours at a time under the hot sun, making bricks out of mud, sand, water, and straw. They maintained the system of ditches, dikes, and canals that were vital to Egypt's survival, because without irrigation the area along the Nile—Egypt's only arable land—would cease to produce. Sometimes they were

assigned to work in the fields.

Because the pharaoh owned all the land and controlled every Egyptian institution, all laborers in Egypt were considered king's servants. There were categories in addition to that of forced laborer, however.

At the lowest level of the social scale were ordinary slaves. Most of them were foreigners too, captured in war or brought into the country by itinerant merchants. They could be owned by individuals as well as by the state and could be hired out or bought and sold like merchandise. They were often branded like cattle. Nonetheless, they seem to have been fairly well treated—if only to maintain their value. They received food, lodging, and a yearly allowance of clothing, linen, and oils.

There was also a class of Egyptian peasants. Technically they were free men and women who could own property, but actually they were not much better off than the slaves. The peasants often worked as serfs on government or temple estates, and in payment they received only a small fraction of what they produced.

In answer to Moses' prayer, the Lord showed him EX. 15:25 a tree, which Moses threw into the water, "and the water became sweet." This miracle may be reflected in an ancient method of making brackish water fit to drink by adding herbs to it.

When the Israelites began to fear that they would all die of hunger in the wilderness of Sin, the Lord promised Moses that the people would have meat that evening and bread in the morning. At twilight "quails came up and covered the EX. 16:13 camp; and in the morning dew lay round about the camp. And when the dew had gone up, there was on the face of the wilderness a fine, flake-like thing, fine as hoarfrost on the ground." EX. 16:15 "What is it?" asked the Hebrews. "And Moses said to them, 'It is the bread which the Lord has given you to eat.' " It is possible that the quails were part of a migrating flock; but what of the manna (*man hu*) that provided food for the 40 years of wandering?

A sugar-rich insect excretion, which is found on tamarisk bushes in the Sinai and known to be edible, has been proposed as manna. Like Moses' God-given bread, the substance appears in the morning. The excretions are produced for only about six weeks a year, beginning early in June.

Under God's protection the Israelites overcame yet another threat to their survival. It was blazing hot by day and bitter cold at night. To-

PLAGUES SENT FROM GOD

The ancient Israelites believed that God sent plagues as punishment for sin and disobedience. Although *plague* in the Bible is often understood to mean pestilence, it can refer to other afflictions directed against an individual, a family, or an entire nation.

In addition to the 10 plagues inflicted on Egypt because the pharaoh refused to free the Hebrews, the Bible also mentions plagues as punishment for the Israelites when they failed to fulfill their covenant with the Lord, which required not just obedience to his commandments but willingness to be disciplined. He punished his people both for disobedience and for stubborn resistance to correction.

In Leviticus the Lord warns the Israelites: "Then if you walk contrary to me, and will not hearken to me, I will bring more plagues upon you, seven-fold as many as your sins [Lev. 26:21]."

The prophets Jeremiah and Ezekiel often threatened the

This innocent-looking clay figure from 14th-century B.C. Egypt scarcely hints at the destruction wrought there by the plague of frogs.

Israelites with disease, war, and famine as punishment from God. Other prophets, and the psalmists as well, referred to various afflictions of the Israelites as plagues. In the Second Book of Samuel, the Lord became angry with Israel and sent an angel to inflict punishment. David built an altar and sacrificed burnt offerings, "that the plague may be averted from the people [2 Sam. 24:21]." The Lord heard his prayer and spared Israel.

Plagues are also mentioned in the New Testament. In Revelation, John describes the "portent in heaven" that appeared in his vision: "seven angels with seven plagues [Rev. 15:1]."

The New Testament affirms that sin leads to suffering, but it also repeats a lesson of the books of Job and Isaiah: that earthly trials are not always a sign of God's anger, nor do they prove that a sufferer has sinned.

Near the temple in Jerusalem, for example, Jesus came upon a man who had been blind from birth. "And his disciples asked him, 'Rabbi, who sinned, this man or his parents, that he was born blind?' Jesus answered, 'It was not that this man sinned, or his parents, but that the works of God might be made manifest in him [Jn. 9:2].' " Jesus then restored the man's sight. God was using a natural affliction to reveal his power and his love.

Safe on dry land, Moses and his people watch as the turbulent waters of the Red Sea swamp the mighty Egyptian Army in this painting by the 16th-century German artist Cranach the Elder.

day's inhabitants, the Bedouins, wear layers of clothing as protection from the sun and at night sleep in goatskin tents, a strategy for survival that the Israelites may well have used in the desert long ago.

How did Moses respond to his people's fear and dissension?

In the wilderness the Israelites had to contend not only with a lack of food and water but also with hostile tribes, venomous serpents, internal strife, and years of homelessness. When their faith faltered, they blamed Moses and challenged his leadership.

After the people broke the covenant by worshiping the golden calf, Moses ordered the loyal sons of Levi to slay the offenders. Exodus says that about 3,000 men were slaughtered and that EX. 32:35 "the Lord sent a plague" to punish the idolaters.

Circling the land of Edom, the people reproached Moses for bringing them into the wil-

derness. The Lord sent fiery serpents that bit and killed many of them. When they repented, the Lord had mercy on them, instructing Moses to "make a fiery serpent, and set it on a pole; and NUM. 21:8 every one who is bitten, when he sees it, shall live." In ancient times the serpent was a symbol of healing (as the entwined snakes of the caduceus are today); in this Exodus account the serpent was a sign of the Lord's healing power.

Arriving at last at the edge of Canaan, Moses sent leaders from the 12 tribes to find out what the land was like. The scouts returned with news that the land flowed "with milk and honey" but NUM. 13:27 also with fearful tales of fortified cities and giant inhabitants. Caleb and Joshua urged the Israelites to trust in the Lord, but to no avail. The people cried out against God and Moses and wished aloud for death. As punishment for their lack of faith, the Lord gave them what they prayed for. All those aged 20 and older, except for Caleb and Joshua, would die as the people wandered in the wilderness for 40 years; only their children would enter the Promised Land.

Prophets of the Lord

One by one, the prophets of the Canaanite god Baal tumble off the cliff after being slaughtered by the Israelites. This illustration is by the 19th-century French artist Gustave Doré.

PROPHET. *The Hebrew word* navi, *the most common biblical designation for a prophet, has its roots in the northern kingdom, or Israel. The word may have originally described prophets who had ecstatic trances, but came to mean prophets who appealed to the people in God's name or on whom God called.*

Roeh and hozeh, *Hebrew words meaning seer or visionary, apparently denoted professional prophets, who promised, for a fee, to summon a vision in which clients' questions would be answered by God. Many of them were disciples of Elijah and Elisha and were known as the sons of the prophets.*

The biblical phrase "man of God" may have meant a certain type of prophet or any true prophet. However, bona fide biblical prophets looked down on diviners, who used superstitious rites to foretell the future, a practice outlawed in Deuteronomy.

When the Judean prophet Amos declared, "I am no prophet, nor a prophet's son [Am. 7:14]," he may have been asking to be known by a title that was more respected in his native region, the southern kingdom. Some scholars suggest that he meant to dissociate himself from the professional prophets of Israel.

Who was the first biblical prophet?

The first person the Bible calls a prophet is the patriarch Abraham. When he and his wife Sarah went to live in the land of King Abimelech, the king took Sarah into his household believing that she was unmarried. Abraham was afraid to speak up; but God appeared to Abimelech in a dream and demanded her return. "Now then re- GEN. 20:7 store the man's wife," God insisted; "for he is a prophet, and he will pray for you, and you shall live. But if you do not restore her, know that you shall surely die, you, and all that are yours."

Although he did not make predictions about the future or in the name of God publicly call upon anyone to repent, as later prophets did, Abraham was a prophet because he interceded with God to save the lives of others. He implored God to spare Sodom, though in the end only Lot and his two daughters survived the destruction of that city.

Why was Moses a great prophet?

At the death of Moses on the threshold of the Promised Land, the author of Deuteronomy pauses to eulogize him: "And there has not aris- DT. 34:10 en a prophet since in Israel like Moses, whom the Lord knew face to face, none like him for all the signs and the wonders which the Lord sent him to do in the land of Egypt, to Pharaoh and to all his servants and to all his land, and for all the mighty power and all the great and terrible deeds which Moses wrought in the sight of all Israel."

DT. 34:10 Moses, then, could communicate directly with God—"face to face"—and mediate for his people, a characteristic that other prophets would emulate, although seldom as frequently or as effectively as Moses. Many times Moses spoke to God in the hope of averting his wrath from the sinning Israelites, most notably after they worshiped the golden calf.

Like later prophets, Moses performed miracles in the service of God. These acts led up to a climactic miracle, the crossing of the Red Sea, which marked the end of Egyptian domination and enslavement of the Israelites. Like all genuine prophetic miracles, those of Moses were performed in the sight of the people.

Moses also carried out other functions that came to be viewed as responsibilities of the prophets. He interpreted God's law, adjudicated disputes, rebuked sinners, and, before his death, foretold the future of his people. Of course, these were not exclusively the prerogatives of prophets. In the Old Testament, for example, priests, Levites, and later scribes expounded on the law; judges and kings resolved conflicts. In the New Testament, Jesus exercised many of the functions associated with Old Testament prophets.

Why were the prophets persecuted?

Many of the prophets were persecuted because they told people in power what they did not want to hear. Speaking in God's name, the prophets criticized monarchs, challenged accepted behavior, and urged social reforms. Sometimes, as with Elijah and his disciple and successor, Elisha, the prophets were much more than mere voices of conscience; they led rebellions and incited destruction of the enemies of the Lord.

The first recorded mass persecution of prophets occurred during the reign of King Ahab in the ninth century B.C. His wife, Jezebel, who rejected 1 KG. 18:4 God in favor of the Canaanite god Baal, "cut off the prophets of the Lord." Elijah escaped this purge and then enraged Jezebel by besting 450 of Baal's prophets on Mount Carmel in a contest ✳

that showed the superiority of God's power over Baal's in front of "all the people of Israel." The 1 KG. 18:20 prophets of Baal were then seized by the Israelites and slaughtered to the last man on Elijah's orders. When news of this humiliation reached Jezebel, she swore to take Elijah's life "by this 1 KG. 19:2 time tomorrow," and the frightened prophet fled into the wilderness. There he eventually found a cave and lived in it until God ordered him to resume his work on behalf of Israel.

Another prophet in Ahab's reign, Micaiah, proclaimed that the king would die fighting the Syrians. Ahab reacted by throwing Micaiah into jail and putting him on a starvation diet of bread and water. But Micaiah's prophecy came true nevertheless. Two centuries later Jeremiah, whose name became a synonym for a pessimist, was mistreated and imprisoned repeatedly for prophesying that the kingdom of Judah was doomed

In this Rembrandt painting, Balaam, a non-Israelite prophet, is being reprimanded by God through the words of an ass because he had beaten the animal.

because of its disobedience to God. In fact, in 587 B.C., Jerusalem fell, Solomon's temple was destroyed, and the people were exiled.

How did Elisha succeed Elijah?

When God told Elijah to stop hiding from the wrath of Jezebel in a cave on Mount Horeb, he also ordered the prophet to seek out the farmer Elisha, 1 KG. 19:16 whom "you shall anoint to be prophet in your place." Traveling together, Elijah and his disciple came to the Jordan River. In front of 50 sons of the prophets (a guildlike society of professional prophesiers), Elijah miraculously split the Jordan by striking the water with his rolled-up 2 KG. 2:8 mantle, "and the water was parted to the one side and to the other, till the two of them could go over on dry ground."

Knowing that God was about to take him, Eli- 2 KG. 2:9 jah asked what he could do for Elisha "before I am taken from you." Elisha replied that he want- 2 KG. 2:9 ed "a double share of your spirit"—a double share being the usual portion of the inheritance of a firstborn son. Elijah said the wish would be granted if Elisha saw exactly how Elijah depart- 2 KG. 2:11 ed. "And as they still went on and talked, behold, a chariot of fire and horses of fire separated the two of them. And Elijah went up by a whirlwind into heaven. And Elisha saw it and he cried, 'My father, my father! the chariots of Israel and its horsemen!' And he saw him no more."

Elisha picked up Elijah's mantle—the traditional hair shirt symbolizing a prophet's calling—and tested whether he had indeed inherited Elijah's powers. He struck the Jordan's waters as Elijah had done. At first nothing happened, 2 KG. 2:14 and the impatient Elisha cried, "Where is the Lord, the God of Elijah?" Then the waters parted, ✳

A French icon shows Elijah ascending in his chariot of fire as Elisha prepares to catch the mantle symbolizing his inherited power.

Elisha passed over, and the sons of the prophets shouted, "The spirit of Eli- 2 KG. 2:15 jah rests on Elisha."

The assertion that Elijah did not die but rather ascended to heaven strongly influenced later Jewish and Christian traditions, which taught that Elijah would return to the earth as the forerunner of the Messiah.

Were Jesus' miracles like those of the prophets?

Many expected Jesus to repeat the earlier miracles of Moses, Elijah, and Elisha. When the disciples James and John asked if Jesus wanted them "to bid fire LK. 9:54 come down from heaven" to consume his enemies, they were evoking the precedent of Elijah, who had called down "the fire of 2 KG. 1:12 God" on King Ahaziah's men. But Jesus declined.

This was not always the case. Elijah and his disciple Elisha each brought a child back to life. Elijah revived a grieving woman's son who had "no breath left in 1 KG. 17:17 him"; the prophet "stretched himself upon the 1 KG. 17:21 child three times . . . and the soul of the child came into him again." In the case of Elisha, he enabled a childless woman to bear a son; then when the boy died some years later, the prophet "lay upon the child, putting his mouth upon his 2 KG. 4:34 mouth, his eyes upon his eyes, and his hands upon his hands; and . . . the flesh of the child became warm . . . and the child opened his eyes." In a very similar act of compassion for a widow whose only son had died, Jesus touched the bier of the youth and told him to rise. "And LK. 7:15 the dead man sat up, and began to speak"—one of three times Jesus revived the dead.

Both Elisha and Jesus miraculously fed many people with scant food. Out of 20 loaves of barley and some fresh grain, Elisha made more than

THE PROPHETS' LAMENT

Being an Old Testament prophet virtually assured an unhappy life. Prophets were often punished for challenging accepted ideas. Moreover, since the people the prophet addressed rarely chose to live up to the standards set by God, frustration and depression were the common lot of the prophets. Several saw no way out but to ask God to take their lives.

During the Exodus, Moses was almost overwhelmed by his responsibility for the Israelites. He told God: "I am not able to carry all this people alone. . . . If thou wilt deal thus with me, kill me at once . . . that I may not see my wretchedness [Num. 11:14]."

Elijah felt a similar sense of failure. After defeating Baal's prophets, he was forced to flee into the wilderness. Sitting under a broom tree, Elijah implored, "It is enough; now, O Lord, take away my life [1 Kg. 19:4]."

Although he never requested death, Jeremiah was torn between the compulsion to speak God's word and frustration over the people's unwillingness to listen. He exclaimed in anguish: "Cursed be the day on which I was born [Jer. 20:14]!"

Perhaps sensing what lay ahead, many prophets at first shrank from speaking for God. Moses, whom many consider the ideal prophet, refused the call no fewer than five times.

Moses' reluctance was echoed by later prophets. When God called Jeremiah to prophesy, Jeremiah responded: "Ah, Lord God! Behold, I do not know how to speak, for I am only a youth [Jer. 1:6]." God touched his mouth, thus assuring Jeremiah that, like Moses, his speech would be divinely guided. Jonah, too, was a reluctant prophet.

In contrast, Isaiah volunteered his services—although first expressing unworthiness. "Woe is me!" cried Isaiah upon receiving a vision of the Lord. "For I am . . . a man of unclean lips [Is. 6:5]." Then an angel purified his lips with a burning coal, and Isaiah enthusiastically accepted his prophetic calling: "Here am I! Send me [Is. 6:8]."

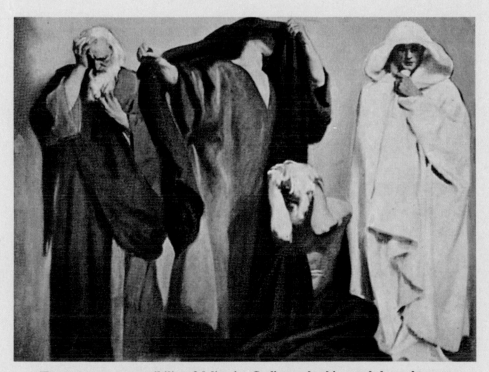

The awesome responsibility of delivering God's word to his people brought some prophets fear and others agony, as shown in a section of a mural by John Singer Sargent depicting Zephaniah, Joel, Obadiah, and Hosea.

enough food to feed 100 men. Jesus, starting with five loaves and two fish, satisfied the hunger of 5,000 people. And when Jesus healed a leper by touching him, it recalled acts of both Elisha and Moses. Elisha cured the leprous Syrian general Naaman by having him bathe in the Jordan River; Moses begged God to heal his sister Miriam's leprosy, and God did so.

How did people decide which prophets to believe?

Since prophecy played such a powerful role in the lives of the ancient Israelites, distinguishing between true and false prophecies was of the utmost importance. The survival of the entire nation could depend on whether a prophecy was the word of God or the fabrication of man. For exam-

A widow welcomes the prophet Elijah, who miraculously brought her son back from the dead, in a painting by Ford Madox Brown.

ple, in the last chapter of the First Book of Kings, the prophet Zedekiah foretold victory for King Ahab in a battle against the Syrians, but Micaiah, the true "prophet of the Lord," prophesied that 1 KG. 22:7 Ahab would be killed and the Israelites defeated. Unfortunately for Ahab and Israel, Zedekiah's prophecy was false.

One strong indication of prophetic authenticity was a rapture of ecstasy, sometimes brought on by music or by dance. But people realized that such raptures could be faked, and sometimes sincere prophets even experienced visions that turned out to be false. When Saul met a band of prophets playing instruments and dancing, "The spirit of God came mightily upon him, 1 SAM. 10:10 and he prophesied among them." Saul's ecstatic prophesying came as a great surprise to the people who knew him, according to the First Book of Samuel, and they asked themselves, "Is Saul also 1 SAM. 10:11 among the prophets?" This question, which the Bible says "became a proverb," has had different in- 1 SAM. 10:12 terpretations. One view sees it as expressing skepticism that Saul's ecstasy made him a true prophet; a more popular reading is that the question probably described people's dawning realization that Saul had "turned into another man," that is, into a 1 SAM. 10:6 genuine prophet of God.

The Book of Deuteronomy attempts to establish criteria for judging the validity of prophetic utterances and declares that the punishment for false prophecy is death. Yet a prophecy that fails to materialize does not necessarily invalidate the prophet, for the predicted event could be far in the future or contingent upon the response of the listeners. Jonah's prophecy of doom for Nineveh did not come true because the people repented of their evil ways.

But even if the prophecy comes true, it is no guarantee of authenticity. If a prophet's "sign or DT. 13:2 wonder which he tells you comes to pass," warns the author of Deuteronomy, "and if he says, 'Let us go after other gods,' which you have not known, 'and let us serve them,' you shall not listen to the words of that prophet."

What did Old Testament prophets say about Jesus' birth?

Telling of Jesus' birth, Matthew writes: "All this MT. 1:22 took place to fulfil what the Lord had spoken by the prophet: 'Behold, a virgin shall conceive and

112

Isaiah, perhaps the most stirring of the Hebrew prophets, from a 12th-century French carving.

new meaning in the passage. He could only conclude that Isaiah was referring to Jesus, who Matthew believed was "God with us," or Emmanuel. MT. 1:23 Further, the fact that Matthew was using the Greek translation of Isaiah, in which the future mother was described as a "virgin," made the MT. 1:23 connection to Jesus' virgin birth even more convincing to him.

Matthew also cites the Old Testament prophet Hosea for his account of the infant Jesus being carried to Egypt: "This was to fulfil what the Lord MT. 2:15 had spoken by the prophet, 'Out of Egypt have I called my son.' " Again Matthew applied the prophetic words to Jesus, investing the ancient passage with new meaning.

Are there prophets in the New Testament?

Because of his teachings and the miracles he performed, Jesus is portrayed as a prophet in the New Testament. It is evident, too, that Jesus considered himself a prophet. When he met with skepticism in his hometown of Nazareth, he responded: "A prophet is not without honor except MT. 13:57 in his own country and in his own house." A passage in the Book of Acts places Jesus on the same level as Moses, who embodied the ideal characteristics of the prophetic calling: "Moses ACTS 3:22 said, 'The Lord God will raise up for you a prophet [Jesus] from your brethren as he raised me up. You shall listen to him in whatever he tells you.' " Matthew reports that Jesus himself called John the Baptist a prophet, "and more than a proph- MT. 11:9 et." And Luke saw John the Baptist as a "prophet LK. 1:76 of the Most High."

Prophecy continues to play a role in the New Testament after Jesus. Paul told the Corinthians, "Make love your aim, and earnestly desire the 1 COR. 14:1 spiritual gifts, especially that you may prophesy." Twelve early Christians at Ephesus, having been baptized by Paul and filled with the Holy Spirit, "spoke with tongues and prophesied." Early ACTS 19:6 Christian prophets also included such figures as Agabus, who foretold Paul's arrest in Jerusalem, and the "four unmarried daughters" of Philip the ACTS 21:9 evangelist, at whose house Paul stayed in Caesarea. The Revelation to John (also called the Apocalypse), the last book of the New Testament, is described in its opening verses as "words of the prophecy," thus identifying John, REV. 1:3 its author, as a prophet.

bear a son, and his name shall be called Emmanuel' (which means, God with us)." The prophet referred to by Matthew is Isaiah.

Like Matthew, many of the early Christians looked to the Old Testament to help them understand the meaning and events of Jesus' life. Matthew's use of Isaiah 7:14 does not change its original meaning—which most Jewish commentators believe was a prophecy that Judah's King Ahaz, beleaguered by Syrian and Israelite enemies, would resist the invaders within a short time after the birth of the child. However, looking back from his knowledge of Jesus, Matthew found ✳

Judges of Israel

Who were the judges?

After the death of Joshua, much of the promised land was not securely held by the people of Israel. Nor were the Israelites firmly united until the time of the kings. For about 200 years, roughly between 1200 and 1000 B.C., various tribal leaders emerged who fought off enemies and tried to keep their people faithful to the covenant with God. These popular heroes became known as the judges, although few of them actually judged in the sense of rendering verdicts.

JG. 17:6; 21:25   "In those days," says the Book of Judges, "there was no king in Israel; every man did what was right in his own eyes." There were 12 judges, of which five are called minor judges because little is said of their deeds. In chronological order, they were Othniel, Ehud, Shamgar, Deborah, Gideon, two minor judges (Tola and Jair), Jephthah, three more minor judges (Ibzan, Elon, and Abdon), and Samson. The succession of judges followed a pattern: the Israelites lapsed into idolatry, for which God punished them with foreign oppressors; when the people repented, he sent a judge to deliver them from their enemies and bring peace. Then the cycle began again.

Which two women helped vanquish a Canaanite army?

Deborah, the only woman judge in the Bible, planned the Israelite attack against a Canaanite army led by Sisera. On the day of battle, the usually tame river Kishon was in flood, bogging down Sisera's 900 iron chariots. The Israelites overwhelmed their better-armed enemy.

Sisera took refuge in the tent of Heber the Kenite. But his wife lulled Sisera to sleep and drove a peg through his head, fulfilling Deborah's prophecy that "the Lord will sell Sisera into the hand of   JG. 4:9 a woman." The Israelite victory destroyed the power of the Canaanite king, Jabin, and turned the struggle to control central and northern Canaan to Israel's advantage.

Why did Gideon take only 300 men to fight thousands?

Thirty-two thousand men answered Gideon's call for revenge against the Midianite raiders who had murdered his brothers. But when the volunteers had assembled, God told Gideon that such a

Seated before the tribal elders, Deborah praises God for the Israelites' victory on Mount Tabor: from a series of biblical tableaux by 20th-century German illustrators.

SAMSON AND DELILAH

Samson's weakness for women was well known when he fell in love with Delilah. Wishing to rid themselves of the Israelite hero, the lords of the Philistines bribed Delilah to discover the secret of his physical power. The first time Delilah cajoled him into telling her "how you might be bound, that one could subdue you [Jg. 16:6]," he told her that tying him with seven fresh bowstrings would make him weak, "like any other man [Jg. 16:7]." While he slept, she bound him as he had instructed, then summoned Philistines to seize him. But, startled out of his sleep, Samson easily snapped the bowstrings. Twice more she tried to wheedle from him the secret of his strength. Both times, of course, he tricked her and was able to evade capture.

Delilah nagged Samson until, "vexed to death [Jg. 16:16]," he told her of his Nazirite vow that prohibited him from cutting his hair. "If I be shaved, then my strength will leave me [Jg. 16:17]." After lulling him to sleep, Delilah called in a man to shave the seven locks of his hair. This time Samson had defeated himself. His captors gouged out his eyes and made him grind grain, walking in circles like an ox.

Samson had his revenge. His hair began to grow back in prison. The blind hero was led to a sacrifice honoring the pagan god Dagon and placed between supporting pillars of the house of worship. Calling on God to restore his strength, Samson toppled the pillars and brought down the entire house on himself and the Philistines—"so the dead whom he slew at his death were more than those whom he had slain during his life [Jg. 16:30]."

huge army could claim that it had defeated the enemy without God's help.

Gideon then selected 300 men, whom he divided into three equal companies, and armed them with trumpets and torches concealed in empty jars. At a predetermined signal the Israelites blew their trumpets, broke the jars, and JG. 7:20 waved their torches, shouting, "A sword for the Lord and for Gideon!" Thinking they were surrounded, the Midianites fled into the desert, where Gideon caught and slew their leaders.

How did Jephthah's desire for victory lead to tragedy?

Threatened by Ammonite attacks, the elders of the region of Gilead asked the outcast Jephthah to help them and offered to make him head of all Gilead. Jephthah agreed and vowed that if he re-JG. 11:31 turned victorious, "whoever comes forth from . . . my house to meet me . . . shall be the Lord's, and I will offer him up for a burnt offering." The battle won, he arrived home, where his daughter rushed out jubilantly to welcome him. Although horrified, he was bound by his vow.

Jephthah's act was not without precedent. The ✳ Bible mentions human sacrifice as early as the story of Abraham. In the reign of Ahaz, the eighth-century B.C. ruler of Judah, children were sacrificed, "according to the abominable practices of 2 CHR. 33:2 the nations whom the Lord drove out before the people of Israel." In Jephthah's view the vow to God made the abominable act unavoidable.

How did Samson differ from other judges?

Most of the judges mentioned in the Book of Judges were military or religious leaders. Samson was neither, nor did he sit in judgment over his people. Nonetheless, he helped the Israelites solidify their hold on Canaan and laid the groundwork for a united monarchy.

Samson's exploits, which give a picture of the rough-and-tumble life on Israel's frontier with the Philistines, have been compared with the epic deeds of such mythological figures as Hercules or the American Paul Bunyan. Samson's reputation stems from superheroic feats: slaying 1,000 Philistines with the jawbone of an ass, for example. He was a loner, a vengeful, free-spirited renegade who singlehandedly took on the Philistines, often motivated by no more than a personal grudge.

John the Baptist

In the wilderness that became home to his ministry, "the word of God came to John [Lk. 3:27]," and he began his mission; a 15th-century Dutch painting.

Why did John perform baptisms?

The man who came to be known as John the Baptist believed that every life must change and MT. 3:8 "bear fruit that befits repentance." Clearly, he was a prophet, with a prophet's call for repentance and the unmistakable hair-shirt garb that had been a prophetic badge since the time of Elijah. To qualify as God's chosen, John preached that it was no longer enough for someone to claim descent from Abraham; people had to show obedience to God and justice to one another in preparation for God's imminent judgment.

The first step to avoid a fiery death, John said, ✳ was to confess one's sins and be plunged into the waters of the Jordan River. John offered this rite to everyone in Palestine and thus earned the title the Baptizer, or Baptist—one who administers baptism.

Why did Herod execute John the Baptist?

In his *Antiquities of the Jews,* written at the end of the first century A.D., the Jewish historian Josephus gave a brief account of John the Baptist's ministry and death. John's sermons had such force, Josephus wrote, that crowds of people "were aroused to the highest degree" and were ready to follow him "in everything they did." John's eloquence alarmed Herod Antipas, the ruler of the Jordan region where John preached, and Herod became convinced that John was fomenting rebellion. He had John arrested and carried in chains to the royal fortress, where the prophet was executed.

Matthew and Mark provide a different version of John's death: the famous story of Salome's dance at Herod's birthday banquet and her request, prompted by her mother, Herodias, for "the head of John the Baptist on a platter." Hero- MK. 6:25 dias was incensed at John for condemning her marriage to Herod on the grounds that she was already married to Herod's half brother Philip.

Regardless of exactly why he was executed, the murder of John the Baptist seems to have left Herod with misgivings. The people believed that John was a prophet, perhaps one of the great ancient prophets raised to life. After John's death it was speculated that Jesus might be John come back to life. Mark and Matthew hint that a guilty conscience led Herod to the conclusion that "John, whom I beheaded, has been MK 6:16 raised."

Was Jesus a disciple of John the Baptist?

Matthew, Mark, and Luke all report that Jesus went to John to be baptized, and it is likely that Jesus began his work within John's circle. Moreover, the Gospels clearly show that Jesus defended the divine authority of John's ministry. Was John, therefore, Jesus' mentor and superior? No, according to the Gospels. "After me MK 1:7 comes he who is mightier than I, the thong of

MK. 1:8 whose sandals I am not worthy to stoop down and untie," Mark quotes John the Baptist as saying about Jesus. "I have baptized you with water; but he [Jesus] will baptize you with the Holy Spirit." Matthew added that John asserted that he himself needed to be baptized by Jesus.

Whatever his initial ties to John, Jesus assumed a completely independent role. Jesus did not baptize, though some of his disciples continued to do so. Whereas John had called people into the wilderness and preached a life of fasting and prayer, Jesus went into the cities and banqueted with Pharisees, tax collectors, and sinners. When his followers asked for instruction in prayer, "as John taught his disciples," Jesus LK. 11:1 gave them a simple new supplication, the Lord's Prayer. Yet Jesus retained the highest respect for John the Baptist, calling him "more than a LK. 7:26 prophet . . . among those born of women none is greater than John."

THE MEANING OF BAPTISM

In the sermon Peter preached on Pentecost, he charged those present: "Repent, and be baptized every one of you in the name of Jesus Christ for the forgiveness of your sins [Acts 2:38]." Some 3,000 people responded to his command, and from that time on baptism was regarded as the initiation rite for anyone wishing to become a Christian.

The word *baptize* comes from the Greek verb *baptizo,* meaning to immerse, go under, or sink. In the earliest Christian rites, baptism meant full immersion in water. By the end of the first century, variations were allowed. Immersion in running water was preferred, but still water was acceptable, with cold favored over warm. If water was scarce, baptism could be performed by pouring water over the initiate's head in the name of the Father, Son, and Holy Spirit.

The Christian sacrament of baptism drew upon the Old Testament tradition of ritual washing for purification. Thus baptism could be thought of as a spiritual bath through which Christians were "washed . . . sanctified . . . justified in the name of the Lord Jesus Christ

and in the Spirit of our God [1 Cor. 6:11]."

Some New Testament writers expressed the meaning of baptism through images that were drawn from the Old Testament. Just as Noah was saved from the waters of the flood, Peter writes, "Baptism . . . now saves you [1 Pet. 3:21]." Paul speaks of the Exodus of the Israelites from Egypt as a baptism "in the cloud and in the sea [1 Cor. 10:2]."

But for early Christians the

ritual of baptism took on its most sacred meaning when it was associated with the death and resurrection of Jesus, becoming a symbol of the victory over spiritual death and the passage to a new life. In baptism the Christian changed into a new person as he "put on Christ [Gal. 3:27]." "All of us who have been baptized into Christ Jesus were baptized into his death," Paul reminded the Romans, "so that . . . we too might walk in newness of life [Rom. 6:3]."

The Gospels relate that a voice and a dove from heaven attended John's baptism of Jesus, shown in this 15th-century fresco.

Apostles and Disciples

Why did Jesus gather disciples?

Many influential figures of ancient times—from Jewish rabbis to Greek philosophers—had pupils who could be called disciples. The pupil served as an apprentice, studying under an admired teacher in the hope of one day becoming renowned himself. Usually it was the pupil who sought out the teacher, but the Gospels emphasize that Jesus sought out his disciples, who formed a diverse group and often seemed unlikely candidates for discipleship: fishermen, tax collectors, zealots, women possessed by demons or of high social standing.

Jesus' disciples were not apprentices striving to master the teachings of the Torah or another body of knowledge. They were emissaries called to give allegiance to Jesus himself in a way that required renunciation of former occupations and even family life. They were important to him not only because they could carry on his work after him, but because they formed a traveling community that practiced the values he proclaimed. They lived and worked and ate among the outcasts, the sick, and the poor. They refused to fast like the Pharisees or John the Baptist's disciples. They sometimes traveled with next to nothing—no staff, bread, or money—equipped with little but their message of the kingdom of God.

How did Simon Peter meet Jesus?

Although the Gospels give three different accounts of Simon Peter's first encounter with Jesus, all share a common thread: the irresistible force of Jesus' appeal. When, according to Matthew and Mark, Jesus spotted two brothers, Simon and Andrew, casting for fish near the shore, MT. 4:19 Jesus simply said to them, "Follow me, and I will make you fishers of men"; without further explanation, MT. 4:20; MK. 1:18 "immediately they left their nets and followed him," apparently not even pausing to stow their gear. Nothing suggests that either brother had seen Jesus before.

The Gospel of John says that when Andrew, a disciple of John the Baptist, saw John point to JN. 1:36 Jesus and say, "Behold, the Lamb of God," he decided to follow Jesus, but he first found his JN. 1:42 brother Simon and "brought him to Jesus," JN. 1:42 who said to him, "So you are Simon the son of ✳

John? You shall be called Cephas," which means rock in Aramaic (the Greek for *rock* is *petros*, hence the name Peter).

In the Gospel of Luke, Jesus first met Simon at Simon's house, where Jesus cured Simon's mother-in-law of a fever. Their second meeting occurred when Jesus was teaching a large crowd by the Sea of Galilee. Hemmed in by the pressing throng, Jesus spotted Simon's empty fishing boat and asked if he could get into it and "put out a LK. 5:3 little from the land" in order to be heard and seen better. When he had finished teaching, Jesus told Simon to row out to deeper water and let down his nets. Simon protested that they had caught nothing all night, "but at your word," he LK. 5:5 said to the man who had healed in his house, "I will let down the nets." Their nets closed around a tremendous school of fish, and Simon felt the presence of awe-inspiring power. As soon as they reached land, Simon and his partners, James and John, "left everything and LK. 5:11 followed" Jesus.

How did John the Baptist's and Jesus' ministries differ?

Preaching by the river Jordan, John the Baptist told the people that God's terrible judgment day was near and called for repentance. A sense of

According to one tradition, Peter and Andrew had been disciples of John the Baptist before Jesus called them to serve as "fishers of men [Mt. 4:19]," as depicted in this sixth-century Italian mosaic.

In his Sermon on the Mount, Jesus teaches his disciples the meaning of perfection: to love as God loves. This detail is from a fresco by Fra Angelico.

LK. 3:9

LK. 7:19

LK. 7:23

apocalyptic urgency infused John's visions of God's impending wrath. "Even now the axe is laid to the root of the trees," he cried; "every tree therefore that does not bear good fruit is cut down and thrown into the fire."

Instead of the terrible punishments that John saw, Jesus taught love and forgiveness. From prison John sent two disciples to ask Jesus, "Are you he who is to come, or shall we look for another?" In response, Jesus pointed to the miracles he was performing and gently challenged John to accept his ministry of healing and preaching good news to the poor. "Blessed is he," Jesus asked the disciples to tell John, "who takes no offense at me."

Were the Apostles revolutionaries?

Little is known about most of the Apostles before they met Jesus, but diverse bits of information have led some scholars to conclude that several were anti-Roman activists or even guerrilla fighters. The case is strongest for Simon (distinguishing

him from Simon Peter), who is called the Cananaean in Matthew and Mark and the Zealot in Luke. Cananaean is the Aramaic equivalent of zealot, and both terms were used to refer to Jews who were zealous defenders of the law. Since the time of the Maccabees in the second century B.C., being zealous for the law usually meant active opposition to foreign domination over the Jewish people; and just before the Jewish revolt against Rome in A.D. 66, one revolutionary party took the name Zealot. That Simon is called a Cananaean, or Zealot, probably indicates that he was actively involved in the anti-Roman opposition of Jesus' day.

Another rebel may have been Judas Iscariot. Some scholars have argued that the name Iscariot is derived from the Latin *sicarius,* or dagger-bearer, a term for a group of political assassins who killed Romans and Roman collaborators in the years before the A.D. 66 Jewish revolt. However, others argue that Iscariot refers to the Judean town of Kerioth, possibly Judas' home.

Because Jesus once called Simon Peter Simon Bar-Jona, there has been speculation that Peter too was a revolutionary. Bar-Jona probably means son of John in Aramaic, but some scholars have linked it to the Semitic terms *biryon* or *baryona*, outlaw or zealot. They point out that Simon Peter carried a sword and was ready to fight the government soldiers who came to arrest Jesus. Another name, Boanerges, meaning Sons of Thunder, which Jesus applied to James and John, may be an indication of those two Apostles' fiery political activism.

Why were some people surprised by how Jesus treated Levi?

Levi (called Matthew in the Gospel of Matthew) was a Jew working as a tax collector for Rome's puppet ruler in Galilee, Herod Antipas. As a Roman collaborator, he was despised by the Jews, who saw him as enriching himself at the expense of his Jewish countrymen.

When Jesus, known for preaching rigorous devotion to God, confronted Levi at his tax office, everyone present, including the tax collector, probably expected a fiery denunciation. But instead Jesus simply said to him, "Follow me." MK. 2:14 Obediently, Levi "rose and followed him." Then MK. 2:14 Jesus shared a meal of fellowship with a whole circle of despised people like Levi.

The local religious teachers demanded an explanation: "Why does he eat with tax collectors MK. 2:16 and sinners?" Jesus himself responded: "Those MK. 2:17 who are well have no need of a physician, but those who are sick; I came not to call the righteous, but sinners."

Which of the disciples did Jesus call Satan?

To be denounced as Satan by Jesus must have been the most devastating reproach imaginable for one of his disciples, and yet that is what happened to Peter. Peter's shame followed his greatest moment of distinction: confessing Jesus to be the Christ, the son of the living God.

The Gospels make clear that the cause of Jesus' censure was Peter's misunderstanding of the meaning of Jesus' mission on earth. At that time many Jews were expecting the appearance of Messiah. They spoke and wrote confidently of his beneficent and powerful rule on the throne of David. He would restore royal power to Israel and remain forever as its glorious king. Peter believed that Jesus would fulfill this prophecy.

But Jesus rejected the traditional messianic role and asserted that he would not rule over a triumphant, just, and happy people. He declared that he must "suffer many things, and MK. 8:31

Fulfilling Jesus' prophecy, Peter makes the first of his three denials to a maid of the high priest in this detail from the cathedral in Siena.

Ironically, Judas betrayed Jesus with a gesture that is synonymous with devotion: a kiss.

be rejected by the elders and the chief priests and the scribes, and be killed." Peter could not endure such dire predictions of Jesus' suffering and began to rebuke him.

In a sharp response Jesus called Peter Satan, MK. 8:33 meaning adversary. "Get behind me, Satan!" he shouted at Peter. "For you are not on the side of God, but of men"—that is, Peter was not willing to accept God's plan for a new kind of messiah who would experience pain and rejection but was looking for one who would come in triumph.

Why did Peter deny Jesus?

Following the Last Supper, Jesus told the Apos-
MK. 14:27 tles, "You will all fall away," but Peter objected
MK. 14:29 strenuously: "Even though they all fall away, I will not." Ever since he had left his fishing nets by the Sea of Galilee, Peter had been a leader among the disciples. Though once he and other Apostles had apparently believed that Jesus would become a powerful political leader of Israel, Peter had come to realize Jesus was a different kind of Messiah, whose greatest power lay not in the political sphere, but in the realm of the spirit. He had accepted the idea that Jesus might be imprisoned or die.

Even when Jesus foretold that Peter would three times deny knowing him, Peter vehemently
MK. 14:31 asserted, "If I must die with you, I will not deny ✳

you." Under trial, however, Peter's loyalty failed, and his Lord's predictions proved true. Surrounded by enemies, he could no longer sustain the courage he had felt walking by Jesus' side.

The Gospel of Luke suggests a more complex set of reasons for Peter's defection. At the Last Supper, Jesus told Peter darkly that "Satan de- LK. 22:31 manded to have you [all the 12 Apostles], that he might sift you like wheat." Jesus' words recall the Book of Job, where Satan gained the right to put Job through severe trials. But Jesus had prayed that Peter's faith would not fail. "And when you LK. 22:32 have turned again," Jesus added, looking beyond Peter's denial, "strengthen your brethren." Jesus recognized that all his disciples would fall when he was arrested, but he pinned his hopes for their recovery on Peter. Although Peter denied Jesus, he was strengthened by his repentance and gave aid and inspiration to his fellow disciples.

All the Gospel writers describe the circumstances of Peter's denials in considerable detail, suggesting that the strength of his later leader-

APOSTLE/DISCIPLE. *The Greek word for disciple (mathetes) is derived from the verb to learn and means a pupil or apprentice.* Apostle *comes from a Greek verb meaning to send out and suggests an emissary.*

The only people in the Gospels called Apostles are the men Jesus sent out to spread his teachings: Simon Peter, James and John of Zebedee, Andrew, Philip, Bartholomew, Matthew, Thomas, James of Alphaeus, Thaddaeus or Judas the son of James, Simon the Zealot, and Judas Iscariot. Paul claimed to be an Apostle and also gave the name to Barnabas and James.

Mark and Matthew use both terms for the Twelve, and Luke says that Jesus called many disciples together and from them chose 12 Apostles. The New Testament mentions other numbers of followers but does not always call them Apostles or disciples. In Luke 10:20, Jesus told a group of 70 that their "names are written in heaven" for spreading his word. In Acts 1:15, Peter asked 120 "brethren" to help choose a replacement for Judas Iscariot.

ship may have been a kind of compensation for the weakness that overcame him after Jesus was led away to face Pilate and Herod.

Why did Judas betray Jesus?

In many ways Judas' motive for betrayal is more of an enigma than Peter's denial of Jesus. According to the Gospel of John, when Jesus foretold at the Last Supper that Judas would betray him, none of the other Apostles grasped what Jesus was saying. Only after Judas' death did they look back and try to understand. In his speech to the faithful gathered in Jerusalem to choose a new Apostle, Peter did not mention Judas' motives but emphasized that his act was a fulfillment of the Scriptures. Similarly, the Gospels of Luke and John assert that Satan was the driving force within Judas and that his betrayal of Jesus was part of God's plan. The Gospel of Matthew implies that greed may have been a motive because of Judas' bargain for 30 pieces of silver.

Some modern scholars have put Judas' motivation down to a sense of alienation and jealousy. His surname, Iscariot, can be translated man of Kerioth, a town in Judea far south of the Galilean homeland of the other Apostles and Jesus. Perhaps Judas always felt he was an outsider.

Another theory is that Judas had misunderstood what kind of Messiah Jesus was. According to this theory, he had expected Jesus to lead a military revolt, and when he saw that Jesus would not use force, Judas felt betrayed and turned Jesus over to the Roman authorities.

How do the Gospels differ about Jesus' appearances after the Resurrection?

All four Gospels agree that the disciples bore witness to Jesus' resurrection, but their accounts vary as to when and where Jesus reappeared and who was present. In the Gospels of Matthew and Mark, only the women experienced the miraculous appearance of an angel at Jesus' tomb. Visiting the tomb at daybreak, the women found it open, and there was an angel sitting on the stone that had sealed the tomb. The angel instructed the women to tell Jesus' disciples that "he is going before you to Galilee; there you will see him." Later, on a mountain in Galilee, Jesus appeared to the remaining 11 Apostles and, as related at the end of Matthew, told them: "All authority in heaven and on earth has been given to me. Go therefore and make disciples of all nations, baptizing them in the name of the Father and of the Son and of the Holy Spirit." MT. 28:7 MT. 28:18

In the Gospel of Luke, the disciples saw Jesus at other places than Galilee. The day of his resurrection he appeared to Peter and also to two disciples who were traveling to Emmaus, a village about seven miles from Jerusalem. Then he appeared to the whole company of Apostles in Jerusalem. As that day drew to a close, Jesus commanded the disciples to "stay in the city, until you are clothed with power from on high." LK. 24:49

Mary Magdalene was the first to see Jesus risen, according to the Gospel of John. Jesus did not show himself to the Apostles until evening, when he suddenly appeared in their midst saying, "Peace be with you." Jesus' series of appearances in Jerusalem were followed by a visit to Peter and six other disciples who were fishing in the Sea of Tiberias. After telling them where to cast their net to make a large catch, Jesus ate breakfast with his disciples, and said to Peter, "Feed my sheep," meaning that Peter was to look after Jesus' ministry and his followers. JN. 20:19 JN. 21:17

CALL. *Occurring some 700 times in the Bible, the word* call *carries several meanings. When God issues a call, it conveys a divine command to human beings. In Isaiah 45:3, God summoned the Hebrews to be his chosen people. "It is I, the Lord, the God of Israel, who call you by your name." Writing to the Philippians, the Apostle Paul spoke of "the upward call of God in Christ Jesus [Phil. 3:14]."*

At times God called individuals to a particular deed or role. Several Old Testament prophets—Amos, Ezekiel, Hosea, Isaiah, Jeremiah, and Samuel—received God's instructions to prophesy in his name. God called Saul and David from obscurity to become Israel's kings. In Galilee the Apostles Peter, Andrew, James, and John answered Jesus' call to join his ministry and become his emissaries. Today members of the clergy speak of being called to the priesthood or ministry or to a new assignment within the church.

THE FIRST CHRISTIAN MARTYR

Stoned to death about A.D. 35, Stephen is called the first Christian martyr. Like many martyrs who came after him, Stephen unflinchingly witnessed—that is, preached the death and resurrection of Jesus—and continued witnessing in the face of death. The connection between witnessing and martyrdom is recognized in the word *martyr,* which is derived from the Greek *martys*, meaning witness.

As a Christian living in Jerusalem in the period immediately following the crucifixion of Jesus, Stephen nevertheless remained a member of the Jewish community, some of whom were Greek-speaking like Stephen. To speak Greek as a first language was a mark of Jews who grew up in the Diaspora (the dispersion of Jews from Palestine that began with the Babylonian exile). Many of these so-called Hellenic Jews came to Jerusalem and worshiped in their own Greek-speaking synagogues where, no less than the native Jews, they took pride in being zealous for the law and for the old religious traditions.

To Hellenic Jews intent on affirming their religious zeal, Stephen was a problem. He did not stop attending their synagogues—yet he preached the new faith of Christianity. Moreover, Stephen was becoming a highly visible Christian, one of seven men, "full of the Spirit and of wisdom [Acts 6:3]," chosen to help the Apostles give food and alms to widows and orphans in Jerusalem.

Stephen became embroiled in religious arguments that were so heated that he was brought before the Sanhedrin, the Jewish supreme council headed by the high priest. There "false witnesses [Acts 6:13]" charged him with blaspheming Moses and God. Stephen's defense was to attack his accusers as disobedient to God, thus confirming the worst rumors the Sanhedrin had heard about him. He had barely finished his speech when he was carried outside the walls of the city and stoned to death.

Present at the execution was an approving young Pharisee named Saul, later known by the name Paul, who was to go on "ravaging the church [Acts 8:3]" until he himself was converted to the new faith.

By portraying Stephen as a man who died unjustly, who was filled with the Spirit and forgave his enemies, the author of Acts was perhaps trying to reflect the death of another martyr, Jesus.

Paul the Missionary

How could Paul claim to be an Apostle?

After the Crucifixion the disciples set strict standards for choosing a new Apostle. In the Book of Acts, Peter told the brethren gathered in Jerusalem that the man who would replace Judas the ACTS 1:21 betrayer must be "one of the men who have accompanied us during all the time that the Lord Jesus went in and out among us, beginning from the baptism of John until the day when he was taken up from us." Not even all of the original Twelve could meet this requirement. There were two suitable candidates, however, Barsabbas Justus and Matthias; both were worthy, and the Apostles eventually chose Matthias by lots.

Paul was aware that not every Christian of his day accepted him as an Apostle. He had probably never seen Jesus before the Resurrection. He claimed his apostleship by divine commission. He said he had been ordained an Apostle by Jesus himself on the road to Damascus, when the risen Christ had appeared and called Paul to take up his ministry. From that moment on, Paul became, in his words, "a servant [literally, a slave] of Jesus Christ, called to be an apostle, set apart for the gospel of God." The many churches that he established and the lives that he helped transform became the living certification of his claim. "If to others I am not an apostle," he wrote in a letter to the church at Corinth, "at least I am to you; for you are the seal of my apostleship in the Lord." ROM. 1:1 1 COR. 9:2

Why did Paul choose to preach among the Gentiles?

Preaching to Gentiles was nothing new for Jews of the Diaspora who, beginning with the Babylonian exile of 587 B.C., had lived outside Palestine and formed far-flung colonies around the Mediterranean and in the Middle East. Many of these Jews had made great efforts, often successful, to win converts to Judaism among the Gentiles and to show similarities between the best of Greek culture and the Jewish Scriptures and laws. As a Jew of the Diaspora, Paul himself might well have tried to win Gentiles to Judaism. But now Paul's mission was different. In addition to confirming Jesus as God's Messiah and God's Son, Paul's vision on the road to Damascus convinced him that he had been chosen to take the message of Jesus to non-Jews. God, he said, "was pleased to reveal his Son GAL. 1:16

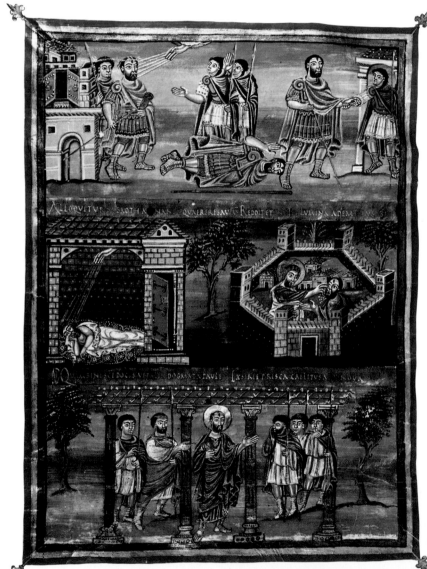

In scenes from a 12th-century manuscript, the disciple Ananias has a vision (top) telling him to visit the blinded Paul (middle). His sight restored, Paul becomes an aggressive missionary.

THE TURNING POINT IN SAUL'S LIFE

Noon was coming on as a band of determined travelers from Jerusalem neared Damascus, the great crossroads of trade and perhaps the oldest city in the world. Their leader, a young Pharisee named Saul, held letters from the high priest empowering him to arrest members of the dangerous heretical sect that was spreading false teachings among Jews, particularly the Jews who had settled outside Jerusalem in cities like Damascus. Calling their sect the Way, these men and women believed that a man named Jesus, who had been executed by the Romans, was the long-awaited Messiah and the Son of God. In Damascus, Saul would hunt down these heretics and return them to Jerusalem for punishment.

Suddenly, a light brighter than the noonday sun shone on Saul, blinding him. He lost his balance and fell helpless in the dirt. Then, just as in the stories he had heard all his life about the Lord

calling Moses or Samuel, a voice spoke: "Saul, Saul, why do you persecute me [Acts 9:4]?" Saul was bewildered; he knew it must be the Lord's voice, but Saul was not persecuting God, but defending him. Stupefied, Saul appealed, "Who are you, Lord [Acts 9:5]?" The most impossible answer that Saul could have imagined filled his ears: "I am Jesus, whom you are persecuting; but rise and enter the city, and you will be told what you are to do [Acts 9:5]."

Saul's life was turned upside down; he knew he had been made Christ's emissary and lived ever after in the light of that revelation. "Whatever gain I had," he told the Christians of Philippi, "I counted as loss for the sake of Christ. Indeed I count everything as loss because of the surpassing worth of knowing Christ Jesus my

This portrait of Paul, the Apostle to the Gentiles, is on a 14th-century vestment.

Lord. For his sake I have suffered the loss of all things . . . in order that I may gain Christ and be found in him [Phil. 3:7]." And to churches in Galatia he wrote: "I have been crucified with Christ; it is no longer I who live, but Christ who lives in me; and the life I now live in the flesh I live by faith in the Son of God, who loved me and gave himself for me [Gal. 2:20]."

to me, in order that I might preach him among the Gentiles." His vision placed him among those Christians who had already begun seeking converts throughout the Mediterranean world. The first Gentile conversion recorded in the Book of Acts had been performed by the Apostle Peter. He had allowed Gentiles who were not proselytes (converts to Judaism) to be baptized. His action came after two significant experiences: first, he had a vision in which God revealed that the Gentiles would share in the new faith; second, the Holy Spirit caused the Gentiles ACTS 10:46 to start "speaking in tongues and extolling God." ✳

Paul reached agreement with Peter, James, and John that he was to be entrusted with the mission to the Gentiles, and he worked systematically to plant the message of Christianity in cities and towns of Asia Minor and Greece: Lystra, Antioch, Troas, Philippi, Thessalonica, Corinth, Athens, Ephesus, and many more. By A.D. 57, he could claim, "from Jerusalem and as far round ROM. 15:19 as Illyricum [present-day Yugoslavia], I have fully preached the gospel of Christ, thus making it my ambition to preach the gospel, not where Christ has already been named, lest I build on another man's foundation."

Who called Paul mad?

For more than two years, A.D. 57–59, Paul languished in prison in Caesarea on charges that he had tried to bring pagans into the inner confines of the Jerusalem temple. Felix, the corrupt Roman governor, was convinced that Paul would eventually offer him a bribe to buy freedom, but he was replaced by a more responsible governor named Festus, who was determined to resolve Paul's case quickly.

Listening to Paul and his accusers (who had been selected by the chief priests and elders in Jerusalem), Festus soon found himself more bewildered than enlightened. When the Jewish king Herod Agrippa II arrived in Caesarea to welcome Festus to his new post, Festus told him that both sides appeared to be debating obscure points of bizarre superstition. Agrippa decided to join Festus in court and hear Paul for himself.

Paul was pleased with the chance to defend himself before a Jewish rather than a Roman ruler because he felt Agrippa would be "especially ACTS 26.3 familiar with all customs and controversies of the Jews." Paul laid out his story and his beliefs without attempting to make them palatable to pagan tastes. He told the court how he, a Pharisee, had persecuted Jesus' followers until the resurrected Jesus had appeared to him and appointed him to bring light to the Gentiles.

Paul's statements appeared erudite nonsense to Festus. "Paul, you are mad!" he shouted. "Your ACTS 26:24 great learning is turning you mad." Festus' reaction did not really surprise Paul, who realized

THE WRITINGS OF PAUL

Paul's only known writings are a series of letters that addressed the specific needs of specific people. Yet those letters had a profound impact on the growth of the early church.

Moving from city to city, Paul would establish a congregation of Christians in one place, then travel on to another. The churches he left behind were often fragile, composed of both Jews and Gentiles who had given up long-standing religious beliefs to join the new community. They had growing pains; they had questions, and often Paul could not return to give his guidance in person. The letters became Paul's long-distance voice, answering inquiries, giving instruction, encouraging, enforcing discipline, transmitting news, cajoling, arguing, warning about dangers, impressing on his readers the fundamental meaning of the Gospel that had made them a community.

Although traditionally all 14

Paul wrote to the Colossians from prison, as shown in a 15th-century miniature.

letters—from Romans to Hebrews in the New Testament —were considered the writings of Paul, today only seven of those are generally accepted as the work of Paul alone: Romans, 1 and 2 Corinthians, Galatians, Philippians, 1 Thessalonians, and Philemon. Authorship of the others is debatable, and the conclusions vary.

Some historians suggest that Paul's disciples wrote letters to the faithful and attributed them to the Apostle; others, that Paul sketched out the ideas for a letter but left it to a coworker to formulate the words; still others believe that for some unknown reason Paul simply changed his ways of expressing himself in some letters.

Considering that every letter of Paul is written for a particular time and place, it is not surprising that today readers may find "some things in them hard to understand [2 Pet. 3:16]." Still, the vision of Christ and the early church community contained in Paul's letters has influenced and inspired Christian theologians and the faithful for 2,000 years.

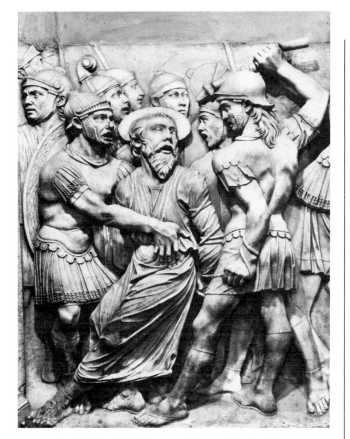

Paul risked his life preaching to the Gentiles. In a 15th-century relief, the Roman tribune arrests him to protect him from a Jerusalem mob.

ACTS 26:25 what a huge gulf lay between Festus' beliefs and his own. Calmly, Paul replied: "I am not mad, most excellent Festus, but I am speaking the sober truth. For the king knows about these things, and to him I speak freely."

ACTS 26:28 The king felt the force of Paul's arguments but was taken aback at Paul's direct appeal to him: "In a short time you think to make me a Christian!" he exclaimed. Soon after, Paul was sent to Rome to stand trial before Caesar. Apparently he remained there under house arrest for two years and was beheaded sometime after A.D. 62.

How did Paul approach the friction between Jewish and Gentile Christians?

Paul insisted that all non-Jews who converted to the new faith need not take on the obligations of the law that would have been required of Gentile proselytes to Judaism. They were not required to be circumcised or to observe the dietary laws.

Many Jewish Christians objected strongly to such a devaluation of the law by those who claimed to be their Christian compatriots. They evidently believed that Jesus, as the Messiah, had come to bring about true fulfillment of God's law, not its annulment. After all, the Scriptures clearly stated that certain practices such as circumcision were part of an "everlasting covenant." GEN. 17:13

Paul countered by saying that Jesus had sent him to the Gentiles not to make them proselytes to the law but simply to "preach Christ." Thus, when a conflict heated up between Jewish and Gentile Christians in the large community in Antioch, Paul argued that the church must not "compel the Gentiles to live like Jews." GAL. 2:14

Did Paul have disciples?

Numerous younger men worked with Paul in his mission and followed his methods and teaching. Most prominent among these were Timothy and Titus, who were Paul's personal emissaries in dealing with church problems. Timothy was from Lystra in Asia Minor. His mother was Jewish, his father Greek, and he became like a son to Paul. "I have no one like him," Paul wrote the Philippians, "who will be genuinely anxious for your welfare." Titus was a Gentile convert who helped Paul deal with several difficult situations. He accompanied Paul to Jerusalem in the midst of the controversy over circumcision and helped win back the Corinthian church after its members had become alienated from Paul. PHIL. 2:20

In addition to Timothy and Titus, Paul mentioned other coworkers in his letters: Lucius, Jason, Sosipater, Tertius, Sosthenes, Silvanus, Epaphroditus, Epaphras, Luke, and Demas. Paul delegated missionary work to his helpers and used them to establish and cultivate churches.

Paul hotly denied that he had disciples in the same sense as Christ. Once, in the church in Corinth, he learned that various groups were claiming, " 'I belong to Paul,' or 'I belong to Apollos,' or 'I belong to Cephas,' or 'I belong to Christ.' " Paul emphatically rejected such dissensions. "Is Christ divided?" he demanded. "Was Paul crucified for you? Or were you baptized in the name of Paul?" No matter how important Paul may have been to the Corinthian Christian community as its founder, he insisted that its members could never be disciples of Paul—all were disciples of Christ. 1 COR. 1:12 1 COR. 1:13

EVERYDAY LIFE

One of the fascinations of reading the Bible is to be transported across time and space to a world at once foreign and familiar. The great moral and religious issues of the Bible make it universal and timeless, and yet those issues are played out in settings that seem enchantingly exotic or suffused with a glow of antique simplicity.

The Bible reflects the everyday life of real people. The more one wants to know the Bible, the more one needs to understand its setting. How did the ordinary people who lived the Bible stories go about their daily routine—what were their houses like, how did they make a living, what did they worry about or take pleasure in? The inhabitants of that land were people like ourselves but with different perspectives from ours, different customs, choices, and aspirations.

One of the first things about the world of the ancient Israelites that the Bible stresses is the importance of the family. People did not usually think of themselves as individuals but as sons or daughters of their parents and as responsible members of their family, clan, and tribe. They maintained extensive genealogical records, and their laws were so structured that families could remain on the same land through generations. The law even provided for those who were struck by financial disaster so that they could regain their ancestral heritage.

Children were vital for survival in this precarious world, and the birth of a child was marked by rites and customs befitting its importance. Women could hardly imagine a greater misfortune than infertility, and some of the Bible's most joyful miracles are those in which God grants a child to a woman who could not otherwise have had one.

As a child grew, he or she was carefully integrated into the tightly woven web of society. Most education took place at home. When schools began to appear, not long before New Testament times, they were offshoots of the synagogues that served as centers of community life and worship. When the time came for marriage, family interests often prevailed over individual wishes. Marriages were arranged by parents, and numerous customs—such as leviratic marriage, wives offering concubines to their husbands, or bans against marriage outside the tribes—served to ensure the continuation of the clan. Even in punishing criminals, the ancient laws gave families a major role. For example, in a society without police or prosecuting attorneys, the family of a murder victim bore the responsibility of avenging the death of its kin, and in certain severe cases an entire family could be punished for the crimes of one of its members. The intention—not always fulfilled—was to organize all of society so that individuals would be encouraged to live by God's law.

Ordinarily, daily life in a biblical village moved to the simple rhythm of sunrise and sunset. Trades and crafts, handed down from father to son to grandson in an economy based largely on barter, changed little over the years. Mothers taught daughters how to clothe and feed their families and raise children. Not even death could sever such powerful ties. When the time came, an Israelite looked forward to resting with his ancestors in a family tomb constructed to hold the remains of many generations.

But the perilous political and geographical position of Israel did not allow the simple rhythms of life to beat without interruption. War frequently burned across the countryside, ranging from raids by the Philistines, Ammonites, and other hostile neighbors to the onslaught of great armies from Egypt, Mesopotamia, Greece, and Rome.

By the time of Jesus, even backwater towns in Galilee and Judea had inexorably become part of the larger Mediterranean world. Jesus left the traditional life of his village and carpenter shop to travel throughout Palestine. His followers in turn took his message along well-traveled roads to the far corners of the Roman empire and beyond. Everyday life had changed. For a woman like Lydia, a trader in cloth and dye—or a tentmaker like the Apostle Paul—daily life involved travel to distant cities and work with new acquaintances. In cosmopolitan centers dominated by Greek and Roman gods, the intimacy of village life was replaced by communities of the faithful gathering in the homes of believers. The simplicity of life in a village like Nazareth could never be regained in the bustle of Antioch, Corinth, or Rome. Still, through the everyday life of the early Christians, the great faith in one God that had been nurtured in the close-knit families and clans of Israel now became the heritage of all the world.

Top left: A 15th-century miniature showing five rabbis.

Tribe and Clan

What was the basic social structure in Old Testament times?

Beginning in the Book of Genesis, an underlying model of social organization for both families and tribes was descent from a common male ancestor, or patriarch: the line of the so-called father's house. In this sense a tribe was a vastly extended family, all of whose members were either descendants of or had married descendants of a man who had lived some time before. A large tribe usually had smaller units, called clans, which were made up of a number of families.

An early Israelite family was often very large, with three or four generations living in the same household. It might have been headed by a great-grandfather, with his wife or wives, including his concubines, his male children and their wives and offspring, and his unmarried daughters, so that the group had family ties of almost every description covering four generations. Moreover, the household was often augmented by a number of unrelated persons, such as alien slaves, prisoners of war, wanderers, and impoverished Hebrews who had sold themselves as slaves for a limited period of time.

The Bible sometimes uses such terms as *father's house, family, clan,* and *tribe* almost interchangeably. This is not surprising in light of the fact that Jacob was the father of the 12 sons whose descendants became the 12 tribes that united to form the nation of Israel. The size of the tribes varied throughout history, but the Old Testament records that around the time of the Exodus "the number of the tribe of Manasseh was thirty-two thousand two hundred" and "of the Levites . . . all the males from a month old and upward, were twenty-two thousand."

NUM. 1:35
NUM. 3:39

How did settling the land change the tribes?

In the time of the tribes, roughly 1200 to 1000 B.C., there was no border-to-border government, no taxation, no standing army. The tribes were united by religion and a tradition of common ancestry going back to Jacob and his 12 sons. Just as the religion survived through periods of migration and conquest, so the structure of society based on common descent endured, even though it was modified by the emergence of a ✳

monarchy in about 1000 B.C. and by gradual urbanization. As more and more unrelated people settled in favored areas of the land, common residence—in towns and cities—joined common descent as an organizing principle in society, and ties of kinship no longer bound tribes so closely. At the same time, rule by a king and a centralized government weakened the authority of tribal leaders and laws.

Why were genealogies important in biblical times?

In a society like that of the Hebrews, which was organized by family, clan, and tribe, one's genealogy was an important part of one's identity. Descent from a respected forefather could bring social, political, and religious prestige.

After the Babylonian exile in the sixth century B.C., genealogies were used to substantiate the property claims of exiles returning to Israel. Also, since only men descended from Aaron could serve as priests, officials consulted genealogies to select candidates to serve in the temple.

In the New Testament, the lineage of Jesus is traced in the Gospel of Matthew to Abraham, and in the Gospel of Luke all the way back to Adam. Genealogies of Jesus were set forth in the Gospels to show that he was a son of David.

How were Hebrew slaves different from other slaves?

Compared with non-Hebrew slaves, who were considered chattel, or property, Hebrew slaves occupied an ambiguous position in the Hebrew family. The Bible recognized that Hebrews were sometimes forced to sell themselves or their children into servitude in order to pay off debts or simply survive, but in Leviticus, God said to Moses, "If your brother becomes poor . . . and sells himself to you, you shall not make him serve as a slave: he shall be with you as a hired servant and as a sojourner." Even so, according to a law given to Moses in Exodus, if a master provided a wife for his Hebrew slave and she had children, "the wife and her children shall be her master's" even if the man was set free.

LEV. 25:39

EX. 21:4

As a rule, foreign slaves were not allowed to buy their freedom, but a Hebrew slave could redeem himself by the payment of his price. In any event, the law called for the release of Hebrew

From the seed of Jesse of Bethlehem (shown reclining in this 16th-century woodcut) sprang a tree of life that produced his son David and grandson Solomon— a royal line crowned by the long-awaited Messiah, Jesus Christ.

slaves in the Sabbath Year, which occurred every seven years. A Hebrew slave could have slaves of his own, as well as other property. A girl might be sold into slavery by her father on the understanding that one of the master's sons, or the master himself, would take her as a wife when she came of age. If the master and his sons reneged, she was freed.

How was property passed from one generation to another?

The Book of Numbers and the Book of Joshua convey God's instructions on how the Promised Land should be distributed among tribes and clans. These allotments were considered binding on future generations, and Hebrew laws and customs dealing with inheritance developed to protect the tribe against the loss of its property.

Keeping land in the tribe began with keeping it in the family. In the Book of Numbers, God gave NUM. 27:8 Moses the basic laws of family inheritance: "If a man dies, and has no son, then you shall cause his inheritance to pass to his daughter. And if he has no daughter, then you shall give his inheri- ✳

tance to his brothers. And if he has no brothers, then you shall give his inheritance to his father's brothers. And if his father has no brothers, then you shall give his inheritance to his kinsman that is next to him of his family." These rules, made in response to a plea by the daughters of Zelophehad to receive part of their father's possessions, established a woman's right to inherit property in the absence of any male heirs.

Female heirs, however, were prohibited from marrying outside the tribe. Moses insisted that "every daughter who possesses an inheritance in NUM. 36:8 any tribe . . . shall be wife to one of the family of the tribe of her father, so that . . . no inheritance shall be transferred from one tribe to another." The custom of levirate marriage—a man's marrying his widowed sister-in-law—also served to keep property within the family.

Just as the Israelites sought to preserve property allotments among the tribes, they believed in maintaining an equitable balance of possessions among families. The traditions of the Jubilee Year expressed this principle. Ideally, at the Jubilee (every 50th year) each family or clan would recover any property that had been lost during the previous 50 years.

Birth

What does the Bible say about childbirth?

Giving birth is described as intense agony. Isaiah, for example, compared Israel's distress under oppressors to the pain of "a woman with child, who writhes and cries out in her pangs, when she is near her time." The Bible acknowledged the dangers of birth to mother and child. Rachel died after the hard labor of delivering Benjamin, and the wife of Phinehas died after giving birth prematurely to Ichabod, the grandson of the priest Eli. Babies were often born in unsanitary conditions, and infant mortality was high.

IS. 26:17

Women in labor were usually assisted by midwives, who were esteemed in the Bible and throughout the ancient world. The midwife would cut the umbilical cord, wash the baby, and then rub its body with salt to toughen the skin, a custom still observed by some people in the Middle East today. The baby was wrapped in swaddling cloths (strips of fabric four or five inches wide and several yards long) in the belief that binding the child's body snugly would make the bones strong.

Although most women had midwives in attendance, Matthew and Luke do not mention one at the birth of Jesus. However, the description of Jesus' birth in a second-century Christian work attributed to James relates that Joseph brought a midwife to Mary shortly after the birth.

How did women regain ritual purity after delivery?

Women who had just given birth were regarded as unclean or impure. The uncleanness was not physical or moral, but meant only that the woman had to observe certain ritual restrictions for a period of time. The new mother could not leave her house for seven days after the birth of a son or 14 days after the birth of a daughter. She was not allowed to touch sacred objects or participate in religious ceremonies for an additional 33 days if she had borne a son or 66 days in the event of a daughter. The Bible gives no explana-

A seventh-century B.C. figurine of a pregnant Phoenician woman.

tion for the two different periods of impurity.

A woman marked the end of her uncleanness with ceremonial offerings. "When the days of her purifying are completed, whether for a son or a daughter, she shall bring to the priest . . . a burnt offering and . . . a sin offering, and he shall offer it before the Lord, and make atonement for her; then she shall be clean from the flow of her blood."

LEV. 12:6

A year-old lamb was preferred for the burnt offering and a young pigeon or turtledove for the sin offering, but poor women were allowed to sacrifice birds for both offerings. Hence Mary sacrificed two turtledoves after the birth of Jesus.

Why were barren women stigmatized?

Infertility was thought to be a curse on a woman (and on a woman only). Having children meant a new generation to care for parents in old age and give them a proper burial, and through children the family line and property could be preserved. Sons were celebrated in the Psalms as "a heritage from the Lord, the fruit of the womb a reward." A woman who was unable to provide her husband with children was looked upon with pity and sometimes scorn, and childless women, such as Rachel and Hannah, were miserable. "Give me children, or I shall die!" cried Rachel to her husband, Jacob. Hannah, the wife of Elkanah, "wept and would not eat" because "the Lord had closed her womb." Eventually Hannah bore a son, Samuel, and Rachel gave birth to Joseph, whereupon Rachel said, "God has taken away my reproach."

PS. 127:3

GEN. 30:1

1 SAM. 1:6

GEN. 30:23

Did miraculous births bring special responsibilities?

The births of many of the Bible's greatest figures—from Isaac to Jesus—were attributed to the intervention of God. Most of these special sons, the result of miraculous pregnancies, were consecrated, either before or at birth, to God's service by their grateful mothers. All but one of

FERTILITY RITES

Fertility was valued throughout the ancient Middle East, but among the covenant people it had only one true source: the Lord. In the Book of Genesis, Abraham speaks of "the children whom God has graciously given [Gen. 33:5]." Although all children—sons and daughters—were acknowledged as God's gifts, in a patrilineal society sons were especially prized. Psalm 127 compares sons to "arrows in the hand of a warrior. . . . Happy is the man who has his quiver full of them." If a woman was barren, her recourse was to petition God to remove the curse that he had placed upon her.

However, fertility lore abounded, and there were many remedies to tempt the desperate. The mandrake plant, in particular, was thought to have properties that aroused desire and stimulated conception. In Genesis, Leah and Rachel evidently believed in the mandrake's power and quarreled over possession of mandrake roots that Leah's son found, but it is clear that God alone enabled the two women to have children by Jacob. In the Song of Solomon, a maiden enticed her lover with the fragrance of mandrakes.

The Israelites were not always successful in resisting the fertility

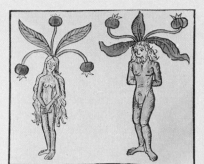

The mandrake herb, a member of the nightshade family, was long regarded as an aid to fertility. Its forked root resembles a human body; its tuft of leaves, a head of hair.

myths and rituals of the Babylonians, Canaanites, Egyptians, and other ancient peoples. Kings of Israel, including Solomon, Omri, and Ahab, and kings of Judah, such as Rehoboam, Jehoram, Ahaziah, and Manasseh, erected shrines to fertility deities. Such apostasy outraged prophets like Jeremiah, who berated Hebrew women for making offerings to a "queen of heaven [Jer. 7:18]," who was in fact an alien goddess. (A number of clay figurines of pregnant women—perhaps statues dedicated to a fertility goddess—have been unearthed at archeological sites in Israel.)

Outside influences challenged but did not break the belief that the true giver of all life was the God of Israel, whose blessings were not obtained by fertility rites but by obedience to his law. "If you obey the voice of the Lord," the Torah promises, "blessed shall be the fruit of your body, and the fruit of your ground, and the fruit of your beasts, the increase of your cattle, and the young of your flock [Dt. 28:2]."

Hannah was deeply distressed because of her infertility; Eli blessed her, and she "conceived and bore a son [1 Sam. 1:20]"—a 12th-century illuminated manuscript.

the sons were born to previously barren women who were usually past childbearing age. The exception was Jesus, born to a young virgin.

In the Old Testament, Sarah, the wife of Abraham, bore Isaac when she was 90, fulfilling God's promise to Abraham to "multiply your descendants as the stars of heaven." Isaac's wife, Rebekah, was barren for 20 years before giving birth to the twins Esau and Jacob, further ensuring the continuation of the line of Abraham. In the next generation Jacob's wife, Rachel, mourned her childlessness for years until God "hearkened to her and opened her womb," producing the indomitable Joseph.

GEN. 22:17

GEN. 30:22

When God ended Hannah's childlessness with the birth of Samuel, she waited only until her son was weaned to deliver him to the priest Eli at the temple. This fulfilled her vow that if she had a son, he would be consecrated to the service of God. The unnamed wife of Manoah in the Book of Judges was also childless and apparently barren; when her son Samson was born, God chose him for a special mission: Samson would "begin to deliver Israel from the hand of the Philistines."

JG. 13:5

In the New Testament, Elizabeth and Zechariah were righteous elderly people who had all but given up hope of having children. But then an angel appeared to Zechariah and announced that Elizabeth would have a son who would bring them "joy and gladness, and many will rejoice at his birth; for he will be great before the Lord." Their son was John the Baptist, who would herald the coming of Jesus.

LK. 1:14

Why were infants buried in city walls?

In excavating the walls of ancient Middle Eastern cities, archeologists have found many infant skeletons interred in burial jars. Opinion is divided on how the infants met their deaths. Some experts think the skeletons are those of babies who were stillborn or died from disease or other unavoidable causes in the first few months of life. In some areas infant mortality may have been as high as 90 percent.

A more sinister theory is that the babies were victims of widespread child sacrifice, and they were buried in the city walls in the belief that their presence would guard against evil spirits. There is possibly a reference in the Old Testament to this practice of "foundation sacrifice." In the First Book of Kings, when Hiel of Bethel was rebuilding Jericho, two of his sons may have been interred in the city structures: "He laid its foundation at the cost of Abiram his first-born, and set up its gates at the cost of his youngest son Segub. . . ."

1 KG. 16:34

This circumcision scene is from the Book of Genesis in a 15th-century Hebrew Bible.

This rebuilding of Jericho had been prophesied and damned by Joshua after he and his men had JOS. 6:26 captured, sacked, and razed the city. "Cursed before the Lord," Joshua said, "be the man that rises up and rebuilds this city, Jericho. "

Was adopting a child a common practice in biblical times?

Adoption was one answer to certain problems resulting from infertility: adopted children could care for their aged parents, for example, and inherit property. Another option was surrogate parenthood. The childless Rachel told her husband, GEN. 30:3 Jacob, to take her maid, Bilhah, "that she may bear upon my knees, and even I may have children through her." There are several other references to children being born on or being placed on the knees of family members. The phrase may refer to an adoption ritual within the family.

Adoption of one kind or another seems to have been an accepted part of life throughout biblical times. Exodus indicates that the child Moses was adopted by the pharaoh's daughter. Centuries later the orphan Esther was reared (though perhaps not formally adopted) by her cousin Mordecai. Adoptions for the purpose of inheritance included those of Joseph's sons Ephraim and Manasseh by Jacob, the children of Manasseh's son Machir by Joseph, and (informally) Ruth's son by her mother-in-law, Naomi.

When were boys circumcised and why?

GEN. 17:10 God told Abraham that "every male . . . that is eight days old among you shall be circumcised." Circumcision was a physical sign of the covenant between God and Abraham. The command included male slaves. Disobedience meant expulsion from the covenant community.

According to Genesis, Abraham was the first Hebrew to perform the rite as a sign of God's covenant, although the practice was observed by other peoples in the Middle East, to whom Jere- JER. 9:25 miah referred as "circumcised but yet uncircumcised." (In the view of Jeremiah and other Jews, circumcision had no religious significance unless done as a sign of their covenant with God.)

Circumcision became a way Jews distinguished themselves from certain of their ene- ✳

As was the custom, baby Jesus was presented in the temple (15th-century fresco by Fra Angelico).

THE DISOBEDIENT MIDWIVES

Midwives were the heroes of what one historian calls the "first recorded case of civil disobedience in defense of a moral cause." It occurred during the Israelites' bondage in Egypt. The pharaoh told the Hebrew midwives: " 'When you serve as midwife to the Hebrew women, and see them upon the birthstool, if it is a son, you shall kill him. . . .' But the midwives feared God, and did not do as the king of Egypt commanded them. . . . [Ex. 1:16]." When the pharaoh accused the midwives of deliberately letting the sons live, the women answered: "Hebrew women are not like the Egyptian women; for they are vigorous and are delivered before the midwife comes to them [Ex. 1:19]." Thus the number of Hebrews grew.

THE MEANING OF NAMES

The ancient Israelites believed that names had mystical powers and that in many ways they reflected the character and destiny of a person.

Usually a baby was named at birth, although by New Testament times parents of sons probably waited until the time of circumcision, eight days later. Either the mother or father selected the name, often with the advice of relatives and neighbors.

Many names incorporated one of God's appellations, showing the parents' devotion to and trust in God. For instance, Jonathan means Yahweh has given; Isaiah, Yahweh is salvation; Elijah, My god [is] Yahweh. Other names were chosen from nature: Leah means wild cow; Rachel, ewe; Deborah, bee. Sometimes cataclysmic events influenced the choice of a name. The priest Eli's daughter-in-law, upon hearing that her husband and father-in-law were dead and that the Philistines had captured the ark of the covenant, named her son

Abraham and Sarah were skeptical that she would conceive; later she bore Isaac (meaning he laughs).

Ichabod, meaning "The glory has departed [1 Sam. 4:21]."

A person usually kept the same name for life, but there are some prominent name changes in the Bible. Often these were made by God and signified an alteration in a person's destiny, for example, "No longer shall your name be Abram, but your name shall be

Abraham; for I have made you the father of a multitude of nations [Gen. 17:5]"; and "As for Sarai your wife, you shall not call her name Sarai, but Sarah shall be her name. . . . I will bless her, and she shall be a mother of nations; kings of peoples shall come from her [Gen. 17:15]."

Starting in the fourth century B.C., when the Israelites came under the influence of Greek and Roman cultures, babies were sometimes given two names, one Hebrew and one Greek or Roman. After the conquest of Asia Minor by Alexander the Great, many Jewish high priests even took Greek names. Paul of Tarsus was a Jew whose Hebrew name was Saul. (He dropped his Hebrew name when he began preaching among the Gentiles.)

The name Jesus is a Greek version of the Hebrew name Joshua, meaning Yahweh's salvation. An angel of the Lord provided the name: "You shall call his name Jesus, for he will save his people from their sins [Mt. 1:21]."

---

1 SAM. 17:26 mies, as when David asked about Goliath, "Who is this uncircumcised Philistine, that he should defy the armies of the living God?" Later the Jews used circumcision to set themselves apart from cultures such as the Greeks and the Romans that sought to absorb them. Eventually, being circumcised came to represent being pure and clean, while not being circumcised meant the opposite. Uncircumcised also connoted something forbidden.

In the early Christian community, the practice was the center of a major controversy as both Jews and others were converted to the new faith. Some Christian missionaries told their non-Jew-

ish converts: "Unless you are circumcised according to the custom of Moses, you cannot be saved." Paul and the other disciples, however, taught that non-Jewish converts were to be accepted into the church without circumcision. Paul told such converts, "If you receive circumcision, Christ will be of no advantage to you." ACTS 15:1 ... GAL. 5:2

Why was it necessary to redeem the firstborn son?

In ancient belief every firstborn, human or animal, belonged to God and by right should be offered up to him. This mandate was expressed in

EX. 13:1 the Book of Exodus after God brought the Hebrews out of Egypt: "The Lord said to Moses, 'Consecrate to me all the first-born; whatever is the first to open the womb among the people of Israel, both of man and of beast, is mine.' "

Israel's God, however, rejected the actual sacrifice of a child. Instead, a ceremony called redemption of the firstborn took place when the son was one month old. (It was felt that if the child survived his first month, he had a good chance of living to adulthood.) The father redeemed his son by paying five shekels to a priest of the temple. The Israelites also believed that God had taken the whole tribe of Levi as his special servants in place of the firstborn sons. A ceremonial "redemption of the son" is practiced among Jews today.

What right of inheritance was often ignored?

DT. 21:17 Among the rules that God gave Moses, there was one dictating the birthright of a firstborn son to a double portion of inheritance, "for he is the first issue of his [father's] strength; the right of the first-born is his." If a man had sons by two wives and he disliked the mother of his firstborn, the law specifically forbade him to give the right to any son but the first one. This edict was violated many times, even though the principle endured. It was through the firstborn sons that family lines continued and that tradition was upheld, and in that sense the first male issue remained special in the eyes of God.

The story of the twins Esau and Jacob is perhaps the best-known Bible story of a younger son usurping what was rightfully his older brother's. Esau was the firstborn twin, but Jacob, with the help of his mother, succeeded in a devious scheme to cheat Esau out of both his inheritance and the family leadership.

In the preceding generation, Isaac, not his older brother Ishmael, received the birthright from Abraham. Jacob continued a family tradition by giving preferential treatment to Judah among the sons of Leah and to the even younger Joseph, son of Rachel. And when Jacob blessed Joseph's two sons, he crossed his arms to put his right hand on the younger Ephraim and thus bestowed a greater blessing on him than on his older brother Manasseh. In addition to these descendants of Abraham in Genesis, many of the great heroes—among them Moses, David, and Solomon—were younger sons.

In this 19th-century painting by Tissot, Jacob impersonates his brother Esau in order to obtain their father's blessing; his mother stands behind him.

Death

Why did Abraham buy land to bury Sarah?

When Sarah died, Abraham wanted more for his wife of over 100 years than a humble grave dug at some spot along the course of their wanderings. He wanted a site that would permanently belong to his clan—where he and each of his descendants could be "gathered to his people." GEN. 25:8

But Abraham and his family, moving from place to place with their herds, owned no property. In the land of Canaan, Abraham was a "stranger and a sojourner" and lived there only GEN. 23:4 with the permission of the established inhabitants such as the Hittites. As wealthy and powerful as he was, Abraham had to ask the Hittites for the legal right to buy or own land.

Since entombment usually followed almost immediately after death, Abraham had to act quickly to secure a burial place for Sarah. At the gate of nearby Hebron, he met with the Hittite GEN. 23:4 leaders and petitioned them, "Give me property among you for a burying place." Bowing before them, he asked for the cave of Machpelah be- GEN. 23:9 longing to a man named Ephron: "For the full price, let him give it to me in your presence as a possession." When Ephron mentioned 400 shek-

els of silver as the value of the cave and land in front of it, Abraham paid at once in full.

The cave of Machpelah became the tomb not only of Sarah, but also of Abraham, Isaac, Rebekah, Leah, and Jacob. Such sepulchers were beyond the means of most families. For the poor (and for criminals and foreigners as well), there were common graves like the one by the brook of Kidron between Jerusalem and the Mount of Olives. It was no more than a series of crude, earth-covered trenches. According to the Gospel of Matthew, the 30 pieces of silver that Judas Iscariot returned to the chief priests were used to buy a potter's field that would become a common graveyard "to bury strangers in." MT. 27:7

Why did Jacob rend his garments?

When a death occurred in a Hebrew household, family members generally expressed their grief by wailing or crying. It was customary to tear one's clothing as a ritual act to signify grief and as a sign to others that one was mourning. If the loss was so devastating that the mourner was plunged into the depths of despair, clothing was occasionally replaced for a time by sackcloth, a rough, uncomfortable material. When Jacob began to tear his clothing upon hearing of the supposed death of his beloved son Joseph, the act did not represent a grief-stricken father who was out of control (although certainly Jacob felt deep grief), but rather a time-honored reaction to death.

Friends and servants were often invited to participate in mourning rituals, which—in addition to wailing and garment rending—could also include rolling about in dirt or ashes as well as the removal of shoes or head coverings. From nearby rooms or rooftops, sympathetic neighbors might add their own shrill cries of grief.

Which of the patriarchs was embalmed?

Embalming was rarely practiced by the ancient Hebrews, who buried their dead quickly. There were exceptions, however. Jacob was embalmed by order of

Joseph and his brothers lay to rest their father's body, wrapped and embalmed in the Egyptian tradition to preserve it during the long journey from Goshen to the family sepulcher in Canaan.

Above the vanquished and bound Satan, Jesus raises Adam and Eve from the endless sleep of the grave to join the saints in heaven in this Byzantine fresco.

his powerful son Joseph, who had become prime minister of Egypt, second in command under the pharaoh. Jacob made a deathbed wish that his body be returned to Canaan, where he could be laid to rest beside his wife Leah, his father (Isaac), and his grandfather (Abraham).

Before the long funeral trip, Joseph evidently authorized for his father the final rites usually reserved for Egyptian nobility: a 40-day embalming ritual and 10 weeks of mourning. Then, with pomp and pageantry that resembled the funeral procession of a pharaoh, the dead patriarch was carried eastward into Canaan and placed in the cave where the remains of his ancestors lay in darkness on their burial slabs.

What were the principal causes of death in biblical times?

Investigations of burial sites indicate that parasitic diseases were major killers in ancient Israel. Infants and children were particularly hard hit, and at least half the population of an average community never lived past the age of 18. Thirty ✳

SHEOL. *The Hebrew word* Sheol *described the region below the earth to which all humanity descended at death. There the dead existed as "shades"— ineffectual, insensate shadows of their living selves. Warriors and kings kept their rank but were powerless, engulfed in darkness, silence, and forgetfulness, a prospect that led Ecclesiastes to conclude ruefully, "A living dog is better than a dead lion. For the living know that they will die, but the dead know nothing [Ec. 9:4]."*

Sheol was not a place of punishment, for both the righteous and the wicked ended there; yet it lacked any of life's satisfactions, since "there is no work or thought or knowledge or wisdom in Sheol [Ec. 9:10]." For the devout the idea of Sheol was particularly painful because it meant no longer praising God. One psalmist implored: "Turn, O Lord, save my life. . . . For in death there is no remembrance of thee; in Sheol who can give thee praise [Ps. 6:4]?"

Angels mourn the death of Jesus in this detail from an embroidered Byzantine tapestry.

touched a corpse. The same procedure was used to purify the possessions of the dead.

For priests, whose days were spent in holy observances among sacred things, the rules were stricter. A priest could not go near a dead body unless it was the body of a member of his immediate family. The high priest was not permitted to go near a corpse at all, even that of a parent.

The ritual defilement resulting from contact with the dead was not equivalent to a lack of virtue or physical cleanliness, but rather an undesirable religious state. Even so, special rules for being "clean" in a ritual sense did not appeal to Jesus, who disagreed with the Pharisees' insistence on ritual purity as a prerequisite to worship: "Evil thoughts, murder, adultery, fornica- MT. 15:19 tion, theft, false witness, slander," Jesus said. "These are what defile a man." (That is, only moral evil made a person impure.)

Which prophet was summoned back from the dead?

The only person in the Bible who though dead spoke with the living was Samuel. He spoke with King Saul when the king consulted a medium reputed to be able to call up the dead. The incident, related in the First Book of Samuel, shows the depths of despair and futility to which the once-powerful Saul had sunk as a result of disobeying God.

It was a desperate King Saul who went in disguise and under cover of darkness to the town of Endor, about 12 miles southwest of Lake Galilee. He was up against a huge Philistine army encamped at nearby Jezreel, and he was certain that his throne would soon be lost. He had already asked, to no avail, for the support and counsel of God. Ironically, in going to Endor, Saul was seeking the help of the very witchcraft that he had earlier banished from Israel after the death of Samuel. His last hope, he felt, was to try to summon Samuel, and he ordered the medium of Endor to raise the prophet from the dead. Immediately Samuel appeared like "a god coming 1 SAM: 28:13 up out of the earth."

As a final blow to the now pitiable king, an angry Samuel told Saul that the Philistines would win the forthcoming battle, Saul and his sons would die during the conflict, and the ambitious young rival, David, would be Israel's new king.

years was the average life expectancy for women, a statistic that has led one observer to comment sadly: "Women in antiquity were a class of humanity in short supply."

In part, Israel's position as a trade and cultural crossroads was to blame for the frequent outbreaks of fearsome plagues, like those described 2 SAM. 24:15 in the Bible as "a pestilence upon Israel" or NUM. 25:4 "the fierce anger of the Lord." Israel was a land bridge for much of the Near East, used by invading armies and by commercial caravans traveling through the region. With the strangers came deadly diseases, including—many scholars believe—the terrifying bubonic plague, which could run rampant in the absence of effective medical and public health practices.

What does the Bible say was wrong with touching a dead body?

The Hebrews believed that touching a corpse made a person unclean for seven days, during which time any contact with sacred objects was forbidden. To remove the taint of defilement, a NUM. 19:9 mixture called "the water for impurity" was prepared under a priest's direction. It consisted of the ashes of a ceremonially slaughtered red heifer mixed with the waters from a clean stream. On the third and seventh days after contact, the mixture was to be thrown on anyone who had ✳

BURIAL CUSTOMS

Among the ancient Hebrews, a proper burial was an important way to show respect for the dead. To wish an enemy to die unburied and unmourned was a heinous curse. For King Jehoiakim's crimes against God, the prophet Jeremiah condemned him to "the burial of an ass . . . dragged and cast forth beyond the gates of Jerusalem [Jer. 22:19]." When Saul's sons were hanged by the Gibeonites and their bodies exposed to scavengers, their mother Rizpah kept vigil by their corpses, fighting off birds and beasts for months until King David intervened and buried their remains.

The more fortunate families owned a burial cave or sepulcher cut out of soft rock. This tomb was usually on the outskirts of their home city. Clothed and wrapped in a shroud, the dead would be carried on a bier to the sepulcher and laid on a stone ledge inside. No coffin was used. A few personal belongings might be placed with the body. On other ledges in the tomb were the remains of ancestors; thus the dead person "slept with his fathers [1 Kg. 11:21]." When only a skeleton remained, the bones were often moved to a receptacle elsewhere in the tomb. This made room for newly deceased family members. The family sepulcher became a symbol of the continuity of a clan. Nehemiah, languishing in exile in Persia, begged to be permitted to return "to Judah, to the city of my fathers' sepulchers [Neh. 2:5]."

Families that could not afford a

The wealthy were buried in underground tombs, such as this one cut into a hillside north of Jerusalem. The entrance was sealed with a circular stone.

Jesus being anointed with oil in a manuscript illumination.

sepulcher dug graves for their dead or simply covered the body with stones and earth. For those too poor to have their own burial site, there were places set aside for the interment of numerous bodies together.

The Israelites normally made no attempt to preserve a corpse, although it was washed and wrapped and sometimes anointed or sprinkled with aromatic herbs, spices, or perfumes. Burial almost always took place within a day of death. Because of the warm climate, decomposition began quickly and, as in the case of the body of Jesus' friend Lazarus, was far advanced within a few days. Although tombs were sealed, Jerusalem allowed none to the west of the city, the direction from which the prevailing winds blew. Cremation, condemned as idolatry in rabbinic literature, was not practiced except in exceptional circumstances.

As the body of a loved one was borne to its burial place, a funeral procession of relatives, friends, and servants followed along, giving vent to cries of anguish and lament. Well-to-do families hired "mourning women" who knew how to "raise a wailing [Jer. 9:18]" and were skilled at singing lamentations. Josephus, the first-century A.D. Jewish historian, observed the custom that "all who pass by when a corpse is buried must accompany the funeral and join in the lamentation."

Marriage

Why did Sarah offer Abraham her slave to bear him a child?

Some 10 years after God promised Abraham progeny who would carry on the line of the covenant people, his wife Sarah had not conceived, and she gave her husband her Egyptian slave Hagar to serve as a surrogate mother. According to the custom of the time, the child (Ishmael) legally belonged to Sarah and Abraham. Hagar's status remained lower than Sarah's, and when Sarah bore her own son, Isaac, she prevailed upon Abraham to send away her surrogate son Ishmael and his mother.

Four of Israel's 12 tribes were descended from slave women given to Jacob by his wives Rachel and Leah, who could not conceive at the time.

How was a wife found for Isaac?

Isaac's father, Abraham, decided that his son should not marry a local Canaanite, but should choose a bride from the region of Haran, where members of Abraham's family had settled. It was the custom to marry fellow clansmen in order to strengthen and perpetuate the clan. To find a wife for Isaac, Abraham sent a trusted servant some 400 miles northward to the city of Nahor near Haran. Daunted by his assignment, the servant implored God for a sign to help him identify a suitable wife for his master's son. Before the servant finished speaking to God, the sign came: a cousin of Isaac's, Rebekah, arrived at the village well and offered the servant a drink.

The girl's father, Bethuel, and elder brother, Laban, agreed that Rebekah could marry Isaac if she wished. When she consented, her family bade her a prophetic farewell: "Be the mother of GEN. 24:60 thousands of ten thousands; and may your descendants possess the gate of those who hate them!" Years later, Rebekah sent her own son, Jacob, to Haran to find a wife.

How could Laban trick Jacob into marrying Leah instead of Rachel?

After working seven years for Laban in order to earn the hand of his daughter Rachel, Jacob was tricked into marrying her older sister, Leah. With Leah's collusion, Laban substituted her—Leah's face evidently obscured by veils—for Rachel in the darkened tent of Jacob, who may have been less than alert after a day of feasting and drinking.

To justify his deceit, Laban cited the custom that an elder daughter married first. Duped by Laban, Jacob fell victim to the same sort of ruse with which he had misled his father, years before, by masquerading as Esau. The Bible does not dwell on this irony, but as told in Jewish folklore, Jacob reproves Leah: "O thou deceiver, daughter of a deceiver, why did you answer me when I called Rachel's name?" Leah answers, "Is there a teacher without a pupil? I learned from your example. Did you not answer your father when he called Esau?"

Jacob soon married Ra-

For Jacob it was love at first sight for Rachel (left), who tends sheep with her sister Leah in this fresco in the Vatican by Raphael.

MARRIAGE CEREMONIES

An 18th-century English plate depicting a Jewish wedding.

A Hebrew wedding was a social occasion rather than a religious or legal one. The bridal couple was formally united at the betrothal when the marriage contract was sealed and the bridal price paid.

Before the festivities, both the bride and groom adorned themselves in their finest clothing and as many jewels as they owned or could borrow. Some of the bride's jewels were probably gifts from the groom or part of her dowry; if her family was wealthy, her dowry might also include a headband of coins. The groom also wore an ornamental headdress—a diadem—on his brow. Their attendants perfumed the couple with scented oils such as aloe, myrrh, and cassia.

Heavily veiled, the bride with her maids of honor left her father's house for the lively procession to the wedding feast at the groom's house. There the guests found a banquet as lavish as the family's finances permitted. Samson's wedding party lasted a week, and the marriage feast that Tobias's in-laws gave for him lasted twice as long.

During the feasting, the couple's parents and friends gave them their best wishes and blessings. Marriage poems, perhaps extolling the beauty of the bride and the happiness of married life, were recited; Psalm 45 and the Song of Solomon, written for royal marriages, appear to be two such poems.

chel as well. Polygamy was legal in ancient Israel, but generally only wealthy men could afford several wives—and they might also have many concubines. Solomon "had 700 wives, princesses, and 300 concubines"; and his son Rehoboam "took 18 wives and 60 concubines." David also had many wives and concubines.

1 KG. 11:3

2 CHR. 11:21

Why did Ruth "propose" to Boaz?

The Book of Ruth offers a fascinating glimpse into the marriage customs of the ancient Israelites. It tells the story of Ruth, a Moabite woman who married a Hebrew. After her husband died, Ruth chose to devote her life to her widowed mother-in-law, Naomi, rather than return to her family in Moab. Penniless, Ruth and Naomi trav-

eled to Bethlehem, where Ruth met Boaz, a prosperous farmer and a kinsman of her mother-in-law and late husband.

Moved by accounts of Ruth's devotion to Naomi, Boaz went out of his way to watch over the younger woman and make sure she got enough food. His fondness for Ruth, Naomi quickly realized, could mean happiness and security for all three of them. By Israelite custom, if a man died without a son to continue his name, the man's brother was expected to marry the widow. If the deceased had no brother, a close relative should assume the responsibility. In these "levirate" marriages (from the Latin word meaning husband's brother), the firstborn son would inherit the first husband's property, a very important consideration in a society that strongly resisted the loss of property to anyone outside the clan.

143

Boaz assures Ruth that he will ask a kinsman to give up claims on her; from a medieval illumination.

Thus Naomi advised Ruth to go to Boaz, and RU. 3:9 Ruth told him to "spread your skirt over your maidservant, for you are next of kin." It was, in effect, a marriage proposal based on the levirate custom; and when Boaz accepted, he explained that marrying Ruth would honor his dead kinsmen (Ruth's husband, Mahlon, and father-in-RU. 4:10 law, Elimelech) and "perpetuate the name of the dead in his inheritance, that the name of the dead may not be cut off from among his brethren and from the gate of his native place." Ruth and Boaz became the parents of a son, Obed, who was the grandfather of David, the celebrated hero-king of Israel. Many generations later, the same line would produce Jesus.

Why did Ezra condemn Jews for marrying non-Jews?

The leader of a group of Jews returning to Jerusalem from exile in Babylonia, Ezra was outraged to find a town filled EZRA 9:2 with "faithlessness," its Jews grown lax regarding their religious obligations. A scribe

Removing a leather shoe symbolized a man's release from a levirate marriage to his kinsman's widow.

well versed in the Torah, Ezra was determined to restore adherence to the law—the discipline that had given his group unity and purpose during the hard years in Babylonia. He insisted that Jerusalem's Jews adopt stringent reforms. The target of the first reform was intermarriage.

Following the destruction of the temple in 587 B.C., many Jews, including priests, had violated the law by marrying non-Jewish women, continuing a practice that had become widespread even before the exile. On his return Ezra assembled all the men of Judah and told them, "You EZRA 10:10 have trespassed and married foreign women, and so increased the guilt of Israel; . . . separate yourselves from . . . the foreign wives." Fearing God's wrath, most of the men divorced their foreign wives. Ezra saw intermarriage as both a sin and a threat. "You shall not make marriages DT. 7:3 with [foreigners]," God told Moses, "for they would turn away your sons from following me." By forbidding intermarriage, Ezra sought to preserve both the ethnic and religious identity of the Jews.

Yemenite and Hasidic brides (left and above respectively) cover their faces, as did the Bible's veiled brides.

What did it mean to be betrothed?

Although the word *betrothal* is often used today to mean engagement, in biblical times it represented an agreement that had more legal weight than a wedding. Marriages were normally arranged by parents. It was the duty of the fathers to arrange the best possible marriage for their children. This involved choosing a bride—often when she was 12 years old—from the groom's own clan. Love was not a basis for matrimony; marriage was a covenant between heads of families.

After a father had chosen a wife for his son, he negotiated the amount of the *mohar*, or bride-price, a sum to be paid to the father of the bride. Fifty shekels of silver was a common offering.

The marriage agreement completed, the couple were betrothed. During the formal betrothal ceremony in front of witnesses, the father and the groom paid the *mohar* and the bride's father gave his assent, saying, as Saul told David, "You shall now be my son-in-law." This private ritual usually preceded the wedding by 12 months.

The betrothed couple were considered husband and wife and were expected to be faithful to each other. The betrothal could be broken only by a formal divorce. Mary and Joseph were betrothed at the time of Jesus' birth, and Matthew calls them husband and wife.

Israel's laws dealt harshly with anyone who ✳

1 SAM. 18:21

LOVE. *Whether referring to God's feeling for his people or to the bonds that tie people to one another,* love *is a powerful word in the Bible.*

In the Old Testament, the Hebrew word ahab *is used to describe many forms of human love: between husband and wife, child and parent, other family members, friends, and neighbors. It encompasses, for example, the lifelong romance of Jacob and Rachel, the loyal friendship of Jonathan and David, Ruth's unbreakable devotion to her mother-in-law, Naomi, and Abraham's feelings for his son Isaac.*

Divine love was the force with which God bound and supported the Israelites. Their destiny and the very essence of their religion and society depended on hesed, *the Hebrew word for the "steadfast love [Ex. 20:6]" of God.*

The New Testament emphasizes God's love for all people, Jews and non-Jews. Paul wrote to the church at Corinth that God's love was the greatest of his gifts; without love, faith and good deeds were meaningless. The Gospel of John points to the coming of Jesus as the most powerful example of God's love: "For God so loved the world that he gave his only Son, that whoever believes in him should not perish but have eternal life [Jn. 3:16]."

145

raped a betrothed woman because it was adultery, for which the penalty was death.

Could a woman initiate a divorce?

DT. 24:1 The law of Moses permitted an Israelite man to divorce his wife if "she finds no favor in his eyes because he has found some indecency in her."

This gave only slightly less latitude to men in ending a marriage than the collection of Babylonian laws called the Code of Hammurabi, which allowed a husband to divorce his wife simply by telling her, "Thou art not my wife." Those words by the husband amounted to a legal divorce decree. Although a woman's adultery or childlessness was a sufficient reason for her husband to divorce her, Jewish women, like Babylonian

PROSTITUTES AND CONCUBINES

Urging marital fidelity, the Proverbs warn men against "the loose woman [Pr. 5:3]" and "the adventuress with her smooth words [Pr. 2:16]." Israelite laws called for severely punishing harlots, but such statutes seem not always to have been strictly enforced.

Although the Bible does not condone prostitution, there are stories of individual prostitutes who were rewarded for behaving more virtuously than people who seemed, on the surface, to be morally superior. For example, the harlot Rahab and her family were spared in the destruction of Jericho because she concealed Joshua's spies. And Jesus, speaking to the priests and elders who questioned his authority, said that "tax collectors and harlots go into the kingdom of God before you [Mt. 21:31]," making the point that the tax officials and prostitutes had repented and accepted his divine authority, while the priests and elders had not.

The Bible reserves its greatest scorn for ritual, or cultic, prostitution, which involved both male and female prostitutes and was supposed to elicit the blessings of fertility from pagan gods. Although Judaism strictly forbade ritual prostitution and fertility cults, the people often could not resist the lure of cultic worship, such as that practiced by the Canaanites and Babylonians. These lapses were condemned in the Old Testament as spiritual harlotry.

Prophets such as Ezekiel and Hosea bitterly compared Israel's infidelity to God with the whorish behavior of the cult prostitutes. Referring to Israel, Ezekiel cried, "She defiled herself with all the idols. . . . She did not give up her harlotry which she had practiced since her days in Egypt [Ezek. 23:7]." To the prophet Hosea, the Lord said, "Go, take to yourself a wife of harlotry and have children of harlotry, for the land commits great harlotry by forsaking the Lord [Hos. 1:2]." Obediently, Hosea wed the prostitute Gomer, who soon deserted him. But when the Lord forgave a repentant Israel, Hosea took back his wife.

The Great Harlot astride the beast, an image in Revelation 17, represented evil forces; from a 13th-century illumination.

*Honoring the marriage of Mary and Joseph, the Italian artist Giotto showed
Joseph with a blossoming rod on which a dove from God had alighted.*

wives, had no right of divorce, and the law placed no clear limits on what was acceptable behavior by a husband. An aggrieved wife's only recourse was to abandon her husband.

However, Mosaic law required Jewish husbands who wished to end their marriages to DT. 24:1 draw up a "bill of divorce"—a public document that allowed the wife to marry any other man except a priest. Although the Old Testament laws permitted divorce, God was seen as frowning on MAL. 2:16 it: "For I hate divorce, says the Lord. . . . So take heed to yourselves and do not be faithless."

In New Testament times, some rabbis taught that only adultery justified divorce, while others allowed reasons as minor as poor cooking. Although Jesus evidently accepted adultery as grounds for divorce, when the Pharisees asked him if it was lawful to divorce one's wife for any MT. 19:6 cause, he answered, "What therefore God has joined together, let not man put asunder."

What was Paul's attitude toward marriage?

Paul considered both married life and single life to be blessed by God. Each person must live in accord with his own special gift from God. ✳

Marriage was to be a relationship of love and mutuality, he wrote in his First Letter to the Corinthians: "The husband should give to his wife 1 COR. 7:3 her conjugal rights, and likewise the wife to her husband. For the wife does not rule over her own body, but the husband does; likewise the husband does not rule over his own body but the wife does."

Great stress came into many marriages when one partner became a Christian while the other remained pagan. Even in such circumstances, Paul urged that a marriage be maintained so long as the pagan partner would agree to it.

Though Paul's praise of the single life that he himself lived has been thought to favor celibacy over marriage, his words were not a universal judgment that an ascetic life of celibacy was better. He emphasized that he was advising the Corinthians for "the present distress" (meaning the 1 COR. 7:26 world's end was thought to be imminent), and it seemed best "for a person to remain as he is" 1 COR. 7:26 and avoid the anxiety of a major life change. "Are 1 COR. 7:27 you bound to a wife?" he asked. "Do not seek to be free. Are you free from a wife? Do not seek marriage." Paul insisted that his views should be taken as advice, not dogma: "I say this for your 1 COR. 7:35 own benefit, not to lay any restraint upon you."

Education

Just as Jewish scholars studied the law in Jesus' time, rabbis ponder the subtleties of the sacred Scriptures in this 19th-century painting by J.A. Lecomte de Nouy.

Did children receive formal schooling?

In Jewish law and tradition, parents had a sacred obligation to educate their children. In earliest times children were taught at home by their parents. During the first century B.C., however, the Jews began to establish schools at synagogues. Only boys (usually aged 6 to 10) were enrolled in these schools; girls remained at home, to be taught by their mothers.

Classes were held in the synagogue, in a room attached to it, or sometimes in the open air. There were no desks or chairs; the pupils simply stood or sat around the teacher. The children learned to read and write, and they studied Scripture, repeating verses over and over. (*Repeat* came to mean teach or learn.)

Religious instruction in the home supplemented school lessons. At home children were taught the meaning of the Sabbath rituals; the significance of the Jewish festivals; and the prayers and practices that were part of the devout Jewish family's daily life.

Parents were also required to pass on the ✳

skills their children would need in life. Girls were trained to run a household; boys learned a trade or occupation. One Jewish sage wrote, "He who does not teach his son a useful trade is bringing him up to be a thief."

How was Jesus educated?

Like all Jewish children, Jesus would have learned much from his parents. Sometime after the age of six he may have gone to a synagogue school, and by the age of 12 showed a precocious knowledge of Scripture when he talked with the teachers in the temple.

Jesus' teachings reveal that he knew the Bible well and could quote from it freely. When he says, "Blessed are the meek, for they shall inherit the earth," for example, he is referring to Psalm 37: "The meek shall possess the land." MT. 5:5

PS. 37:11

Who taught in the schools?

The synagogue school was conducted by the *hazzan* (keeper of the scrolls). As an assistant to the head of the synagogue, he per-

RABBI. *Derived from the Hebrew word rab, meaning great, rabbi is literally translated my master. The word does not appear in the Old Testament; in the New Testament, however, it occurs frequently.*

In Jesus' time, rabbi was a term of respectful address that the people frequently used when they spoke to their religious leaders. In the Gospels of Matthew, Mark, and John, Jesus is addressed as rabbi by his disciples and other people. Jesus harshly criticized those who took pride in being called rabbi in public; he warned his disciples, "You are not to be called rabbi, for you have one teacher, and you are all brethren [Mt. 23:8]."

Eventually, the word's meaning changed; today, the title rabbi designates a person who is ordained to interpret and to pass on the teachings of the Torah and the Talmud and to be the spiritual leader of a Jewish community of worship.

training and specialized knowledge, they were an elite group—a kind of intellectual aristocracy—and they wielded considerable authority. Scribes made up a large segment of the Sanhedrin, Judaism's highest court, and many held office in synagogues and local judicial bodies.

The scribes had three main responsibilities. They preserved and interpreted the law, applying it to daily life; they helped judge cases in the courts; and they taught the Torah and the oral law to students. Since the scribes were not paid for their work in the Sanhedrin, and were not supposed to accept money for teaching, many were merchants, craftsmen, or even laborers.

Scribes were scholars who might also be priests or might belong to one of the two influential religious groups, the Sadducees and the Pharisees. As a mark of their status, the scribes dressed like the nobility in flowing robes with long, fringed tassels. Ordinary people revered them, addressed them as "Rabbi," and stood up when they passed.

formed various tasks during public worship, such as handing the Torah and other scrolls to the reader. He probably recited prayers and blessings on certain occasions, such as funeral ceremonies. He also announced the start of the Sabbath and the festivals by blowing a shofar three times from the roof of the synagogue.

LK. 4:20   The Gospel of Luke tells of the time Jesus read the Sabbath lesson from Isaiah and then "closed the book, and gave it back to the attendant." This attendant was the *hazzan*.

Who were the scribes?

Before the Babylonian exile, scribes were government officials or others who held positions because of their ability to read and write. They performed such tasks as keeping records, writing letters, and copying documents. During the exile, priest-scholars such as Ezra studied and copied the Hebrew Scriptures, and the role of the scribe took on a specifically religious meaning. By the time of Jesus, the scribes were professional Torah scholars and interpreters of the law, both oral and written. Because of their intensive ✳

Among the Babylonian exiles, scribes like Ezra, pictured in a seventh-century miniature, kept the law from being forgotten.

War and the Military

Did the Israelites have a standing army?

Early in the period covered by the Old Testament, every man was a potential soldier. He changed from shepherd or farmer to warrior simply by picking up his weapon at the sound of the shofar wailing over the hills. Larger families were capable of fielding 50 armed men for defense and raids, while the tribes deployed battalion-sized units known as thousands. In wartime the tribes were led by charismatic chieftains believed to be chosen by God. Warfare was primitive, training was rudimentary, and tactics were simple.

This model of military organization, which might be described as a tribal militia, suited the needs of a wandering people. Tribal leaders called the army into being when the need arose and disbanded it when danger was past.

With this foot-soldier militia, carrying swords, spears, bows, and slings, the Hebrew nation crossed the desert and occupied Canaan. For about two centuries, down to the time of King Saul, such an army fought nearly constant bloody wars with its enemies. But Saul saw the need for change.

Saul recruited a standing army and began to build a corps of professional soldiers. His successor, David, used mercenaries and probably introduced the chariot, which the Philistines already used with great effectiveness. Solomon completed the shaping of a professional army and, by mounting archers and spearmen on chariots, established a swift and maneuverable fighting force.

With the change to mobile warfare came Solomon's commitment to a large support system: full-time horse trainers, foragers, stable hands, and garrison troops; barracks and stables; maintaining trade routes to bring fine horses south from what is now Turkey; and manufacturing and repairing chariots and other weapons.

Did "holy war" originate in the Bible?

To the Israelites who saw themselves as God's chosen people, war was holy because God had declared that their enemies were his enemies. He was their leader in battle. They carried the ark of the covenant as a symbol of the presence of God. They spoke of him as "a man of war" and "the Lord of hosts [armies]." EX. 15:3 / 1 SAM. 15:2

When the Hebrews mobilized for war, they consulted oracles and prophets to be sure that God approved of their aims. When they conquered, they sometimes "devoted" the spoils of victory—that is, sacrificed them to God. This might mean the execution of every man, woman, and child of the enemy or the slaughter of the male captives and enslavement of the children and females and the burning or destruction of houses and livestock.

The Book of Joshua portrays Israel's conquest of Canaan as a holy war. At Jericho, Joshua ordered the entire city and its inhabitants to be "devoted to the Lord for destruction; only Rahab the harlot and all who are with her in her house shall live, because she hid the messengers [spies] that we sent." JOS. 6:17

How were espionage and psychological warfare used in wartime?

With enemies or potential enemies at all points of the compass, the Israelites had a pressing need for accurate

Fired by Gideon's words, the Israelites charge the Midianite forces in this scene from a series of 20th-century German postcards.

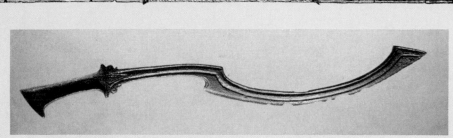

Discovered at Shechem, this sword dating from 2000 to 1500 B.C. might have been used by a Canaanite warrior against the Israelites.

ISRAEL'S NEIGHBORS

The Israelites left Egypt for "a good and broad land, a land flowing with milk and honey, to the place of the Canaanites, the Hittites, the Amorites, the Perizzites, the Hivites, and the Jebusites [Ex. 3:8]."

When the Israelites arrived, Canaan was made up of a loose confederation of tribes and city states. In spite of Joshua's conquest of their territory, these peoples had not been subjugated and remained a constant threat to the Israelites for centuries to come. (The name *Canaanite* can refer either to one specific tribe or to all the diverse groups that lived in the land of Canaan.)

Most of these small tribal groups occupied particular regions. For example, the Hittites lived around Hebron and Beersheba; the Perizzites in the forested hill country of Ephraim; the Hivites in the town of Gibeon and a few other areas; and the Jebusites, in Jerusalem.

Meanwhile, other nations surrounded Israel and often threatened it from the outside. In the Sinai Desert were the Amalekites and Midianites, nomadic peoples who had fought the Hebrews as they crossed the wilderness and who continued to raid Israelite settlements well into the period of the kings.

East of the Jordan River and the Dead Sea were the Edomites, Moabites, and Ammonites. Though the Edomites were descendants of Esau, they were Israel's bitter enemies. Israel disdained the Moabites and the Ammonites as descendants of Lot's daughters by incest with their father. These two nations had joined forces to subdue Israel during the period of the judges, but Moab, Ammon, and Edom were all reduced to vassal status within David's empire.

To the west were the Philistines, who had invaded Canaan about the same time as the Hebrews. They were concentrated in a league of five cities on the southern coast of Canaan and eventually gave their name to the whole land: Palestine.

Challenged by the Israelites and the Philistines, the power of the Canaanites declined until, by the 12th century B.C., they retained firm control of only the maritime kingdom of Phoenicia, whose main cities were Tyre and Sidon.

A grisly tally. To keep track of the number of enemy dead, Egyptian scribes in this relief count a mound of severed hands.

intelligence. They used spies to reveal enemy positions and recruited collaborators who could open the enemy's gates or disclose its intentions.

JG. 7:15 When outnumbered, the Israelites often chose to avoid risking more men than necessary. Like Gideon routing "the host of Midian" with 300 men, they made a weapon of surprise and terror, rushing an enemy camp at night with war cries and trumpet blasts and torching the tents. They intimidated enemies with fearless acts of heroism, as when a daring two-man assault by Jonathan and his armor-bearer on a Philistine post at
1 SAM. 14:15 a rocky pass caused "panic in the camp, in the field, and among all the people."

Nor was psychological warfare unknown to Israel's enemies. The Assyrians propagandized the Hebrews in their own language and used such terror tactics as displaying prisoners who had been tortured and impaled.

What was a chariot city?

To consolidate his power and ensure a peaceful commerce, Solomon set up a chain of fortified bases for his chariot army. These were the famed "chariot cities" of the Old Testament. They were 1 KG. 10:26 six in number: Hazor, Megiddo, Gezer, Lower Beth-horon, Baalath, and Tamar. Solomon also quartered a chariot force in Jerusalem.

At Megiddo archeologists have found a complex of rooms and courtyards that could have been facilities for about 450 horses. The stables,

---

DAVID AND GOLIATH

Jesse of Bethlehem sent his youngest son, David, with food to his older brothers, who were fighting with King Saul against the Philistines in the valley of Elah, some 15 miles away. David reached the Israelite encampment just as the two armies were preparing for battle. Dropping his supplies, he ran into the ranks to greet his brothers.

While they were talking, the Philistine champion Goliath, the giant of Gath—standing nearly 10 feet tall and wearing a bronze coat of mail that weighed about 150 pounds—came forward and shouted a challenge to the Israelites. He dared them to send a champion to oppose him in single combat. "If he is able to fight with me and kill me, then we will be your servants," he said, "but if I prevail against him and kill him, then you shall be our servants and serve us [1

Sam. 17:9]." Hearing this, the Israelites fled. All, that is, except David. Moved by the spirit of God, he asked boldly, "Who is this uncircumcised Philistine, that he should defy the armies of the living God [1 Sam. 17:26]?"

Upon hearing David's words repeated in the camp, King Saul sent for him. Confidently, David volunteered to meet Goliath in hand-to-hand combat. To prove that his offer was serious, David told Saul how with his bare hands he killed the lions and bears that attacked his flock. "The Lord who delivered me from the paw of the lion . . . will deliver me from the hand of this Philistine [1 Sam. 17:37]."

Armed only with a sling and five smooth stones in a pouch, David set out to meet Goliath. Watching him approach, the Philistine taunted David. "Come to me,"

Goliath sneered, "and I will give your flesh to the birds of the air and to the beasts of the field [1 Sam. 17:44]."

Unshaken by the giant's threats, David replied, "This day the Lord will deliver you into my hand [1 Sam. 17:46]." With his sling he hurled a stone at the forehead of the giant. Goliath fell facedown on the ground. David ran up to the body, pulled out the giant's sword, and beheaded him. When they saw that David had slain their champion, the Philistines scattered, pursued by the Israelites.

Throughout Israel people sang about the tens of thousands slain by David. And indeed the death of Goliath was only a suggestion of the many victories David would earn on the field of battle, which would eventually lead to his succeeding Saul on the throne of Israel.

Throwing off his cumbersome armor, David races forward to do battle with Goliath;
in the background, the Philistines and the Israelites urge on their champions.

if that is what they really were, date from the reign of Ahab, who may have rebuilt Solomon's structures, just as elsewhere Solomon rebuilt stables that had existed before his reign.

Biblical and archeological evidence indicates that Solomon had some 1,400 chariots, each drawn by two horses with a third in reserve, and 12,000 charioteers and support troops. Although they never fought a major battle, this chariot force must have been a formidable deterrent to enemies contemplating a challenge to Israel's control of the lucrative trade routes from Persia and the East to the Mediterranean.

Why did Herod the Great need a fortress network?

The future Herod the Great was an official under the Hasmonean ruler Hyrcanus II, a client king of Judea, controlled by Rome, but in 40 B.C. Herod was forced to flee Jerusalem when an invading Parthian army overthrew Hyrcanus and put his nephew Antigonus on the Judean throne. Backed by Rome, Herod returned, defeated Antigonus in 37 B.C.—and proceeded to construct forts and refortify old sites, like the bastion of Masada, in a massive program of national security. The forts served, too, as prisons for Herod's enemies.

In Jerusalem, Herod rebuilt the temple citadel and renamed it Antonia after his benefactor in ✳

Rome, Mark Antony. From Mount Carmel in the north to the Nabatean border on the south, he maintained more than half a dozen major strongholds. His master creation was Herodium, rising from a man-made hilltop about five miles southeast of Bethlehem. There, in 4 B.C., with great military pomp, Herod was carried up 200 marble steps on a solid gold bier to his tomb.

SHIBBOLETH. *The modern meaning of* shibboleth *comes from the clever stratagem devised by the Gileadite leader Jephthah after defeating the Ephraimites. During battle the Gileadites had taken control of the crossings on the Jordan River. When the retreating Ephraimites attempted to disguise their identity and sneak back into their own country, they were halted by Jephthah's sentries, who asked them to say the password:* shibboleth.

The Ephraimites spoke a different dialect of Hebrew from the Gileadites and pronounced the sh *sound in* shibboleth *as* s. *When the Ephraimites mispronounced the password, responding with "sibboleth," they revealed their identity and were slain by the Gileadites.*

Living by the Law

Unaware of their divinity, Abraham lavishes hospitality on God's angels; a 15th-century icon.

What does "the law of Moses" mean?

LK. 10:25 When a man asked Jesus, "What shall I do to
LK. 10:26 inherit eternal life?" Jesus replied: "What is written in the law? How do you read?" The man quoted from Deuteronomy and Leviticus the commands to love God and love one's neighbor,
LK. 10:28 and Jesus concurred: "You have answered right; do this and you will live."

In addition to its moral message, the exchange illustrates how intimately many Jews knew "the law," the term used for the most authoritative part of their Scriptures—Genesis, Exodus, Leviticus, Numbers, and Deuteronomy. These books are also known by other names, such as the Books of Moses, the Torah, and the Pentateuch (meaning five scrolls).

The law appears in several overlapping codes woven into the history of Israel. The biblical core laws, the Ten Commandments, are given twice, once in Exodus and again in Deuteronomy. ✳

Alongside the Ten Commandments stands "the EX. 24:7 book of the covenant" in Exodus 21–23, which includes a wide variety of particular laws.

The Book of Leviticus centers around a distinctive body of laws sometimes called the Holiness Code (Chapters 17–26) because it is dominated by God's command, "You shall be holy; for LEV. 19:2 I the Lord your God am holy." The holiness laws are surrounded by smaller collections of regulations concerning sacrifices, feasts, priests, and purity that make up the Priestly Code.

The longest single code is the summation in Deuteronomy 12–26. This may have been "the 2 KG. 22:8 book of the law" found in about 620 B.C. during Josiah's repairs of the temple. Although it and all of the codes included ancient traditions, they were probably assembled into their five-book form during the time of the Babylonian exile.

Why did hospitality carry the force of law?

Throughout the ancient Mediterranean world, travelers separated from their families faced the risk of mistreatment. Because of such anxiety—

TORAH. *Although traditionally the word* torah *has been translated into English as law, it more accurately describes a body of religious instruction than a codified system of law.*

Because most of the religious instruction for Israel is embodied in the first five books of the Bible, these came to be called the Torah (or the law). In Judaism this written Torah was supplemented by a growing body of oral tradition, which guided the interpretation of the written Torah. Eventually, even the "oral Torah" was put into writing and is embodied in the Mishnah, the Talmud, and other works of rabbinic literature.

In early Christianity a controversy arose over whether the followers of the new faith should accept the Torah as binding law. While many Jews who became Christians continued to follow the Torah, others, notably Paul, argued that the Torah's instructions must not be imposed as law on Gentiles who became Christians.

EVERYDAY LIFE

JOSIAH, LEGAL REFORMER

Crowned king of Judah at the age of eight, Josiah inherited a kingdom corrupted by foreign influences. Idolatry had replaced the law of Moses, and religious and moral life had crumbled.

The child king matured into a leader who "did what was right in the eyes of the Lord [2 Chr. 34:2]." When he was 20, Josiah initiated a vigorous campaign to purge idolatry from Judah and to restore the temple in Jerusalem. In the midst of the

temple's renovations, a "book of the law [2 Chr. 34:14]" was discovered. When it was read to Josiah, he grieved that the people had strayed so far from Yahweh's laws. He sought advice from the prophet Huldah on how to avert God's wrath; the only consolation she offered was that Judah's destruction would not come in Josiah's lifetime.

Gathering all of Jerusalem's inhabitants, Josiah pledged to reinstate

God's laws and to fight the corruption that had crept in under his predecessors. Josiah's reforms restored the code of laws that had governed the Israelites since the Exodus and made Jerusalem the center of worship again. "Before him there was no king like him, who turned to the Lord with all his heart and with all his soul and with all his might, according to all the law of Moses; nor did any like him arise after him [2 Kg. 23:25]."

shared by all who had to travel—customs of hospitality came to have almost the force of law.

Genesis clearly approves of the hospitality of Abraham and Lot when strangers (who turned out to be angels) came, as Lot said, "under the shelter of my roof." By contrast, the people of Sodom showed their depravity by trying to attack and rape the strangers. Rather than violate the code of hospitality by letting the mob have the strangers, Lot offered his daughters instead.

GEN. 19:8

Jesus' disciples often traveled without money or food or extra clothes, counting on the hospitality of the people to support them. "Do not neglect to show hospitality to strangers," counsels the Letter to the Hebrews, "for thereby some have entertained angels unawares."

HEB. 13:2

What taxes did the Israelites pay?

In the early stages of Israel's history there were evidently no civil taxes. Religious offerings financed the expenses of maintaining the sanctuary and priesthood. With the rise of a monarchy in the 10th century B.C. came the first substantial taxes. These were paid with crops, animals, and conscripted labor. Under King David, Israel became strong enough to exact tribute from sur-

rounding peoples. For a while this helped to limit the taxes paid by the Israelites, but King Solomon's ambitious programs increased the tax burden. With the decline and division of the monarchy and the ensuing centuries of domination by foreign powers, the Israelites endured a variety of taxation systems, many of them oppressive.

When the Romans took over direct rule of a region (as opposed to working through a client king like Herod the Great), they regularly conducted a census, or enrollment of households and estates. Two kinds of taxes were then imposed: a tax on agricultural produce, *tributum soli* (land tribute), and a *tributum capitis* (head tax), which included both a poll tax on every person and a property tax. Excise taxes were also imposed on imported and exported goods.

The Gospel of Luke recounts that at the time of Jesus' birth, Joseph and Mary went to Bethlehem to "be enrolled" for taxation. A relatively poor carpenter like Joseph probably owned no land that yielded produce and thus would have had to pay only the *tributum capitis*, which included a property tax of perhaps 1 percent on belongings that he and Mary had accumulated.

LK. 2:1

In A.D. 6, when Herod the Great's son, Archelaus, was deposed for misrule, Roman governors took over direct control of Judea and Samaria.

155

The first such governor, Quirinius, ordered a tax enrollment in the region, and the taxes began to be paid directly to Rome. This sparked a short-lived rebellion against paying taxes directly to pagan rulers. In the Book of Acts, Luke mentions ACTS 5:37 "the census" and the uprising it caused.

What advantages did Roman citizenship have?

In the regions conquered by Roman armies, Roman citizenship provided a measure of security and was much sought after. A tribune ACTS 22:28 who arrested Paul in Jerusalem told him: "I bought [my] citizenship for a large sum," at ACTS 22:28 which point Paul informed the tribune, "I was born a citizen."

Though Paul in his letters never mentions being a Roman citizen, the Book of Acts tells how citizenship gave him legal leverage in dangerous situations. For instance, when the tribune in Jerusalem was about to interrogate Paul while brutally scourging him—calculated to beat some sort of confession out of him—Paul stopped the soldiers in their tracks by asking a centurion, ACTS 22:25 "Is it lawful for you to scourge a man who is a Roman citizen, and uncondemned?"

Several years earlier in Philippi in Macedonia, city magistrates had hastily ordered Paul and his compatriot Silas beaten with rods and thrown into prison. When the officials sent word the next day to release them, Paul refused to leave until he received a public apology because, he said, "They have beaten us publicly, uncon- ACTS 16:37 demned, men who are Roman citizens."

After his arrest in Jerusalem and transfer to Caesarea, Paul, by using his right as a Roman citizen to "appeal to Caesar," avoided being sent ACTS 25:11 back for trial in Jerusalem, where he feared he would be assassinated. Unfortunately, Paul's eventual trial before Caesar evidently led to his execution. But even in his final moments, Roman citizenship spared him the horror of execution by crucifixion, according to tradition a fate suffered by Peter. It is more likely that Paul was beheaded, as the law stipulated for executing a citizen.

What did Jesus teach about the law?

Jesus' teaching about the law appeared to have two distinct sides. On the one hand, he showed himself obedient to the law and instructed people on how to practice their prayers, fasting, and almsgiving. Moreover, he staunchly avowed that the law's commandments should be obeyed: "Whoever then relaxes one of the least of these MT. 5:19 commandments . . . shall be called least in the kingdom of heaven."

On the other hand, Jesus taught a kind of obedience that aroused the opposition of many who considered themselves devoted to the law. He centered all obedience to God and God's law on two commands of the Torah: love for God with

In this fourth-century relief, Jesus hands a scroll of law to Peter. Paul stands on the left.

A LAWYER'S QUESTION

Speaking to a crowd, Jesus said that to obtain eternal life you must love "your neighbor as yourself [Lk. 10:27]." A lawyer, seeking to justify himself as a candidate for eternal life, stood up and asked, "And who is my neighbor [Lk. 10:29]?" In answer, Jesus related the parable of the Good Samaritan.

On the road from Jerusalem to Jericho, a band of robbers waited to ambush an unsuspecting traveler. The bandits leaped on him, stripped him, and left him for dead.

Soon after the incident, a priest came down the same road and saw the wounded man lying in the ditch. Under Jewish law, if the man was already dead and the priest touched the corpse, the priest would be defiled; he would have to undergo seven days of ritual cleansing, which would interfere with his temple duties. To avoid the problem, the priest crossed to the other side of the road and continued on his way.

A short while later, a Levite who served in the temple came along and saw the injured man. He too crossed to the other side

Only the Good Samaritan grasped the true meaning of God's law; a painting by van Gogh.

of the road to avoid contact.

Later in the day, a Samaritan was journeying along the road. When he saw the wounded man, he stopped and bandaged his wounds. The Samaritan then took the man to an inn where he could care for him. Before he left the next day, he gave the innkeeper some money and said, "Take care of him; and whatever more you spend, I will repay you when I come back [Lk. 10:35]."

When asked by Jesus, even the young lawyer had to admit that it was the Samaritan, a foreigner scorned by the Jews for unorthodox customs, who had kept the spirit of the law. The priest and the Levite had turned their backs on one of their own people because they were preoccupied with rules and rituals.

MT. 22:40
MK. 2:22
JN. 5:18

one's whole being and love for one's neighbor as oneself. "On these two commandments depend all the law and the prophets." He called his teaching a "new wine" that could not be put into "old wineskins." He "broke the sabbath" by putting human needs, such as the need for healing or even the desire to eat, above the hallowed ban on every form of work. He rejected many of the accepted views of ritual purity and impurity, going so far as to state—in apparent opposition to ✳ the dietary laws—that "whatever goes into a man from outside cannot defile him." MK. 7:18

Finally, his manner of teaching astonished many who heard him because it did not fit the conventions of religious instruction, "for he taught them as one who had authority, and not as their scribes." The scribes quoted the written law and the oral tradition. Jesus based the authority of his teaching upon his own word, not upon the sayings of those who had gone before. MT. 7:29

Crime and Punishment

Truth is Jesus' defense as the high priest Caiaphas interrogates him before the Sanhedrin—a dramatic scene from a 14th-century altarpiece in the Siena Cathedral.

Was it a crime to break one of the Ten Commandments?

The Ten Commandments set the basic standards of religious and moral conduct for every Israelite, but they did not constitute criminal law. They provided no specific penalties for their violation. In the sections of Exodus and Deuteronomy that give the commandments, God speaks of the blessings that obedience brings and of the guilt or possible divine punishment that results from disobedience, but the rewards and penalties are God's choice, not society's.

Other sections of the law, however, treat the acts prohibited by the Ten Commandments as punishable crimes. For example, the Bible mandates penalties for murder, theft, bearing false witness, and adultery.

EX. 20:8 Even the positive commands to "remember
EX. 20:12 the sabbath day" and "honor your father and your mother" became the basis for severe criminal penalties. Working on the Sabbath or striking or cursing one's parents could bring a death sentence. The religious duties with which the Ten Commandments begin were also the foundation ✳ for numerous laws that authorized death for worshiping other gods (or encouraging others to do so) and blaspheming the name of God.

When did innocents suffer for the crimes of the guilty?

In general, Israel's judicial procedures followed the principle of individual responsibility: "The fa- DT. 24:16 thers shall not be put to death for the children, nor shall the children be put to death for the fathers." But if the crime brought moral corruption on the entire nation, God might punish many people with a plague or a defeat in battle. Then, to turn the Lord "from his burning anger," the JOS. 7:26 community might execute everyone in the offender's family—as in the exemplary case of Achan, who stole some of the booty from Jericho that had been "devoted" (dedicated) to God.

How were criminals tried?

From ancient times the judicial system of Israel centered in the elders of the community, who sat in judgment at the city gate. These individuals

158

were heads of families and clans who dealt with all types of disputes, including criminal accusations. If the elders were upright and just, the system worked well, but the prophets often found AM. 5:12 reason to condemn those "who afflict the righteous, who take a bribe, and turn aside the needy in the gate."

The elders heard the arguments of both the accuser and the accused, each of whom could summon witnesses and present documents or other tangible evidence. Though the laws of the land contained no explicit presumption of innocence, legal traditions favored the accused. Most criminal trials required at least two witnesses for a conviction. If the convicted one was to be executed by stoning, the witnesses had to take responsibility for their testimony by casting the first stones. Witnesses who committed perjury suf-

THE CODE OF HAMMURABI

Sometime in the 18th century B.C., five centuries before Moses ascended Mount Sinai to receive the law, the Babylonian king Hammurabi climbed the steps of the temple of Esagila in Babylon to erect a black stone stela, nearly eight feet high, inscribed with his laws for the kingdom. A relief carved at the top of the stone showed Hammurabi standing before the god of justice to receive his scepter as king and lawgiver.

Hammurabi styled himself "the king of justice" who would "promote the welfare of the people" and "cause justice to prevail in the land" so that "the strong might not oppress the weak." His stela listed some 282 rulings on a wide range of criminal and civil issues. The list concluded with mighty curses on anyone who altered or rescinded his judgments. Hammurabi's stela stood in place for about 600 years before it was carted off to Susa by conquering armies.

Hammurabi's laws appear to be not so much a systematic and comprehensive code as a selection of the king's legal judgments. Numerous subjects such as homicide, arson, regulation of sales, and ordinary marriage procedures are hardly

Excavated in Iran by French archeologists in 1902, the pillar bearing Hammurabi's Code now stands in the Louvre.

touched. The code seemed to assume the existence of a vast body of unwritten common law that regulated everyday life. Though not so extensive or well-preserved, similar legal codes of nations around Babylonia have been discovered, dating from both before and after the reign of Hammurabi.

In style Hammurabi's laws were all casuistic law, describing what was to be done in particular cases—for example, "If a man accused another man and brought a charge of murder against him, but has not proved it, his accuser shall be put to death." Cases of personal injury were judged by the "eye for an eye" principle (*lex talionis*), except that distinctions in social class could modify the penalty. The code stated that "If a man of the upper class has knocked out a tooth of a man of his own rank, they shall knock out his tooth. If he has knocked out a commoner's tooth he shall pay one-third mina of silver."

Hammurabi's laws were quite different from the law of Moses, although both had roots in the broad common law of the ancient Middle East. Hammurabi's code was royal law and did not bear the dominant religious stamp of Israel's law or claim to be a revelation of divine law. It did not blend religious and ritual requirements together with civil and criminal law, nor did it see the law as part of a covenant between God and the people.

fered the punishment that would have been imposed on the accused.

The trial of Naboth in 1 Kings shows both how the system worked and how it could be corrupted. Naboth owned a vineyard that King Ahab and his queen, Jezebel, wanted. To "the elders and the nobles who dwelt with Naboth in his city," Jezebel sent a letter under the king's seal commanding them to obtain false testimony from two witnesses who would say that Naboth had cursed God and the king. Less concerned with justice than with pleasing their rulers, the elders complied and immediately carried out the punishment. Seizing Naboth, they "took him outside the city, and stoned him to death with stones."

1 KG. 21:8

1 KG. 21:13

How was the judicial system organized?

According to 2 Chronicles, in the ninth century B.C. King Jehoshaphat of Judah instituted a formal judicial system in major cities and appointed presiding judges. Jehoshaphat also set up an appeals court in Jerusalem that was composed of religious and secular leaders: "Levites and priests and heads of families of Israel." When this court tried religious matters, the chief priest presided; when it heard "the king's matters," a judge was "the governor of the house of Judah."

2 CHR. 19:8

2 CHR. 19:11

2 CHR. 19:11

At times, in the manner of Solomon, the kings made themselves the court of last resort; but Je-

DEBTS AND DEBTORS

The Mosaic law—God's commands to his people—is destroyed by sinners; a German illustration.

Lending money was looked upon as a humanitarian act of assistance to a poor neighbor in financial difficulty rather than a commercial banking enterprise. Mosaic law forbade the lender to charge interest to a fellow Israelite but did allow a pledge as security for the loan. Often the pledge was a symbolic personal item, such as a garment, but it could also amount to such substantial collateral as the use of an ox or a donkey or even control of fields or vineyards for the duration of the loan. Such potentially ruinous pledges were condemned by prophets and teachers of the law.

Once a loan was made, if the debtor was unable to pay, everything that he possessed, including his children and his own person, could be seized by the lender. The prophet Elisha rescued a widow, for example, whose husband had left debts behind. She begged the prophet for help because "the creditor has come to take my two children to be his slaves [2 Kg. 4:1]."

If the debtor or his children were sold to a fellow Israelite who followed the Mosaic law, they had to give a maximum of six years of indentured service before being released. If, however, they were sold to the slave trade, they had no protection. Nehemiah instituted a program to try to buy back "our Jewish brethren who have been sold to the nations [Neh. 5:8]."

Some Israelites, like the band of men who surrounded David in hiding from King Saul, became outlaws to escape servitude for unpaid debts. Others fled the country and spent years in exile because of their indebtedness.

hoshaphat evidently assumed no such role. The priests, assisted by cadres of Levites serving as officers of the court, were considered authoritative interpreters of the law.

During the Roman rule of Palestine, the Sanhedrin (or Great Sanhedrin) became the highest court of the Jews in Jerusalem. Although historians do not agree on the exact scope of the Sanhedrin's duties, powers, and jurisdiction, most authorities believe that it dealt with a variety of judicial, legislative, political, and religious matters. Its officials, sometimes described as sages, seem to have included priests, laymen, and scribes, presided over by the high priest. The name Sanhedrin is derived from the Greek word for council, *synedrion*.

What was a city of refuge?

The custom of blood vengeance in ancient Israel meant that if one person killed another, the nearest kinsman of the victim had a right, indeed a responsibility, to slay the killer. The kinsman, NUM. 35:19 whom the law called "the avenger of blood," did not need to consider whether or not the slaying had been accidental; he needed to know only that his kin had been killed and who did it.

This code of retaliation operated in much of the Middle East, but was modified in Israel by the NUM. 35:13 establishment of "cities of refuge." Six cities—three on each side of the Jordan—were designated asylums for fugitives from blood vengeance. Served by good roads, one or the other of the cities was relatively easy to reach from any part of the country. *(See map above right.)*

If the avenger slew the killer, that was usually the end of the matter. If the killer slew the avenger, presumably another avenging kinsman would take up pursuit. But if a killer reached a city of refuge, he was then entitled to a trial to determine if he had killed intentionally. If he was found guilty of intentional murder, nothing could save him, not even the time-honored asylum given a fugitive who clung to the horns of a sacred altar. He was executed by the avenger, evidently in whatever way the avenger chose.

A verdict of accidental killing did not entirely free the slayer from the threat of retribution. He was protected from the avenger, who still had the right to kill him, only so long as he remained inside the city of refuge. The fact that he had spilled human blood could not be overlooked, ✳

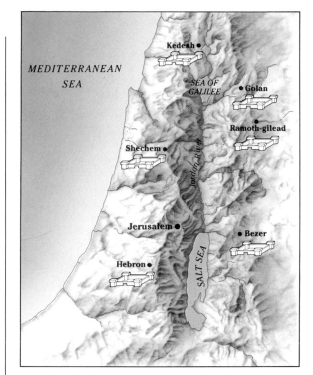

Having divided Canaan among the tribes, Joshua set aside six cities of refuge for fugitives.

as the Book of Numbers stated: "Blood pollutes NUM. 35:33 the land, and no expiation can be made for the land, for the blood that is shed in it, except by the blood of him who shed it." However, one eventuality could at last remove the threat of death from the unintentional slayer, and that was "the death of the high priest who was anointed NUM. 35:25 with the holy oil." The high priest's death was evidently believed to atone for the original killing or to substitute for the death of the manslayer.

When was the death penalty used?

In Israel's law death was required for crimes against human life and against God. Thus blasphemy against the holy name of God, profaning the holy Sabbath, or any form of idolatry, including sorcery or necromancy, and violations of sacred property brought death.

Capital crimes against human life included malicious murder (not manslaughter), wanton negligence, such as letting a dangerous ox run loose until it killed someone, and kidnaping a person for purposes of slavery. Another kind of capital crime against human life pertained to of-

THE TRIAL OF JESUS

According to the Gospel of Mark, Jesus was arrested in the middle of the night during the feast of Passover and brought before the Sanhedrin, Jerusalem's highest court, to answer to the alleged crime of blasphemy. The whole council of elders "sought testimony against Jesus . . . but they found none [Mk. 14:55]." Numerous false witnesses testified, but no two agreed—the mandatory number for a conviction.

The high priest questioned Jesus directly: "Are you the Christ, the Son of the Blessed?" Silent until then, Jesus responded, "I am." At this the high priest tore his garments. "Why do we still need witnesses?" he cried to the council. "You have heard his blasphemy. What is your decision?" Unanimously, they found Jesus guilty and "deserving death [Mk. 14:61]."

The next morning "the chief priests, with the elders and scribes, and the whole council held a consultation; and they bound Jesus and led him away and delivered him [Mk. 15:1]" to the Roman governor, Pontius Pilate. Questioning Jesus, Pilate elicited nothing that warranted the death penalty. "Are you the King of the Jews?" Pilate asked, to which Jesus responded, "You have said so [Mk. 15:2]," and would say no more in his own defense, "so that Pilate wondered [Mk. 15:5]."

Following a Passover custom, Pilate then asked the crowd to decide whether he should release one of "the rebels in prison [Mk. 15:7]" named Barabbas or "the King of the Jews [Mk. 15:9]." Although the crowd chose the rebel, Pilate summarily condemned Jesus to be scourged and "delivered him to be crucified [Mk. 15:15]."

The Gospels vary in their accounts of the accusation and trial of Jesus. All agree, however, that it was Pilate who gave the order for Christ's execution, not the Sanhedrin.

Scavenging birds descend upon Achan, stoned for his disobedience to God, in a Doré etching.

fenses against one's parents. A third category encompassed many violations of approved sexual relations such as adultery, incest, sodomy, and bestiality.

How were criminals executed?

Most judicial executions were carried out by stoning. In earlier times, the criminal may have been killed by a crowd hurling stones small enough to be thrown. Later, stonings involved pushing the victim headlong off a precipice at least 10 feet high; then the principal witness smashed his chest with a large stone. Only if he remained alive would other stones be cast.

The Bible mentions many other forms of capital punishment. Burning was the penalty if "a man takes a wife and her mother." It was also the fate of a priest's daughter who "profanes herself" and "profanes her father" by becoming a prostitute. Kings evidently executed enemies by sword or spear, sometimes by having them beheaded, as Herod did John the Baptist. Hanging usually

LEV. 20:14

LEV. 21:9

LEV. 21:9

referred to the public exposure of the body of a criminal after death. In Persia, however—as in the story of Esther—it meant execution by impaling the body on a tall stake. In New Testament times, hanging meant crucifixion.

How were lesser crimes punished?

For many noncapital crimes, the law of Moses imposed specific punishments. Compensation for theft, for example, was two to five times the amount stolen. If a thief could not make good the total amount, he could be sold into slavery.

Courts imposed various corporal punishments. A man could be flogged with up to 40 strokes of a rod while he lay face down. Scourgings, or severe whippings, were sometimes given with sharp objects attached to the whip ends. Not surprisingly, scourging could be fatal.

For some lesser crimes, Israel's law authorized physical mutilation under the principle EX. 21:24 "eye for eye . . . wound for wound." Only the wrongdoer suffered such a penalty, however, in contrast to the Code of Hammurabi, which sometimes called for punishment of a wrongdoer's kin; for example, if a man caused the death of his debtor's son, his own son was executed.

Imprisonment was seldom, if ever, used as a punishment, although people were frequently held in prison, sometimes for a number of years, while they awaited a hearing.

How did Rabbi Gamaliel save the Apostles?

ACTS 4:13 To the members of the Sanhedrin, Jerusalem's highest council, the "uneducated, common men" who led the followers of Jesus of Nazareth had become an embarrassment and a nuisance. The head of the Sanhedrin, who as high priest was the chief religious authority in the land, had them arrested to stop their preaching, but the Apostles escaped from prison, and as their trial was scheduled to begin, they were found "standing ACTS 5:25 in the temple and teaching the people."

When the Apostles were rearrested and brought to trial, the high priest firmly reminded them of the court's injunction that they cease teaching. The unrepentant brashness of Peter and the others so infuriated the Sanhedrin, however, that most of its members "were enraged ACTS 5:33 and wanted to kill them," but then the voice of Gamaliel was heard. He was a famous "teacher ACTS 5:34 of the law, held in honor by all the people," the most prominent Pharisee of his time.

He calmly reminded the court of how similar movements had come to nothing in the past, and he counseled trust in God. "If this plan or this ACTS 5:38 undertaking is of men, it will fail; but if it is of God, you will not be able to overthrow them. You might even be found opposing God!" His words assuaged the court, and even though they suffered a beating, the Apostles went free, able to preach again.

The Roman practice of crucifixion was viewed as the most degrading form of execution; the Gospel story inspired this Swiss painting of Jesus' ordeal.

Work, Home, and Family

What were the common occupations?

For thousands of years, most of the people of Palestine made their living from the land. By Jesus' time, much of the land was held by wealthy absentee landlords. A typical tenant farmer in an area such as Galilee would have a small field for grain (mostly wheat or barley), a vineyard that yielded grapes for wine and raisins, and an olive grove to produce oil. Some vegetables planted between the grapevines, and perhaps fig trees, would fill out the farmer's crops.

The marginal growing regions were the domain of herders with sheep, goats, and sometimes cattle. The life of a herder changed little from the days of Abraham to the time when shepherds visited the infant Jesus in Bethlehem. Other than the herds that provided meat, milk, and clothing, oxen were raised for plowing, and donkeys and camels for beasts of burden.

Jobs in the villages centered around the necessities of life. With a utilitarian elegance but little embellishment, potters shaped local clay into the vessels needed for everyday use. (Pottery shards cover practically every archeological site in the ancient world.) Carpenters were all-purpose woodworkers. Smiths, working in bronze and iron, made plowshares, tools, and vessels, and in time of war, swords, spearheads, and armor. Stonemasons went wherever a construction project was under way. The spinning and weaving of fabric for clothing was done primarily by women, though some weavers were men.

Certain places attracted a specialized work force. Most of Palestine's fishermen lived around the Sea of Galilee. (The people did little fishing in the Mediterranean.) The temple at Jerusalem meant employment for hundreds of priests and Levites.

Difficult as it may be to imagine, those who had some choice in the kind of work they did were fortunate. A large part of the population in the ancient world consisted of slaves. Whether through war, debt, or other circumstances, they were reduced to doing whatever work their owners demanded.

Why were tax collectors especially despised?

Never popular in any age or nation, taxes became especially hateful in Israel and Judah when weak kings taxed their subjects for gold and silver that then went to pay extortionate tribute to powerful foreign empires such as Egypt, Assyria, or Rome. In effect, the people were taxed to keep their puppet rulers from being deposed by outside forces.

In New Testament times, the Romans received taxes either directly or through vassal kings such as the Herods. The Apostle Matthew had once worked as a tax agent for Herod the Great's son, Herod Antipas, who sent some tax monies to the Roman emperor. In Judea, where Rome ruled through its own governors, a chief tax collector such as Zacchaeus—a short man who Luke reports climbed a tree in order to see Jesus enter Jericho—worked directly for Rome.

Jews like Zacchaeus who became tax collectors were pariahs in their society. Viewed as collaborators and enforcers of Roman domination, they were despised by their countrymen, who longed for political independence.

Furthermore, tax collectors were hated because of the corruption and extortion that permeated the extensive Roman tax apparatus, which allowed unscrupulous agents to keep a portion of whatever amounts they collected with little fear of prosecution. A clue to the scope of the dishonesty involved is found in the story of Zacchaeus, to whom Jesus said, "Make haste and come down ✳ LK. 19:5

Their fishermen's stamina and courage would serve Andrew and Peter (here in a 12th-century painting) well in their work as Apostles.

In an Italian fresco, Jacob's flocks drink the "still water" in Laban's trough. As Leah and Rachel (right) arrive with their herd, a servant adds well water to the trough.

THE GOOD SHEPHERD

The shepherd tending his flock is a vivid and familiar image in the Bible. Shepherds and sheep are mentioned more than 300 times, beginning with the first "keeper of sheep [Gen. 4:2]," Adam's son Abel. The greatest heroes of Israel's past—Abraham, Moses, David, Amos—were shepherds, and the Scriptures even portrayed God in this way: "The Lord is my shepherd, I shall not want; . . . He leads me beside still waters; he restores my soul [Ps. 23:1]."

Hard work and worry filled the shepherd's life, as Jacob reminded his uncle, Laban: "By day the heat consumed me, and the cold by night, and my sleep fled from my eyes [Gen. 31:40]." The shepherd had to nurse sick and weak sheep, gather the young lambs that couldn't keep up with the flock, and "carry them in his bosom [Is. 40:11]." With a heavy spiked club, he drove off wild animals and thieves. He was constantly moving his flocks in search of grazing land and pools of water. (The "still waters" of Psalm 23 refer to the premise that sheep will drink standing water but balk at a swiftly flowing stream.) At night the shepherd soothed the

Artfully rendered in a fifth-century statue, the good shepherd returns his lost sheep to the fold.

flocks by playing his flute.

In his teaching, Jesus readily drew on the image of the kind shepherd caring for defenseless sheep. Speaking to the Pharisees, Jesus said, "I am the good shepherd. The good shepherd lays down his life for the sheep [Jn. 10:11]." The crowds coming for healing appeared to him "harassed and helpless, like sheep without a shepherd [Mt. 9:36]." His disciples who spread his teachings were "sheep in the midst of wolves [Mt. 10:16]." To help people understand the urgency of his ministry, he compared the shepherd searching for a lost sheep with his mission to save sinners. "If a man has a hundred sheep, and one of them has gone astray, does he not leave the ninety-nine on the mountains and go in search of the one that went astray? And if he finds it, truly, I say to you, he rejoices over it more than over the ninety-nine that never went astray [Mt. 18:12]."

LK. 19:7 [from the tree]; for I must stay at your house to-day." So remorseful did this "sinner" feel after being singled out by Jesus that he promised to LK. 19:8 give half his property to the poor, "and if I have defrauded any one of anything, I [will] restore it fourfold." In later Jewish law, tax agents were treated as traitors and robbers; they could not testify in court, nor could their money be accepted by charities.

A shepherdess spins wool with her distaff in this fourth-century mosaic.

Finally, many Jews concerned about purity shunned tax collectors because their continual contact with Gentiles made them ritually unclean. To be a tax collector in Jewish society was comparable to being a sinner who flouted the law.

What work did women do?

In practically every household, women carded wool and prepared flax for linen; they spun thread and yarn, using hand spindles with stone or clay whorls; they did basic dyeing and wove cloth on vertical looms; they sewed family garments and kept the clothes clean by "treading" (trampling on) their laundry in streams or public pools. In large, wealthy households numerous servants under the direction of the mistress of the house might manufacture clothing to be sold by city merchants. For the most part, only luxury garments were bought outside the household.

Women were occupied too with keeping bread in the mouths of their families. Poor women often gathered grain—like Ruth—by "glean- RU. 2:23 ing" the remnants left by the reapers. They also threshed and winnowed the grain and ground it into flour, using a handmill or even a primitive mortar and pestle. Women carried the water for their household from a spring or well, mixed it with flour to make the dough, kneaded it, and baked the bread. They usually rose before dawn

RUTH GLEANING

Ruth and her mother-in-law, Naomi, returned to Bethlehem in April, at the start of the barley harvest. For a widow and a foreigner like Ruth, gleaning was one of the few ways to earn a living. The law required farmers to leave some of the harvest in the fields "for the poor and for the sojourner" [Lev. 19:10] to gather.

Rising at dawn, Ruth joined the widows, orphans, and poor who waited to collect the grain left along the edges and in the corners of the field by the reapers, as they walked up and down, rhythmically swinging their sickles. The servants followed the reapers and tied the stalks into sheaves.

In the late morning Boaz came out to greet his workers and spotted Ruth among the other gleaners. Boaz knew that this young Moabite had left her family and native land to care for Naomi and her devotion moved him. He invited her to stay with his workers and glean only on his land. At mealtime Ruth joined the reapers for some bread, roasted grain, and wine. When she went back to the fields, Boaz told his men to leave extra grain for her to pick up. By evening Ruth had gathered an ephah (about half a bushel) of grain. Ruth's gratitude for Boaz's kindness and generosity led soon after to their marriage.

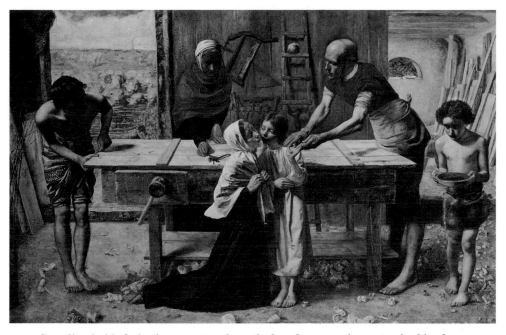

Standing in his father's carpentry shop, the boy Jesus receives a tender kiss from his mother in a scene conceived by the British painter John Everett Millais.

to build the fires for cooking. In larger households, the mistress of the house might also supervise a vineyard and the making of wine.

The role of women to which the society attached the most importance, however, was bearing and raising children. Having children gave a woman status, and she and her husband began educating them at an early age in the values and traditions of their people.

How did a carpenter like Jesus practice his trade?

A carpenter in a small town like Nazareth was probably skilled in making everything from small carved implements to parts of houses. His workshop might be a first-floor room, open to the street, with his family living behind or above it. His principal tools for shaping wood were an adze, an iron saw the size of a large knife, a mallet and some chisels, a bow drill, a heavy stone hammer, a shaver, and a lump of sandstone for smoothing. During working hours he might be found sitting on the floor, holding his work in place with his feet as he worked with his hands.

Most of his time was probably spent crafting yokes for oxen, sturdy wooden plows, threshing ✳

NEW WINE INTO OLD BOTTLES. *When Jesus said that "no one puts new wine into old wineskins [Mk. 2:22, Lk. 5:37]," he was telling the Pharisees that his teaching and way of life were incompatible with how they believed the old law should be interpreted and enforced. An attempt to make them compatible would destroy both—the Pharisees' "old wineskin" would burst as the "new wine" of Jesus' teaching fermented and expanded. The expression "new wine into old bottles [Lk. 5:37]" comes from the King James version of the Gospel; newer texts use the more precise word* wineskin.

Anyone familiar with the winemaking of the time would have immediately understood Jesus' message. When the grape juice began to ferment, the wine was transferred from vats into skins, or leather bottles, where the process continued. During fermentation certain gases, such as carbon dioxide, were released. While new wineskins expanded, old ones tended to be more brittle, and instead of stretching, could break, spilling and ruining the wine.

To commemorate Jesus' Last Supper with his Apostles, early Christians shared bread and wine at the **agape,** *or love feast, as in this Roman carving.*

quired to build houses, which were made with stone or mud-brick walls, carpenters might have been called upon to place wooden beams that supported roof structures. They found work too on large public buildings, such as synagogues and market centers.

When Jesus began his ministry, he may have already worked for as many as 20 years in the carpenter's shop. His craft is known because Mark relates how the people of Nazareth doubted Jesus' wisdom and asked, "Is not MK. 6:3 this the carpenter?" In Matthew's account, the townspeople ask, "Is not this the carpenter's MT. 13:55 son?," indicating that Joseph was a carpenter.

boards, winnowing forks, and other implements for farmers. Often he alone made all the manufacturing decisions, beginning with the selection and cutting of the tree from whose wood he fashioned the final product. In addition to farm implements, he might be asked to make benches, chairs, beds, boxes, coffins, and carts. Carpenters in seacoast towns became boatbuilders.

Although woodworking was not usually re-

What were the main foods?

A passage from Deuteronomy concisely sums up the staples of the Israelite diet: "For the Lord your DT. 8:7 God is bringing you into a good land . . . a land of wheat and barley, of vines and fig trees and pomegranates, a land of olive trees and honey." Wheat and barley grains were made into bread, the staff of life, without which no meal was considered complete. Loaves were usually round and fairly flat (although leavening was provided by fermented dough) and baked over coals in outdoor clay ovens. The grains might also be simply roasted. In the First Book of Samuel, the young David takes a meal of "parched grain" to 1 SAM. 17:17 the encampment of his older brothers, soldiers in the service of King Saul.

Farmers cultivated lentils, beans, onions, garlic, and cucumbers. Greens such as lettuce, endive, chicory, and mustard grew wild. In addition to the fruits mentioned or alluded to in Deuteronomy (grapes, raisins, pomegranates, and figs), the people also ate dates, either fresh or dried.

From grapes came Palestine's principal agricultural product, wine. It was drunk full-strength or watered down, and several types (including the sparkling variety) are mentioned in the Bible. Second to wine in trade importance was the oil

DAILY BREAD. *In his Sermon on the Mount, Jesus told those gathered to pray that God "give us this day our daily bread [Mt. 6:11]." Look to God, he was saying, to provide the necessities of everyday life.*

Throughout the ancient Middle East, bread was the primary food. Families often went without meat, but bread was considered indispensable. Biblical writers frequently used it as a metaphor for all food. When Ezekiel warned Israel of the famine and hardship to come with Jerusalem's fall, he said that God would "break the staff of bread [Ezek. 4:16]," meaning God would destroy the Israelites' means of survival. In the New Testament, Jesus chose bread to symbolize spiritual nourishment: "I am the bread of life; he who comes to me shall not hunger [Jn. 6:35]."

pressed from olives, which was used for cooking, lighting, washing, and ritual anointing.

Milk from goats, sheep, and sometimes cows was abundant, and the people drank it fresh or soured or made it into butter and cheese. Eggs came from partridge, quail, geese, chickens, and pigeons. Salt was used both as a preservative and a seasoning, and spices such as coriander, cumin, dill, and sesame were common. Honey was harvested from the hives of wild bees.

Lamb and goat meat was available but usually cost too much to be served regularly. Beef and veal were even more of a luxury and were reserved for feasts of the wealthy. From the River Jordan and the Sea of Galilee came fish, which were eaten fresh or preserved in salt.

Dietary laws in the Torah proscribed certain foods. Meat could come only from animals that had cloven hooves and chewed their cuds. This excluded pigs, which are not cud chewers. A slaughtered animal had to be carefully bled so that a person did not eat its blood. Fish that had fins and scales were permitted, but not shellfish. Some birds were allowed; but others, such as eagles, vultures, and gulls, were not.

How did people dress?

"And the Lord God made for Adam and for his wife GEN. 3:21 garments of skins, and clothed them." If those first clothes were like the ones believed to have been worn in early biblical times, their design was similar for men and women. As the ages passed, differences developed between how the sexes dressed, and by the time of Deuteronomy the law forbade wearing the clothes of the opposite sex: "A woman shall not wear anything that DT. 22:5 pertains to a man, nor shall a man put on a woman's garment." Distinctions arose too between the clothes of the rich and poor, not so much

FORMAL BANQUETS

Major festive and social events in biblical times often centered around meals whose purpose transcended merely sharing food.

The host usually invited his friends, relatives, and wealthy neighbors, expecting them to return the favor. Jesus had a different sort of guest list in mind, one that would bring spiritual rewards to the host, when he said, "Invite the poor, the maimed, the lame, the blind, and you will be blessed, because they cannot repay you [Lk. 14:13]."

Attendants washed the hands and feet of arriving guests and anointed them with fragrant oils. The early Israelites sat cross-legged on the ground to dine, but by Jesus' time banquetgoers had adopted the Greco-Roman

The bitter herbs eaten at Passover, shown in a Spanish illumination, remind Jews of slavery's bitter taste.

manner of reclining on couches. The most desirable seats, those immediately to the right of where the servants served the food, were reserved for guests of the highest social rank.

The banquet menu often featured wine mixed with honey, followed by rich delicacies. The choicest and largest portions went to the guest of honor.

For entertainment there was music, storytelling, and dancing. Guests often remained and talked long into the night; to leave too early was an insult to the host. King Ahasuerus of Persia and his guests once carried this courtesy to an extreme: his banquet for state officials lasted 180 days.

in the cut of the garments but in the kind of fabric used and how it was decorated.

In New Testament times, many adults wore a simple tunic as an undergarment. The tunics of men were usually open-necked, sleeveless, and knee-length; women's came to the ankles. Early tunics were made of leather or flax. Later ones were of coarse wool or linen for the poor and finely woven linen or silk for the wealthy.

Over the tunic Jews wore a cloaklike garment resembling a sheet with a hood, which typically was made of wool. These cloaks were plain or striped and could double as blankets at night. A girdle or belt (often embroidered) encircled the tunic or outer garment. All but the very poor wore sandals, and both men and women had some kind of headgear as protection against the sun and the other elements.

What colors were popular in clothing in biblical times?

The Israelites were skilled in the art of fabric dyeing. Because linen was difficult to dye, most colored garments were made from wool, possibly cotton (although its use in early times is doubtful), and, for the upper classes, silk. Using plant, animal, and mineral substances and various methods of treatment and drying, artisans created clothes in blue, black, red, yellow, green, and white. The most popular—and expensive—colors were hues of purple, which were made with dyes that came from murex mollusks found in the Mediterranean Sea. The garments of women were usually more colorful than men's.

The higher the status of the wearer, the more elaborate the decoration of the garment, espe-

Top: A bust of a stylish Syrian woman in the third century. Middle: A cosmetics bowl. Bottom: Phoenician beads.

cially around the hem. The priestly robe of Aaron, the brother of Moses, was to be embroidered in this manner: "On its skirts you shall EX. 28:33 make pomegranates of blue and purple and scarlet stuff . . . with bells of gold between them."

The Book of Judges, telling of Sisera's mother waiting in vain for her son to come home from a battle between the Canaanites and Israelites, reveals how highly prized were the decorative fabrics of the Israelites. Thinking that Sisera was delayed because he was collecting booty from the Israelites, she wonders if he is bringing "dyed stuffs for JG. 5:30 Sisera," and "two pieces of dyed work embroidered for my neck as spoil?"

What kinds of jewelry were customary?

Both men and women wore bracelets, necklaces, and rings, especially for celebrations and holy days. Although in some Middle Eastern cultures both men and women wore earrings and nose rings, among the Israelites only the women did. Men wore rings as symbols of authority and for use as seals. An Israelite woman's jewelry might consist of beads made from shells or crystalline rocks; pendants carved out of animal bone; and bracelets, anklets, rings, nose rings, and earrings of bronze. As a rule, only the rich owned jewelry fashioned from gold, silver, and precious stones.

What cosmetics were used?

To make many of their cosmetics, the Israelites ground certain minerals into a powder, which they then mixed with water or gum to make a paste. One form of eye paint, for example, contained crushed green malachite and galena (lead sulfide), a bluish-gray mineral. Red ocher, an iron compound, may have been the base for the first known rouge. Other cosmetics came from plants. The crushed leaves of the henna tree yielded a reddish dye used on the feet, hands, nails, and hair.

People rubbed perfumed oils into their hair and on their bodies not only to smell pleasant (frequent baths being uncommon) but also to protect their skin from the burning sun. Common fragrances added to oils included myrrh, frankincense, saffron, cinnamon, balm of Gilead, rose, jasmine, balsam, and mint. Men and women of all social classes used these scented oils, although it was not considered proper for scholars to appear perfumed in public.

Does the Bible condone personal adornment?

Although both men and women used perfumed oils, and women used eye paint and other makeup, beautification for immoral or wanton purposes was frowned upon in the Bible. Isaiah prophesied that God would punish the women of Jerusalem who were "haughty . . . glancing wantonly IS. 3:16 with their eyes" by taking away all their jewelry, perfume, and fancy clothes. And Jeremiah used the image of a gaudily attired harlot to berate his idolatrous nation: "What do you mean that you JER. 4:30 dress in scarlet, that you deck yourself with ornaments of gold, that you enlarge your eyes with paint?"

The New Testament provided another perspective on beautifying oneself: "Let not yours be 1 PET. 3:3 the outward adorning with braiding of hair, decoration of gold, and wearing of fine clothing, but let it be the hidden person of the heart with the imperishable jewel of a gentle and quiet spirit, which in God's sight is very precious."

What were the popular games and sports?

The recreational activities mentioned in the Bible were primarily feasts, festivals, and other celebrations, where people enjoyed themselves play-

*The Holy Family prepares for Passover in this
19th-century work by the English artist Dante Gabriel Rossetti.*

MUSICAL INSTRUMENTS

Praise the Lord!" sings Psalm 150, ". . . with trumpet . . . with lute and harp . . . with timbrel . . . with strings and pipe . . . with loud clashing cymbals!" Instrumental music often accompanied Israel's worship, celebration, and lamentation.

The only biblical instrument still used in Jewish religious services is the shofar, a hollowed ram's horn. Its piercing wail heralded the beginning of the Sabbath and the new year, and called the Israelites to arms in times of war. Another horn, the trumpet, introduced temple sacrifices and ceremonies. Made from metal such as silver or gold, it was usually played in pairs, although when Solomon brought the ark into the temple, an ensemble of

Top: David's lyre most likely resembled this modern one. Bottom: An Egyptian hand rattle.

120 trumpeters played "in unison in praise and thanksgiving to the Lord [2 Chr. 5:13]."

Stringed instruments were popular both in the temple and in aristocratic homes. David's harp was probably a lyre, an instrument dating from about 2400 B.C. Woodwinds included the pipe, a kind of primitive clarinet, and a double reed instrument similar to a modern oboe. Drums, cymbals, rattles, and gongs provided rhythm. Hebrew women played the timbrel, a flat hand drum. When Saul returned from fighting the Philistines, the women rushed out, "singing and dancing . . . with timbrels, with songs of joy, and with instruments of music [1 Sam. 18:6]."

ing music, singing, and dancing. Also popular were storytelling contests and the posing and solving of riddles. The sixth-century B.C. prophet Zechariah foretold the return of happier times when the Lord would again dwell in Jerusalem: ZECH. 8:5 "And the streets of the city shall be full of boys and girls playing in its streets." In the Gospels of Matthew and Luke, Jesus refers to children piping and dancing in the marketplaces.

Archeology has provided some glimpses into the everyday recreations of ancient times. Game boards of wood, stone, or ivory have been found at several sites in the Middle East. One common game, known in Egypt, was called 58 Holes. It was played on a violin-shaped board into which the holes were drilled. Archeologists have also unearthed ancient games similar to checkers and backgammon.

It is likely that some hunting was done for sport; and wrestling and archery provided recreation, in addition to conditioning and training for soldiers.

How did Paul use sports images in his writing?

Paul spent most of his life—and did most of his work for the church—in and around the cities of Greece and Asia Minor. In those cities athletic contests were a centuries-old tradition, and this partly explains why the footrace became one of Paul's favorite analogies both for his own ministry and for the lives of his converts. When Paul urged the Christians at Corinth to run like racers competing for a prize, they no doubt thought of the ancient games still held in their own city, in which the winner was crowned with a wreath of wild celery symbolizing the glory of his achievement. "Every athlete exercises self-control in all things," Paul reminded them. "They do it to receive a perishable wreath, but we an imperishable [one]." 1 COR. 9:25

In other letters Paul described himself in his life and work as continually striving toward the Christian ideal. "Forgetting what lies behind and PHIL. 3:13

straining forward to what lies ahead," he wrote, "I press on toward the goal for the prize of the upward call of God in Christ Jesus. Let those of us who are mature be thus minded."

Paul saw the strenuous regimen of Greek athletes as a positive model of self-discipline, struggle, and focused exertion that could inspire his converts. He compared the commitment of his life to the prepa-
1 COR. 9:26 ration of a boxer for the games. "I do not box as one beating the air" as an untrained fighter would, he observed. Instead, as though he were training with a tough and skill-
1 COR. 9:27 ful sparring partner, "I pommel my body and subdue it, lest after preaching to others I myself should be disqualified."

From the bloody gladiatorial spectacles of the Romans, however, Paul drew another kind of inspiration. In them he saw an analogy to the general suffering and humiliation of early Christians. He de-
1 COR. 4:9 scribed the Apostles as "men sentenced to death; because we have become a spectacle to the world, to angels and to men."

An ebullient David dances and plays the pipe in this mosaic, as he did during the procession into Jerusalem with the ark.

Why did roofs have a special significance in the Bible?

With most families living in crowded, one-room houses, roofs provided an extra dimension to the home. In fact, one of the laws handed down from Moses concerned making roofs safe for
DT. 22:8 people: "When you build a new house, you shall

The names of these dogs were inscribed on the clay figurines in the seventh century B.C.

make a parapet for your roof, that you may not bring the guilt of blood upon your house, if any one fall from it."

Reached usually by an outside stair or ladder, rooftops were good for ripening fruits and vegetables, drying flax, and no doubt drying the wash too. They could be used for praying or for sleeping when the heat made indoor quarters uncomfortable. A roof could also be a social center, a place to gossip with one's neighbors, and a spot from which to survey the passing scene. From such a vantage point, David saw Bathsheba bathing, and his lust for her was aroused.

Most roofs were flat, consisting of rafters overlaid with branches that were plastered with mud. After a rain, cylindrical rollers were used to pack the mud down again. The flimsy construction of ancient roofs is illustrated in the Gospel's story of Jesus healing the paralytic in Capernaum: "And they came, bringing to him a paralytic car- MK. 2:3 ried by four men. And when they could not get near him because of the crowd, they removed the roof above him; and when they had made an opening, they let down the pallet on which the paralytic lay."

Travel

How and why did people travel in Bible times?

GEN. 12:1 "Go from your country and your kindred and your father's house," God ordered Abraham, "to the land that I will show you. And I will make of you a great nation. . . ." Dutifully, Abraham set out on a 400-mile journey from his father's tents in Haran to the land of Canaan. His trip was most likely made on foot, accompanied by donkeys carrying the family's possessions.

Travel was not easy in ancient times. Until the Romans built extensive roads, there were little more than footpaths along which people and beasts of burden slowly picked their way. Because there was safety in numbers, travelers joined caravans when possible. Some of the caravans, with as many as 1,500 camels, stretched for miles. Led by a rider on a donkey, they moved at approximately three miles per hour.

Despite its hazards and rigors, travel was necessary to carry on trade, escape war and famine, find work, maintain family ties, and make religious pilgrimages.

How were travel and the spread of Christianity linked?

The Roman Empire often persecuted Christians. Yet, unwittingly, the Romans also removed barriers in Christianity's path. They established a single political regime stretching from Britain to the deserts east of the Holy Land, so that a citizen needed no permits to travel over much of the known world. And across the same vast area, the Romans created a trading network, thereby propagating the language of commerce, which happened to be Greek. The result was that a Christian missionary needed to speak only one language to be understood virtually anywhere in the empire.

The Romans also made sea travel safer by subduing the pirates of the Mediterranean. And they built—over five centuries—53,000 miles of highways and 200,000 miles of secondary roads. One traveler on those roads and sea-lanes was the missionary Paul. In his journeys throughout the Holy Land and Asia Minor and to Greece and Italy, Paul was "three 2 COR. 11:25 times . . . shipwrecked"; and he faced "danger from rivers, danger from robbers 2 COR. 11:26 . . . danger in the city, danger in the wilderness, danger at sea . . . toil and hardship . . . hunger and thirst." Yet Paul's missionary work would have been even more difficult if the Romans had not built roads and tamed the pirates.

The Holy Family's fearful flight to Egypt, shown in this Flemish work, may have taken three weeks.

What city was situated "in the center of the nations"?

Fenced in by rugged terrain, the site of Jerusalem seems more suited to a fortress than to a commercial and cultural center. Yet by Jesus' time, Jerusalem was a bus-

ANCIENT ROADS

Beginning as simple cattle and sheep paths to serve the needs of a nomadic people, the network of roads crisscrossing the Holy Land developed through the centuries into an impressive system of trade routes connecting the kingdoms of Egypt, Mesopotamia, and Asia Minor. The two most important arteries, the Way of the Sea (Via Maris) and the King's Highway, coursed north to south through Palestine.

From its southern end, the Way of the Sea ran from Memphis in Egypt to Gaza, north along the Mediterranean coast through Tyre and Sidon, then east to Aleppo in Syria. Here it joined a major road linking the valleys of the Tigris and Euphrates in the east with Asia Minor in the west. When Joseph and Mary fled Palestine with Jesus after Herod decreed the death of young male children, it is likely they took the Way of the Sea from Gaza across the Sinai Desert toward Egypt.

South from Damascus the King's Highway penetrated the heart of Palestine, winding east of the Jordan River, the Sea of Galilee, and the Dead Sea. The

Begun in 312 B.C. and built to last, the 360-mile-long Appian Way was ancient Rome's main military and commercial link to the south. This section of the road is near Rome.

lower segment branched west, joining Palestine with Egypt, and south, running between Petra and the Red Sea ports.

A number of lesser roads crossed the Holy Land east and west, connecting such coastal towns as Ascalon, Joppa, and Caesarea with Jerusalem and the interior. In central Palestine other routes carried traffic from the eastern deserts.

During his ministry Jesus walked hundreds of miles on this irregular grid of highways and footpaths. He went to Jerusalem for the religious festivals, visited the coastal cities, and walked the paths connecting the villages on the Sea of Galilee, such as Bethsaida, Magdala, and Chorazin.

tling city of perhaps 100,000, giving more than religious significance to God's phrase "center of the nations." Jerusalem's emergence as a trading center was hindered by its hilly location, but from the time of David, it attracted traders, scholars, and perhaps most important, people such as Mary and Joseph, who took Jesus there as a boy for Passover and other observances.

Jerusalem under Roman rule was a diplomat-ic, military, and administrative center; it also blended Hebrew and Greek cultures. The city was a religious center as well, since it contained the temple that the Jews believed to be God's dwelling place on earth. And it was in Jerusalem, finally, that Christ was crucified and resurrected, giving the city special meaning to a new community of believers that would eventually spread around the world.

EZEK. 5:5

Time and Measurement

A medieval artist portrayed Hezekiah's "dial of Ahaz" as a water clock, which tells time by measuring water dripping from a reservoir.

What did the law of Moses say about weights and measures?

In Deuteronomy, God warned against fraudulent weighing and measuring: "You shall not have in your bag two kinds of weights, a large and a small. . . . A full and just measure you shall have; that your days may be prolonged in the land which the Lord your God gives you. For all who . . . act dishonestly, are an abomination to the Lord your God." In Leviticus, a similar command was given concerning the use of accurate standards of measurement: "You shall have just balances, just weights, a just ephah, and a just hin."

DT. 25:13

LEV. 19:36

How did Abraham buy land from the Canaanites?

Though God promised the whole of Canaan to Abraham and his descendants, the only part of the Promised Land that Abraham ever actually ✳ owned was a place that he purchased as a sepulcher for the body of his wife, Sarah. For this he bought a cave near Hebron from Ephron, a native of the region.

Ephron said he was willing to give the burial site to Abraham, but Genesis emphasizes that Abraham paid the full purchase price. Probably using a balance scale, Abraham measured out silver—most likely in the form of rings or bracelets—weighing 400 shekels (about 10 pounds), "according to the weights current among the merchants." By carefully following accepted business practices, Abraham seemed to be making sure that there could be no challenge to his claim on this plot in the ancestral lands of the Canaanites.

GEN. 23:16

What calendar did people use in Jesus' time?

The year A.D. 1 marks Jesus' birth, the turning point of the ages from a Christian view. But A.D. 1 did not acquire its present significance until more than 500 years after Jesus, when a monk devised a calendar that began with the year he calculated Jesus had been born: *anno Domini I*, or in the year of our Lord 1. Actually the monk erred by four to seven years in dating Jesus' birth.

Several kinds of calendars were used in the Roman Empire. Scholars of that era numbered the years from the time Rome was supposedly established—to them, A.D. 1 was 754. A different method was used for most Roman legal documents, which carried the names of the two chief magistrates presiding over the Senate. Because these consuls served concurrent one-year terms, their names in effect told the year. (A document of A.D. 1 would have been signed by both C. Caesar, son of Augustus, and L. Aemilius Paullus, son of Paullus.) Still other systems gave the year in the reign of a ruler. In A.D. 1, documents in Jerusalem would have been dated the fourth year of the reign of Archelaus, son of Herod the Great; in Nazareth, the fourth year of Herod Antipas, another of Herod's sons. Anywhere in the Roman Empire, A.D. 1 could have been called the 27th year of Emperor Augustus.

Many ancient peoples worked out some sort of compromise between a lunar calendar, in which the year had 12 months and about 354 days, and a solar calendar, which followed the cycle of the seasons over a year of 365¼ days. Israel after the exile used Babylonian names for the months and perhaps also followed the Babylonian practice of adding an extra month every few years to keep the lunar calendar, which determined the feast days, in synchrony with the seasons. This ensured that the calendar date for, say, a harvest festival would continue to occur around the time of the actual harvest. By Jesus' time the Roman Empire had generally adopted the Julian calendar. Named for Julius Caesar, it used a 365-day solar year, with every fourth year having 366 days.

How did people tell time without clocks?

Before the invention of mechanical clocks, it was hard to keep track of short periods of time. In ancient Israel the concept of the hour was unknown. The Israelites divided the daytime into its

GEN. 18:1 natural segments: dawn, "the heat of the day,"
GEN. 3:8 "the cool of the day," and "evening, the time
GEN. 24:11 when women go out to draw water." Nighttime was divided into three watches.

IS. 38:8 The nearest thing to a clock in the Bible is "the dial of Ahaz" by which King Hezekiah told the
IS. 38:1 time. When Hezekiah was "at the point of death," he appealed to God, and through Isaiah,
IS. 38:5 God promised to add "fifteen years to your [Hezekiah's] life." As a sign that he would do as he
IS. 38:8 said, the Lord ordered Isaiah to tell Hezekiah, "I will make the shadow cast by the declining sun on the dial of Ahaz turn back ten steps." Once

thought to refer to a sundial such as archeologists have found in ancient Palestine, modern research has shown that the word translated *dial* actually means steps or stairs. This indicates that Hezekiah marked time by noting how a shadow, perhaps one cast by a building in his palace complex, moved along a flight of steps.

By the time of Jesus, it was commonplace to divide the daytime into 12 hours. The hour, however, was not a fixed unit of time as it is today, but one-twelfth of the period between sunrise and sunset. Thus an hour in summer (which would be about 70 minutes today) was substantially longer than an hour in winter (about 50 minutes today). To tell the time, one counted from sunrise (the first hour) to noon (the sixth) to sunset (the twelfth).

Byzantine weights were usually composed of bronze, with the value inscribed on top.

FULL AND JUST MEASURES

Unit in the Bible	Equivalent
Weight:	
Beka Ex. 38:26	³⁄₁₀ oz.
Shekel 1 Sam. 17:7 .... 2 bekas	²⁄₅ oz.
Mina 1 Kg. 10:17 .... 50 shekels	1¼ lb.
Talent 1 Chr. 22:14 .... 60 minas	75 lb.
*Pound Jn. 12:3	⁷⁄₁₀ lb.
Length:	
Finger Jer. 52:21	³⁄₄ in.
Hand-breadth Ex. 25:25 .. 4 fingers	3 in.
Span Ezek. 43:13 .... 3 handbreadths	9 in.
Cubit Gen. 6:15 .... 2 spans	18 in.
*Fathom Acts 27:28	6 ft.
*Stadia Rev. 21:16	200 yd.
*Mile Mt. 5:41	⁹⁄₁₀ mi.
Volume:	
Log Lev. 14:10	²⁄₃ pint
Omer Ex. 16:36 .... ¹⁄₁₀ ephah	²⁄₃ gal.
Hin Ezek. 46:14 .... 12 logs	1 gal.
Ephah, or Bath .... 6 hins	6 gal.
Ru. 2:17, Kg. 7:26	
Cor, or Homer .... 10 ephahs	60 gal.
2 Chr. 2:10; Num. 11:3	
Coinage:	
Denarius Mt. 20:2	1 day's wage
Silver shekel 2 Sam 24:24	4 denarii
Gold shekel 1 Chr. 21:25	15 silver shekels
Gold mina Ezek 45:12	50 gold shekels
Gold talent 2 Chr. 36:3	60 gold minas
*Penny Mt. 10:29	¹⁄₁₆ denarius

**New Testament unit*

KINGS AND CONQUERORS

The clamor of marching armies reverberates through biblical history as it did across the plains and hills of Canaan. The Israelites believed God had set aside that ribbon of earth at the western end of the Fertile Crescent as the land he would give to the descendants of Abraham. To the predatory eyes of conquerors it was a vital crossroads of trade, a point at which caravan routes converged and fortunes could be made. To the ancient Israelites, however, such concerns were far less important than the land itself. Over and over, they told the stories of how God had delivered them from slavery in Egypt and led them to this "land flowing with milk and honey [Ex. 3:8]." Even though Canaan was occupied by peoples stronger than the Israelites, God miraculously enabled them to capture walled cities and make the land their own.

The ancient Israelites saw themselves as a theocracy, a society ruled by God alone in accordance with his law. But a secure and ordered life was threatened by belligerent rivals all around—Philistines, Midianites, Amorites, and others. The loose tribal confederacy that might have fostered an age of freedom under God's rule instead ushered in a time of oppression and anarchy, when "every man did what was right in his own eyes [Jg. 17:6]." Ultimately, the people demanded a leader strong enough to defend them from invaders. They wanted a king.

With sorrow for the lost ideal, the prophet Samuel opened a new era by anointing a tall, handsome young man named Saul as Israel's first king. Samuel soon grew disenchanted with Saul, however, and secretly anointed a second claimant to the throne, the young shepherd David. In the great drama that ensued, the tragic death of Saul coincided with the rise of David, a valiant and charismatic leader who would live on in the people's memory as their greatest king. David took advantage of the declining strength in Assyria to his north and Egypt to his south and extended Israelite rule over an ever greater area.

Solomon, David's son and successor, rode the crest of his father's triumphs through a period of royal prosperity and ambitious building, including the construction of the first temple. But Solomon's reign also spawned excesses that alienated much of the populace, and his headstrong son Rehoboam oversaw the collapse of a thriving kingdom into two weak and warring rivals, Israel and Judah. Worse yet, Israelite strength was sapped by this rift just as Assyria and Egypt were showing signs of renewed life and aggressiveness.

The two poorly organized little kingdoms lived for generations in dread of Assyria's fearsome armies, each one calculating how much independence it dared to assert according to the weakness or strength of successive Assyrian kings. Ultimately the northern kingdom of Israel lost this cat-and-mouse game in 721 B.C. The 10 northern tribes were swallowed up by Assyria and their people deported into permanent exile, a fate seen by the biblical narrators as God's decisive judgment of the people's idolatry.

More than a century later, much the same judgment befell Judah, this time at the hands of the rising Babylonian empire. Rather than being dispersed beyond recovery, however, the Jews exiled to Babylonia struggled fiercely to maintain and strengthen their identity. The ebb and flow of history also came to their aid as a Persian upstart named Cyrus conquered Babylonia in 539 B.C. and reversed the policy of exiling defeated peoples. Many Jews gradually returned to Jerusalem to rebuild the temple, determined to recapture the dream of a theocracy. Many others remained abroad and established strong Jewish communities in cities from Spain to Mesopotamia.

War again swept through the region as Alexander the Great overthrew Cyrus' distant successor in 333 B.C. Hellenistic rule was imposed on the Jews first from Egypt, governed by Alexander's successors the Ptolemies, then from Syria, controlled by another line of successors, the Seleucids. When a Syrian king tried to force the Jews to abandon the law of Moses, however, rebellion blazed, led by Judas Maccabeus, and the Jews gained their independence for the first time in more than four centuries. Judas' successors restored a Jewish kingdom that prospered for a time, but ultimately could not resist the imperial expansion of the greatest of the ancient empires: Rome. The last kings to sit enthroned in Jerusalem were men who owed their power entirely to the Roman emperor.

The land of Israel had endured dominion from all directions, but the writers of both Old and New Testaments were sure of one thing: events in that much-contested place were more significant than any in the world's great power centers. The land of promise never climbed to the pinnacle of imperial glory, but its greatest leaders—from the shepherd-king to the carpenter acclaimed as "king of kings [Rev. 17:14]"—have exercised more influence over human history than any pharaoh or caesar.

Top left: King Solomon, from a 12th-century Latin Bible.

The Land of Promise

What stopped the Israelites at the edge of the Promised Land?

After almost a year at Mount Sinai, the Israelites had become restless and resentful. As they made their way north toward the Promised Land of Canaan, they complained of the hardships of the journey. Twelve scouts were sent ahead to investigate Canaan. Ten came back with negative reports—the land was indeed bountiful and beautiful, NUM. 30:32 they said, but it "devours its inhabitants"; the people liv- NUM. 13:32 ing there were "men of great stature . . . and we seemed to ourselves like grasshoppers, and so we seemed to them." Not only were the Canaanites giants, they also looked like better soldiers.

Only two of the scouts urged invasion. Caleb NUM. 13:30 said simply: "We are well able to overcome it." NUM. 14:8 And Joshua added: "If the Lord delights in us, he will bring us into this land."

Displeased with the people's lack of faith in him, God decided the entire generation was not up to the challenge of conquering the Promised NUM. 14:22 Land: "None of the men who have seen my glory and my signs which I wrought in Egypt and in the wilderness . . . shall see the land." But instead of giving up his plans completely, God decreed that the people wander for 40 years; then he would bring in their children's generation, so that the world would see his faithfulness (and the people's lack of faith). Because they believed in God's promise, only Caleb and Joshua were allowed to enter Canaan.

Why were Moses and Aaron barred from the Promised Land?

The action that disqualified Moses and Aaron is vividly described in Numbers 20. When the people needed water in the desert, God instructed Moses and Aaron to take Moses' famous rod, stand before a large rock, and tell it to yield water. Instead of following God's command, Moses ✳

A stained glass panel shows Moses' spies returning with huge grapes, proof of Canaan's bounty.

turned on the complaining multitudes and vented his frustration with them: "Hear NUM. 20:10 now, you rebels; shall we bring forth water for you out of this rock?" Then, lifting his hand, he struck the rock twice with the rod.

Surprisingly, the water gushed forth, and the people and the animals drank. This miracle was a turning point in God's treatment of Moses and Aaron. Moses had given credit for the miracle to himself instead of God. "Because NUM. 20:12 you did not believe in me," God said, "to sanctify me in the eyes of the people of Israel, therefore you shall not bring this assembly into the land which I have given them."

Grace and pathos mark Moses' last hours, told at the end of Deuteronomy. He climbed a high mountain called Nebo, and spread before him was all of the Promised Land. To the north he could see beyond the Sea of Chinnereth (Galilee) to "Gilead as far as Dan," to the south and DT. 34:1 east the great deserts, and on the west the Mediterranean. Then "Moses the servant of the Lord DT. 34:5 died there" and was buried by God himself.

Was Canaan truly a land of milk and honey?

In commissioning Moses to lead the people out of Egypt, God spoke of the agricultural richness and diversity that awaited them in Canaan; this was confirmed by reports of the region's fabulous productivity that had long circulated in the ancient Middle East. The Egyptian "Story of Sinuhe" (c. 1900 B.C.) described Canaan as "a good land. . . . Figs were in it, and grapes. It had more wine than water, plentiful was its honey, abundant its olives. Every kind of fruit was on its trees. Barley was there and emmer wheat. There was no limit to any [kind of] cattle."

However, the Israelites could not just walk into Canaan and start enjoying all its natural bounty. The Canaanites were already settled in the fertile, well-watered river valleys, and they were ready and able to fight off intruders. Thus for many years the Israelites farmed the fringe areas, which were forested, hilly, and dry. These uncultivated areas, often covered with wildflowers and native vegetation, were lands of milk and honey in the sense that they were suitable for bees and grazing livestock but not for growing crops.

It took time—probably several generations—to clear the forested hills and construct terraces that would prevent the runoff of precious water, minimize erosion, and provide level surfaces for planting and cultivation. Drought was common in the region, and the distribution of rainfall was almost impossible to predict. The odds were that in any year some people somewhere in Canaan would be suffering the effects of drought.

Moses had prepared his people for these challenges by telling them, "The land which you are entering . . . is not like the land of Egypt . . . where you sowed your seed and watered it with your feet." In time, the Israelites developed irrigation and other dry-farming methods and became masters of coaxing crops out of the arid land.

Thus "land flowing with milk and honey" did not necessarily mean an earthly paradise. It could mean a wild region inferior to productive farmland. When the prophet Isaiah used a similar image to describe hard times to come, "Every one that is left in the land will eat curds and honey," the people understood his message. IS. 7:22

DT. 11:10

EX. 3:8

What miracle allowed the Hebrews to cross the Jordan?

Crossing the Jordan marked the official entry of the Israelites into the Promised Land, and the first chapters of the Book of Joshua emphasize the event's immense historical and religious importance. It was a dangerous time of the year to cross because "the Jordan overflows all its banks throughout the time of harvest," but God assured Joshua, "As I was with Moses, so I will be with you," and the people followed. JOS. 3:15 JOS. 3:7

During the crossing, the priests carried the ark of the covenant, representing the power of God, and as "the feet of the priests bearing the ark were dipped in the brink of the water," the river parted. "The waters coming down from above stood and rose up in a heap . . . and those flowing down toward the sea . . . were wholly cut off." The priests took the ark to the middle of the dry riverbed and "all Israel," including "forty thousand ready armed for war," crossed over to JOS. 3:15 JOS. 3:16 JOS. 3:17; JOS. 4:13

For 30 days the children of Israel mourned Moses, who died in the land of Moab within sight of the Promised Land he could never enter; a detail from a fresco in the Sistine Chapel.

The collapse of Jericho before the Hebrew invaders and their sacred ark is vividly depicted here by Edmund Dulac.

naanite strongholds. As Joshua planned his attack, he had an experience that closely paralleled Moses' encounter with the burning bush. A heavenly messenger with a sword in his hand appeared and told Joshua, "Put off your JOS. 5:15 shoes from your feet; for the place where you stand is holy"—words that almost exactly duplicated those spoken to Moses in Exodus.

Jericho was prepared for a siege, but the Israelites had other ideas about how to take the city. Once a day for six days, the soldiers marched around the city accompanied by seven priests with seven trumpets. "And the armed men went be- JOS. 6:9 fore the priests who blew the trumpets, and the rear guard came after the ark, while the trumpets blew continually." On the seventh day the Israelites marched seven times around the city, and then on Joshua's orders "the people JOS. 6:20 raised a great shout, and the wall fell down flat." Joshua's army poured into the city and demolished it as a sign of devotion to their Lord.

Recent archeological analyses of Jericho's ruins indicate that the city was completely destroyed in about 1400 B.C., some 150 years before the date most widely accepted for Joshua's invasion. Several of the findings, however, are similar to the biblical accounts. The destruction took place at the time of the spring harvest, the walls were destroyed, and the city was burned but apparently not plundered.

JOS. 4:18 the plains of Jericho. When the priests with the ark of the covenant came out of the river, "the waters of the Jordan returned to their place and overflowed all its banks, as before."

The separation of the waters of the Jordan clearly recalled the crossing at the Red Sea in the time of Exodus—an earlier instance of the Lord's presence at a decisive historical moment. Moreover, Joshua was seen as the new Moses, who with God behind him would lead the people in the conquest of Canaan.

How did Joshua destroy Jericho?

The capture of Jericho was Joshua's first major military objective after crossing the Jordan. Once the Israelites controlled Jericho, they could advance into the Jordan Valley and attack other Ca-

How quickly did the Israelites conquer Canaan?

Scholars suggest that the Israelites may have migrated into the land of Canaan little by little from surrounding areas. If that was so, the conquest involved a gradual incursion of seminomadic clans drifting into Canaan and taking over areas not strongly defended by the Canaanites. This idea finds support in the many biblical references to the Canaanite peoples after the Israelites arrived. Had the Canaanites not been around, there would seem to have been little need for the continual warnings against intermarriage and worshiping pagan gods.

The very first verse of Judges, the book that follows Joshua, indicates how much more there was to do after Joshua's conquests. "After the death of Joshua the people of Israel inquired of the Lord, 'Who shall go up first for us against the Canaanites, to fight against them?' " The many conflicts that make up the rest of the Book of Judges are the answer to that opening question. Though the occupation of Canaan may have been gradual, it was punctuated with fierce and bloody battles, as the books of Joshua and Judges attest. Archeological evidence has confirmed the stories of warfare at Ai, Lachish, Hazor, and other biblical battle sites.

JG. 1:1

"NO MERCY TO THEM"

To the Israelites the conquest of the Promised Land called for special rules of war. The Canaanites were no ordinary enemy. Not only did they worship gods that were offensive to the Lord, they also were firmly entrenched in the land God had promised to his chosen people. According to Deuteronomy, God demanded annihilation of the Canaanite culture: "When the Lord your God gives them over to you, and you defeat them; then you must utterly destroy them; you shall make no covenant with them, and show no mercy to them [Dt. 7:2]."

Because it was God who gave them victory, the Israelites believed that everything they captured—people, animals, treasure—belonged to God. These spoils of war, which might otherwise have been split among the victors, were "devoted" to God, forever removed from human use. "No devoted thing . . . shall be sold or redeemed; every devoted thing is most holy to the Lord [Lev. 27:28]."

The condition of being reserved for God was called *herem* in Hebrew. The nations of Canaan were *herem* because, God said, "they would turn away your [Israel's] sons from following me, to serve other gods [Dt. 7:4]."

In the most extreme form of

An eighth-century B.C. stone relief shows the Assyrians' brutal treatment of their prisoners.

herem, as at Jericho, the Israelites followed the command to "save alive nothing that breathes [Dt. 20:16]," but *herem* seldom meant utter destruction of people and property. At Ai, God allowed his people to divide "its spoil and its cattle [Jos. 8:2]."

Parallels to Israel's concept of *herem* were practiced by other nations in the Middle East. Mesha, a ninth-century B.C. king of Moab, boasted that he had massacred the entire Israelite population of Nebo as a sacrifice to his god, Ashtar-Kemosh.

Three Great Kings

What part did Samuel play in establishing the monarchy?

The last of the judges, Samuel was a national leader, a priest, and a seer or prophet. His role in establishing a kingship reveals the division of the Israelites into pro- and antimonarchical factions.

At first, Samuel opposed the Israelites' desire for a monarch, seeing it as a rejection of God's sovereignty. He warned of the demands a king could make: military conscription, forced labor, heavy taxes. The day would come, said Samuel, 1 SAM. 8:18 when "you will cry out because of your king . . . but the Lord will not answer you."

Samuel also felt that the demand for a king constituted a repudiation of his own leadership. Deeply hurt, he made the people publicly declare that he had always treated them fairly and never used his high position for personal gain. Nevertheless, once God had assured him that a king was acceptable, Samuel proceeded to help find and install Israel's first monarch, Saul.

What made people believe Saul would be a worthy king?

The son of Kish of the tribe of Benjamin, Saul was an unlikely choice for king of Israel. He was not from a dominant tribe like Judah, which might have been expected to provide a king, but from what he called "the least of the tribes of 1 SAM. 9:21 Israel." Although he was tall, handsome, and wealthy, he was shy and had no political ambitions. Through a series of vivid episodes (which may represent separate traditions), 1 Samuel reveals how Saul was transformed into a military leader with an unchallenged claim to be king.

In the first episode, God brought Saul and the prophet Samuel together by having Saul sent with a servant in search of lost asses. The servant led Saul to Samuel, who was revered as a seer with the ability to find what was lost. Saul was unaware that destiny awaited him and that God had told Samuel to expect this man of Benjamin: "You shall anoint him to be prince over my peo- 1 SAM. 9:16 ple Israel." The next day, as Samuel anointed Saul with oil, he informed Saul of God's choice. Thus began Saul's transformation. "God gave 1 SAM. 10:9 him another heart" and "the spirit of God came 1 SAM. 10:10 mightily upon him." People began to ask, "Is 1 SAM. 10:11 Saul also among the prophets?"

The second episode describes the public disclosure of God's decision. Without revealing that he had already anointed someone, Samuel gathered the people at Mizpah to select a king by lot: such a method, it was believed, left the choice to God. The lots inexorably picked the tribe, the

---

DAVID'S MUSIC CALMS THE SPIRIT OF SAUL

Darkness settled over King Saul's soul as he sat in his fortress in Gibeah, for "the Spirit of the Lord departed from Saul, and an evil spirit from the Lord tormented him [1 Sam. 16:14]." Depression and paranoia were robbing Saul of his ability to function as king. Alarmed at their ruler's deterioration, Saul's servants urged him to find a skilled musician to play the lyre and drive away the evil spirit.

Seemingly by chance, one of Saul's servants knew of such a person—David, the son of Jesse. Not only was David a musician; he was also a "man of valor, a man of war [1 Sam. 16:18]," a prudent young man blessed by God. Saul dispatched messengers to Jesse requesting David's presence.

At court the youth soon gained the king's affection. The music from David's lyre eased Saul's troubled mind, "so Saul was refreshed, and was well, and the evil spirit departed from him [1 Sam. 16:23]." In battle David fought at Saul's side as his personal armor-bearer. Saul sent word to Jesse that he wanted David to remain in his service, "for he has found favor in my sight [1 Sam. 16:22]." The bitter irony for Saul was that he had taken to his heart the very man destined to be the king's undoing. In obedience to God's wishes, the prophet Samuel had already anointed David as king in Saul's place.

family, and finally the individual—Saul.

1 SAM. 10:22 But where was he? He had "hidden himself among the baggage." The people brought

1 SAM. 10:24 him out to shouts of "Long live the king!" though many were skeptical of his ability.

His anointing and selection by lot did not immediately alter Saul's life, however, and he returned home. Then one day he heard that an Ammonite army had besieged an Israelite city and threatened to gouge out one eye of every male inhabit-

1 SAM. 11:6 ant. The "spirit of God" seized Saul again. He rallied the men of Israel to arms and saved the city, thereby silencing the skeptics. The people met at Gilgal and honored their new king with feasts.

Who was Saul's constant critic?

Practically from the moment they met, Saul found Samuel very difficult to please. Samuel's attitude perhaps combined his ambivalence about monarchy with his dismay over Saul's behavior. Reasons enough for Samuel's displeasure can be found in 1 Samuel, where Saul is described in some detail as being disobedient to God—and rash and foolish besides. In contrast, Saul's military victories over the enemies of Israel are

1 SAM. 14:47 only summarily praised: "Wherever he turned he put them to the worse. And he did valiantly . . . and delivered Israel out of the hands of those who plundered them."

Time and again Saul's battlefield successes collapsed into religious failures. For instance, as Saul prepared for his first engagement against the heavily armed Philistines, he mustered the ragtag Israelite army at the shrine of Gilgal so that Samuel could offer a preparatory sacrifice. Samuel had told Saul to wait for him seven days, but at the end of that time Samuel had not come. Saul's troops were so outnumbered and terrified that many were deserting, and the Philistines threatened to strike at any moment. Saul therefore decided that he must perform the duties of the priest. He proceeded to offer the sacrifice

1 SAM. 13:12 himself to gain "the favor of the Lord." Soon after, Samuel arrived, giving no explanation for his lateness, and angrily prophesied that Saul's foolish disobedience to God would cost him the ✳

The music of David's lyre comforts the brooding Saul, reclining on a leopard skin in this painting by W.L. Taylor.

kingdom. Thus, even before Saul's first victorious battle against the Philistines, Samuel informed him that God had decided to deny Saul and his descendants "kingdom over Israel for ever."

1 SAM. 13:13

Saul evidently acted with good intentions and plainly with considerable success, but it was not enough for Samuel. The aged prophet always demanded more exacting obedience and fiercely condemned him. Saul became despondent. With God and Samuel against him, he could not maintain his mental and emotional balance.

Who was the second king of Israel?

When Saul died in a disastrous defeat on Mount Gilboa, three of his sons, including Jonathan, his firstborn, were slain with him; his son Ish-

ACTS 13:22
"I have found in David the son of Jesse a man after my heart, who will do all my will."

The Books of Samuel consistently portray David as a man who is good-hearted. Through his years as the undeserving victim of Saul's hatred, David remained loyal to Saul, who was God's anointed king of Israel, refused to do him harm, and genuinely mourned his death. At the same time, David was a heroic figure who fought for God's people, almost always dispensed justice without self-interest, was faithful in his friendships and true to his promises. He was the friend of God's prophets and priests and sought to guide his actions by God's will.

Yet the Bible does not make David a sinless paragon of virtue. There is no attempt to justify his uncontrolled lust, which led to adultery with Bathsheba, or his subsequent arranging of the death of her husband Uriah on the battlefield. Also his decision to conduct a national census brought a pestilence from God that killed some "seventy thousand men." Still, David's heart nev- 2 SAM. 24:15 er became permanently hardened by power. He recognized his sins, showed repentance, and asked for forgiveness. In Psalm 51, said to have been composed by David after the death of Uriah, the speaker prays, "Create in me a clean PS. 51:10 heart, O God, and put a new and right spirit within me. Cast me not away from thy presence."

PHILISTINE. *The original Philistines inhabited the southwest coast of Palestine and were constantly at war with neighboring nations until Israel subdued them in the 10th century B.C. As archenemies of Israel, they are portrayed unfavorably in the Bible. The books of Judges, Samuel, and Kings contain numerous examples of their barbarism in the war with Israel. The prophet Ezekiel spoke of the "malice of heart" and "never-ending enmity [Ezek. 25:15]" of this warlike nation. Zechariah called the Philistines a "mongrel people [Zech. 9:6]."*

Philistine entered modern usage in 17th-century Germany, where university students looked down on the local populace as brutish and uncultured, and called them Philister, *the German equivalent of* Philistines. *Through the years the meaning evolved to describe anyone who was narrow-minded, materialistic, and unenlightened.*

bosheth (also called Ish-baal or Esh-baal) was not at Gilboa and survived. Saul's commander, Abner, installed Ish-bosheth as king over all the northern tribes of Israel, even though the Philistines dominated much of the area. Meanwhile, in 2 SAM. 2:4 the south, "the men of Judah . . . anointed David king over the house of Judah." During the years Saul's son ruled Israel, he and his supporters viewed David as a rebel and traitor. As 2 Samuel 2 SAM. 3:1 records, "There was a long war between the house of Saul and the house of David." Only after two assassins slew Ish-bosheth at his noontime rest was David's victory assured.

In what sense was David a man after God's "own heart"?

Samuel warned Saul that his dynasty would not 1 SAM. 13:14 continue because "the Lord has sought out a man after his own heart; and the Lord has appointed him to be prince over his people." Later, when Samuel went to anoint one of Jesse's sons, God indicated that his choice might be surpris- 1 SAM. 16:7 ing because "the Lord looks on the heart." In the New Testament, God's testimony was expanded: ✳

A silver plate from Constantinople shows Samuel anointing the head of young David, Israel's future king.

A Hebrew contract bears the image of Jerusalem encircled by mountains.

JERUSALEM: CITY OF DAVID

The Jebusite stronghold of Jerusalem, or Jebus, as it was known, had held out against the surrounding Israelites for centuries. Lying near the border of Israel and Judah, the city provided the perfect spot for David to establish the central capital of a united Israel, unlike his old capital of Hebron, which lay deep inside Judah.

The citadel was so strongly fortified, however, that the Jebusites boasted that "the blind and the lame [2 Sam. 5:6]" could

defend it. But David attacked through an opening that was probably thought impassable. He sent men through a near-vertical water shaft that connected the fortress to the Gihon spring outside the walls. Archeologists have uncovered this shaft: it would have made for a difficult—and almost certainly unexpected—point of attack.

David took the narrow hilltop "stronghold of Zion" and renamed it "the city of David [2 Sam. 5:7]." Rather than kill the inhabitants,

he made allies and aides of many of them.

Since David was creating a new capital, he repaired its fortifications and built his house of cedar there. But most important, he brought the ark of the covenant out of years of obscurity, and with a grand procession led it to a place of honor in Jerusalem. Thus he began the process that transformed a Jebusite stronghold into "Jerusalem, the holy city [Is. 52:1]."

How did David build his empire?

David's military skill, honed in years of struggle and backed by the newly reunited tribes of Israel, quickly turned the tide of defeat that had undermined Saul's reign. In two major battles David 2 SAM. 5:20 overwhelmed the Philistines "like a bursting flood" and further humiliated them by capturing their sacred idols.

With the Philistines subdued, David consolidated his control of Canaan. He reduced Moab to paying tribute, placed garrisons among the Edomites, and subjugated the Ammonites. Thus ✳

those pagan neighboring nations that had plagued Israel in earlier centuries were now its vassals.

With a solid power base in Canaan, David began to expand his kingdom. He was fortunate in that as he began his empire building, the larger empires of Egypt and Assyria were both in decline under weak rulers. Egypt was divided between north and south and had lost most of its influence in Canaan. Assyria, defending itself against Aramaean, or Syrian, raiders from the west and southwest, was unable to mount conquests.

Moving northward, David defeated a coalition of Aramaean tribes, which gave him all of Syria, including the great trade and cultural center of

187

Damascus, and lands stretching to the Euphrates. The irony of his victory is that David may have weakened the Aramaeans enough to take pressure off Assyria and allow it to gather new strength for its imperial ambitions. Two centuries later, Assyrian forces conquered Israel.

Why did David's dynasty become part of Israel's religion?

2 SAM. 7:5 After he brought the ark of the covenant to Jerusalem, David wanted to build a temple for it—"a house" to replace the tent in which the ark was kept. But David's plan did not entirely meet with God's approval. Rather than David building God a house, God would build a house for David by establishing his descendants as the permanent 2 SAM. 7:16 rulers of Israel: "Your house and your kingdom shall be made sure for ever before me; your throne shall be established for ever." As part of that pledge God would allow David's son, Solo- 2 SAM. 7:13 mon, to "build a house for my name"—the Jerusalem temple.

Thus a divine promise, God's covenant with David, was believed to bind together the Davidic dynasty, the temple, and the city of Jerusalem. Not all the people, however, accepted the idea of an everlasting union of their nation, religion, and David's descendants. The northern tribes rebelled against David's grandson Rehoboam and gave up worshiping at the Jerusalem temple, preferring shrines such as Bethel that were hallowed by associations with the patriarchs.

When the last of David's royal descendants was overthrown by Babylon in the early years of the sixth century B.C., the apparent breach of God's promise caused the consternation reflect- PS. 89:39 ed in Psalm 89. Had God "renounced the cove- PS. 89:39 nant" with David and "defiled his crown in the dust"? The confidence that God would not do so laid the basis for the expectation that a future descendant of David, an anointed king, the Messiah, would once again sit on David's throne.

How could Solomon, a younger son, inherit David's throne?

Dynastic struggles plagued the later years of David's reign. First, David's eldest son Amnon was killed by order of Absalom, David's third son, because he had raped Tamar, Absalom's sister and Amnon's half sister. David's second son Chileab had apparently died, and Absalom, now the eldest, was so impatient to take over that he led a

---

Intrigued by stories of King Solomon's fabulous wealth and wisdom, the queen of Sheba is shown in this 15th-century panel traveling from Arabia to Jerusalem to meet the renowned monarch.

rebellion that nearly overthrew David. As the battle turned against Absalom, however, he fled on 2 SAM. 18:9 a mule and, passing under an oak tree, "his head caught fast in the oak, and he was left hanging."

That made Adonijah, David's fourth son, next in line. As the aged king lay dying, Adonijah and his powerful supporters, including Joab, feasted in anticipation of his coronation.

But one of David's younger sons, Solomon, held a trump card. His mother, Bathsheba, was David's favorite wife. Backed by the prophet Nathan and Zadok, a senior priest, she reminded the dying king that he had once promised the throne to her son. Bathsheba's argument prevailed. David ordered the immediate anointing of Solomon as king. The news cut short Adonijah's feast, and his guests fled in fear.

What seeds of ruin did Solomon sow?

In many ways the reign of Solomon was a golden age—a wise king sat on a secure throne, and there was prosperity in Israel. As later chroniclers looked back at Solomon's rule, however, they saw signs of weakness and decay.

In pushing Israel's diverse society toward a centralized empire, Solomon demanded more efficient tax collection, which in turn required the establishment of administrative districts. The new districts, however, did not correspond to the

Author of 3,000 proverbs, King Solomon is framed by his temple in this 15th-century manuscript.

old tribal territories, undermining tribal strength; and worse, Solomon apparently exempted his native Judah from taxation. Resentment over these acts may have fueled the rebellion that marred Solomon's final years.

Solomon's ambitious building projects, requiring ever greater use of forced labor gangs, also created stresses that hastened the end of Israel's golden age. Although David had pressed subjugated peoples into forced labor, Solomon took the highly controversial step of conscripting the Israelites themselves, sending vast numbers of them to Lebanon to get wood and stone for his buildings. The hatred generated by this perceived enslavement of free Israelites was a bitter heritage for Solomon's son, Rehoboam.

The empire that David had built by military prowess Solomon tried to maintain by dynastic marriages. Each foreign princess he married, however, brought along her ancestral deities and the altars and sanctuaries associated with them. With cosmopolitan tolerance Solomon often worshiped with his pagan wives. In so doing, the great builder of the renowned temple of God in Jerusalem became a major patron of a whole pantheon of pagan deities. For Israel's historians this excess of Solomon above all others sowed the seeds of destruction for the united kingdom of Israel.

A Land Divided

Why did Israel split into two kingdoms after Solomon's death?

When Solomon died, it fell to his son, Rehoboam, to deal with the old rivalries between the northern and southern tribal regions. One of the leaders of the northern contingent was Jeroboam. Once an official in charge of forced labor under Solomon, he had rebelled and fled to Egypt. With the change of leadership in Jerusalem, Jeroboam returned to Israel.

Jeroboam and other northern leaders called Rehoboam to the city of Shechem in the north, where they petitioned him to relax the harsh conscription and taxation policies of his father. 1 KG. 12:6 Instead of listening to the counsel of the "old men," Rehoboam followed the advice of his 1 KG. 12:8 peers, the "young men." His response was harsh 1 KG. 12:14 and scornful: "My father made your yoke heavy, but I will add to your yoke; my father chastised you with whips, but I will chastise you with scorpions [whips with studs]."

The northern tribes answered with rebellion. When Rehoboam sent out Adoram, his taskmaster, to conscript laborers, the people of the north stoned Adoram to death. Rehoboam was forced to flee in his chariot to Jerusalem, where he began to build an army to subdue the rebels.

Rehoboam called off an invasion, however, when the prophet Shemaiah told him that God commanded, "You shall not go up or fight 1 KG. 12:24 against your kinsmen the people of Israel." In addition to following God's orders, Rehoboam's decision was militarily sound. Invading the northern region, whose population and territory were greater than Judah's, promised no certain victory.

Thus the kingdom united under David and Solomon broke in two. The Davidic dynasty ruled the southern kingdom of Judah, with its center at Jerusalem. The people of the northern kingdom, henceforth called Israel, crowned Jeroboam their ruler, and he made Shechem his royal city.

Did the political split affect how people worshiped?

In establishing a new monarchy in the north, Jeroboam and his supporters rejected Jerusalem not only as a political center but also as a religious one and set up new holy places for worshiping God at Bethel and Dan. In a sense, this was a restoration of earlier practices, since both Bethel and Dan had long histories as the sites of religious shrines for Israel's tribes; but Jeroboam had more than his people's religion in mind. At stake, he felt, was his very survival: "If this people 1 KG. 12:27 go up to offer sacrifices . . . at Jerusalem, then the heart of this people will turn again to their lord, to Rehoboam king of Judah, and they will kill me."

In the eyes of those faithful to the Jerusalem temple, Jeroboam was guilty of apostasy for constructing golden calves (young bulls) in Bethel and Dan. It is possible, however, that Jeroboam and his people saw the images as serving the same purpose as the great golden cherubim (likely in the form

King Jeroboam risks the wrath of God by sacrificing at a rival shrine in this 18th-century painting by Jean-Honoré Fragonard.

THE KINGS OF JUDAH AND ISRAEL

Judah	Date	Israel
REHOBOAM	922 B.C.	JEROBOAM
Egypt invades Jerusalem, the capital of Judah.		Establishes temples at Bethel and Dan.
ABIJAM	915 B.C.	War between Israel and Judah.
ASA	913 B.C.	
Destroys pagan sanctuary established by his father.		
	901 B.C.	NADAB
	900 B.C.	BAASHA
Allies with Syria against Baasha. Builds new cities.		
	877 B.C.	ELAH
	876 B.C.	ZIMRI/OMRI
		Omri establishes Samaria as the capital.
JEHOSHAPHAT	873 B.C.	Period of prosperity and expansion.
Establishes judicial system.		
	869 B.C.	AHAB
		Joins Judah against Syria; Elijah prophesies.
	850 B.C.	AHAZIAH
JEHORAM	849 B.C.	JEHORAM
		Allies with Jehoshaphat against Moab.
AHAZIAH/ATHALIAH	842 B.C.	JEHU
Ahaziah joins Jehoram of Israel against Syria.		Fights against the worship of Baal; Elisha active as prophet.
JEHOASH	837 B.C.	
Repairs temple. Syria takes Gath, threatens Jerusalem.		
	815 B.C.	JEHOAHAZ
		In constant battle against Syria.
	801 B.C.	JEHOASH
AMAZIAH	800 B.C.	Jehoash battles Amaziah.
Supports law of Moses.	786 B.C.	JEROBOAM II
		Israel's boundaries restored.
UZZIAH (Azariah)	783 B.C.	Period of prosperity.
Fights the Philistines.		
	746 B.C.	ZECHARIAH
Jotham becomes regent.	745 B.C.	SHALLUM/MENAHEM
JOTHAM	742 B.C.	
Establishes cities; Isaiah and Micah active as prophets.		Menahem pays tribute to Assyria
	738 B.C.	PEKAHIAH
	737 B.C.	PEKAH
		Fights Assyria.
AHAZ	735 B.C.	
Fights Syria and Israel and loses. Sends tribute to Assyria.		Assyria takes parts of Israel; many deported.
	732 B.C.	HOSHEA
		Pays tribute to Assyria.
	721 B.C.	**Fall of Samaria.**
HEZEKIAH	715 B.C.	
Rebels against Assyria; institutes religious reform.		
MANASSEH	687 B.C.	
AMON	642 B.C.	
JOSIAH	640 B.C.	
Establishes religious reform.		
JEHOAHAZ/JEHOIAKIM	609 B.C.	
Pays tribute to Egypt.		
JEHOIACHIN	598 B.C.	
Jerusalem taken by Babylonia; many deported.		
ZEDEKIAH	597 B.C.	
Fall of Jerusalem.	587 B.C.	

An eighth-century B.C. Syrian inlay.

Thrown from her window on Jehu's orders, Jezebel is devoured by dogs as shown in this 17th-century stained glass window from an English church.

JEZEBEL. *Ruthlessly corrupt, King Ahab's Phoenician wife Jezebel epitomized vice and immorality in the Bible. Her bloodthirsty campaign to wipe out Israel's religion and replace it with the Canaanite fertility cult earned her lasting infamy. Today jezebel implies a wanton, wicked woman.*

Jezebel met a gruesome end at the hands of Jehu, an Israelite general chosen by God to be king of Israel and destroy King Ahab's line. At Jehu's command, the palace eunuchs hurled Jezebel from her window. The palace dogs ate her body, leaving only "the skull and the feet and the palms of her hands [2 Kg. 9:35]."

Jehu's name, too, has a modern connotation: a jehu is a fast or reckless driver. In the biblical episode, a palace sentry spied a chariot approaching at breakneck speed and observed, "The driving is like the driving of Jehu . . . for he drives furiously [2 Kg. 9:20]."

of winged bulls) that stood in Solomon's temple in Jerusalem. This possibility seems to be dismissed by the historians of the Hebrew Bible. They consistently favor the southern kingdom and the Davidic dynasty and condemn the northern kingdom for its failure to worship God at the Jerusalem temple.

Why was Israel known as the land of Omri?

Under the Omride dynasty in the ninth century B.C., the northern kingdom, Israel, may have surpassed even the heyday of Solomon's united kingdom in wealth and prosperity, though not in territory. However, the Bible gives scant notice to the reigns of Omri and his son Ahab, and the mention of any northern kings, especially Ahab, is almost always an occasion to condemn them for promoting the cult of Baal.

Much nonbiblical evidence suggests that the Omride reign was in some ways the high point of Israelite history. Long after the dynasty had fallen, Assyrian records continued to call Israel "the land of Omri." Archeological records also indicate that under the Omride kings the northern city of Samaria reached a zenith of splendor.

Considered in political rather than religious terms, Omri seems to have been a strong and able ruler who strengthened his country against the Syrians through an alliance with the king of Tyre and reconquered Moab. He developed a cordial relationship with Judah that brought some years of peace and mutual prosperity, which continued under Ahab and his Judean counterpart, Jehoshaphat. Then, when Jehoram, Jehoshaphat's successor in the south, married "the daughter of Ahab," the two royal families 2 KG. 8:18 became related by marriage. The Omride dynasty effectively ended with the deaths of Ahaziah and Jehoram and Jehu's subsequent slaughter of everyone who was associated with the house of Ahab.

How did the northern kingdom of Israel come to an end?

From the outset of the divided kingdom, the northern kingdom held an advantage. Its strategic location, straddling the trade routes between Egypt and the eastern empires, encouraged economic development. By contrast, the southern kingdom of Judah was something of a backwater. However, pressures from within and without kept Israel in constant political turmoil, and while it probably outstripped the southern kingdom in wealth and political clout for most of its existence, Israel lacked the stability to stand up to the increasing encroachments of its powerful neighbors. The Bible also attributes Israel's decline to its worship of alien gods.

In the eighth century B.C., from beyond the Euphrates, the Assyrian Empire reasserted itself, and, under Tiglath-pileser III (called Pul in the Bible), it became a dominant power. His conquests created a realm of vassal states and provinces, bringing virtually the entire Middle East under Assyrian control.

Assyria's takeover of Israel started gradually but ended with severe subjugation. The Bible reports that Menahem, king of Israel, began to pay tribute to Assyria. Menahem's son and successor was Pekahiah, who ruled just two years before being murdered by the usurper Pekah, who broke with Assyria and was then himself slain and replaced by Hoshea. According to biblical and nonbiblical sources, Hoshea was a vassal of Assyria, but eventually he too rebelled. Apparent-

Because he refused to repent for his sins, Nebuchadnezzar lost his kingdom and was condemned to graze like an ox.

ly, the Assyrian rulers had had enough of unruly kings. Led by Shalmaneser V (Assyrian emperor, 727–722 B.C.) and Sargon II (721–705 B.C.), Assyrian forces destroyed Samaria and (as reported in an inscription by Sargon II himself) carried away 27,290 of its inhabitants into captivity. This ended the existence of the northern kingdom of Israel as an independent nation.

Why did Nebuchadnezzar attack and destroy Jerusalem?

After defeating the Egyptian forces at Carchemish in 605 B.C., the Babylonians became the new masters of what had once been the Assyrian Empire. The kingdom of Judah under King Jehoiakim became one of the numerous vassal states paying tribute to Babylonia. But following a battle in 601 B.C. in which Egypt bested Babylonia, Judah and several neighboring states surmised that the Babylonians' power had waned, and they and their neighbors rebelled. This was a major blunder. Nebuchadnezzar (circa 605–562 B.C.) regrouped his forces and mounted a swiftly successful siege of Jerusalem. In 597 B.C. his army plundered Solomon's temple and decimated the society by deporting to Babylon "10,000" skilled 2 KG. 24:14 workers, leading citizens, and the king of Judah, Jehoiachin, and his family.

Nebuchadnezzar then placed Zedekiah, Jehoiachin's uncle, on the throne. Soon Zedekiah also became involved in a conspiracy against Babylonia (a plot opposed by the prophet Jeremiah). In the ensuing war Jerusalem suffered a siege lasting a year and a half. Finally, when the inhabitants of the city were beginning to starve, the wall of Jerusalem was breached on the ninth of Tammuz (July), 587 B.C.

Nebuchadnezzar made an example of the city. He deported its remaining inhabitants to Babylon; and on the ninth of Av (August), 587 B.C., his forces razed Jerusalem, including the center of Jewish national and religious identity, Solomon's temple. Zedekiah, the rebellious vassal king, received a brutal punishment: "They slew the sons 2 KG. 25:7 of Zedekiah before his eyes, and put out the eyes of Zedekiah, and bound him in fetters, and took him to Babylon." With the end of the kingdom of Judah, the awesome responsibility of preserving the Jewish heritage fell to the captives deported to Babylon.

Babylonian Exile

How was the exile of Judah different from the exile of northern Israel?

For inhabitants of the northern kingdom, the two Assyrian deportations in 732 and 721 B.C. meant their end as a distinct people. Much of the dispersed population lost its identity among the Assyrians, vanishing into memory as the Ten Lost Tribes. By contrast, the Babylonian exile was only an interlude—traumatic but temporary—in the continuing existence of Judah, whose people became the only surviving remnant of the original united Israelite nation.

Several factors accounted for these different circumstances. In the north, Assyria maintained the economy of the conquered region by importing colonists to repopulate the cities. Babylon, on the other hand, simply let Judah languish for decades, impoverished and depopulated. The Assyrian policy radically altered the ethnic, cultural, and religious character of the northern kingdom, eventually producing the Samaritan people, while Babylonian policy ultimately allowed the Jews to reassert their national identity.

Just as important was Judah's own internal development. Unlike Israel, which was divided into rival tribes and clans with little real unity, Judah had spent four centuries under a stable Davidic dynasty based in the great unifying center of Jerusalem. At the time of their exile, the Jews of the south had a deep devotion to the Mosaic law, the temple, and Jerusalem that helped to sustain their culture. Indeed, the exile, far from diluting their traditions, encouraged these Jews to focus on them more clearly.

Why does the Bible refer to Cyrus as God's "anointed"?

The Persian king Cyrus was one of history's brilliant upstarts, a vassal king who by 539 B.C. had conquered the Medes and the even mightier Babylonians. When he took over the vast realm of Babylonia, Cyrus reversed the policies of deportation and destruction that had long been in force. Practicing tolerance toward the diverse peoples of his empire, he supported the restoration of many ruined sanctuaries. In line with that policy, Cyrus in 538 B.C. authorized the Jews in Mesopotamia to return to Jerusalem and rebuild their temple, even replacing the sacred vessels of silver and gold that Nebuchadnezzar had plundered. Little wonder, then, that the Book of Isaiah describes Cyrus as God's "anointed." IS. 45:1

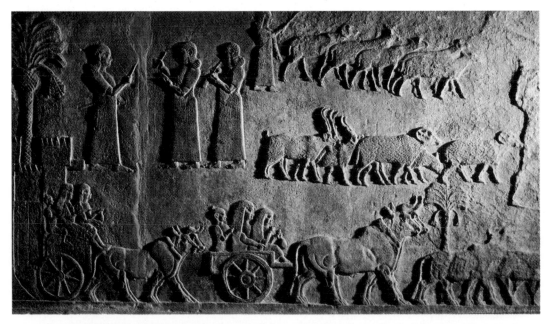

Assyrian officials count the flocks seized for King Tiglath-pileser III as deportees are carted away to repopulate other parts of the empire in this eighth-century B.C. relief.

SCATTERING OF A PEOPLE

A Jew traveling to any major city and most smaller towns across the Roman Empire could be confident of finding Jewish compatriots who would give him lodging, direct him to the local synagogue, and help him to find food that did not violate the dietary laws. Early in the first century A.D. the Greek geographer Strabo wrote of the Jews: "This people has already made its way into every city, and it is not easy to find any place in the habitable world which has not received this nation."

At that time probably 60 to 70 percent of all Jews lived outside Palestine, and major Jewish communities in Babylonia, Egypt, and Asia Minor had existed for several centuries. The Diaspora had begun with the Babylonian exile and the flight of many Jews to Egypt in the early sixth century B.C. But during the period of Hellenistic rule from the late fourth century B.C. onward, commerce and the fortunes of war caused many Jews to migrate throughout the Hellenistic empires and as far west as Rome and Spain.

By the first century B.C., the largest and most exemplary Diaspora community was in the Egyptian city of Alexandria. Jews came from all levels of society, worked in all areas of crafts and commerce, and included a few very wealthy families. For example, Alexander Lysimachus was a chief financial administrator in Egypt rich enough to plate the gates of the temple in Jerusalem with gold and silver; his brother, the philosopher Philo, was a prolific author and the most brilliant contributor to a long tradition of Jewish literature in Alexandria.

Under foreign rule Jews knew both tolerance and persecution: above, an Istanbul synagogue built under Ottomans.

The Jews in Alexandria formed a peaceful community with their own governing authorities but did not share full Alexandrian citizenship. In the first century A.D., when they strove to gain citizens' rights (without agreeing to worship the city's pagan gods), violent anti-Jewish riots broke out. Many Jews were murdered and their synagogues ruined.

Similarly, in other parts of the Mediterranean world the Jews were usually accepted as an ancient people with their own distinctive culture and religion, but they were always outsiders in pagan society. Political or economic conflicts could precipitate persecutions or expulsions. Each Jewish community developed its own way of maintaining peace with the surrounding culture.

Besieged for the second time by Nebuchadnezzar's army, Jerusalem's citizens held out for months before their walls finally crumbled beneath the battering ram.

How did the exile affect Judaism as a whole?

The Babylonian exile sharply redirected the flow of Israel's history. Judah, previously an independent monarchy, was reduced to a colonial province. Even with the restoration of the temple in Jerusalem, Jewish history would thereafter follow a double path of two cultures: the Jews of Palestine and the Jews of the Dispersion.

The exile had shaken cherished beliefs in the invulnerability of the temple, God's earthly dwelling place. But it also fostered a new emphasis on the universality of God, who would be with his people wherever they went. It forced Jews, wrenched from the safety of homeland, to choose between their belief in one God and the easy apostasy of polytheism. Strict observance of the Sabbath, circumcision, and the other rites of the law were increasingly stressed as the marks of a loyal Jew. Tradition became a living reality, a defense of Jewish identity in a threatening world.

Even greater emphasis was placed by the Jews on preserving their heritage in writing. Traditions that had been handed down orally from one generation to the next, often in different versions, were set down on scrolls. The oracles of the prophets, the regulations of the priests in the lost temple, and the histories of the nation from Joshua to 2 Kings all took shape. The people of Israel were becoming "the people of the book."

What attitudes did the Jews have toward their exile?

The long exile produced reactions ranging from anger and despair to acceptance and hope. One of the most poignant psalms gives voice to the exiles' longing: "If I forget you, O Jerusalem, let PS. 137:5 my right hand wither! Let my tongue cleave to the roof of my mouth, if I do not remember you, if I do not set Jerusalem above my highest joy."

Along with this yearning for home—and rage at the Babylonians and others who had destroyed Jerusalem—was a feeling of resignation, especially among those who viewed the captivity as an act of divine punishment, not as an imperial conquest. "Thus says the Lord of hosts," Jere- JER. 29:4 miah wrote in a famous letter to the exiles: "Build houses and live in them; plant gardens JER. 29:5 and eat their produce. Take wives and have sons and daughters. . . . Seek the welfare of the city where I have sent you into exile, and pray to the Lord on its behalf, for in its welfare you will find your welfare."

How did the dispersion of the Jews aid early Christianity?

Spanning the ancient world from India to Spain, the Diaspora proved crucial to the survival of the infant Christian faith. By the first century A.D., the Hebrew Scriptures had been translated for the use of Diaspora communities into Greek and Aramaic, the languages of international commerce and culture. The Greek translation, called the Septuagint, soon became the standard scripture for Christians, whose New Testament was also written in Greek.

At the same time, synagogues of the Dispersion provided models for the organization and worship services of fledgling Christian congregations. Indeed, many early churches were offshoots of synagogue congregations and were made up largely of converted members.

Just as important, many of the key teachings of Christianity had been given special emphasis in the Jewish Diaspora—for example, the doctrine of monotheism. The Jews of the Dispersion, stressing the universality of God and his rightful authority over all nations, had developed arguments to defend their belief in one God against the colorful pantheons of pagan religions.

THE STRATEGY OF DEPORTATION

Most of the great empires of the ancient world used the threat of exile, deportation, or dispersion to keep vassal nations in submission. By dissolving an entire population, or simply removing the upper classes that could lead a rebellion, imperial overlords killed the seed of defiance before it could take root.

As early as the 18th century B.C., the famous legal code of Hammurabi had cursed any ruler who violated its statutes, calling on the gods to bring about "the destruction of his city, the dispersion of his people . . . the disappearance of his name and memory from the land!" Inscriptions left by victorious kings from then on boast of mass deportations. One Hittite king uprooted 15,000 subjects in one year and 66,000 in another. In the 13th century B.C. Rameses II of Egypt reportedly moved entire populations around in every direction. At about the same time, Shalmaneser I, Assyria's first great warrior-king, recorded that he banished the young people of

Tears of the exiles flow into the waters of Babylon in a 12th-century miniature.

Urartu to Assyria and exiled another 14,400 from the middle Euphrates region. Beginning in the ninth century B.C., every Assyrian king who fought foreign campaigns used the exile of defeated populations as a means of consolidating the victory.

Thus when Tiglath-pileser III captured a large portion of Israel

in 732 B.C., it was all but inevitable that "he carried the people captive to Assyria [2 Kg. 15:29]." Eleven years later, when the stronghold of Samaria was captured, 27,290 more people were deported, according to an inscription set up by Sargon II. In their place Sargon settled deportees from other defeated nations, including Arab tribes, Babylonians, and Syrians. The Babylonian kings who overthrew the Assyrian Empire in 612 B.C. carried on the tradition, and King Nebuchadnezzar removed Jews from the southern kingdom of Judah in 597 and 587 B.C.

Long after these exiles of Old Testament times, similar methods were used to weaken and subdue the Jews. After the Judean revolt against Rome in A.D. 66–70, thousands of Jews were shipped off to serve as slave laborers or to be killed in gladiatorial shows. Finally, after the revolt led by Simon Bar Kochba from A.D. 132 to 135, all Jews were deported from Jerusalem and banned from entering the city; pagan colonists were settled in their place.

Return to Zion

Did all the Jews return from Babylon?

By the time King Cyrus allowed them to return to Jerusalem and rebuild their temple, most Jews in Babylon were too young ever to have seen their ancestral homeland. Almost a human life span had passed from the first exile in 597 B.C. to Cyrus' liberating decree of 538 B.C. Though the Jews knew that they lived in exile, they also knew that their Babylonian community represented their people's elite. Their law and tradition, more than the Jerusalem temple, gave them their identity. For these reasons many Jewish families decided to remain permanently in Babylon.

Still, soon after Cyrus' edict a group of Babylonian Jews returned to Jerusalem. Their leader was Sheshbazzar, who may have been a son of King Jehoiachin. Another expedition, led by Zerubbabel, set out in 522 B.C. According to the Books of Ezra and Nehemiah, nearly 50,000 Jews went with Zerubbabel.

After Zerubbabel's expedition more than seven decades elapsed before Nehemiah arrived in Jerusalem shortly after 445 B.C. Between Zerubbabel and Nehemiah, there may have been a few sporadic migrations, but they were probably not extensive, for the vitality of the Jewish community in Babylon seems to have been unaffected.

Why did it take so long to rebuild the temple?

In his original effort to rebuild the temple, Sheshbazzar succeeded only in laying the foundations. It appears that his temple project never received the funds "from the royal treasury" that Cyrus EZRA 6:4 had promised. Local opposition probably developed toward what was plainly the ambitious goal of a single religious group, and there seems also to have been a lack of commitment by the Jewish community during harsh economic times.

Eighteen years after Sheshbazzar's return, the appointment of Zerubbabel as Judah's governor in 520 B.C. coincided with rising public sentiment to rebuild the temple, a desire fanned by the prophets Haggai and Zechariah. The people lived in "paneled houses," Haggai scolded, HAG. 1:4 "while this house [the temple] lies in ruins."

However, Tattenai, the Persian governor of "Beyond the River," refused to believe that Zerubbabel had royal permission to rebuild. He insisted on a search for Cyrus' original decree in the royal archives in Babylon. The document was found; Darius I proclaimed that the temple's cost "be paid to these men in full and without EZRA 6:8 delay from the royal revenue"; and Zerubbabel, supported by the prophets and his high priest Jeshua, completed the second temple in 515 B.C.

What was Nehemiah's mission?

While serving in the trusted position of cupbearer to the Persian king Artaxerxes I (465–424 B.C.), Nehemiah learned that Jerusalem still lay in ruins. Zerubbabel's temple presided over broken city walls and a people "in great trouble and NEH. 1:3 shame." This news so upset Nehemiah that he begged for a royal appointment to rebuild "the NEH. 2:5 city of my fathers' sepulchres." Surprisingly, the king assented.

When he arrived in Jerusalem, Nehemiah was able to inspire the people to "rise up and build" the walls of the NEH. 2:18 holy city. The people had to endure ridicule, threats, and raids from the neighboring Samaritans, Ammonites, and Philistines, but in a mere 52 days of all-out determination the walls were soundly reconstructed, and Jerusalem became a defensible capital, a proud city once more.

Nehemiah served as governor of Judah in two separate terms. During those years he labored hard to restore justice to Judeans who had been impoverished by oppressive debts and

The Cyrus Cylinder, a cuneiform record, tells how the Persian king helped the Jews return to their homeland.

*The scribe Ezra reads the law
in this fresco taken from a ruined
Syrian city, Dura-Europos.*

shocked to find religious pluralism and tolerance of mixed marriages. When he discovered that "the holy race has mixed itself with the peoples of the lands," he wrote, "I rent my garments and my mantle, and pulled hair from my head and beard, and sat appalled." EZRA 9:2 EZRA 9:3

By intense moral pressure, Ezra persuaded many Jewish men, including some in the high priestly families, to divorce the non-Jewish "foreign women" and to disown their children. The rigor with which Ezra was willing to nullify the ties of over a hundred men to their wives and children and to splinter their families dramatically illustrates his extreme commitment to rooting out a lax religious mentality and reconstituting a nation based on devotion to the law. EZRA 10:44

Ezra had the law publicly read and interpreted for the people, and they began to celebrate the annual Feast of Booths and gathered for a national day of covenant renewal that included the confession of sin. Ezra's reforms left a permanent mark on the nation. His tenure was a major step toward Judea becoming a theocracy founded on the teaching of the priests and scribes.

ZION. *Determined to eradicate the last vestige of Canaanite power in Palestine, David attacked and captured "the stronghold of Zion, that is, the city of David," an event described in 2 Samuel 5:7. This passage refers to the Jebusite fortress on the southeastern hill of pre-Israelite Jerusalem. After Jerusalem was made Israel's religious and political capital at the beginning of the 10th century B.C., Zion became a synonym for the entire city.*

To Jews scattered by the Babylonian exile in 587 B.C., Zion, the holy city, symbolized their lost homeland and sovereignty. Zion, or Jerusalem, had been the site of the temple, God's earthly dwelling place. Psalm 137 laments the exile: "By the waters of Babylon, there we sat down and wept, when we remembered Zion." But the prophet Zechariah spoke of Israel's return, when "the Lord will again comfort Zion and again choose Jerusalem [Zech. 1:17]."

The Zion of the New Testament is the Jerusalem of the age to come—the "holy city" described in Revelation 21:2.

taxes and to establish a strong Jewish identity in the region. Still, his lasting memorial was his first mission: rebuilding the walls of the holy city.

How did Ezra alter the Jewish community?

Ezra's mission was to re-establish religious purity and obedience to the law among the Jews of Judah. In his commission from King Artaxerxes, Ezra was described as a priest, "the scribe of the law of the God of heaven." The term *scribe* meant that his position was similar to that of a government secretary or minister today. Thus Ezra was a royal minister for matters involving Jewish law. EZRA 7:12

Like Nehemiah, Ezra had been raised in Babylon in the spirit of rigorous devotion to the law and its traditions. Arriving in Judea, he was ✳

The Maccabees

Who were the Maccabees?

"Maccabees" is the popular designation for the family of Mattathias and his five sons, who ignited a revolt against Syrian persecution in 166 B.C. and eventually won independence for the Jewish nation. The name may come from the nickname "the Hammer" (in Aramaic, *maqqabah*), given to the most famous son, Judas Maccabeus. The family was also called the Hasmoneans after an ancestor named Hasmoneus.

When Antiochus IV struck down the law of Moses, he sent out officers to force Jews to join 1 MACC. 2:21 in pagan sacrifices and "desert the law." In the town of Modein north of Jerusalem, an officer encountered Mattathias, an elderly priest who re-1 MACC. 2:24 fused such apostasy. Mattathias so "burned with zeal" that he slew an apostate Jew on the pagan 1 MACC. 2:27 altar, then shouted, "Let every one who is zealous for the law . . . come out with me!"

Mattathias and his sons left everything they owned, fled to the rocky hills, and began to gather an army. They were joined by a group of zealous Jews called Hasideans, or pious ones, who saw the guerrilla war as a religious crusade. With a patchwork of diverse groups, the Jewish forces began to harass the Syrian oppressors.

A mask of Antiochus IV, whose persecution of the Jews ignited the Maccabean uprising.

Why was Judas Maccabeus a national hero?

When Mattathias lay dying shortly after the revolt had begun, he bypassed his older sons and named his third son, Judas, the new leader, calling him "a mighty warrior from his youth." 1 MACC. 2:66

Judas turned the revolt against persecution into a full-scale revolution for Jewish independence. In 166 B.C. he defeated Apollonius, the Syrian governor of Samaria, and captured Apollonius' sword, which he used "in battle the rest 1 MACC. 3:12 of his life." In 164 B.C. after a series of victories against some of the best generals in the Syrian kingdom, Judas regained control of the temple in Jerusalem and purified and rededicated it—a momentous event that has been celebrated ever after in the festival of Hanukkah. Judas continued to beat off Syrian attacks for years, but in 160 B.C., vastly outnumbered by a major Syrian army, he was slain in battle.

How long did the Hasmonean kingdom last?

Although Judas Maccabeus had recaptured the Jerusalem temple in 164 B.C., the Syrians held parts of the city for another 20 years. After his brother Simon finally expelled them, he was acclaimed as high priest and military commander. Simon's son John Hyrcanus (134–104 B.C.) took the same offices and consolidated national security by conquering neighboring regions of Judea. He forced the Idumeans in the south to convert to Judaism, thereby bringing into the nation the clan that would produce King Herod the Great.

Though he maintained Jewish independence, John Hyrcanus leaned increasingly toward Greek culture. His son Aristobulus I (104–103 B.C.) took the title of king and, while admiring Greek ways, forcibly converted the people of northern Galilee to Judaism, making it the Jewish region that it was in Jesus' time. Aristobulus I was succeeded by his hated brother Alexander Janneus (103–76), and Alexander in turn by his widow Salome Alexandra. After Alexandra died in 67 B.C., the dynasty was torn by internal warfare between her sons. One of them, Hyrcanus II, persuaded the Romans to intervene in the conflict, but once the Roman army under Pompey had arrived in 63 B.C., it would not leave. Jewish independence lasted 101 years after the recapture of the temple.

Determined to root out Judaism from his empire, Antiochus IV ordered the desecration of the temple and made war on Jerusalem's inhabitants, shown in the left-hand panels of a medieval illumination; led by Judas, the Maccabees took revenge on Seleucid troops in the right-hand panels.

A CLASH OF EMPIRES

The aftermath of Alexander the Great's conquests left Palestine bracketed by two powerful kingdoms: at the end of the fourth century B.C. the dynasty of the Ptolemies ruled Egypt to the south, and the Seleucid dynasty held Syria to the north.

Ptolemy I, one of Alexander's finest commanders, quickly took control of wealthy Egypt after his leader's death. There he established a kingdom run by a Greek and Macedonian elite with Alexandria as its capital. Ptolemy and his successors labored to make Egypt a center of Hellenistic culture, science, and education.

The Ptolemies seized control of Palestine in 301 B.C. and held the territory until 198 B.C. For the most part, they allowed the Jews to run their own affairs as a temple state. The high priest headed the Jewish government, and the law of Moses as applied by the priests and scribes served as its constitution.

In Syria, Seleucus, another of Alexander's commanders, established a vast kingdom that eventually reached from eastern Mesopotamia to the Aegean Sea.

War elephants march across a coin from Seleucus I's reign.

One of the ablest of Seleucus' successors was Antiochus III, called the Great, who in 198 B.C. wrested control of Palestine from the young Ptolemy V. At first Antiochus continued the same tolerant rule that the Ptolemies had allowed, but he soon suffered a serious defeat at the hands of the Romans and was forced to pay enormous war reparations. Attempts to confiscate funds from the temple in Jerusalem increased resentment toward Syria and encouraged a pro-Egypt faction among the Jewish aristocracy.

The animosity intensified during the reign of Antiochus IV (175–164 B.C.), who styled himself Epiphanes, meaning god manifest. He appointed a pro-Syrian high priest in Jerusalem, Jason, who immediately introduced Greek laws and customs. Among pious traditionalist Jews, there was a particularly strong reaction against the Syrian king and the many powerful Jewish "hellenizers" like Jason.

When Antiochus saw that his Jewish antagonists supported his Egyptian enemies, he responded violently. In 167 B.C. he banned obedience to the law of Moses entirely and required all Jews to conform to pagan practices. A Jew who kept dietary laws or the Sabbath or had a son circumcised could be punished by death. Worse, in their sacred temple Antiochus set up a pagan altar for sacrifices to the Olympian Zeus. The Jews felt that the temple itself had been desecrated and called the altar a "desolating sacrilege [Mt. 24:15]." Instead of humbling devout Jews and destroying Judaism, however, Antiochus' extremist policies ignited the Maccabean uprising in 166 B.C. that brought a century of Jewish freedom.

Herod and Rome

Herod appears to study Mary and Joseph as census officials interview the couple in a 14th-century mosaic from the Church of St. Savior in Istanbul.

CHRISTIAN. *Originally, Christian may have been a term that followers of Jesus associated with being scorned and persecuted. It occurs only three times in the New Testament and always seems to be used by non-Christians. Acts 11:26 places the origin of the term in Antioch around the fourth decade of the Christian era. The original Greek term, Christianos, combined the word Christ with the ending -ianos, a suffix derived from Latin and meaning belonging to or slave of.*

Before the end of the first century A.D., simply being a Christian could be a capital crime. A passage in the First Letter of Peter exhorted: "If one suffers as a Christian, let him not be ashamed, but under that name let him glorify God [1 Pet. 4:16]." The Roman historian Tacitus reflected popular prejudice when he described the "notoriously depraved Christians" whom Nero executed in A.D. 64 and spoke of "their guilt as Christians, and the ruthless punishment it deserved." Although to be labeled Christian could mean a death sentence, the believers began to call themselves Christians as a badge of honor.

Who was responsible for Herod the Great's political connections with Rome?

Herod's formidable career was built on the accomplishments and connections of his father, Antipater, a top government official. In a small country like Judea, political survival depended on picking the right side in the shifting struggles among powerful overlords, especially during the century-long Roman civil war. Like his father, Herod showed exceptional acumen in choosing masters who would further his ambitions.

Antipater had risen to power by allying himself with Hyrcanus II, one of the last of the Hasmoneans, who was locked in a dynastic fight with his brother Aristobulus II for the throne and high priesthood of Judea. Antipater's role as the right arm of Hyrcanus impressed Julius Caesar, who made Antipater a Roman citizen and the procurator (financial administrator) of Judea.

In 47 B.C. Antipater named his 25-year-old son Herod governor of Galilee. As energetic as his father, Herod set about clearing out bands of brigands in the region and, according to the ancient historian Josephus, gained the admiration not only of local citizens but of the governor of Syria, a cousin of Caesar's.

202

How did Herod, an Idumean, become king of the Jews?

After the assassination of Julius Caesar in 44 B.C. (and the poisoning of Herod's father a short while later), Herod's long friendship with another powerful Roman, Mark Antony, led to a high political appointment under Hyrcanus, the chief priest and ethnarch of Judea. Meanwhile, Herod had improved his political stature by becoming engaged to Mariamne, a princess of the royal Hasmonean family.

In 40 B.C. the army of Parthia, Rome's archrival, invaded Palestine, overthrew Hyrcanus, and put his nephew on the throne. Herod barely escaped from Judea with his life and fled to Rome. There Mark Antony and Octavian (later to become Augustus Caesar) cordially received him

PAX ROMANA: PEACE BACKED BY POWER

Roman armies marched relentlessly across the Mediterranean world in the second and first centuries B.C., forcing nation after nation to surrender to Rome's military might and forging a mighty empire that would last for hundreds of years.

With the death of Julius Caesar, the Roman republic, already unsteady, collapsed from civil strife among powerful rival generals; and war raged among the factions of such notables as Pompey, Brutus, Cassius, Lepidus, Mark Antony, and Cleopatra, until finally Octavian emerged victorious, becoming the first Roman emperor.

As *princeps*, meaning first citizen or prince, Octavian labored tirelessly to restore political tranquillity. Although he lacked the brilliance of some of his predecessors as a military strategist, his skillful reorganizing of the administration of the Roman Empire created a foundation for lasting peace and a framework for industrial, economic, and cultural progress

that came to be known as the *Pax Romana*, or Roman peace.

The triumph of Octavian, or Augustus (the Exalted), as he came to be called, over his enemies ushered in a long period of prosperity from about A.D. 30 to 180. This era of well-being did not signify an end to Rome's imperialism, however. It was by the threat of force that Augustus and his successors preserved peace and stability in an empire that eventually covered well over a million square miles. Rome did not hesitate to brutally suppress two major Jewish revolts in A.D. 70 and 135. Foreign taxes helped pay for public services, roads, and aqueducts at home. Nevertheless, Rome adopted a liberal attitude toward vanquished peoples, permitting provinces some self-government and allowing them to keep their religion and customs.

Augustus had desired to be the empire's prince of peace, and a generation of war-weary citizens

Wings spread majestically atop an army standard, the eagle symbolized the power and glory of Rome.

was happy to proclaim him its savior. In gratitude the Roman senate erected the magnificent Altar of Augustan Peace *(Pax Augusta)*. It memorialized the harmony of peoples under a Roman emperor whose piety and beneficence maintained peace with the gods.

Throughout most of the empire, travelers and traders moved safely over well-built roads and well-protected sea lanes, and the *Pax Augusta* also brought security from invasion, just laws, and effective administration. Under the umbrella of the Roman peace, Christianity as well as other movements spread with ease across the empire.

The infamous massacre of Jewish children ordered by King Herod is portrayed in this 16th-century wood painting.

and presented him to the senate, which unanimously appointed him king of Judea in the expectation that he could win the region back from the Parthians.

Over the next three years, using both local and Roman forces, he drove out the Parthians and their puppet king and captured Jerusalem and Judea. In 37 B.C. the 36-year-old Herod sat unchallenged on his throne as king of the Jews.

Was Herod a good ruler?

Herod began his 33-year reign with eight years of ruthlessly consolidating his power and ended it with an equal period of murderous family feud- ✳

ing as he weakened with disease and near madness. The middle years, however, were a period of prosperity and relative security in which Herod's most memorable works were accomplished. In honor of Augustus, he built the hellenized cities of Caesarea on the Mediterranean Coast and Sebaste (Greek for Augustus) on the site of Samaria, which had been destroyed by John Hyrcanus by 107 B.C. He founded other cities and fortresses in honor of his late parents and brother; and he built aqueducts, theaters, palaces, parks, and numerous public buildings such as the tomb of Abraham in Hebron. But the project that brought him the greatest fame was the magnificent reconstruction of the Jerusalem temple, on which work began in 20 B.C.

Why did Herod rebuild the temple?

Though Herod was a third-generation Jew, his Jewish political opponents cast doubt on his ethnic origins because his grandfather, a member of an Idumean clan, had been forcibly converted to Judaism by John Hyrcanus. As king of the Jews, Herod had reason to demonstrate his ties to Judaism in a dramatic way. The temple built by Zerubbabel 500 years earlier had been renovated a century before Herod's time, but it remained a modest structure. It did not match the growing splendor of Jerusalem or express for Jews the majesty of their deity. Herod set out to defuse his religious opposition and at the same time enhance the glory of his kingdom by rebuilding the temple with an opulence that even Solomon might not have imagined. The result was the largest and perhaps most impressive temple complex of the ancient world. "Whoever has not seen Herod's building," ran a popular saying, "has never seen anything beautiful."

According to historical evidence, Herod allowed only specially trained priests—reportedly 1,000 of them—to work on the construction of the temple itself, and their work was carried out behind curtains that hid the holy site from prying eyes. The temple was completed in a year and a half without interrupting the daily sacrifices. Herod dedicated it with a sacrifice of 300 oxen and great celebrations. The construction and decoration of the surrounding grounds and buildings in the temple complex continued for a number of years.

How was Palestine governed in Jesus' time?

By the time of Jesus' ministry little remained of the kingdom of Herod the Great. In northern Palestine three distinct regions bordered the Sea of Galilee. To the southeast was the Decapolis, a league of 10 self-governing cities, each thriving as a center of Hellenistic culture under the general supervision of the Roman governor of Syria. To the northeast was the predominantly non-Jewish area of Gaulanitis, ruled by Herod's son Philip, who had been granted this territory by Rome and given the title tetrarch, meaning a regional ruler of lesser status than a king. Unlike his father, Philip was praised for his modest and peace-loving disposition and his readiness to aid any person in need of justice. West of the sea lay Galilee, ruled by Philip's brother Herod Antipas, an ambitious and canny politician whom Jesus called "that fox." Both Philip and Antipas controlled their own economies, paying taxes directly to Rome.

I.K. 13:32

Palestine west of the Jordan and south of Galilee (formerly Samaria and Judah) made up the Roman province of Judea, which was nominally subordinate to Syria, but had its own Roman governor (prefect). Taxes were based on the Roman census carried out when the province was organized in A.D. 6 after Herod's son, Archelaus, was banished.

Did the Romans give Jews religious autonomy?

The governors appointed by Rome held supreme military, financial, and judicial authority and had broad administrative powers. This left a wide scope for misrule, and Judea repeatedly suffered from inept, corrupt, or malicious governors.

As a practical matter, however, the governors regularly allowed institutions such as the Sanhedrin court in Jerusalem self-government in local and religious affairs. Jewish national leadership was vested in the high priest, who was appointed by the Roman governor. For the most part the governor intervened judicially only in affairs of a political nature, leaving the everyday administration of justice wholly to the Jewish officials in charge of applying the law.

MASSACRE OF THE INNOCENTS

As old age weakened his body and mind, Herod the Great grew paranoid about threats to his throne. When foreign "wise men [Mt. 2:1]" arrived in Jerusalem, inquiring, "Where is he who has been born king of the Jews [Mt. 2:2]?", a title reserved for Herod alone, Herod "was troubled, and all Jerusalem with him [Mt. 2:3]." These wise men had been following a star that had led them finally to Jerusalem. Herod's own priests and scribes informed him that prophets had foretold the birth of a ruler in Bethlehem.

Pretending that he too wished to honor the child, Herod asked his visitors to return to him when they had found the infant king. But the wise men were warned in a dream that Herod intended to murder the child, and after they had seen the baby Jesus, they left Judea secretly.

Enraged that he had been deceived, Herod ordered his soldiers to "kill all the male children in Bethlehem and in all that region who were two years old or under, according to the time which he had ascertained from the wise men [Mt. 2:16]." His atrocious deed fulfilled the words of the prophet Jeremiah: "A voice was heard in Ramah, wailing and loud lamentation, Rachel weeping for her children; she refused to be consoled because they were no more [Mt. 2:18]."

Between 10 and 20 children may have been murdered, according to some sources, but the one Herod sought survived. The holy family fled to Egypt and stayed until Herod died. Jesus' escape parallels that of another infant in the Bible: in Egypt, Moses was saved from the pharaoh's decree that all male Hebrew babies be thrown into the Nile.

THE MIRACULOUS AND THE UNSEEN

The Bible shows us a world in which ordinary life is continually touched by divinity, merging the visible world of home, family, politics, and war with the unseen world of divine and miraculous power. It unites these two seemingly separate spheres because God, who is all-seeing and all-knowing, infuses everything, everywhere, with a sense of wonder and the miraculous.

The prominence of all kinds of wonders in the Bible has inspired generations of readers, though the common assumptions about the meaning of miracles have changed over time. People today often think of miracles as events that defy the laws of nature. Everyday occurrences, like the rising and setting of the sun, follow from natural causes, but a miracle occurs when God intervenes and alters the course of nature.

In the period when the Bible was written, however, people did not believe that day-to-day events occurred by impersonal "laws of nature." Rather they believed that God directly governs nearly everything that happens in the world. God maintains "seedtime and harvest . . . day and night [Gen. 8:22]." He feeds "the birds of the air [Mt. 6:26]" and clothes "the lilies of the field [Mt. 6:28]." In a sense the entire world is miraculous, and each event from the least to the most significant shows the power of God.

The miracles recounted in the scriptures were not considered violations of natural laws but rather signs that revealed God's ever-present sovereignty. Usually God's power stays hidden, remaining behind the scenes, but sometimes, in extraordinary moments, he emerges suddenly and dramatically, evoking both trepidation and awe.

Miraculous events provide the framework for the entire biblical history from God's creation of the world to his deliverance of Israel from Egypt, to the coming of Jesus Christ and his resurrection from the dead, to the last universal judgment before the throne of God. The Bible ignores the ordinary barriers of time that limit human perceptions. It reaches back into an eternity before creation and forward to eons beyond the present world. Within that vast time frame the Bible often describes especially important moments in history when God showed his presence through a miracle worker such as Moses or Elijah or Jesus. The accounts of their miracles help the believer to discern the divine purpose that is at work as the stories of the Bible unfold.

By lifting their eyes beyond the workaday world, the Bible gives hope to people struggling with the ups and downs of life. The prophetic visions grant humans a glimpse of the divine glory of God's heavenly court on the one hand and the demonic horrors of hell on the other. And all this immense expanse of biblical vision is portrayed in images so vivid that they capture the imagination of everyone. A basic purpose of this almost endless vista is to help a person recognize the power of good and evil in the world. The human struggle with love and hate, justice and oppression, righteousness and sin is played out on a cosmic stage. The moral battles that take place in everyday society and in the human heart are mirrored in the unseen world by the opposing forces of angels and demons. Satan, who in the Old Testament accused the blameless Job of self-serving righteousness and put him through bitter trials, ultimately appears in the Bible as the master of demonic armies who opposes the work of Christ, torments individuals through evil spirits, and makes people slaves to sin. The image of such consummate evil helps the believer to grasp why his own moral struggles can be so difficult and painful and why evil is so destructive.

This cosmic perspective of the Bible is never credited to its human authors, but always to divine disclosures that break the barrier separating ordinary life from the unseen realm of God. Visions, dreams, and the thundering pronouncements of prophets become God's instruments to guide and shape the hopes of the people. The Bible shows that God alone holds the key to the future, and he chooses his own moments of revelation—whether an enigmatic dream foretelling famine to a pharaoh, a vision in the temple sending Isaiah to warn his people of coming disaster, an angelic appearance to Mary announcing the birth of the Messiah, or a series of apocalyptic visions seen by John on the island of Patmos.

Through all the trials and disasters of human history, the Bible urges believers to be confident that the ultimate future belongs to God. It foresees an end when all evil is overcome and the conflicts and injustices of human life are resolved. Then the wall between the ordinary visible world and the miraculous and unseen will dissolve—as the Apostle Paul said, "Now we see in a mirror dimly, but then face to face [1 Cor. 13:12]."

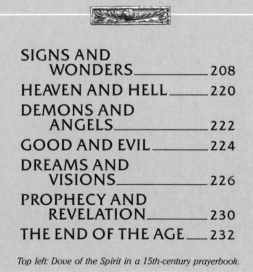

Top left: Dove of the Spirit in a 15th-century prayerbook.

Signs and Wonders

Who are the Bible's great miracle workers?

At the time of the Israelites' flight from Egypt, God gave them their first great miracle worker, Moses, who was often assisted by his brother Aaron, whom Moses felt he needed as a spokesman. A pattern was set: miracles in the Bible occur during periods of crisis or transition, as when miracle after miracle marked Joshua's conquest of Canaan—from the parting of the Jordan River, to the fall of the walls of Jericho, to the sun standing still at Gibeon as a sign that God was on Joshua's side in his victorious battle against the five Amorite kings.

Two of the greatest miracle workers were Elijah and Elisha, born after the tumultuous division of Israel into northern and southern kingdoms. The Books of Kings show how their work helped the Israelites keep their faith alive when it was threatened by the worship of the pagan god Baal. Numerous miracles took place during the tragic Babylonian exile in the sixth century B.C. For example, the Book of Daniel tells how Daniel's friends, Shadrach, Meshach, and Abednego, survived the fiery furnace after refusing to worship King Nebuchadnezzar's golden image. Later Daniel himself, condemned by the plotting courtiers of King Darius, was miraculously spared in the lions' den. Daniel and his friends became an inspiration to the people of Judah as they endured foreign domination.

The greatest number of miracles, however, occurred during the ministry of Jesus ("Miracles of Jesus," page 214) and the spread of his Gospel in the early church. The miracle workers included not only Jesus but also Peter, Paul, and others.

What devices did miracle workers use?

It is clear in the Bible that any object employed in performing a miracle derived its power directly from God. The most famous of these was Moses' staff, or rod, which repeatedly enabled him to accomplish God's plan. The staff changed into a snake, brought on plagues, parted the sea, made water flow from a rock, and performed other feats in the hands of Moses and Aaron.

Like Moses' staff, the prophet's mantle of Elijah became an instrument for enacting God's miracles. By striking the water with the mantle, both Elijah and Elisha made the Jordan River part. Elisha also used a branch to make an axhead float, salt to purify water, and flour to remove poison from stew. Always, however, such devices were understood to be extensions of God's power, not powerful in themselves.

How did miracles establish Moses as leader of his people?

When God sent him to lead the Israelites to freedom, Moses was an 80-year-old who had been absent from both his own people and the court of Egypt for 40 years. As a mere mortal, he might have been unconvincing as a liberator, but God granted him the power to give signs and perform miracles and thereby establish his leadership. When Moses cast his rod upon the ground, it "became a serpent," and when he put his hand EX. 4:3 inside his cloak, it came out "leprous, as white EX. 4:6 as snow," but returned to normal after he put

---

MIRACLE. *The English word* **miracle** *comes from the Latin noun* **miraculum**, *meaning a wonder. The verb form of this noun means to be astonished, which is the human response to a remarkable, inexplicable event such as a miracle. The fourth-century theologian Augustine defined a miracle as something "above the hope and power of them who wonder."*

Both the Old and New Testaments use terms like "works and mighty acts [Dt. 3:24]" and "mighty works [Mk. 6:2]" to describe miracles. Frequently, the compound phrase "signs and wonders [Ex. 7:3; Acts 4:30]" is used to convey the idea of a portent, symbol, or sign of some greater reality and truth. The Gospel of John regularly calls the miracles of Jesus "signs [Jn. 2:11]."

Today the word **miracle** *describes an occurrence that contradicts scientific laws, but the Bible does not regard a miracle in this way. In the Bible, a miracle refers to a startling, extraordinary, or totally unexpected event in which believers see the hand and special power of God at work in the world.*

THE PRACTICE OF MAGIC

In the ancient world, magic was widely condemned but even more widely practiced. Rulers often feared and banned the private practice of magic lest spells or charms be turned against them, but the same rulers might employ skilled diviners, sorcerers, and magicians for their own purposes. Most people seemed to believe that occult powers really existed and could be used to see the future, cast spells, or contact the dead.

The law of Moses condemned "anyone who practices divination, a soothsayer, or an augur, or a sorcerer, or a charmer, or a medium, or a wizard, or a necromancer [Dt. 18:10]." Yet magicians obviously flourished. When Isaiah lists the leaders of Jerusalem and Judah, he places "the judge and the prophet" alongside "the diviner . . . the skilful magician and the expert in charms [Is. 3:2]." Manasseh, one of the longest-reigning kings of Judah, "practiced soothsaying and augury, and dealt with mediums and with wizards [2 Kg. 21:6]."

Not only kings but also the people looked to magicians for help. When the armies of Babylon were threatening Judah, Jeremiah warned the people that their "prophets," "diviners," "dreamers," "soothsayers," and "sorcerers [Jer. 27:9]" were deceiving them with assurances that they would not be conquered.

The early Christians also condemned the practice of magic. The Book of Acts tells how a convert in Samaria named Simon, who may have aroused suspicion because he "had previously practiced magic in the city . . . saying that he himself was somebody great [Acts 8:9]," tried to buy from Peter the ability to bestow the Holy Spirit on anyone by laying on his hands. On Cyprus, Paul denounced a Jewish magician named Elymas Bar-Jesus, who was evidently an adviser to the Roman governor. Acts further relates how in the city of Ephesus Paul's preaching and "extraordinary miracles [Acts 19:11]" so impressed "both Jews and Greeks [Acts 19:17]" that "a number of those who practiced magic arts brought their books together and burned them in the sight of all; and they counted the value of them and found it came to fifty thousand pieces of silver [Acts 19:19]."

This ancient magician wears a headdress of ibex horns.

Granted wondrous powers by the Lord, Moses made a bronze serpent that could miraculously heal snakebites.

As a whirlwind lifts Elijah up to heaven,
Elisha inherits the prophet's mantle.

much convince the pharaoh as awe him with the overwhelming display of God's power.

No sooner had Moses and the freed slaves left Egypt than the people began to complain about their lot and challenge Moses' leadership. Once more, through one miraculous sign after another, God showed his approval of Moses as their leader. Moses parted the sea, provided food and water in the wilderness, and most important, gave his people their new law at Mount Sinai.

When individuals or groups challenged Moses' authority—whether his cousin Korah and his large band of supporters or his brother and sister, Aaron and Miriam—God defended Moses by miraculously punishing his detractors. As the Bible says of Moses, no other person was "like him for all the signs and the wonders which DT. 34:11 the Lord sent him to do."

EX. 7:13 it again inside his cloak. When Moses and Aaron went before the pharaoh, their signs proved unconvincing because the "pharaoh's heart was hardened." However, the pharaoh heeded Mo-
EX. 7:16 ses' plea to "let my people go" after Egypt was struck by 10 plagues. The plagues did not so

What did the miracles of Elijah and Elisha accomplish?

The stories of the lives and miracles of Elijah and Elisha, the greatest of the prophets of God in the ninth century B.C., were handed down through

THE TELLING OF MIRACLES

Most of the miracle stories in the Bible, especially in the Gospels, are remarkably brief, considering the amazing events they describe. Typically, these stories had been retold many times before they were written down in the Bible and contained only the details necessary to understand the story.

Usually, miracle stories have three parts. The first part describes the situation that demands a miracle. If it is a healing miracle, the severity of the disease or the ineffectiveness of an earlier treatment may be emphasized. If it is a nature miracle, the danger of the

Ministering to ills of
the body as well as the soul,
Jesus cures a deaf man in this
14th-century miniature.

situation may be pointed out—the Israelites trapped between the Egyptian army and the Red Sea or the disciples caught in a fierce storm on the Sea of Galilee.

Next comes the actual performance of the miracle. Often some detail makes the story distinctive. Moses lifts up his rod and stretches out his hand over the sea to divide it. Jesus acts through a word or touch. For example, when he raised Jairus' daughter from the dead, he took her by the hand and said, "Little girl, I say to you, arise [Mk. 5:41]."

A miracle story closes with a report of the success of the miracle and often the reaction of those who observed it.

In this 17th-century Flemish painting, God exercises his absolute power over natural forces in the creation of the world, splitting the day from night and shaping the earth and its heavens.

many generations and were woven into the Books of Kings during the Babylonian exile in the sixth century B.C. Though Elisha was Elijah's direct spiritual heir, and both prophets showed deep compassion for their people and merciless opposition to their enemies, they emerge as different kinds of miracle workers.

Elijah was a passionate reformer who single-handedly challenged paganism. He punished Israel's King Ahab for worshiping the rain and storm god Baal by invoking a drought on the area. During the drought Elijah had to hide out as a fugitive from the king. Before he prayed for the drought to end, however, he challenged Ahab's 450 pagan prophets to a miracle contest on Mount Carmel. Elijah stood alone against the pagans as hour after hour they implored Baal to send his fire to burn their offering. When they were exhausted, the lone prophet prayed, and fire immediately descended, devouring his offering and even the altar on which it lay. Then Elijah promptly killed all 450 of Baal's prophets.

Elisha, on the other hand, worked miracles that served the people. He made Jericho's water wholesome by throwing salt into it, gave water to the parched army of Israel and Judah, and drove ✳

back the Syrian army by striking the soldiers blind. And to save a widow's children from being taken as slaves by a creditor, he caused her oil jar to fill every empty vessel she could find with valuable oil, which she sold to pay her debts.

How was God's power manifested in nature?

Throughout the Bible all of the forces of nature are understood to have been created and controlled by God. Nature miracles do not necessarily depart from the ordinary course of natural events but are miraculous because they occur at a propitious moment, changing the expected outcome of an event.

When the Israelites attacked the Philistines, for example, a terrifying earthquake struck, causing the enemy to panic; and an earthquake was also responsible for opening the prison in Philippi where Paul and Silas were held. Samuel called "upon the Lord, that he may send thunder and 1 SAM. 12:17 rain" on the wheat harvest to show the Israelites that "your wickedness is great . . . in asking for 1 SAM. 12:17 yourselves a king." Even the simple act of a caterpillar eating the leaves of a tall plant was seen

"Behold, I will rain bread from heaven for you [Ex. 16:4]." In a 15th-century painting by Roberti, the Israelites pause in their wanderings to gather nourishing manna from the desert.

as a miracle of God because the tree happened to be shading the prophet Johah, whom God wished to reprimand.

Yet many nature miracles in the Bible reach far beyond the expected course of events. The floods in Noah's time, for example, were said to have covered the earth's highest mountains by more than 20 feet. When Moses parted the Red EX. 14:22 Sea for the Israelites, the waters became "a wall to them on their right hand and on their left." Joshua even called for the sun to stand still while a battle continued at the siege of Gibeon. Jesus' similar mastery over nature was manifested by walking on water, causing a tree to wither, and changing water to wine.

When did God provide food for the hungry?

The only miracle of Jesus' ministry recorded in all four Gospels is the story of feeding a throng of 5,000 men, women, and children with only five barley loaves and two fish, which were to have been the simple lunch of a boy in the crowd. The miracle expressed Jesus' compassion for the MK. 6:34 people, "because they were like sheep without a shepherd." Not long afterward, according to Matthew and Mark, he performed a similar miracle, this time feeding more than 4,000 people who ✳

had wandered with him for three days in the desert. Both times there was food left over.

These miracles of Jesus recalled the time the Old Testament prophet Elisha fed a hundred people with 20 small barley loaves with food to spare. In a time of famine Elisha also purified a poisoned pot of stew belonging to a company of prophets by simply throwing flour into it. The prophet Elijah not only saved a widow and her son from starvation by providing them with a perpetual supply of flour and oil, but also he himself was miraculously fed by ravens and angels.

The largest miraculous meal, however, is that of the people of Israel during their 40 years in the wilderness. According to Exodus, they lived on a substance called manna, "like wafers made with EX. 16:31 honey," which fell from the sky six days a week, "fine as hoarfrost on the ground." During some EX. 16:14 periods this diet was supplemented by quail that came and "covered [their] camp." EX. 16:13

When did God send fire from heaven?

"The Lord your God is a devouring fire," Moses DT. 4:24 told the people of Israel. Heavenly fire is one of the most frequent symbols of God's power in the Bible. When God first appeared to Moses, it was "in a flame of fire out of the midst of a bush." EX. 3:2

God guided his people during their Exodus in a "pillar of fire" by night, and descended on Mount Sinai "in fire."

EX. 13:21

EX. 19:18

At least four times the Bible describes divine fire that consumed a sacrifice, thereby demonstrating God's approval of the offering. When Aaron was first consecrated as high priest, "fire came forth from before the Lord and consumed the burnt offering." The Books of Chronicles tell of similar events when David first erected an altar on the site of the future temple and when Solomon later dedicated his lavish temple. The most dramatic of these sacrifices, however, was Elijah's water-drenched offering on Mount Carmel—it was wholly devoured by divine fire in the presence of hordes of pagan priests.

LEV. 9:24

Fire from heaven could also be the instrument of God's punishment. Sodom and Gomorrah fell under a rain of "brimstone and fire from the Lord out of heaven." Divine fire consumed several groups of sinners during the Exodus and destroyed companies of soldiers who came to arrest Elijah. The Book of Revelation pictures the ultimate end of all forces of evil, when "fire came down from heaven and consumed them."

GEN. 19:24

REV. 20:9

What water miracles does the Bible describe?

The Genesis account of creation describes the first biblical water miracle as God divides the raging flood of primordial chaos into waters above and below, thereby bringing order to the world. Many of the subsequent biblical water miracles reflect the imagery of that account. The great deluge plunged the entire creation, except for Noah and the animals and people on his ark, back into chaos. On their way to Canaan the Israelites' path was twice blocked by water—at the Red Sea and at the flooding Jordan River. In both cases God divided the threatening waters to allow them first to escape from the Egyptians and then to enter the Promised Land. Elijah, too, parted the waters of the Jordan in order to rendezvous with a chariot of fire, and Elisha demonstrated his prophetic powers by dividing the waters yet again on his return to the Jordan. In the New Testament, the stormy Sea of Galilee threatens Jesus' disciples, and Jesus overcomes the danger by calming the storm and by twice walking on the roiling waters.

Other biblical miracles frequently revolve ✳

JESUS WALKING ON THE WATER

When early Christians faced harsh oppression and felt the need for help, they remembered the story of Jesus coming to aid his disciples on the stormy Sea of Galilee.

Wild winds blew against them as the disciples labored to cross the water to the town of Bethsaida. It was past 3 A.M. and they had been rowing since nightfall, when the crowds with Jesus had gone home, filled with a meal of bread and fish that he had provided from practically nothing. Jesus had sent the disciples ahead in the boat while he went to a hilltop to spend a few hours in prayer.

Their hope was fading when behind their boat a dim, gray, fluttering figure appeared in the moonlight. Terror struck. "It is a ghost [Mt. 14:26]!" they cried.

But as they stared, paralyzed, a familiar voice called out, "Take heart, it is I; have no fear [Mt. 14:27]." Afraid to believe what they heard, Peter responded, "Lord, if it is you, bid me come to you on the water [Mt. 14:28]." "Come [Mt. 14:29]," was the response. With his eyes on Jesus, Peter stepped out upon the raging waves. But the instant his eyes turned from Jesus, fear caught him and he sank. Only Jesus could lift him up.

The moment Jesus reached the boat, the wind dropped to stillness. His presence had removed the disciples' fear and the danger. They rowed to shore in wonder.

around water as the life-sustaining drink so necessary in an arid land. The first great plague against Egypt was when Moses turned the Egyptians' water into blood—an abomination to drink. By contrast, three times during the period of the Exodus, Moses gave the Israelites water—once by making bitter water sweet, twice by

THE MIRACLES OF JESUS

Miraculous Event	Matthew	Mark	Luke	John
Heals people before the Sermon on the Mount.	4:23		6:17	
Cleanses a leper.	8:1	1:40	5:12	
Heals a centurion's servant.	8:5		7:1	
Heals the fever of Simon Peter's mother-in-law.	8:14	1:29	4:38	
Heals and casts out demons.	8:16	1:32	4:40	
Stills a storm.	8:23	4:35	8:22	
Casts out demons at Gadarene.	8:28	5:1	8:26	
Heals and forgives a paralyzed man.	9:1	2:1	5:17	
Raises Jairus's daughter.	9:18	5:21	8:40	
Heals a woman with a hemorrhage.	9:20	5:25	8:43	
Heals two blind men.	9:27			
Casts out a demon.	9:32		11:14	
Heals a man with a withered hand.	12:9	3:1	6:6	
Heals and casts out demons by the sea.	12:15	3:7		
Heals a blind and mute demoniac.	12:22			
Feeds 5,000 people.	14:13	6:32	9:10	6:1
Walks on water.	14:22	6:45		6:16
Heals at Gennesaret.	14:34	6:53		
Heals a woman's daughter in the region of Tyre and Sidon.	15:21	7:24		
Heals people on the mountain.	15:29			
Feeds 4,000 people.	15:32	8:1		
Heals an epileptic after the disciples failed.	17:14	9:14	9:37	
Causes a fish to appear with the temple tax in its mouth.	17:24			
Heals large crowds in Judea.	19:2			
Heals the blind at Jericho.	20:29	10:46	18:35	
Heals the blind and lame in the temple.	21:14			
Causes a fig tree to wither.	21:18	11:12		
Appears to his disciples after his resurrection.	28:9	16:9	24:13	20:14
Casts out demons in the synagogue at Capernaum.		1:23	4:33	
Heals sick people in his own country.		6:5		
Heals a deaf man with a speech impediment.		7:31		
Heals a blind man at Bethsaida.		8:22		
Causes Peter to net a tremendous catch of fish.			5:1	
Raises a widow's son at Nain.			7:11	
Heals many people in the presence of John the Baptist's followers.			7:21	
Heals a woman bent for 18 years.			13:10	
Heals a man with dropsy.			14:1	
Cleanses 10 lepers.			17:11	
Restores the ear of the high priest's servant.			22:51	
Changes water into wine.				2:1
Heals an official's son.				4:46
Heals a lame man at the Pool of Beth-zatha.				5:2
Heals a man born blind.				9:1
Raises Lazarus.				11:1
Causes disciples to net a great catch of fish.				21:4

bringing water from a rock. Elisha provided water for the city of Jericho and later for Israel's army. Jesus took such miracles one step further by turning water into wine.

Which animals talk?

Only two animals in the Bible speak. The first was the serpent in the Genesis account of the Garden of Eden. By telling Eve she would not die if she ate the forbidden fruit, the serpent enticed her to disobey God. For this, God condemned the serpent to move on its belly and eat dust.

The other animal that spoke was the donkey belonging to a Mesopotamian seer named Balaam. The Moabites had hired Balaam to prophesy against their enemies, the Israelites, thereby arousing God's ire. A comic episode demonstrates Balaam's foolishness. On the road to Moab an angel blocked his way, but only the seer's donkey could see the sword-wielding apparition. When the donkey refused to budge, Balaam beat it with his staff. God "opened the mouth of the ass," and it began to complain to Balaam about its unjust and abusive treatment.

NUM. 22:28

How did God influence the outcome of battles?

The fulfillment of God's promises to Abraham meant freeing a nation of slaves from their bondage to Egypt and leading them to conquer territory long held by Canaanite peoples. The people of Israel recalled how God had fought their battles, and they sang of how God had "triumphed gloriously" over the pharaoh's chariots: "The horse and his rider he has thrown into the sea." When the Israelites were attacked by the Amalekites, the people prevailed as long as Moses, bearing "the rod of God," held his hands aloft.

EX. 15:1
EX. 15:1
EX. 17:9

When the Israelites invaded Canaan, God immediately granted them a miraculous victory over Jericho, but he brought them defeat at Ai because a soldier had stolen some of the Jericho booty that according to the law belonged to God. Later God again fought for the Israelites against the five Amorite kings whose armies attacked the city of Gibeon. The Amorites suffered a barrage of "great stones from heaven," and the sun "stayed in the midst of heaven" while Israel won a decisive victory.

JOS. 10:11
JOS. 10:13

During the time of the Judges, God used Gide- ✳

Jesus' miraculous powers are recorded in three 15th-century miniatures by Liberale. From top: at Bethsaida he feeds the 5,000; cured, a leper kisses Jesus' feet; and a mute boy receives the gift of speech.

on's force of 300 men to defeat a host of Midianites. And he gave Samson superhuman strength so he could defeat 1,000 Philistines singlehanded. In some battles against the Philistines, God intervened with thunder or earthquakes. David attributed his victory over Goliath to divine intervention, but divine intervention also brought about Saul's defeat by the same Philistines.

Later an attacking Syrian army was struck blind by Elisha's prayer, while another panicked 2 KG. 7:6 and fled when God made them hear "the sound of a great army." When the greater Assyrian army 2 KG. 19:35 under Sennacherib attacked Judah, an "angel of the Lord" intervened directly and slew 185,000 of the Assyrians in their camp.

Did miracles always lead to belief in God?

Once, when some of Jesus' opponents asked him to perform a miraculous sign, evidently to MT. 12:39 prove his ministry's validity, Jesus answered, "An evil and adulterous generation seeks for a sign," and he refused to perform a miracle.

Though miracles have often been considered a sure proof of God's presence, the Bible recounts incidents in which signs and wonders failed to bring about faith in God. For example, when God was angry with the Israelites in the NUM. 14:11 wilderness, he asked, "How long will they not believe in me, in spite of all the signs which I have wrought among them?" Even in the case of JN. 2:23 Jesus, the Gospel of John notes, "many believed in his name when they saw the signs which he did; but Jesus did not trust himself to them"— implying that their faith based on signs was somehow shallow or inadequate.

MT. 24:24 Jesus warned his followers that "false prophets will arise and show great signs and wonders, so as to lead astray, if possible, even the elect." Though signs and wonders have an important place in the biblical narratives, they are never considered sufficient in themselves to create or to guarantee faith in God.

What was the first miracle that Jesus performed?

The first miracle that Jesus performed, as told in the Gospel of John, was different from any other of his miracles. He had just returned to Galilee from the Jordan River and John the Baptist when

he and his followers received a wedding invitation, perhaps from a family friend or kinsman, since Jesus' mother was also there.

During the long celebration—often such feasts lasted seven days—a major social embarrassment arose for the hosts: their supply of wine ran out, threatening to bring the festivities to a halt. When Jesus' mother learned of the situation, she informed her son. As frequently happens in the Gospel of John, Jesus' response was both surprising and seemingly mysterious: "O JN. 2:4 woman, what have you to do with me? My hour has not yet come." It is clear that for Jesus more was at stake in that moment than just the embarrassment of the hosts.

Though Jesus' words seemed to indicate unconcern, his mother nevertheless told the servants, "Do whatever he tells you." Jesus told JN. 2:5 them to fill six stone jars with water—something over 120 gallons—and then "draw some out, JN. 2:8 and take it to the steward of the feast."

At some unknown moment before the water reached the steward's lips, it had become wine. The steward had no idea where this fresh supply had come from. The happy festival continued, and the miracle went largely unheeded. Only Jesus' disciples recognized what had happened. In the midst of feasting, dancing, and singing, Jesus had "manifested his glory; and his disciples be- JN. 2:11 lieved in him."

Who performed healing miracles?

Most of the miracles of healing in the Old Testament occur when God reverses a plague or punishment that he has imposed. For instance, Abraham's prayer brought healing to Abimelech, whose household God had stricken with barrenness. Moses prayed for the healing of Miriam, who had been punished with leprosy, and he set up a bronze serpent to heal those who were dying because of a plague of fiery serpents. When King Jeroboam stretched out his hand against a prophet, the hand withered, but it was restored by the prophet's prayer.

Rarely is anyone healed of a natural disease in the Old Testament. One instance was when Elisha told a Syrian commander named Naaman that his skin disease could be cleansed by dipping his body seven times in the Jordan.

In the New Testament, healings are the pre-

*To honor Asclepius, god of medicine, Greeks cured of an illness adorned
the temple walls with images of the affected body parts.*

MEDICINE IN BIBLE TIMES

Medicine and physicians were frowned on in the Old Testament because the Hebrews thought people should rely on God for health and healing. Diseases were seen as punishments for rebellion against God: "The Lord will smite you with consumption, and with fever, inflammation, and fiery heat . . . with the boils of Egypt, and with the ulcers and the scurvy and the itch, of which you cannot be healed [Dt. 28:22]."

In treating illness, people used herbal folk remedies, which included oils and unguents such as the famous "balm [Jer. 8:22]" of Gilead. Isaiah prescribed "a cake of figs [Is. 38:21]" for King Hezekiah's boil. Isaiah also spoke of "bruises and sores and bleeding wounds" that needed to be "pressed out, or bound up, or softened with oil [Is. 1:6]."

The early Israelites were not served by professional physicians, and they distrusted physicians of other nations. King Asa of Judah, suffering from diseased feet, was condemned because "he did not seek the Lord, but sought help from physicians [2 Chr. 16:12]."

However, the Book of Sirach, from about 200 B.C., shows a growing respect for medicine. All "healing comes from the Most High [Sir. 38:2]," Sirach asserts, but God has given skill to the physicians, and "by them he heals and takes away pain [Sir. 38:7]." The wise man who is sick will "pray to the Lord [Sir. 38:9]" and "offer a sweet-smelling sacrifice [Sir. 38:11]," but he will also "give the physician his place [Sir. 38:12]."

In the New Testament, Mark's account of a woman who had had "a flow of blood for twelve years [Mk. 5:25]" says she had suffered "under many physicians, and had spent all that she had, and was no better but rather grew worse [Mk. 5:26]." Such experiences were not uncommon, given the limited medical knowledge of even the most advanced physicians of the era.

In the days of early Christianity most physicians were associated with the Greek god Asclepius, under whose aegis scores of temples were founded. His symbol, snakes entwined around a staff, is still the emblem of the medical profession. These temples, such as those at Epidaurus in Greece or Pergamum in Asia Minor, were a combination of health spa, medical school, and healing shrine. Votaries often believed that they were healed by dreams from Asclepius as they slept.

RAISING LAZARUS FROM THE DEAD

The Gospel of John tells that Jesus was teaching east of the Jordan River when he received word that his close friend Lazarus was seriously ill. Lazarus lived with his sisters Mary and Martha in the town of Bethany, near Jerusalem. Not long before, Jesus had narrowly escaped arrest and stoning in Jerusalem, but he serenely finished two more days of work in the region and set off for Bethany.

When he arrived at his friends' home, Lazarus had been in the tomb for four days. Martha, who was well aware of Jesus' healing powers, greeted him pointedly: "Lord, if you had been here, my brother would not have died [Jn. 11:21]."

At the tomb Lazarus' friends surrounded Jesus. They could not understand why he had failed to use his healing power. Jesus wept, sharing their grief.

Then unexpectedly Jesus said, "Take away the stone [Jn. 11:39]." Martha spoke what everyone was no doubt thinking: it was too late for even Jesus to help: "Lord, by this time there will be an odor, for he has been dead four days [Jn. 11:39]." Jesus insisted, however, saying, "Did I not tell you that if you would believe you would see the glory of God [Jn. 11:40]?" The stone was removed.

Then, standing before the gaping mouth of the burial cave, Jesus thundered, "Lazarus, come out [Jn. 11:43]." It was never too late for the one who could say "I am the resurrection and the life [Jn. 11:25]." The raising of Lazarus, who struggled from the tomb still bound in his shroud, was only a sign pointing to the deeper truth that death itself had been conquered: "Whoever lives and believes in me shall never die [Jn. 11:26]."

dominant miracle, and all are cures of natural diseases. When John the Baptist sent two disciples to inquire about the meaning of Jesus' ministry, Jesus responded by performing healings: LK. 7:21 "In that hour he cured many of diseases and plagues and evil spirits, and on many that were blind he bestowed sight. And he answered them, 'Go and tell John what you have seen and heard: the blind receive their sight, the lame walk, lepers are cleansed, and the deaf hear.' " Healings MT. 8:17 by Jesus, the Gospel of Matthew asserts, "fulfill what was spoken by the prophet Isaiah, 'He took our infirmities and bore our diseases.' "

The Gospels report that Jesus urged those he healed not to tell anyone of their recovery. Apparently he did not want the healings interpreted as proof of the validity of his teachings; rather, they were a visible sign of the compassion that characterized his ministry.

Were only the faithful healed?

When Jesus was preaching in Galilee, a woman whose hemorrhaging had continued for years LK. 8:44 touched the fringe of his garment "and immedi-✳ ately her flow of blood ceased." "Daughter," said MK. 5:34 Jesus to the woman, "your faith has made you well; go in peace." Several times in the Gospels, Jesus points to a connection between the faith of individuals and their restoration to health. However, the Gospels do not suggest that faith alone brings about a miraculous healing. The woman who touched Jesus' garment, for example, was healed by "power" that came from Jesus after LK. 8:46 her faith had made her reach out to him.

Sometimes a person was made well by the faith of others. Jesus healed a paralyzed man when he saw the faith of the four men who had carried him. Blocked by the press of the crowds, the four boldly climbed the roof above Jesus, made a hole in the roof, and let their friend down to Jesus. Another time, Jesus was so impressed with the faith of an army centurion that he healed the man's servant.

What miraculous events occurred at Jesus' death?

The Gospels of Matthew, Mark, and Luke tell how Jesus' death was marked by ominous changes in nature. All three report that at noon,

MK. 15:33 as Jesus hung on the cross, "there was darkness over the whole land," and the gloom lasted until his death three hours later. All three also tell of a MT. 27:51 mysterious event in which "the curtain of the temple was torn in two, from top to bottom."

Matthew also says that at the moment of Jesus' MT. 27:52 death a great earthquake struck, and "the tombs also were opened, and many bodies of the saints who had fallen asleep were raised, and coming out of the tombs after his resurrection they went into the holy city and appeared to many."

John is the only Gospel that does not tell of any miraculous signs surrounding Jesus' death.

How many times are the dead restored to life in the Old Testament?

Among the several different occasions when the dead are brought back to life, three occur in the Old Testament. When a widow who had given food and shelter to the prophet Elijah lost her only son to a severe illness, the prophet 1 KG. 17:22 stretched out over the child, prayed, and "the soul of the child came into him again, and he revived." In much the same way, Elisha prostrated 2 KG. 4:35 ed himself on the dead son of a couple who had given him lodging, and "the child sneezed seven times, and the child opened his eyes." Even after his own death, Elisha's ability to restore life remained powerful, according to an incident relat- 2 KG. 13:21 ed in the Second Book of Kings: "As a man was being buried, lo, a marauding band was seen and the man was cast into the grave of Elisha; and as soon as the man touched the bones of Elisha, he revived, and stood on his feet."

When are people raised from the dead in the New Testament?

The Gospels tell of three miracles in which Jesus restored the dead to life. Once, like Elijah, he raised the only son of a widow, stopping the funeral procession on its way to the burial. On another occasion he was summoned to heal a sick girl, but as he was traveling to her, word came that the girl had died. Jesus came to the child, took her by the hand, and raised her up. The most detailed account of Jesus raising the dead is the resurrection of Lazarus in the Gospel of John. Matthew describes a mysterious related ✳

This Russian icon shows Jesus, surrounded by his ancestors, raising Adam and Eve to life.

occurrence when he refers to many saints rising at the time of Jesus' crucifixion.

Both Peter and Paul followed the lead of their master in raising the dead. Peter raised a widow named Tabitha or Dorcas, who was well known for her acts of charity. During a long sermon that Paul preached in a third-floor room, a young man named Eutychus (meaning lucky), who was sitting in a window, fell asleep, and plunged to the ground. Though he was "taken up dead," ACTS 20:9 Paul embraced him and announced that "his life ACTS 20:10 is in him. . . . And they took the lad away alive."

The story of Jesus' resurrection is different from all the others. Jesus' healing power raised the dead to life, but they still faced physical death later. The New Testament teaches that Jesus was raised to eternal life. Paul and others saw Jesus as the "first fruits" of the final resurrec- 1 COR. 15:20 tion at the close of the age. "In Christ shall all be 1 COR. 15:22 made alive," Paul wrote. "Christ the first fruits, 1 COR. 15:23 then at his coming those who belong to Christ."

Heaven and Hell

In this detail from "The Last Judgment" by Fra Angelico, friends and family joyfully greet one another in heaven as cherubic angels frolic in their midst.

How are the wicked punished in hell?

Which is the worse fate of a person condemned to suffer in hell? Is it the physical torment of scorching heat rising from the lake of fire and sulfur into which, according to the Book of Revelation, the earth's sinners are thrown? Or is it the total and eternal isolation from God, the hopeless despair of never knowing his love?

The idea of punishment after death for earthly sins grew gradually in biblical times, and the image of fire as hell's ultimate punishment began to take hold as early as the third century B.C. Jesus made dramatic use of that image in his parable of a rich man who ignored the beggar Lazarus at his gates—only to see after his own death Lazarus LK. 16:22 cradled in "Abraham's bosom." Crying out desperately for deliverance from the fire of torment, the rich man pleads to Abraham for a visit from LK. 16:24 Lazarus so that he may "dip the end of his finger in water and cool my tongue, for I am in anguish in this flame."

A condemned soul looks out through the gates of hell.

What does heaven look like?

Although the actual shape and dimensions of heaven are never clearly described by the Bible writers, there is unanimity on one central point: heaven is the dwelling place of God. Moses instructs the Israel- DT. 26:15 ites to ask God: "Look down from thy holy habitation, from heaven, and bless thy people." And Jesus in the Sermon on the Mount addresses God with the words: "Our Father MT. 6:9 who art in heaven."

People in biblical times, like others through the ages, craved knowledge of heaven's appearance, but the Old Testament provides only tantalizing glimpses of the celestial realm surrounding the throne of God. In the Book of Exodus, Moses and the elders of Israel saw God's throne resting on "a pavement of sapphire" in the firmament. EX. 24:10 More dramatic is the vision of Ezekiel: "Above EZEK. 1:26 the firmament over their heads there was the likeness of a throne, in appearance like sapphire." The throne was in the shape of a chariot with gleaming wheels within wheels driven by four cherubim.

REV. 4:2 Reminiscent of Ezekiel's vision is the testimony of John, the writer of Revelation: "And lo, a throne stood in heaven, with one seated on the throne! And he who sat there appeared like jasper and carnelian, and round the throne was a rainbow that looked like an emerald. . . . From the throne issue flashes of lightning, and voices and peals of thunder, and before the throne burn seven torches of fire, which are the seven spirits of God; and before the throne there is as it were a sea of glass, like crystal." Many traditional Christian images of heaven derive from later passages REV. 21:2 in Revelation, in which John describes "the holy city, new Jerusalem, coming down out of heaven REV. 21:18 from God"—a city built of "pure gold, clear as glass," whose wall was composed of jasper, whose foundations were adorned with jewels, and whose gates were made of pearl. There the blessed will eat from the tree of life, and God REV. 21:4 himself "will wipe away every tear from their eyes, and death shall be no more, neither shall there be mourning nor crying nor pain any more, for the former things have passed away."

What is the heavenly court?

Just as numerous biblical passages make clear that heaven is God's dwelling place on high, so the Bible indicates repeatedly that he does not dwell there in solitude. Quite the contrary. God presides over a host of angels waiting in attendance to communicate his commands and promises to earth's inhabitants below.

One breathtaking vision of the heavenly court is described by Isaiah: "I saw the Lord sitting IS. 6:1 upon a throne, high and lifted up; and his train filled the temple. Above him stood the seraphim; each had six wings: with two he covered his face, and with two he covered his feet, and with two he flew." Another was related by the prophet Micaiah: "I saw the Lord sitting on his throne, 1 KG. 22:19 and all the host of heaven standing beside him . . . and the Lord said, 'Who will entice Ahab, that he may go up and fall. . . ?' And one said one thing, and another said another. Then a spirit came forward and stood before the Lord, saying . . . . 'I will go forth, and will be a lying spirit in the mouth of all his prophets.' And he said, 'You are to entice him . . . go forth and do so.' "

ANCIENT COSMOLOGY

One of the fundamental mysteries that religion must explore is the origin of the universe—how it was formed and how it works. The Genesis description of the cosmos leaves many details unclear, but it provides an overall picture of how the flat disk of land called earth fitted into the greater scheme of things. Below the earth, which was surrounded by flowing waters, lay the realm of the dead. Rising from the earth were massive pillars that held up the firmament, a large, solid dome in which God had placed the sun, moon, and stars "to give light upon the earth, to rule over the day and over the night [Gen. 1:17]." Above the firmament were vast waters, as well as storehouses of snow, hail, and winds that could be released upon the earth through "the windows of the heavens [Gen. 8:2]." Higher still was heaven, where God reigned supreme, looking with favor or disfavor on the actions of people below.

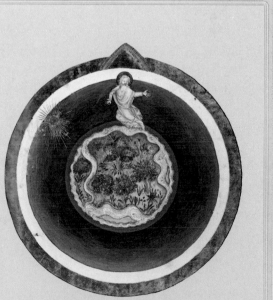

Gazing down from heaven, God appears satisfied with his handiwork, a lush world enclosed by waters and illuminated by the sun shining in the firmament.

Demons and Angels

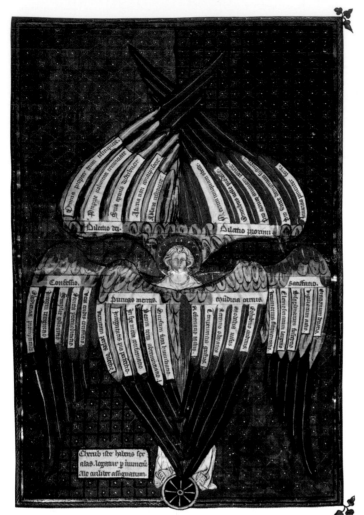

Mighty seraphim guard God's throne: "Four living creatures, each of them with six wings [Rev. 4:8]."

Who is Satan?

The Hebrew name Satan has come to mean the spiritual being who opposes God. The word in itself means accuser or adversary and sometimes appears in the Bible as a common noun. It was translated into Greek as *diabolos* (in English, devil).

Several Old Testament passages represent Satan as one who accuses people of wrongdoing, rather than as the embodiment of wickedness. Zechariah describes him as a prosecuting angel in the trial of "Joshua the high priest standing before the angel of the Lord." In Job, the "Satan" cynically charges that Job serves God for gain.

Characterizations of Satan greatly expanded ✳

ZECH. 3:1
JOB 1:6

following the Babylonian exile. The persecution and the suffering of people who were devoted to God's law raised the specter of an evil power behind the injustice in the world. After 200 B.C., Jewish writings increasingly described Satan as a leader of the forces of evil.

The idea of Satan as an evil being continues in the New Testament. As Jesus prepared for his messianic mission in the wilderness, he confronted Satan the tempter. "Begone, Satan!" Jesus finally cried, and "the devil left him." In the Book of Revelation, Satan is ultimately defeated after battling with the archangel Michael.

MT. 4:10
MT. 4:11

How are angels ranked?

Angels are usually portrayed as attendants of the heavenly court. Their role was to worship God and carry out the divine will on earth.

Some Old Testament passages mention classes of angels, including cherubim and seraphim. After the Babylonian exile, angels came to be seen as warriors against Satan. Reflecting the military model, they began to be ranked; the New Testament suggests classes such as "thrones or dominions or principalities or authorities."

COL. 1:16

The Bible names only a few angels. Gabriel appears in the Book of Daniel and the Gospel of Luke; Michael, in Daniel, Jude, and Revelation. (In Jewish tradition, Michael is Israel's guardian angel.) Raphael, Uriel, and Jeremiel appear in the Apocrypha, which, like Revelation, refers to numerous unnamed angels and archangels.

How did the idea of demons change in the Bible?

Pagan gods were once called demons. Many ancient Israelites believed that the gods of Canaan were real entities, less powerful than God himself but still able to affect their lives for good or ill, as when Israel's faithless "sacrificed to demons which were no gods." Later the Apostle Paul stated: "What pagans sacrifice they offer to demons and not to God."

DT. 32:17
1 COR. 10:20

222

DESCRIPTIONS OF SATAN

Accuser of our brethren	Rev. 12:10
Adversary	1 Pet. 5:8
*Ancient serpent	Rev. 12:9
Angel of the bottomless pit	Rev. 9:11
*Beelzebul	Mt. 10:25
Belial (meaning worthless one)	2 Cor. 6:15
Day Star, son of Dawn (Lucifer in King James Version)	Is. 14:12
Deceiver of the whole world	Rev. 12:9
*Devil	Mt. 4:1
The evil one	Mt. 13:19
Great dragon	Rev. 12:9
God of this world	2 Cor. 4:4
Liar and the father of lies	Jn. 8:44
Prince of demons	Mt. 9:34
Prince of the power of the air	Eph. 2:2
*Ruler of this world	Jn. 12:31
*Satan	1 Chr. 21:1
*The tempter	Mt. 4:3

* Occurs more than once in the Bible

By the first century A.D., demons were thought of more generally as evil spirits controlled by Satan. Jesus stated that when he cast out demons MT. 12:28 "by the spirit of God," he was showing God's kingdom to the world.

How did Jesus cast out demons?

Ancient peoples believed that demons could be ACTS 19:13 cast out by "exorcists" who invoked the authority of a deity. But Jesus was different because he cast out demons on his own authority. Even ACTS 16:16 Paul, in expelling "a spirit of divination" from a ACTS 16:18 slave girl, did not do so on his own but "in the name of Jesus Christ."

LK. 4:33 Luke relates an incident in which a man "who had the spirit of an unclean demon" approached Jesus in the synagogue of Capernaum. The man LK. 4:34 shouted, "What have you to do with us, Jesus of Nazareth? Have you come to destroy us?" Jesus LK. 4:35 commanded, "Be silent, and come out of him!" ✳

The demon threw the man down and departed.

Mark tells of a man of Gerasa possessed by many demons. When Jesus asked him his name, the demoniac replied, "My name is Legion; for MK. 5:9 we are many" and begged Jesus to "send us to MK. 5:12 the swine," since a herd was nearby. Whereupon Jesus "gave them leave. And the unclean spirits MK. 5:13 came out, and entered the swine; and the herd, numbering about two thousand, rushed down the steep bank into the sea, and were drowned."

Who accused Jesus of being in league with Satan?

Believing that all spiritual power came from either God or Satan, several of Jesus' opponents among the Pharisees and scribes decided that when Jesus seemed to threaten orthodoxy, he was getting his instructions from Satan.

For example, when Jesus healed on the Sabbath or allowed himself to be touched by "a LK. 7:37 woman . . . who was a sinner," his critics said he was working with Satan, or Beelzebul. Jesus replied that "if Satan casts out Satan, he is divided MT. 12:26 against himself; how then will his kingdom stand?" Then, turning the question back on them, he asked, "If I cast out demons by Beelze- MT. 12:27 bul, by whom do your sons cast them out?"

After a 40-day fast, Jesus still resists Satan, who has tempted him to turn stones into bread; a 12th-century painting.

223

Good and Evil

Why is there evil in the world?

While completely accepting the idea that God is a righteous God who desires only the good for his people, many believers have echoed Jeremiah's question, "Why does the way of the wicked prosper?" or, conversely, why do the righteous suffer at the hands of the wicked? One line of thought proposes that since God is the creator of all, then he must also be responsible for evil. Yet how can a God who is good cause evil? Some biblical writers suggest that God uses suffering to chasten and discipline his people, but this interpretation does not seem to explain all instances of suffering. Another idea, exemplified by the story of Job, is that suffering is a divine mystery beyond human understanding.

JER. 12:1

A dualistic view of two competing forces—good versus evil—emerged in Judaism toward the end of Old Testament times and is clearly evident in the New Testament. The battle against evil was expressed in terms of God versus Satan: for example, God's forces are described as being clothed in an "armor of light," while Satan rules "the dominion of darkness." The New Testament teachings hold that though evil may gain dominance for a time, God will eventually bring about its destruction and create a new heaven and a new earth. Thus evil and suffering, though real and powerful, are also ephemeral and subject to the power and plan of God. Suffering may be seen as a sign of the eventual defeat of evil as exemplified by the suffering of Jesus Christ.

ROM. 13:12
COL. 1:13

How is evil punished and good rewarded?

Some of the Bible's most famous stories make it clear that on certain occasions God intervened in human affairs to deliver a direct punishment for evil or a reward for good. The destruction of Sodom and Gomorrah and the blessings received by Abraham, for example, demonstrated that the direct intervention by God in the lives of people was an ever-present possibility. This possibility was central to the thinking of many of the psalmists and Old Testament prophets.

Yet it is also clear that God did not always punish the wicked and reward the righteous. The view that came to prevail was that God's ultimate reward for good and his punishment of evil would occur not in our day-to-day lives but rather according to a divine schedule. At the end of time, a day of judgment would come. Evil would receive its final punishment then and would be banished from the presence of God; and righteousness would be rewarded with eternal joy "in the age to come."

LK. 18:30

Lot's wife is turned to salt for looking back at the destruction of Sodom after God has forbidden a last glance.

What are the evil spirits?

The idea of evil spirits occurs in the miracle stories of the Gospels in which Jesus heals someone who is ill

THE PAINFUL LESSON OF JOB

Job was a man renowned for his piety and blessed by God with prosperity. When the Lord praised Job before the heavenly council, Satan, in his role as prosecuting angel, questioned the depth of Job's piety and was allowed to test it.

In the throes of an agonizing illness, after losing his wealth and family, Job is visited by three friends—Eliphaz, Bildad, and Zophar. They tell him that his misfortune must surely be deserved and that he should accept it as a manifestation of divine justice. Eliphaz asks, "Can mortal man be righteous before God? Can a man be pure before his Maker [Job 4:17]?" Job, who knows he is righteous, cries out against the injustice of his suffering: "I will speak in the anguish of my spirit; I will complain in the bitterness of my soul [Job 7:11]." A fourth friend, Elihu, berates Job for questioning God's justice: "God is greater than man. Why do you contend against him [Job 33:12]?" God then rebukes Job from out of the whirlwind: who is he to question God? "Where were you when I laid the foundation of the earth [Job 38:4]?" Eventually, Job comes to understand that he must accept the fact that God's ways are mysterious, and thus neither he, his friends, nor anyone else can presume to explain the deeds of God. He repents of his harsh words. At the end, Job is rewarded anew for his piety and restored to prosperity.

MT. 8:16 or "possessed with demons" by casting out an evil spirit. The New Testament describes evil spirits as having the power to dominate individual men and women and the supernatural ability

MK. 1:24 to recognize Jesus as "the Holy One of God." However, biblical writers stress that compared to divine power, the forces of evil are weak and inferior, whether they appear as demons, pagan gods, or in some other form. All such demonic forces are rendered powerless before God.

What are the wages of sin?

When the Apostle Paul wrote in his letter to the Romans, "For the wages of sin is death," he was ROM. 6:23 personifying sin as the master of those people who chose to serve it. But the wages sin paid were destructive because they meant death. Sin, not God, was responsible for death. A few sentences earlier in the same letter, Paul had pointed out that people who "were slaves of sin . . . ROM. 6:20 were free in regard to righteousness," but he then immediately asked what such freedom was really worth if "the end of these things is death." ROM. 6:21 The opposite of servitude to sin, Paul said, was servitude to God, a paradoxical kind of slavery in which an individual could find new freedom and dignity.

There was an even greater reward for those who had been set free from sin and become slaves of God: "The return you get is sanctifica- ROM. 6:22 tion and its end, eternal life. For . . . the free gift of God is eternal life in Christ Jesus our Lord." The overall context in this passage is that of apocalyptic belief in an eventual end to the world. At that time a new heaven and new earth will be created.

REPENTANCE. *Central to the meaning of repentance is an active turning away from sin and a return to God, which involves a change in the way one thinks and behaves. In the Old Testament, when calamity struck or the people strayed from obedience to God, prophets speaking for God challenged the Israelites to repent. "Return, faithless Israel [Jer. 3:12]," Jeremiah cried, and Ezekiel demanded, "Turn back, turn back from your evil ways [Ezek. 33:11]." In the New Testament, John the Baptist preached "a baptism of repentance for the forgiveness of sins [Mk. 1:4]," and Jesus urged repentance as the way to prepare for the arrival of God's rule: "The kingdom of God is at hand; repent, and believe in the gospel [Mk. 1:15]."*

Dreams and Visions

In this medieval French carving, God's angel appears to the Wise Men in a dream after they have seen the baby Jesus.

Are dreams and visions different?

The Bible treats revelations in dreams and visions as practically identical. Both are used to describe ways in which God breaks through everyday reality to communicate his will to the people. Although dreams refer to experiences during sleep and visions are usually applied to something seen when a person is awake or in a trance, the distinction is not always maintained. GEN. 46:2 Dreams are often called "visions of the night." DAN. 7:1 The Book of Daniel tells how he "had a dream and visions of his head as he lay in his bed."

God's message was always more important than whether the person receiving it happened to be awake or asleep. Jeremiah condemns prophets who "speak visions of their own minds" and JER. 23:16 prophesy lies, saying, "I have dreamed!" JER. 23:25

To whom does God talk in dreams?

The evidence of the Bible suggests that one did not have to possess special spiritual gifts in order to experience divine revelations in dreams. Just about anyone—even idol worshipers and evildoers—could receive such messages. In addition to communicating through dreams with such well-known figures as the patriarchs Abraham, Jacob, Joseph, and many prophets, God used dreams to reveal his will to people like ✳

Abimelech, the Gentile king of Gerar, warning him to release Abraham's wife Sarah, and Jacob's unscrupulous uncle, Laban, telling him not to harm the fleeing Jacob. The Book of Numbers tells how God communicated with a pagan prophet, the Mesopotamian priest-diviner Balaam: "And God came to Balaam NUM. 22:20 at night and said to him, 'Only what I bid you, that shall you do.'" Dreamlike visions persuaded Balaam to obey the Lord's will and bless Israel rather than curse it.

The New Testament, too, relates how God used dreams to send ordinary people messages. In the Gospel of Matthew an angel of the Lord appeared to Joseph before and after the birth of Jesus. Matthew also tells how the "wise men from the East" were "warned MT. 2:1 in a dream not to return to Herod"; and how the wife of the Roman governor, Pilate, dreamed that her husband should "have nothing to do with MT. 27:19 that righteous man," Jesus.

What happened to Saul when he tried to summon the spirit of Samuel?

Since it seemed to ancient peoples in the biblical world that almost anyone could be the recipient of a message from God, it became common practice among some to try to bring about such communication through induced trances or professional prophets.

The First Book of Samuel describes how Saul, the first king of the Israelites, when faced with a military invasion by the Philistines, "inquired of 1 SAM. 28:6 the Lord," but got no response, "either by 1 SAM. 28:6 dreams, or by Urim, or by prophets." Desperate for any kind of supernatural guidance, Saul asked his servants to find him "a woman who is 1 SAM. 28:7 a medium, that I may go to her and inquire of her." When they found a "medium at Endor," 1 SAM. 28:7 Saul asked her to summon the spirit of the deceased prophet Samuel. Saul himself had banned this practice because God had warned that anyone who turned to a medium would be cut off "from among his people." The angry Sam- LEV. 20:6 uel told Saul that not only would he suffer defeat but that he would die.

Who was the first great interpreter of dreams?

The Bible's best-known interpreter of dreams was Joseph. Held in an Egyptian prison on false charges, Joseph listened to two fellow inmates—the pharaoh's former chief butler and chief baker—relate their strange dreams. The GEN. 40:9 butler had dreamed "there was a vine before me, and on the vine there were three branches; as soon as it budded, its blossoms shot forth, and the clusters ripened into grapes." In his dream the butler was holding the pharaoh's cup and saw himself pressing the grapes into the cup and placing it in the pharaoh's hand. According to Joseph, the dream meant that in three days the man would be restored to his post as chief butler. The baker had dreamed of three cake baskets, one on top of the other, on his head. There were birds eating out of the top basket. Joseph said that in three days "Pharaoh will . . . hang GEN. 40:19 you on a tree; and the birds will eat the flesh from you." Both predictions came true.

Two years later, the pharaoh himself had a troubling dream, but "there was none who could GEN 41:8

INTERPRETING DREAMS

Ancient peoples had little doubt that divinities communicated with human beings through the medium of dreams. In biblical times, Egyptians, Babylonians, Assyrians, and Greeks, as well as the Hebrews, relied on such messages for guidance and carried out prescribed ritual practices, such as sleeping in designated holy spots, to bring on divinely inspired visions.

Some of the dreams reported in the Bible are so explicit that they need no interpretation. For example, there is no ambiguity about the promises in Abraham's visions that he will have children. But there are other biblical dreams whose meanings are shrouded in allegory and symbolism. They puzzle and perplex the dreamer, who calls for the help of interpreters.

The Bible indicates that the Egyptian pharaoh and the Babylonian kings Nebuchadnezzar and Belshazzar employed professional dream interpreters in their courts, although none

God warned the pharaoh of the coming famine in a dream that only Joseph could interpret.

matched the interpretive powers of the Israelite heroes Joseph and Daniel. Neither of these men took personal credit for his special skill, however. Joseph said to the pharaoh's officers, "Do not interpretations belong to God [Gen. 40:8]?" and Daniel told King Nebuchadnezzar, "There is a God in heaven who reveals mysteries [Dan. 2:28]." To both Joseph and

Daniel their ability to interpret dreams was a God-given skill that enabled them to convince even kings of God's supreme power.

"Dream books," with explanations of dream symbols, apparently used by professional interpreters in Egypt and Mesopotamia, have survived the centuries. For example, a 13th-century B.C. manuscript from Thebes explains that seeing oneself "plunging into the river" means being purged of evil. The sight of the moon shining promises divine forgiveness. A large cat indicates a large harvest. Looking into a deep well portends possible imprisonment.

Even if a dream reveals the future, the Bible warns, the people are not to take it as God's word if the interpreter or seer urges them to abandon the one true God and worship idols. "That prophet or that dreamer of dreams shall be put to death, because he has taught rebellion against the Lord your God [Dt. 13:5]."

Bathed in celestial light, the angel Gabriel interprets Daniel's bewildering visions of the world's end in this 18th-century painting.

interpret it." The chief butler told him of the ability to read dreams that Joseph had shown in prison. Summoned by the pharaoh, Joseph revealed the dream as a warning of famine to come—and how to survive it. The grateful pharaoh elevated Joseph to the post of Egypt's prime minister.

What was Daniel's reward for interpreting Nebuchadnezzar's dream?

When Nebuchadnezzar, the Babylonian king, had a puzzling dream, he challenged "the magi- DAN. 2:2 cians, the enchanters, the sorcerers, and the Chaldeans [a caste of wise men]" of his court to describe and interpret it. None could do so. Then Daniel, an Israelite court official, offered his services as an interpreter of the king's dream.

The dream began with "a great image . . . of DAN. 2:31 exceeding brightness" that had a head of gold, breast and arms of silver, a belly and thighs of bronze, legs of iron, and feet a mixture of iron and clay. As the dreaming king watched, a stone struck the image, cracking it to pieces, and then the stone "became a great mountain and filled DAN. 2:35 the whole earth." Daniel gave this interpretation: the various metals were kingdoms that would follow Babylonia. The stone that broke them was the kingdom of God, which would last forever.

So impressed was Nebuchadnezzar that he

DANIEL'S VISION OF THE FOUR BEASTS

Waking from a terrifying dream, Daniel feverishly wrote down everything he could remember. He had seen "four great beasts [Dan. 7:3]"—perhaps signifying the Babylonian, Median, Persian, and Greek empires—rise out of a churning sea. The first "was like a lion and had eagles' wings [Dan. 7:4]." The second, a bear, held between its teeth three ribs. Another resembled a leopard with wings. The last creature was "terrible and dreadful [Dan. 7:7]," with iron teeth and 10 horns on its head. While Daniel watched, the beast sprouted an 11th horn that had eyes and a mouth.

A heavenly court then appeared, and "one that was ancient of days [Dan. 7:9]" took the seat of judgment. "A thousand thousands served him, and ten thousand times ten thousand stood before him [Dan. 7:10]."

Daniel asked someone in the crowd to explain and was told, "These four great beasts are four kings who shall arise out of the earth [Dan. 7:17]." The fourth beast would destroy the others, and from his line 10 kings would rise. After them would come a ruler who would "speak words against the Most High [Dan. 7:25]." For a time that ruler would prevail, but God and his saints would ultimately triumph.

DAN. 2:48 gave Daniel "many great gifts, and made him ruler over the whole province of Babylon, and chief prefect over all the wise men of Babylon."

How did visions help Mary and Joseph?

The Gospel of Luke describes the angel Gabriel visiting the Virgin Mary in a waking vision and LK. 1:31 telling her, "You will conceive in your womb and bear a son, and you shall call his name Jesus."

Matthew gives special prominence to dreams and visions in his account of Jesus' birth. When Joseph, who was betrothed to Mary, found out MT. 1:19 that she was with child, he "resolved to divorce her quietly" because he believed she must have MT. 1:20 had relations with another man. But "an angel of the Lord appeared to him in a dream" and told him, "Do not fear to take Mary your wife, for that which is conceived in her is of the Holy Spirit."

MT. 2:13 After the Wise Men visited the baby Jesus, "an angel of the Lord" came to Joseph in a dream and instructed him to flee with his family to Egypt so that Herod would not be able to harm the infant. After Herod's death, the angel appeared to Joseph and said, "Rise, take the child MT. 2:20 and his mother, and go to the land of Israel, for those who sought the child's life are dead."

How did revelations guide Paul's ministry?

Paul, once a persecutor of Christians, became an Apostle of Jesus Christ because of a vision on the road to Damascus and thereafter had an "abun- 2 COR. 12:7 dance" of "visions and revelations of the Lord." It 2 COR. 12:1 was a dream that caused him to leave Asia Minor and travel to Greece to preach the Gospel, a journey that introduced Christianity to Europe and changed the course of history. Then, when persecuted in the Greek city of Corinth, Paul again had a dream in which God spoke to him: "Do not ACTS 18:9 be afraid, but speak and do not be silent; for I am with you, and no man shall attack you to harm you." Similar dreams and visions persuaded Paul to go to Jerusalem and then to Rome.

Hearing a voice yet seeing no one, the people flee from Paul, struck blind on the road to Damascus in his encounter with the resurrected Jesus.

Prophecy and Revelation

REVELATION. *A revelation is an act of disclosure or enlightenment. In the Bible this word usually concerns God's revelations to humans. God reveals himself or his message in many ways. He appears and speaks directly to individuals in the Bible, including Abraham, Moses, and Jesus. At other times he appears in dreams, or his message is revealed to humans by angels or prophets. In a general sense many biblical writers believed that historical events revealed God's intent, and that good events were a message of God's blessing and bad events an expression of God's judgment. In time the written books of the Bible came to be seen as the vehicle of God's revelation to humans. In the New Testament the writings of the Old Testament are called "the oracles of God [Rom. 3:2]," while Jesus is described as God's newly revealed "Word [Jn. 1:1]." A few of the biblical writings claim to record God's direct words, as when prophetic passages begin, "Thus says the Lord [Jos. 7:13]"; nevertheless, both Jewish and Christian traditions regard all of the biblical writings as the word of God.*

What was the difference between divination and prophecy?

In a general sense the difference between divination and prophecy lies in the initiator of a communication between a human and God. Divination in the Bible occurs when a person asks a question of God and God responds by giving a sign whose meaning can be interpreted; for example, when priests and others occasionally find answers to their queries in the flight of birds or the entrails of sacrificial animals. Prophecy, on the other hand, is initiated by God, who conveys his message to people through a chosen messenger, typically but not always a prophet.

Although the practice of divination was generally looked upon with disfavor by the ancient Israelites, there were exceptions. According to the Book of Genesis, on the second return trip of Joseph's brothers from Egypt to Canaan, Joseph ✳ secretly planted a silver cup in Benjamin's bag as a means of divination. It was from the silver cup, said Joseph's steward, that "my lord drinks, and by this that he divines." GEN. 44:5 Apparently Joseph dropped things into the wine- or water-filled cup and then noted the results.

The most common form of divination involved Urim and Thummim. These were probably sticks cast by the priests, which, somewhat like the heads-or-tails of tossing a coin, could be said to give a yes or no answer to a particular question. There are few references to lots in the New Testament, although "they cast lots" for Jesus' cloth- LK. 23:34 ing, and the remaining Apostles "cast lots" to ACTS 1:26 determine who would replace Judas.

When did prophecies cease?

Prophesying began to decline after the fall of Judah to the Babylonian armies in 587 B.C. The prophets had an important role in Israelite society, but as the society crumbled after the Babylonian devastation, so also did the once secure place of the prophet. The last great prophets, Ezekiel and the anonymous seer frequently called Second Isaiah (author of Chapters 40 to 55 in the Book of Isaiah), gave a message of hope to exiles in Babylon. After the return to Judah from Babylonian exile began in 538 B.C., there was a short-lived (520–518 B.C.) resurgence of prophecy represented by Haggai and Zechariah, followed by Malachi, probably some time between 500 and 450 B.C. Corresponding to the decline in prophetic activity was the increasing authority of the

This ancient clay model of a liver guided Babylonian priests as they sought to divine the future by examining animal entrails.

Attended by a host of angels, the God of Isaiah's prophecies rules over a new Israel, returned from its exile, in an 11th-century illumination.

sacred writings—the Hebrew Bible. In time the sacred writings, rather than the words of living prophets, came to be seen as the vehicle of God's word.

What Old Testament prophecy was fulfilled at Pentecost?

At the first Pentecost after the death, resurrection, and ascension of Jesus, an astonishing thing happened. The Apostles and others were ACTS 2:2 meeting in Jerusalem, when "suddenly . . . the Spirit gave them utterance," and they found they could be understood by the foreign residents of ACTS 2:6 Jerusalem, each of whom "heard them speaking in his own language." The Apostle Peter then explained to the bewildered audience what had just occurred. He paraphrased a passage from JL. 2:28 the Book of Joel: "And it shall come to pass afterward, that I will pour out my spirit on all flesh; your sons and your daughters shall prophesy, ✳

your old men shall dream dreams, and your young men shall see visions." Joel's prediction that prophecy would return was thus fulfilled, according to Peter, by this miracle at Pentecost.

How was the fall of the Roman Empire predicted in the Bible?

The Book of Revelation, which was written around A.D. 95 during the reign of the Roman emperor Domitian, foretells the fall of the Roman Empire in colorful and symbolic language. It was a time when Christian churches were suffering under Roman repression. In Revelation 13, the terrible beast that rises out of the sea is a symbol of the Roman Empire. The seven heads of the beast stand both for the seven hills of Rome and for the city's seven emperors. Men worship the beast because it wields authority on earth. This evil beast, with the harlot seated on it, is called Babylon, which was a code name for Rome in the Jewish and Christian literature of the period. The writer sees in his vision a time when the beast and its allies will battle the Lamb (Christ), who will conquer them. After the beast is captured, it is "thrown alive into the lake of fire that REV. 19:20 burns with sulphur." The symbolic evocation of the fall of Rome and of Christ's eventual victory gave hope and strength to Christians of the day.

How did Jesus prophesy his rejection and execution?

As the disciples looked back on all Jesus had told them about his coming ordeals, they were amazed at how slow they had been to understand. After the fact, it was clear that he had foreseen all and had told them explicitly what would happen. They remembered that once when he was alone with them, avoiding crowds so that he could spend precious hours teaching them, he had stated, "The Son of man will be delivered MK. 9:31 into the hands of men, and they will kill him; and when he is killed, after three days he will rise." Thunderstruck, they could not comprehend what their master was saying and "were afraid to ask MK. 9:32 him" for fear of what they might learn. At times, Jesus had even told of his rejection by the chief priests and execution by Gentiles. But only after the disciples had seen him crucified and resurrected did they grasp the reality of his words.

The End of the Age

At the climax of the final battle, Satan and his hideous cohort will be thrown into "the lake of fire and sulphur . . . and they will be tormented day and night for ever and ever [Rev. 20:10]."

What will happen on the day of the Lord?

Writing out of the hope and pain of Israel's history, the prophets of the Old Testament foresaw a day when God would intervene forcefully in the world—a day often called "the day of the Lord." At that fateful time, God would bring an end to injustice and oppression. He would "punish the world for its evil, and the wicked for their iniquity," but he would also "judge between the nations, and . . . decide for many peoples," and a new time of salvation would begin when nations would "beat their swords into plowshares and . . . nation shall not lift up sword against nation, neither shall they learn war any more."

The day of the Lord is most frequently described in the Bible as a dark judgment day, "cruel, with wrath and fierce anger, to make the earth a desolation." Sometimes the complete destruction of the world is envisioned: "All the earth shall be consumed; for a full, yea, sudden end he will make of all the inhabitants of the earth"; but other passages counter the horror of

(margin references: AM. 5:18, IS. 13:11, IS. 2:4, IS. 2:4, IS. 13:9, ZEPH. 1:18)

these prophecies with the promise of renewal: "I create new heavens and a new earth; and the former things shall not be remembered or come into mind. But be glad and rejoice for ever in that which I create."

How will the world end according to the Bible?

In early Christianity the day of the Lord came to be understood as "the day of the Lord Jesus," that is, the day when Jesus would return as the judge of the world. Jesus explains that "no one knows" the day or the hour when this will happen, "not even the angels of heaven, nor the Son, but the Father only," and he asserts that the day will come very suddenly "for the Son of man is coming at an hour you do not expect."

Paul describes this moment as "the end, when [Jesus] delivers the kingdom to God the Father after destroying every rule and every authority and power." Even death, "the last enemy," will be destroyed. This passage in 1 Corinthians emphasizes God's final triumph over evil.

Other passages describe the end of the world in physical terms. The Second Letter of Peter says that "the heavens will pass away with a loud noise, and the elements will be dissolved with fire, and the earth and the works that are upon it will be burned up." But the faithful can expect "new heavens and a new earth in which righteousness dwells." Revelation, too, envisions a new heaven and earth after "the first heaven and the first earth had passed away."

The end of the world then is portrayed as a time when God pours out his wrath against human wickedness but also offers hope for those who are just and faithful. The visions of spiritual transformation and physical destruction and rebirth picture the future world as a place in which God will be "everything to every one."

(margin references: IS. 65:17, 1 COR. 5:5, MT. 24:36, MT. 24:36, MT. 24:44, 1 COR. 15:24, 1 COR. 15:26, 2 PET. 3:10, 2 PET. 3:13, REV. 21:1, 1 COR. 15:28)

JOHN'S VISION ON PATMOS

The author of the Book of Revelation identifies himself only as John, a servant of God, a prophet, and "your brother [Rev. 1:9]." He addresses his opening remarks to the "seven churches that are in Asia [Rev. 1:4]"—meaning the Roman province of that name in western Asia Minor. His manner is that of a church leader writing to reassure his flock; in fact, he names the congregations in the same order a courier would follow carrying a letter from city to city. John also says he is "on the island called Patmos on account of the word of God and the testimony of Jesus [Rev. 1:9]," banished to that Aegean island by Roman authorities for preaching Jesus' message. His exile occurred at a time of official persecution, most likely under the emperor Domitian (A.D. 81–96), though possibly under Nero (A.D. 54–68) or Vespasian (A.D. 69–79).

This much has been deduced about the author of Revelation—but much remains uncertain. One question is whether John of Patmos was the same person traditionally identified as Jesus' beloved disciple, believed to be the author of the Gospel of John and the three Epistles of John. Since at least the time of the Christian bishop Irenaeus (A.D. 180–200), an influential school of thought has held that John of Patmos and John the disciple of Jesus were indeed the same man. Many scholars have challenged this conclusion, however, finding the Fourth Gospel and the Book of Revelation too different in both writing style and intellectual tone to have been produced by the same author.

In the end, modern readers of Revelation are probably less concerned with such questions than with gaining some insight into John of Patmos and his message. Revelation not only records the dramatic visions God commanded John to write down, but also conveys the burning intensity of his spirit, the passion for Christian truth and for the inevitable day of judgment. Indeed, it is difficult not to feel John's overpowering wrath against those who persecuted the church and exiled him—against Rome itself, "the great harlot . . . bedecked with gold and jewels and pearls, holding in her hand a golden cup full of abominations . . . drunk with the blood of the saints and the blood of the martyrs of Jesus [Rev. 17:1]."

Exiled to the island of Patmos, John is seemingly in a trance as he records his apocalyptic visions in this 17th-century painting by Velázquez.

John wrote from Patmos to the seven churches (red dots) in Asia Minor.

What Is the Second Coming?

The Savior who came to earth as an infant born in a stable and wrapped in swaddling cloths will return as the Son of Man, appearing in glory on the clouds. This was announced to the disciples by two angels on the day of the ascension: "Jesus, who was taken up from you into heaven, will come in the same way as you saw him go." He would arrive, moreover, in a manner befitting the occasion, "with a cry of command, with the archangel's call, and with the sound of the trumpet of God."

ACTS 1:11

1 TH. 4:16

The *Parousia*, or second presence, of Jesus Christ was eagerly awaited by the early Christians, who interpreted his various sayings to mean that he would return soon—before the death of his own earthly generation. Paul himself advised the Corinthians that "the appointed time has grown very short," and spoke to the Thessalonians of "we who are alive, who are left until the coming of the Lord."

1 COR. 7:29

1 TH. 4:15

As decade after decade passed, these hopes were reinterpreted to teach a life of continual

A demon whispers in the ear of the antichrist, standing above the multitude, in this 15th-century painting.

ANTICHRIST. *The word* antichrist *is used only in 1 and 2 John, where one "who denies that Jesus is the Christ [1 Jn. 2:22]" is termed an antichrist. But when John said the "antichrist is coming [1 Jn 2:18]," he was speaking of a widely held belief that an emissary of Satan would herald Jesus' return, deceive believers by posing as the Christ, and be defeated. Biblical passages interpreted as references to the antichrist include Jesus' warning regarding false messiahs who say "I am the Christ [Mt. 24:5]," Paul's description of the "man of lawlessness [2 Th. 2:3]," and the beast whose "number is six hundred and sixty-six [Rev. 13:18]."*

readiness. Christians came to see the delay as God's mercy at work, giving sinners a chance to repent before it was too late. They remembered that Jesus had said that his coming would be as sudden as lightning—unexpected and unpredictable. "Of that day and hour no one knows, not even the angels of heaven."

MT. 24:36

The delay of the *Parousia* has invested the whole history of Christianity with hope. It has encouraged Christians to look beyond the present to a fulfillment of the grandest promise imaginable. For men and women of faith, the expectation of the Second Coming has ruled out despair.

What Is the Last Judgment?

From the day when God expelled Adam and Eve from Eden, the Bible shows that mankind has faced a series of judgments from God. The Lord judged Cain for the murder of his brother, loosed the flood upon a sinful world, leveled Sodom and Gomorrah, and allowed his chosen people to be sent into captivity in Babylon.

But the greatest judgment of all was an event that lay in the future: the climactic reckoning in the final days, when every soul's fate will be pronounced by God through his Son and each person will receive the verdict that God has promised from the earliest Scripture. "All the tribes of the earth will mourn," Jesus told his followers, "and they will see the Son of man coming on the clouds of heaven with power and great glory; and he will send out his angels with a loud trum-

MT. 24:30

On the day of the Last Judgment, as envisioned here by the French artist Jean Cousin the Younger, the souls of meek and mighty alike are to be lifted up from the dead and judged by the risen Christ.

pet call, and they will gather his elect from the four winds."

The promise was carried into the Christian era through the extensive writings of Paul, who assured the Thessalonians that God would deal out tribulation to those who tormented the believers, and cast into the flames those who did not know God or failed to heed the words of Jesus. This dire forecast was balanced by the promise of a place in the kingdom of God for the believers, ✳ and Paul urged those in Thessalonica to give thanks that they had been chosen for salvation.

The prelude to judgment was the resurrection of the dead, the saved and damned alike. Christian belief has varied on this point. One interpretation holds that each person is judged and his destiny fixed at death—but his eternal sentence is pronounced at the Last Judgment, the day when history and time cease and the kingdom of God is established throughout creation.

235

THE MESSIAH

A great theme that binds the Old and New Testaments together is the expectation of the Messiah. The hope for a Messiah begins to gain strength in the later books of the Old Testament and becomes the main idea of the New, centering on Jesus Christ.

The terms *Messiah* and *Christ* derive respectively from the Hebrew and Greek words meaning anointed. They are rooted in the ancient ceremony of consecration, which bestowed special authority on a leader by anointing him with oil. The early Israelites believed that their kings and high priests were men set apart by an anointing blessed by God. When Babylonian armies conquered the Jews and disrupted the monarchy and the priesthood, the people fervently prayed for a Messiah to rule over them. They envisioned him as a mighty king descended from the great King David.

But as generations and centuries passed, their hopes were not fulfilled. As one of the writers of the Proverbs observed, "Hope deferred makes the heart sick [Pr. 13:12]." Even in the second century B.C., when Jewish independence was finally restored after many generations of foreign rule, no Messiah arose. The kings of Judea could not fulfill their people's dream because they were not descendants of David.

Yet the hope that the line of David would bring forth a Messiah would not die. One of the songs in a nonbiblical collection known as the Psalms of Solomon, written in the first century B.C., implored God to raise up for the Jews "their king . . . to rule over Israel your servant. And gird him with strength to crush unrighteous rulers; to cleanse Jerusalem from the Gentiles that trample her in destruction." People expected the Messiah to be a man anointed with God's spirit, with a special commission to bring blessedness to them. Many believed that the Messiah's wisdom and justice would be so great that even pagans would turn to God. The same Jewish psalm continued, "The Gentiles will come from the corners of the earth to see his glory . . . and to see the glory of the Lord."

The New Testament is founded on the faith that Jesus Christ was the fulfillment of such prophecies. But at every stage of the story of Jesus, the New Testament emphasizes the unusual character of this surprising Messiah. Yes, he was descended from David, but he hardly seemed royal. He was born not to a princess of Israel's ruling house, but to a young woman who was betrothed to a village craftsman. His birth was celebrated not by courtiers, but by lowly shepherds and Wise Men of foreign birth. Known as the son of a carpenter, he became a traveling teacher and directed his words of blessing and comfort mostly to the poor and outcast.

Jesus spoke the language of the common people, not of their rulers, and he taught God's will through images drawn from the lives of farmers and fishermen, housewives and herders. He chose for disciples men of no social prominence or power, some of them completely uneducated. Even when his miraculous deeds brought him fame and crowds of needy people thronged around him, he refused to make any attempt to turn popular adulation into political power. He came into repeated conflict with those who held both political and religious authority in Palestine.

The Gospels show that even the disciples, his most devoted followers, were perplexed by parts of Jesus' ministry, especially his talk of his own approaching suffering and death. And when he was crucified and Pilate posted the title "the King of the Jews [Jn. 19:19]" over Jesus' head for all passersby to see, the title was a ridiculing charge against him, not an affirmation of a hope fulfilled.

Jesus' followers, including his closest disciples, at first found it difficult to accept any kind of suffering for the Messiah. Crucifixion was widely regarded as the most debasing of punishments of the times. Even after Jesus' resurrection, his disciples expected him to literally "restore the kingdom to Israel [Acts 1:6]"; but Jesus instructed them that such matters were in God's hands and that they were to be his witnesses not just to Israel but "to the end of the earth [Acts 1:8]."

Gradually the early Christians began to see that Jesus both fulfilled and transformed the ancient hope for a Messiah. They came to understand the true significance of the resurrection. By raising him from the dead, God showed that the crucified Jesus was truly the Christ and his Son. Jesus' message and ministry did not end; the hope of the Messiah, transformed and filled with new life, spread to the whole world. Jesus had turned upside down all the expectations of glory and military might that had become an integral part of the messianic hope, but paradoxically he had thereby created a new hope, more universal, more powerful, and ultimately more glorious.

Top left: "The Crucifixion," a 14th-century altar, Florence.

Birth and Childhood

Quietly adoring, Mary and Joseph contemplate the newborn Jesus in this 15th-century painting; at the upper left, an angel brings the good news of the Messiah's birth to the startled shepherds.

What do the Gospels tell us about Jesus' birth?

Only Matthew and Luke provide details about what has become one of the most celebrated and treasured stories in the Bible: the birth of Jesus. Mark and John are silent on the subject, beginning their narratives with John preaching his baptism of repentance in the wilderness.

Both Matthew and Luke emphasize that Jesus was miraculously born of a virgin named Mary, that Mary was betrothed to Joseph, a man of the house of David, and that the child was born in Bethlehem, the city of David—all in fulfillment of Old Testament prophecies. In addition, however, each provides material from which Christian tradition has been able to shape a cohesive narrative of a helpless infant threatened by an evil tyrant but guarded and nurtured by adoring parents in order that he may achieve his destiny of saving mankind.

Luke tells of the angel Gabriel's announcement to Mary at Nazareth that she will give birth, a revelation that she greets with the beautiful psalm known as the Magnificat. As the time of Jesus' birth approaches, the emperor Augustus decrees a census that takes Joseph and Mary to Bethlehem. With no place to stay, Mary gives birth in a stable. An angel proclaims the birth to shepherds, who hasten to worship the child. After 41 days, the parents take the infant to Jerusalem for presentation at the temple and then return to Nazareth.

Matthew gives none of these details, recounting instead a series of dreams in which an angel of the Lord appears to Joseph. In the first he learns that his betrothed has conceived of the Holy Spirit. In the second, following the child's birth and the visit of "wise men from the East," MT. 2:1 Joseph is warned to escape the wrathful jealousy of Herod by fleeing with his family to Egypt. In the third and fourth dreams, after Herod's death, Joseph is told that it is safe to return to the land of Israel—not to Bethlehem in Judea, where Herod's son Archelaus reigns, but rather to Nazareth in Galilee.

When was Jesus born?

The event on which the entire Christian calendar depends cannot be precisely dated. The only two Gospel writers to mention the birth of Jesus, Matthew and Luke, do not say when it occurred—either because the information was not available to them or because their Christian contemporaries were not particularly interested in such data.

Both Matthew and Luke say that Jesus was born during the reign of Herod the Great, who is known to have died in 4 B.C. But Luke also sets the birth at the time of a census that was taken when Quirinius was the Roman governor in Syria. Quirinius took office in A.D. 6—10 years after Herod's death. Historians generally follow the common testimony of the two evangelists and date Jesus' birth one to three years before Herod's death.

The month and day of the birth are also unknown. Various traditions have supported March 28, April 18 or 19, and May 29—mostly because shepherds watching their flocks in the fields suggests spring. In time, Jesus' birth seems to have become linked to the winter solstice: December 25 in the Julian calendar, January 6 in the Egyp-

The Magi, the first Gentiles to worship Jesus, pursue the star of Bethlehem in a 13th-century stained glass at Canterbury Cathedral, England.

tian. First included in a Roman liturgical calendar for the year 336, December 25 was accepted in both eastern and western churches by the end of that century.

Who were the Magi?

A magus was originally a member of a caste of people dwelling to the east of the Holy Land who led a life of self-denial, studied astrology, and interpreted dreams. By Jesus' time, the term was applied to any wise man or magician seeking the truth about God and the universe.

In the Gospel of Matthew it is significant that the Wise Men from the East are magi. As foreigners and experts on the stars, they confirm for the world the sign in the heavens pointing to the long-awaited birth of the king of the Jews. Although the evangelist does not give their names or their number, later tradition held that there were three Wise Men and that their names were Caspar (or Gaspar), Melchior, and Balthasar. Matthew lists the Wise Men's three gifts to the infant Savior, gold, frankincense, and myrrh, which were thought by some medieval interpreters to symbolize Jesus' kingship, divinity, and ultimate death as a man.

CELEBRATING JESUS AS THE MESSIAH

Having promised a devout old man of Jerusalem named Simeon that he would not die until he had seen the Messiah, the Holy Spirit led Simeon to the temple on the day when the Holy Family came for Mary's ritual purification, 41 days after the birth of Jesus.

According to Luke, Simeon took the infant into his arms, blessed God, and said, "Lord, now lettest thou thy servant depart in peace, according to thy word; for mine eyes have seen thy salvation which thou hast prepared in the presence of all peoples, a light for revelation to the Gentiles, and for glory to thy people Israel [Lk. 2:29]." Mary and Joseph marveled at what Simeon said, but then he went on to warn Mary of the suffering that was to come, as well as the glory, telling her, "And a sword will pierce through your own soul also [Lk. 2:35]."

At the same hour the aged prophetess Anna, coming on the scene, also gave thanks to the Lord and began to tell about the child "to all who were looking for the redemption of Jerusalem [Lk. 2:38]."

What was the star of Bethlehem?

In the belief that God manifests his will through nature, biblical interpreters have sought an explanation in astronomical findings for "the star in the East" that brought the Wise Men to Bethlehem. Some people speculate that it could have been a nova, or exploding star, such as the one that was observed in the Southern Hemisphere in 1987. Chinese astronomers recorded a nova in the year 5 B.C.

Johannes Kepler, the renowned German astronomer, calculated that a highly visible convergence of the planets Saturn and Jupiter, such as the one he observed in 1603, would also have occurred in 6 or 7 B.C. Still others have demonstrated that Halley's Comet would have been visible over Palestine in 12 B.C.

Conclusive evidence that would link any of these astronomical phenomena to the birth of Jesus is lacking—especially since Matthew describes a moving star that "came to rest over the place where the child was." Nevertheless, the theories do lend scientific plausibility to the biblical account of magi following a heavenly body that was remarkable either for its newness or its brightness.

EGYPT AS A PLACE OF REFUGE

When King Herod threatened the life of the infant Jesus, an angel appeared to Joseph in a dream to give a warning: "Rise, take the child and his mother, and flee to Egypt, and remain there till I tell you [Mt. 2:13]."

Why Egypt? From ancient times the lush Nile Valley, the lifeline of Egypt's ancient civilization, had attracted refugees from the far more arid land of Canaan. Genesis tells how Abraham, soon after arriving in Canaan for the first time, faced a famine and went to stay in Egypt.

Egypt was next a refuge from famine for Jacob and his sons. But the wealth of Egypt became a snare. Jacob's descendants remained along the Nile for generations, until a pharaoh came to power who enslaved them, and the Lord had to deliver them.

In later times the rebellious Jeroboam escaped King Solomon's reach by fleeing to Egypt until he could return after the king's death and lead the revolt of the northern tribes of Israel. Still later, when the Babylonians were deporting Jews to Mesopotamia, a contingent escaped to Egypt, taking the prophet Jeremiah with them.

Joseph, Mary, and the infant Jesus, therefore, were following a well-worn path when they trekked southwest along the coastal road to the hospitable and protective banks of the Nile to escape Herod's edict.

Mary tenderly cradles Jesus in Fra Angelico's painting of the Holy Family's escape into Egypt.

In a painting by Holman Hunt, Mary and Joseph find Jesus, displaying wisdom far beyond his years, earnestly discussing the law with the temple's learned men.

What do we know of Jesus' life between 12 and 30?

Although Jesus is the single most influential individual the world has ever known, 30 of the 33 years of his life are an almost total blank. The Gospels of Matthew and Luke tell of his birth, and Luke adds one important incident that occurred when he was 12. Thus the so-called hidden years are subject to conjecture.

We know from Luke's account of young Jesus' journey with his parents to Jerusalem for Passover that Joseph and Mary were devout Jews and that Jesus was already intensely interested in the Torah. It is probable that his religious studies continued and laid the groundwork for his later teachings about the law. The most likely conclusion to be drawn from the lack of information on Jesus' childhood is that it passed uneventfully. No doubt Jesus lived the life of a Galilean boy of the first century A.D.

The Gospels mention that Joseph and Jesus were both carpenters. But since Jesus never mentions carpentry in his teaching, should one surmise that he did not particularly like the craft and perhaps was glad to leave it behind?

It would be fascinating to know more about Jesus' years of growth and learning. The Gospels, however, look only at the result: a brief ministry that transformed the world.

JESUS AMONG THE TEACHERS

Having celebrated the feast of Passover in Jerusalem, Joseph and Mary had started home for Nazareth when they discovered that 12-year-old Jesus was not among the crowd of people with whom they were traveling. They returned to search for the boy and on the third day found him, "sitting among the teachers, listening to them and asking them questions [Lk. 2:46]."

According to Luke, the boy's parents were amazed, and his mother asked him, "Son, why have you treated us so [Lk. 2:48]?" His response baffled Joseph and Mary, for what he said was "Did you not know that I must be in my Father's house [Lk. 2:49]?" And by "Father," it is clear, he did not mean Joseph.

Nonetheless, Jesus went home with his parents and "increased in wisdom and in stature, and in favor with God and man [Lk. 2:52]."

The Ministry

Does the Bible say that Jesus and John the Baptist were related?

Because the King James Version of the Bible, published in 1611, was for so long the most widely accepted one in English, it has been believed for nearly four centuries that Jesus and John were cousins. According to the King James translation, the angel of God says to Mary: "And, behold, thy cousin Elizabeth, she hath also conceived a son in her old age."

LK. 1:36

Modern scholars, however, translate the Greek differently, identifying Elizabeth, the mother of John the Evangelist, as merely a kinswoman of Mary's. It is perhaps worth noting that it is unlikely that the two were first cousins, since Mary was a young virgin and Elizabeth was a woman "advanced in years."

LK. 1:7

What language did Jesus speak?

The Gospel of Mark, thought to be the oldest of the four Gospels, gives clear evidence of Jesus having spoken Aramaic. His final cry from the cross, "*Eloi, Eloi, lama sabachthani?*" is in Aramaic and is translated by Mark as "My God, my God, why hast thou forsaken me?" Other Aramaic phrases in Mark are the words used by Jesus to raise the daughter of the head of the synagogue ("*Talitha cumi*," translated as "Little girl, I say to you, arise") and the command used to heal a man of deafness and a speech impediment ("*Ephphatha*," translated as "Be opened").

MK. 15:34

MK. 5:41

MK. 7:34

Aramaic, a sister language of Hebrew and one just as ancient, had come to dominate everyday communication throughout the Middle East during the Assyrian, Babylonian, and Persian em-

Satan offers to give all the world's kingdoms to Jesus in this medieval miniature by the Sienese artist Duccio. Jesus rejects the tempter, and God's angels rejoice.

pires. Hebrew in these late Old Testament times was gradually relegated to scholarly discourse—in particular, to interpretation of Scripture—and to religious ceremonies. While Hebrew never disappeared from everyday use entirely, the common language of the Jews of Palestine in the time of Jesus was Aramaic.

A boy of Jesus' intelligence would almost certainly have memorized the Hebrew Scripture, and most scholars believe that he could at least read that language. Indeed, Luke tells of Jesus standing up in the synagogue at Nazareth to read from the prophet Isaiah.

It is also possible that he knew some Greek. The conquests of Alexander the Great in the fourth century B.C. had brought Greek culture to the Holy Land, and the language of commerce and diplomacy in Jesus' time was Greek. Mark has Jesus conversing with a Greek woman, and in John's Gospel some Greeks seek an interview with him. Two of Jesus' disciples have Greek names, Andrew and Philip, and—though Jesus most likely taught in Aramaic—nearly all his sayings were handed down in Greek.

As for Latin, the language of the Romans who ruled Palestine in the time of Jesus, there is no evidence that he knew it.

Where did Jesus' ministry take place?

Although Jesus seems to have been almost always on the move during his ministry and the principal locations of his work are well known, his itinerary can be only roughly sketched from the information in the Gospels.

Jesus' hometown was Nazareth, an obscure village in the rocky hills of Galilee, away from any main trade route. His first miracle took place in the equally obscure village of Cana, 12 miles north. Jesus was at home in such Galilean villages, and most of his ministry took place in the towns and countryside around the Sea of Galilee.

Near the beginning of his ministry, Jesus moved to the town of Capernaum, on the north
MK. 1:39 shore of the sea, and it became his base as "he went throughout all Galilee, preaching in their synagogues." It was at Capernaum, a principal trading center for the region ruled by Herod Antipas, that Jesus met Levi, one of Herod's tax collectors, and where he also healed a centurion's servant. Two miles eastward, the Jordan flows ✳

THE TEMPTATION OF JESUS

Before beginning his public ministry, Jesus spent 40 days fasting in a remote wilderness area. While there, the devil tempted him three times.

In the first confrontation, the devil appealed to Jesus' hunger: "If you are the Son of God, command this stone to become bread [Lk. 4:3]." Jesus answered with a citation from Deuteronomy 8: "It is written, 'Man shall not live by bread alone [Mt. 4:4; Lk. 4:4].' "

In the second temptation (Luke placed it third), the devil took Jesus to Jerusalem, to the highest part of the temple, and said, "If you are the Son of God, throw yourself down [Mt. 4:6]." The devil then quoted from Psalm 91: "He will give his angels charge of you [Mt. 4:6]," and "On their hands they will bear you up, lest you strike your foot against a stone [Mt. 4:6]." Jesus answered: "You shall not tempt the Lord your God [Mt. 4:7; Lk. 4:12]."

Finally, the devil took Jesus to a high mountain and showed him "all the kingdoms of the world and the glory of them [Mt. 4:8]," and said, "All these I will give you, if you will fall down and worship me [Mt. 4:9]." Jesus answered, "Begone, Satan [Mt. 4:10]!" and cited a verse from Deuteronomy 6: "You shall worship the Lord your God, and him only shall you serve [Mt. 4:10]." At this point, Matthew and Mark say that angels came and ministered to Jesus. Luke adds ominously that the devil departed "until an opportune time [Lk. 4:13]."

The temptations have been interpreted as three ways to be a messiah that Jesus rejected: he decided not to appeal to people's physical needs; he chose not to perform spectacular but superficial miracles; he elected not to make political and military conquests.

into the Sea of Galilee, and just beyond lay the town of Bethsaida, the home of Peter, Andrew, and Philip. Westward down the coast was Magdala, the home of Mary Magdalene, who became a devoted follower after Jesus freed her from demonic possession. Farther down the coast was Tiberias, Herod's capital, the probable home of Joanna, the wife of Herod's steward, who left the comforts of court life to follow Jesus.

Occasionally Jesus traveled beyond Galilee. To the south and east across the sea lay the league of 10 Greek cities known as the Decapolis, where Jesus healed a man with so many demons that he called himself Legion. Jesus also trekked northwest to the Phoenician areas of Tyre and Sidon, north to the source of the Jordan River at the Greek city of Caesarea Philippi, as well as south into Samaria.

How often Jesus traveled to Jerusalem after his ministry began is a matter of some dispute. The Gospels of Matthew, Mark, and Luke only speak of the single climactic journey to Jerusalem that led to his confrontation with the temple authorities and his execution by the Romans. The Gospel of John, on the other hand, mentions three journeys from Galilee to Jerusalem and depicts much of Jesus' ministry as occurring in Judea and Jerusalem. It even places Jesus' dramatic action of driving the money changers from the temple early in his ministry rather than at the end, as the other Gospels have it.

To whom did Jesus preach?

LK. 4:18 At the beginning of his ministry Jesus rose in the synagogue at Nazareth to read from Isaiah: "The Spirit of the Lord is upon me, because he has anointed me to preach good news to the poor. He has sent me to proclaim release to the captives and recovering of sight to the blind, to set at liberty those who are oppressed."

Much of Jesus' ministry took place by the Sea of Galilee, where several of his disciples were once fishermen.

Closing the book, he added that the words of the ancient prophet were that day fulfilled. When John the Baptist sent disciples to ask him if he was the Messiah, Jesus instructed the messengers to tell John that he had come to preach good news to the poor.

Throughout his ministry Jesus drew crowds of the humble, the afflicted, and the outcast. In a rigidly stratified society that frequently dealt harshly with the lowly, Jesus took pains to address himself to the lame, the blind, the scorned, and the penniless; he even spoke to tax collectors, prostitutes, and sinners. But Jesus also preached to the rich and powerful, challenging their smug belief that they were the favored of God. When a pious and wealthy man asked what had to be done to gain eternal life, Jesus advised him to sell all that he had and give it to the poor; freedom from possessions was the "one thing" MK. 10:21 the man lacked.

Yet more important, Jesus addressed his message to all those persons who allowed themselves to receive it or, as he is quoted in several places in the Gospels, "If any man has ears to MK. 4:23 hear, let him hear."

Did the Nazarenes believe in Jesus?

Long ago the writer Aesop observed that "familiarity breeds contempt." Jesus similarly summarized his own experience when he returned to his hometown of Nazareth after gaining some fame in his ministry. He cited the proverb, "A MK. 6:4 prophet is not without honor, except in his own country, and among his own kin, and in his own house."

His neighbors in Nazareth were possibly nettled because Jesus failed to remain a village carpenter, as would have been expected of Joseph's son. When he began teaching with an astonishing sense of authority that they could not understand, they asked, "Where MK. 6:2

"Christ Preaching," a 17th-century etching by Rembrandt, explores the diverse effects of Jesus' words on a group of listeners.

did this man get all this? . . . Is not this the carpenter, the son of Mary and brother of James and Joses and Judas and Simon, and are not his sisters here with us?" Mark notes that "they took offense at him" and that Jesus "marveled because of their unbelief."

MK. 6:3
MK. 6:6

Probably Jesus also had friends among the townspeople of Nazareth, and his family clearly felt concern for his welfare; once, when people began to say Jesus was mad and "beside himself," they tried to take him in hand, evidently to bring him home.

MK. 3:21

The Gospel of John notes that "even his brothers did not believe in him." Jesus' relation to those whom the Gospels call his brothers and "his sisters" became the object of considerable controversy beginning in the fourth century. As the doctrine of the perpetual virginity of Mary became widely accepted, the persons referred to in the Gospels could no longer be understood to be children of Mary, Jesus' mother. They were often, therefore, said to be either his cousins or stepbrothers and stepsisters, the children of Joseph by a previous marriage.

JN. 7:5

MK. 6:3

Why did Jesus so often ask that his miracles and mission be kept secret?

Readers of the New Testament have often wondered why Jesus insisted so frequently that news of his great spontaneous acts of healing should not be spread. A similar but perhaps more intriguing puzzle is why Jesus insisted that his disciples not reveal that he was the Messiah. Scholars eventually came to call this second injunction the messianic secret.

In the first chapter of Mark, Jesus, "moved with pity," healed a leper but asked him to speak of it to no one—a command the man disregarded, bringing people to Jesus "from every quarter." Jesus knew that his miraculous powers would obscure his messianic mission, that people were unlikely to understand that his acts of mercy were meant to demonstrate qualities of kindness, forgiveness, and trust. It was the message and not the miracles that counted.

MK. 1:41

MK. 1:45

As for the messianic secret, again Jesus demonstrated his understanding of human frailty by insisting that even his disciples wait until his ministry was fully completed and they saw its outcome before they proclaimed him a messiah.

Why did Jesus teach in parables?

To enlist the imagination of his listeners in coming to an understanding of the kingdom of God, Jesus spoke in parables. By using figurative language and striking illustrations, he was able to reach deeper into their hearts and minds than he could have done by giving them moral advice or exhorting them to obedience. In the small body of Jesus' preserved teaching, more than 40 parables can be counted.

Jesus' parables involve at least two levels of meaning. In the first, the colorful story itself, Jesus drew on every level of his contemporary society, from servants to farmers to travelers to bridesmaids to kings. To give a hint of the second, deeper level of meaning, Jesus frequently MT. 13:31 used a simile, such as "The kingdom of heaven is like. . . ." or used a parable to answer a probing question, such as "Who is my neighbor?" But LK. 10:29 often, the second level of meaning was to be supplied by the listener.

Jesus was aware that not everyone could or would be caught up in his parables or accept his teaching. He even used a parable to explain this fact, telling of a sower scattering seed in a field. All around him seed is lost: to birds, to rocky ground, to choking thorns. But where the seed falls on good ground—that is, receptive listeners—it multiplies thirty-, sixty-, a hundredfold.

For many the parables would remain just puzzling little stories, heard but not really understood. But Jesus' disciples treasured them, knowing that they opened doors to enlightenment that otherwise might have remained shut.

What was the Sermon on the Mount?

Rather than the record of a single homily delivered on a specific occasion, the long passage in

JESUS HEALS THE PARALYTIC

Jesus' reputation as a healer was well known. At times he could hardly move for the throngs around him—the sick, the lame, the curiosity seekers, those who wanted to hear more of his distinctive teaching. News that he was in Capernaum drew such a crowd that it jammed the house where he was teaching and blocked the door. When four men approached carrying a paralyzed friend, they saw immediately that they had no hope of breaking through the thicket of spellbound listeners.

Then one of them had a desperate idea. They climbed an outside stairway and positioned themselves so that they could remove the roof above the area where Jesus sat teaching. One may well imagine that Jesus stared up in astonishment as earth and bits of wood started to shower down, light broke through, and a pallet carrying a paralyzed man was lowered. Gazing through the hole were four men whose eyes told Jesus of the faith that had led them to this extreme action.

Everyone no doubt expected the man to be healed immediately, but instead Jesus looked at him and said, "My son, your sins are forgiven [Mk. 2:5]." The man still lay paralyzed, and the minds of the scribes sitting there started whirring: "It is blasphemy! Who can forgive sins but God alone [Mk. 2:7]?"

His opponents could not deny his healings, but they called his claim to forgive blasphemous. Thus the man who came through the roof became a demonstration, "that you may know that the Son of man has authority on earth to forgive sins [Mk. 2:10]." "Rise," Jesus commanded the paralyzed man, "take up your pallet and go home [Mk. 2:11]." The dense crowd parted as the man stood and walked out. The people had never seen anything like it, and they "glorified God [Mk. 2:12]."

In the parable of the prodigal son, illustrated here by the Flemish painter Roelandt Savery, Jesus evoked the idea of God the father forgiving his children who repented their rebellious ways.

Matthew known as the Sermon on the Mount appears to be a compilation by Matthew of some of the most characteristic and essential teachings of Jesus. A shorter passage in the Gospel of Luke presents many of the same ideas, often in similar language, but sets the sermon on level ground instead of on a mountain. Taken together, the similarities and differences in the two accounts reinforce the impression that these were attempts to summarize Jesus' revolutionary message, in which he offered trust in an accessible God as a relief from fear and anxiety.

It is perhaps difficult for a modern reader to appreciate how radical the sermon would have appeared to Jesus' contemporaries. For Jesus was not content to uphold the ancient law that focuses on such antisocial behavior as adultery and murder. Rather he sought the cause of such behavior and asked for a new kind of person: one who does not commit murder because he can control his anger; one who does not commit adultery because he does not harbor lust.

Jesus' parables, like the story of the sower depicted in this 13th-century stained-glass panel, employed familiar routines to teach profound truths.

Though his society frowned upon rabbis talking publicly to women and upon Samaritans in general, Jesus spoke freely with the Samaritan woman at the well; a fourth-century Roman catacomb painting.

Because the Sermon on the Mount contains the Lord's Prayer, the Beatitudes, and the Golden Rule, it is justly famous. However, it is the heart of Jesus' teaching not because of these, but because it invites believer and skeptic alike to find the source of good and evil conduct. That source lies, as Jesus preached, within the heart. Only by a purity of heart can people learn to love even their enemies and become true children of the MT. 5:45 "Father who is in heaven."

What did Jesus mean by "the kingdom of God"?

The prayer Jesus offered the crowds during his Sermon on the Mount suggests succinctly what MT. 6:10 is meant by the kingdom of God: "Thy kingdom come. Thy will be done, on earth as it is in heaven." God's will, he is saying, must rule in the world he created.

Jesus' understanding of God's kingdom had many facets, and many of his sayings point to different aspects of the kingdom of God (in Mat-
LK. 6:20 thew, the kingdom of heaven): "Blessed are you
MK. 10:15 poor, for yours is the kingdom of God." "Whoever does not receive the kingdom of God like a
LK. 18:25 child shall not enter it." "It is easier for a camel to go through the eye of a needle than for a rich man to enter the kingdom of God."

But Jesus never tried to give a comprehensive ✳

definition of the kingdom of God or to limit it to a specific timetable. He spoke of it not only as something coming in the near future but also as something already present in his own ministry. "Repent, for the kingdom of heaven is at hand," MT. 4:17 he said on one occasion. "The kingdom of God LK. 17:20 is not coming with signs to be observed; nor will they say, 'Lo, here it is!' or 'There!' for behold, the kingdom of God is in the midst of you."

When he wanted to explain the kingdom of God, Jesus used similes. God's kingdom is like a "treasure hidden in a field," a valuable pearl, or a MT. 13:44 grain of mustard seed that grows into a tree. Through such parables Jesus discouraged his disciples from understanding the kingdom of God simply as a doctrine about the end of the age and helped them to see it as a present reality and a continual quest. "Seek first his kingdom MT. 6:33 and his righteousness," Jesus urged them, "and all these things shall be yours as well."

Why was it unusual for Jesus to talk with a Samaritan woman?

It was noon on a hot day, but when Jesus requested a drink of water from a Samaritan woman at Jacob's well near Shechem, she was astounded—as were his disciples, who "marveled JN. 4:27 that he was talking with a woman." Jesus' request was startling because it was considered improper for a man to address in public a woman not related to him. As his ministry continued, however, the disciples were to learn that Jesus regularly rejected the conventions that barred him from talking to women. He taught women as freely as he did men, and his traveling circle of disciples came to include several women whose lives he had changed.

The conversation at the well was doubly shocking because it was with a Samaritan. The religious and political hatred between Jews and Samaritans dated back centuries. In Jesus' time, Jews traveling through Samaria to Jerusalem often did not feel welcome to enter a town, because—as the woman at the well observed— JN. 4:9 "Jews have no dealings with Samaritans." Not only did Jesus flout such conventions on this occasion, but he even held up the Good Samaritan as an example of the fulfillment of God's command to love one's neighbor. When they wished to express their outrage at his teaching, Jesus' JN. 8:48 opponents once said, "Are we not right in saying that you are a Samaritan and have a demon?"

Because Jesus had treated her with respect, the Samaritan woman took his message back to her village. Its inhabitants asked him to stay with JN. 4:41 them for two days, "And many more believed because of his word."

What did Jesus teach about the power of faith?

For Jesus, faith meant trust in God—the belief that he was near and cared for his creatures. Those who lacked faith suffered anxiety and fear MT. 6:25 for their well-being. "Do not be anxious about your life, what you shall eat or what you shall drink. . . . Consider the lilies of the field," Jesus MT. 6:30 told his disciples. "If God so clothes the grass of the field . . . will he not much more clothe you, O men of little faith?"

Too often Jesus discovered that his disciples MT. 8:26 were such "men of little faith." Their trust in God failed in the face of a storm at sea or when they confronted a boy in convulsions that they could not heal. As Jesus approached the child, his fa- MK. 9:22 ther begged, "If you can do anything, have pity on us and help us." Jesus replied, "If you can! All things are possible to him who believes." The father cried in desperation, "I believe; help my unbelief!" Immediately Jesus healed the boy. ✳

Since faith is trust in God, and "with God all MT. 19:26 things are possible," Jesus could use highly dramatic language to describe the power of faith. "If MT. 17:20 you have faith," he told his disciples, ". . . you will say to this mountain, 'Move from here to there,' and it will move; and nothing will be impossible to you."

Faith, however, did not mean using God to change things. Rather, it meant trusting and submitting to God's will. As Jesus prayed in the Garden of Gethsemane, "Abba, Father, all things are MK. 14:36 possible to thee; remove this cup from me; yet not what I will, but what thou wilt."

Whose faith did Jesus single out for praise?

Jesus was quick to recognize genuine faith, and he found it in unlikely candidates. He praised

BEATITUDE. *A beatitude is a blessing that one person confers upon another. Many beatitudes in the Old Testament bestow God's favor on someone who lives according to spiritual principles: for example, "Blessed is the man who walks not in the counsel of the wicked [Ps. 1:1]."*

Less conventional, however, are the Beatitudes of Jesus contained in the Sermon on the Mount. Jesus confers God's favor on those suffering situations that seem the opposite of blessedness. In Matthew 5, Jesus blessed the spiritually impoverished; those in mourning; the meek and vulnerable; those to whom righteous and just treatment is denied; those who do not retaliate but show mercy; the pure of heart; the peacemakers; the persecuted.

The version in Luke 6 contrasts four blessings with four woes: Blessed are you who are poor, who hunger, who weep, who are hated; woe to you who are rich, have plenty to eat, have a good time, enjoy popularity.

The Beatitudes of Jesus have been called end-time, or eschatological, blessings. They are promises of God's vindication as his kingdom replaces the enthroned powers and raises up those most in need of divine protection and deliverance.

Jesus confers with Moses (left) and Elijah (right) in Titian's powerful vision of the Transfiguration. The Apostles, crouching below, shield their faces from the blinding radiance streaming from the mountaintop.

the faith of a sinful woman who wept at his feet during a banquet and that of a blind beggar named Bartimaeus who persisted in calling out to him when others told him to be silent.

Two individuals in particular earned Jesus' admiration for their faith; remarkably, neither was a fellow Jew. One was a centurion who approached Jesus in Capernaum, urgently telling him of a slave of his who was paralyzed and on the verge of death. Jesus was ready to go to the house of this Gentile to heal his servant when the MT. 8:8 man stopped him. "Lord, I am not worthy to have you come under my roof, but only say the word, and my servant will be healed." Jesus was MT. 8:10 amazed. "Truly," he said to those following him, "not even in Israel have I found such faith."

Again when Jesus sought seclusion by withdrawing to the Phoenician city of Tyre, north of Galilee, a Greek woman sought him out and begged him to heal her daughter of demonic possession. Matthew records Jesus' uncharacter- MT. 15:24 istically harsh response: "I was sent only to the lost sheep of the house of Israel. . . . It is not fair to take the children's bread and throw it to the ✳

dogs." The woman kept her daughter's need paramount and swallowed her pride. "Yes, Lord," she said, "yet MT. 15:27 even the dogs eat the crumbs that fall from their master's table." Now Jesus was taken aback. "O wom- MT. 15:28 an, great is your faith!" he exclaimed, and he healed her daughter instantly.

What was the Transfiguration?

Peter had confessed his belief that Jesus was the Messiah, but Jesus commanded that no one be told of it. To his astonished disciples he revealed that he must go to Jerusalem, where he would "suffer many things MT. 16:21 from the elders and chief priests and scribes, and be killed, and on the third day be raised."

About a week later he took Peter, James, and John to a mountaintop. There the awestruck disciples saw their leader suddenly transformed into a figure of almost blinding radiance. Moses and Elijah—representing the law and the prophets—appeared, speaking with Jesus, and from a luminous cloud moving above came a voice saying, "This is my MT. 17:5 beloved Son, with whom I am well pleased; listen to him."

The story of the Transfiguration appears in the Gospels of Matthew, Mark, and Luke, but not in the Gospel of John. The mystical event is clearly a turning point in the life of Jesus or, as one scholar has termed it, a point of no return. Soon afterward, according to Luke, Jesus sensed that the days that were to mark the climax of his mission were drawing near, and "he set his face to LK. 9:51 go to Jerusalem."

What is "the great commandment"?

As Jesus was answering questions in the temple, a lawyer rose to test his knowledge by asking for

SYMBOLS OF CHRISTIANITY

In speaking to his followers, Jesus referred to himself as "the living bread which came down from heaven [Jn. 6:51]," "the good shepherd [Jn. 10:11]" who leads his flocks to salvation, and "the true vine [Jn. 15:1]." Through these vivid images Jesus sought to reveal his identity and the meaning of his ministry.

After the death of Jesus his followers continued to teach and preach in his name. The first symbol adopted by the early Christians to signify their belief in the Messiah and the new faith was probably the fish. It recalled the baptismal waters, the loaves and fishes, and Jesus' own invitation to the disciples to become "fishers of men [Mt. 4:19]." The Greek word for fish, *ichthys,* is an acrostic for "Jesus Christ, Son of God, Savior"; the first letters of each word in the phrase read in order form the word *ichthys.*

The fish symbol appeared in Christian meeting places in the catacombs in Rome and on Christian tombs and doorposts, but how it became such a widespread symbol for Christianity remains unclear. In the first few centuries of church history during the Roman persecutions, the fish may have been a secret symbol of Christian identification.

The cross, on the other hand, was not associated with Christianity until the fourth century A.D. Understandably, the early Christians may have been reluctant to glorify an object connected with such a shameful punishment. During the reign of Constantine the Great (306–337), the first Christian Roman emperor, the cross was adopted as a sacred Christian symbol. As reported by the church historian Eusebius, Constantine "saw with his own eyes the trophy of a cross of light in the heavens above the sun, and bearing this inscription, 'Conquer by this.'" On the strength of his vision, Constantine marked the shields of his soldiers with Chi Rho—the first two letters of the Greek word for Christ, which form the shape of a cross—and won a decisive battle.

A later legend concerns Constantine's mother, Helena. Supposedly, she discovered the cross of Jesus in Jerusalem, which the legend says was identified by a miracle—a corpse stretched out on the true cross came back to life. Constantine abolished crucifixion as a legal Roman punishment during his reign. Both the cross alone and representations of Christ on the cross began to be used more and more as the definitive Christian symbol.

Bearing Christ's monogram, the Greek letters Chi and Rho, this cross was carved onto a fourth-century Roman sarcophagus.

Two symbols of Christian faith, the fish and the cross, are shown in this Coptic sculpture from an Egyptian cemetery.

A hand that is raised in blessing is fixed at the center of this medieval cross from Turkey's Scented Church.

MAMMON. *The word* mammon *is evidently from an ancient Aramaic term meaning wealth, riches, or property. Later, it became a synonym for* treasure, *which is the meaning it had in Jesus' time.*

Jesus' famous saying "You cannot serve God and mammon [Mt. 6:24]" warns of the tension between service to God and the pursuit of money and possessions. Jesus sharpens the point about the corrupting power of possessions when he contrasts mammon *with God as two mutually exclusive claims on a person's ultimate loyalty: a slave cannot have two owners; what happens when the slave receives contradictory orders?*

Jesus personified the power in mammon, *but he does not hold it up as a pagan god or demon. There is the suggestion that when a person "owns" anything, this possession has a way of exercising its own control.*

It was not until the Renaissance that mammon *became the personification of greed—for example, Sir Epicure Mammon, the greedy, sensual knight in Ben Jonson's play* The Alchemist.

MT. 22:36 clarification of a much-discussed point: "Teacher, which is the great commandment in the law?"

Jesus responded first by reciting one of the most frequently quoted passages of the Torah, the call to Israel to believe in one God alone and to love God with all the powers of heart, mind, and soul. But to this first and greatest commandment Jesus added a second, quoting a less em-

MT. 22:39; MK. 12:31 phasized passage from Leviticus: "You shall love your neighbor as yourself." On these two, he told the lawyer, depended "all the law and the prophets." When his interrogator agreed, adding that to love one's neighbor was worth more than all the burnt offerings and sacrifices, Jesus com-

MK. 12:34 mended him: "You are not far from the kingdom of God."

According to the version of this event in Mark, no one dared ask Jesus any more questions. Luke has the lawyer asking Jesus to define *neighbor*, which he does by telling the parable of the Good Samaritan.

What was Jesus' attitude toward Roman rule in Judea?

When Jesus left Galilee for Judea, he was aware of some of the atrocities committed against his fellow Jews by Pilate, the Roman prefect there. He was told, for example, of a group of Galileans who had been murdered in the temple in the very act of sacrificing and "whose blood Pilate LK. 13:1 had mingled with their sacrifices." The Gospel says little of Jesus' reaction except that he rejected any suggestion that the misdeeds of the victims were somehow to blame for their sufferings.

In Jerusalem his focus was not on Pilate and the Romans but on the temple and the faith of his own people. Still, some of the Pharisees and Herodians who evidently supported Roman rule tried to trap him into making an anti-Roman statement that might be used to prosecute him. Enticing him with syrupy praise for his truthfulness and impartial disregard for human authorities, they set the trap by asking, "Is it lawful to MT. 22:17 pay taxes to Caesar, or not?" If Jesus said no, as they hoped, that alone might be enough to bring down the wrath of Pilate. But if he said yes, he risked alienating those of his followers who chafed under Roman taxation.

Recognizing their guile, Jesus responded with a trick of his own. He asked them whose picture and name were on the coin they used to pay the tax. When they said "Caesar's," he turned their MT. 22:21 response against them, telling them to "render therefore to Caesar the things that are Caesar's, and to God the things that are God's."

Despite such confrontations, Jesus' attitude toward the Romans does not seem to have been much different from that of most Pharisees. They could never really approve of Roman rule but were willing to live with it, believing it was God's will, just as the domination by Babylon and Persia had been in the past. At Jesus' trial before Pilate, the Gospel of John tells that he responded to Pilate's threats by saying, "You would have no JN. 19:11 power over me unless it had been given you from above."

When did opposition to Jesus begin to appear?

People had difficulty knowing what to make of Jesus. He fitted into none of the known religious parties and made a point of stripping bare the inadequacies of respected spiritual leaders such as the Pharisees and scribes. He called for religious renewal but not by requiring rigorous purity and obedience to the regulations of the Torah, as did most other reformers. Because he was different, Jesus ultimately aroused opposition from almost every powerful group within his nation.

The first conflict developed early in his ministry when the influential Pharisees realized that Jesus rejected their vision of a holy nation that maintained purity, fasting, and rigorous observance of the Sabbath. Jesus, on the other hand, ate with sinners, ignored ritual washing, and rejected fasting. He refused to stop his healings on the Sabbath and defended his disciples who gathered grain on the holy day. To the Pharisees and many professional interpreters of the law, such actions expressed a disregard for God's commandments that should not be tolerated in one who was acclaimed as a prophet.

When Jesus left Galilee to go to Jerusalem, the opposition and dangers increased. He outraged the powerful religious establishment by disrupting the temple's business, turning away money changers, driving out animals, and accusing the priests of making God's house "a den of rob- MT. 21:13 bers." When they asked his authority for such offensive acts, he refused to give any. The popular following that Jesus enjoyed evidently aroused real fears in them that an uncontrollable uprising might erupt because of Jesus and that "the Ro- JN. 11:48 mans will come and destroy both our holy place and our nation."

How long did Jesus' ministry last?

This question has been disputed by scholars for centuries, without any satisfactory resolution of the controversy.

According to the three Synoptic Gospels (Matthew, Mark, and Luke), the ministry could have lasted but a single year; they speak of Jesus celebrating only one Passover. John, however, mentions three distinct Passovers, which suggests a ministry of up to three years in length. However, since the Gospels do not give a clear chronology for this period of Jesus' life, it is impossible to say which view is the correct one.

Likewise, the year of Jesus' death remains uncertain. Dates ranging from A.D. 27 to 34 have been suggested by scholars.

"Let him who is without sin among you be the first to throw a stone [Jn. 8:7]," Jesus tells the scribes and Pharisees urging him to judge an adulterer; a painting by G. B. Tiepolo.

The Last Days

Down this dusty road leading to the Golden Gate in the Jerusalem temple's east wall (background), Jesus rode his donkey.

Why did Jesus enter Jerusalem on a donkey?

Jesus made special arrangements to enter the city of Jerusalem at the beginning of the Passover festival on a donkey rather than on foot. "Go into the village opposite you," he instructed his disciples, "and immediately you will find an ass tied, and a colt with her; untie them and bring them to me."

MT. 21:2

Both Matthew and John explain the significance of Jesus' entrance, for this was how the Old Testament prophet Zechariah had foretold the arrival of the Messiah: "Lo, your king comes to you; triumphant and victorious is he, humble and riding on an ass, on a colt the foal of an ass." The messianic symbolism was immediately clear to the holiday crowds gathered in Jerusalem. Spreading their garments and branches cut from trees along the road in front of Jesus, they shouted, "Blessed is he who comes in the name of the Lord!"

ZECH. 9:9

MT. 21:9

Why did Jesus overturn the tables of the money changers in the temple?

By his triumphal procession into Jerusalem, Jesus created a major disturbance and with it implicitly challenged the ruling chief priests and the Sadducees. His next move, the symbolic cleansing of the temple, struck at the heart of the Sanhedrin's authority.

In the courtyard of the Gentiles, the outermost portion of the temple in Jerusalem, merchants conducted a thriving trade in pigeons, lambs, and other sacrificial items people needed to make the offerings required by Mosaic law. For a fee, money changers converted foreign currency into the proper coins to pay the temple tax. These practices were authorized by the high priest and temple officials, who received a portion of the revenue. Nevertheless, when he entered the courtyard with his disciples, Jesus scattered the tables and chased out the merchants and money changers. As the crowd looked on, he recalled the words of the prophet Jeremiah, who had rebuked the temple authorities of his day in the very same court for similar reasons: "Has this house, which is called by my name, become a den of robbers in your eyes?"

JER. 7:11

What is the significance of the bread and wine at the Last Supper?

The Gospels record that Jesus called the bread he shared with the Apostles "my body" and the wine "my blood." The cup of wine, he said, symbolized a "new covenant" like the ancient covenant God had made with the people of Israel at Mount Sinai.

MT. 26:26

MK. 14:24

LK. 22:20

In ancient societies, entering into a solemn agreement often involved some kind of blood sacrifice. After Moses had read the law to the people, he made offerings to God and sprinkled the altar and the people with the blood of the sacrifices. The Letter to the Hebrews explains that just as the Old Testament covenants were ratified with sacrificial offerings, the new covenant announced by Jesus required that his blood be shed. But whereas the Israelites had to make repeated offerings to atone for their sins under the covenant of Moses, Jesus under the new covenant would die once and expiate sin forever.

The anonymous author of the Letter to the Hebrews explains that Jesus' death had much greater value than that of sacrificial animals. "For if the sprinkling of defiled persons with the blood of goats and bulls and with the ashes of a heifer sanctifies for the purification of the flesh, how much more shall the blood of Christ . . . purify your conscience from dead works to serve the living God."

HEB. 9:13

Obeying Jesus' instructions to his disciples to "do this in remembrance of me," the early Christians shared bread and wine to reaffirm their unity as Christians and their fellowship, or communion, with each other. Reenacting the events of the Last Supper, the Holy Communion service of the church commemorated the new covenant and bound members to each other as well as to God.

LK. 22:19

What became of Judas Iscariot?

The fate of Jesus' betrayer has remained one of the Bible's most intriguing mysteries. The New Testament offers two very different explanations. According to Matthew, Judas repented of his deed and attempted to return the 30 pieces of silver to the chief priests and the elders, saying, "I have sinned in betraying innocent blood." When they

MK. 27:4

scorned his repentance, Judas flung the money on the temple floor and went away to hang himself. Since it was unlawful to put blood money in the temple treasury, the chief priests used it to buy a field for the burial of strangers.

The Book of Acts, however, says that Judas himself bought a field with the money and suffered a gruesome death there, "falling headlong he burst open in the middle and all his bowels gushed out." The author of Acts agrees with Matthew in calling the plot of land purchased with the tainted money "the Field of Blood."

ACTS 1:18

MT. 27:8; ACTS 1:19

Who was the high priest at Jesus' trial?

Prominent in Jesus' arrest, trial, and execution was the cunning Caiaphas, who served as high priest from A.D. 18 to 36. Coming from a long and prominent line of high priests in Judea, Caiaphas became high priest three years after his father-in-law, the powerful Annas, five of whose sons also held the office of high priest. It appears that Annas continued to exert influence over temple matters through his son-in-law, for—according to John—Jesus was first questioned at the house of Annas before being sent to Caiaphas.

As John tells it, the chief priests and the Pharisees had become concerned that Jesus' popular-

At the Last Supper, Jesus broke bread with his disciples (left) and washed their feet (right). The bright hues and flat perspective of this illumination in the sixth-century Rossano Codex are typically Eastern.

ity was undermining their authority; more important, they feared that the Romans might perceive the noisy crowds around Jesus as the beginning of a riot

JN. 11:47 and retaliate against all Jews. "What are we to do?" they asked. "For this man performs many signs. If we let him go on thus, every one will believe in him, and the Romans will come and destroy both our holy place and our nation."

JN. 11:49 Caiaphas answered them: "You know nothing at all; you do not understand that it is expedient for you that one man should die for the people, and that the whole nation should not perish." Convinced by Caiaphas, the chief

JN. 11:53 priests and Pharisees "from that day on" plotted how to put Jesus to death.

Why did Pilate deliver Jesus to Herod?

In the course of questioning Jesus, Pontius Pilate, who was the Roman governor in Palestine, learned that the prisoner was a Galilean and therefore was legally under the jurisdiction of the Roman ruler of Galilee, Herod Antipas. Conveniently, Herod, a son of Herod the Great, was in Jerusalem at the time, so Pilate directed that Jesus be taken to him for judgment. Herod questioned Jesus at length but became frustrated and contemptuous of him when he refused to speak a single word in reply. As a gesture of derision, Herod put beautiful

Jesus endures the spiritual torment at Gethsemane in this Renaissance painting by the Florentine master Botticelli.

robes on Jesus and then sent him back to Pilate.

"Because he had heard about him," Herod LK. 23:8 had wanted to meet the famous teacher and miracle worker for a long time and "was hoping to see some sign done by him." He was so pleased by the Roman governor's actions that he and Pilate "became friends with each other that very LK. 23:12 day, for before this they had been at enmity with each other."

What crime was Jesus charged with?

In the hearing before the Sanhedrin, Jesus' accusers found him guilty of blasphemy and "con- MK. 14:64 demned him as deserving death." But nothing that Jesus said or did in the Gospels constituted blasphemy under known Jewish law. To claim to be the Messiah—even to call oneself the son of God—was not blasphemous.

When Jewish officials brought Jesus before ✳ Pontius Pilate, they phrased their charges in po-

ABBA. *In Aramaic,* abba *was what a small child called his or her father. Jesus used this intimate term when praying to God and perhaps taught his disciples to do so by beginning the Lord's Prayer with it.*

The Aramaic term was used in the Greek New Testament in Mark's account of Jesus' prayer of agony at Gethsemane, and twice in Paul's Letters to the Romans and the Galatians. In these books, abba *survived among early Christians as a term signifying that they were children of God.*

LK. 23:2

litical rather than religious terms, stating that Jesus was "perverting our nation, and forbidding us to give tribute to Caesar, and saying that he himself is Christ a king." The Gospels agree on

MT. 27:11

one charge that Pilate asked Jesus about: "Are you the King of the Jews?" Jesus' answer neither confirmed nor denied the charge. However, since crucifixion was a punishment reserved for the most serious crimes of treason against Roman authority, it would seem that in the end Jesus was executed for political insurrection.

Why did Pilate allow the crowd to choose between Barabbas and Jesus?

Pilate's motives and behavior in the arrest, trial, and crucifixion of Jesus have perplexed many students of the Bible. Perhaps no act of Pilate's is more puzzling than his offering the crowd a choice between releasing Jesus and a man named Barabbas, who had fought and killed someone in an anti-Roman insurrection in Jerusalem. One explanation is that Pilate saw that Jesus was popular with the crowds and that the aristocratic chief priests had brought him to trial

MT. 27:18

"out of envy." In this view, Pilate clearly preferred that Jesus be released rather than the insurrectionist and hoped that Jesus' popularity would lead the crowd to condemn the dangerous rebel Barabbas. However, the chief priests had no difficulty in stirring up the crowds to call for Barabbas and thereby condemn Jesus.

According to the Gospels, this drama was based on a custom by which a Jewish prisoner was released at Passover. Such a custom could only have been carried out at the pleasure of the Roman governor, who held absolute control over all prisoners and executions.

When and where was Jesus crucified?

We know that Jesus died sometime between A.D. 26 and 36 because those are the years Pontius Pilate served as governor of Judea. All four Gospels agree that Jesus was crucified on a Friday and that his body had to be removed from the cross before sundown, which marks the beginning of the Jewish Sabbath. But whereas the Synoptic Gospels have the execution taking place on Passover, John says that Passover was on ✳

THE AGONY IN THE GARDEN

After the Last Supper, Jesus and his disciples walked toward the Mount of Olives. Jesus seemed agitated and troubled. He had said many strange things at supper, among them that one of the Twelve would betray him and that Peter would deny knowing him three times "before the cock crows [Mt. 26:34]."

When they reached the place called Gethsemane, Jesus took Peter, James, and John aside and said, "My soul is very sorrowful, even to death; remain here, and watch with me [Mt. 26:38]." Going farther on, he knelt, and full of anguish over his impending rejection and death, he prayed, "My father, if it be possible, let this cup pass from me [Mt. 26:39]."

When Jesus returned, he found his disciples sleeping. "So, could you not watch with me one hour?" he asked. "Watch and pray that you may not enter into temptation; the spirit indeed is willing, but the flesh is weak [Mt. 26:40]." He left them then and went back to his meditations. The Apostles fell asleep a second time. Embarrassed, they could offer Jesus no excuse when he returned. Once more Jesus went away to pray to his father in heaven, saying, "If this cannot pass unless I drink it, thy will be done [Mt. 26:42]."

Strengthened by his prayer, he returned to the Apostles, who had yet again surrendered to fatigue. "Are you still sleeping and taking your rest [Mt. 26:45]?" he asked them. There, in the mild Jerusalem evening, he sensed the approach of Judas and the mob; the events he had foretold at the evening meal were beginning. "Behold, the hour is at hand, and the Son of man is betrayed into the hands of sinners. Rise, let us be going; see, my betrayer is at hand [Mt. 26:45]."

JN. 19:31 Saturday, "for that sabbath was a high day."

Because Passover always occurs during the full moon in the month of Nisan (March/April), astronomers can easily calculate when a full moon occurred on a Friday or Saturday during the years of Pilate's governorship. They give four possible years for Jesus' death: A.D. 27, 30, 33, or 34, with many favoring A.D. 30, when he probably would have been in his mid-thirties.

The place of execution was the grisly Golgotha, a Semitic word usually taken to mean skull, or the place of a skull (and translated into Latin as *calvaria*). Commentators have speculated that Golgotha was so named because it was a place covered with the skulls of executed criminals or because the shape of the hill on which it was located resembled a skull.

From hints in the Gospels it is assumed that Golgotha was near a road just outside the city gates. Time has altered the local geography so radically that the actual site cannot be identified with any certainty, although Jerusalem's Church of the Holy Sepulchre is the place hallowed by tradition.

How long did Jesus suffer on the cross?

According to the Gospel of Mark, Jesus was raised on the cross at "the third hour" (9 A.M.) MK. 15:25 and "uttered a loud cry, and breathed his last" MK. 15:37 shortly after "the ninth hour" (3 P.M.). Pilate was MK. 15:34 astonished when he learned that Jesus had died after only six hours on the cross. Often victims of

ROME'S MAN IN JUDEA

Appointed by the emperor Tiberius, Pontius Pilate served as the prefect, or governor, of Judea, Samaria, and Idumea from A.D. 26 to 36. The reason for his rise to political power is unclear; most likely, as the son of a good Roman family, he was an officer in a Roman legion who gradually ascended the diplomatic ladder.

Although the Gospels say little about Pilate's character, events recorded by the Jewish writers Josephus and Philo suggest that he was an ambitious and hot-tempered young man. His dealings with the Jews demonstrated indifference to the rights of a subjected people. When Pilate first marched into Jerusalem, his military escort carried standards emblazoned

Firm in his mission, Jesus suffers the scorn of Pilate in a 19th-century painting by the Russian artist Nikolai N. Ge.

with the emperor's image. This outraged the Jews, who resented any form of idolatry. They retaliated by besieging the governor's palace; when Pilate threatened violence to end the

demonstration, the Jews lay down in the streets, prepared to die rather than endure pagan images in their city. Another time Pilate raided the temple treasury to fund a new aqueduct. Thousands died in the resulting riots.

During major Jewish festivals, when the influx of people increased the likelihood of civil disturbances, Pilate moved his residence from Caesarea to Jerusalem. There he held court, hearing complaints and issuing judgments, and it was there that the Sanhedrin would have brought Jesus.

The fact that Pilate's term of office lasted 10 years suggests that his superiors must have considered him a competent administrator. However, his peremptory way of handling the Jews finally led to his downfall. After he ordered the annihilation of a Samaritan mob, he was recalled to Rome. The circumstances of his last years and death are unknown.

Almost transfigured in this colossal painting by Gustave Doré, a 19th-century artist famed for his sense of the sublime, Jesus strides toward his destiny, symbolized by the cross below.

this cruel form of execution lingered in excruciating pain for up to two or three days.

Twice during the agony of his crucifixion, Jesus was offered something to drink. First, upon reaching Golgotha, his executioners offered him wine mixed with myrrh or gall, which may have served as a painkiller, but he refused it. Later, as his strength flagged, Jesus cried out, "I thirst." The soldier who lifted a vinegar-soaked sponge to Jesus' lips was fulfilling the words of Psalm 69: "For my thirst they gave me vinegar to drink."

Meanwhile, his garments had been divided among the soldiers, who cast lots to see who would get his seamless tunic, thus fulfilling the words of the psalmist: "They divide my garments among them, and for my raiment they cast lots."

Two other men were crucified alongside Jesus. One sneered at Jesus' apparent helplessness, but the other asked to be remembered when "you come into your kingdom." Out of respect for Jewish law, the executioners were prepared to dispose of their victims before sundown ✳

so that Jews would not have to break the Sabbath to remove their bodies. They hastened the two criminals' death by breaking their legs. But when the soldiers discovered that Jesus had already died, one of them stabbed him in the side to make certain he had expired. John points out that Jesus' legs had not been fractured in fulfillment of the command in Exodus that the bones of the Passover lamb are not to be broken, while the stab fulfilled Zechariah's prophecy, "When they look on him whom they have pierced, they shall mourn for him, as one mourns for an only child, and weep bitterly over him, as one weeps over a first-born."

What was the inscription on the cross?

A victim condemned to crucifixion in Roman times was often forced to wear a *titulum* around his neck, an inscription describing his crime that was later attached above his head on the cross.

JN. 19:28

PS. 69:21

PS. 22:18

LK. 23:42

ZECH. 12:10

Exhausted and reviled, Jesus bears his cross toward Golgotha in this 15th-century miniature from a Dutch book of hours.

New Testament accounts do not agree on the exact wording of Jesus' *titulum*, but it apparently called him King of the Jews in Hebrew, Latin, and Greek.

Pilate's sarcastic wit was responsible for the wording of Jesus' *titulum*. Members of the Sanhedrin objected that some people might mistake JN. 19:21 the meaning unless the inscription read "This man said, I am King of the Jews." But Pilate dis- JN. 19:22 missively replied, "What I have written I have written." The Roman governor wanted it to be clear to the Jews that Rome would not tolerate any rival authority in Palestine; what he had done to Jesus he would do to any man who claimed to be king of the Jews.

Who witnessed Jesus' death?

Because Golgotha was just outside the city, many Jews witnessed the execution of Jesus, the most prominent among them being the chief priests, the scribes, and the elders who came to revile him. To their number can be added curious passersby and unspecified bystanders, one of whom—according to the Gospels of Matthew and Mark—was the soldier who offered Jesus ✳

his last drink, the sponge soaked with vinegar.

Looking on from afar were acquaintances of the condemned man and many women "who MT. 27:55 had followed Jesus from Galilee, ministering to him." Among them were Mary Magdalene, Mary the mother of James and Joseph, the mother of the sons of Zebedee, and Salome. According to John, a mournful group that included Mary the mother of Jesus and "the disciple whom he JN. 19:26 loved" (thought to be John himself) drew near enough to speak to him. Before surrendering to death, Jesus commended the care of his mother to John, the only one of his male disciples to have shared in the ordeal.

In addition to the Roman soldiers who carried out the execution and the two criminals also being crucified, there are two others mentioned in the Gospels who were likely witnesses. Simon of Cyrene may have lingered at Golgotha after being recruited to carry Jesus' cross there. And since it was Joseph of Arimathea who went to ask Pilate for Jesus' body, it is possible that this "good and righteous man" had observed the fi- LK. 23:50 nal agony on the cross of the man he secretly revered.

What were Jesus' last words on the cross?

As he hung from the cross, the Gospels record, Jesus uttered what have come to be known as the seven last words, although they are actually complete sentences.

Matthew and Mark include only what seems to be a cry of abandonment and despair: "My God, MT. 27:46 my God, why hast thou forsaken me?" However, biblical scholars point out that this is the first line of Psalm 22, a prayer for deliverance from mortal pain that concludes with a ringing expression of faith.

The last three words in Luke give eloquent testimony to three qualities of Jesus: his compassion and willingness to forgive, his generosity in reaching out to all mankind, and his obedience to the will of God. "Father, forgive them; for they LK. 23:34 know not what they do," he cried out as the soldiers raised him on the cross to die. To the man being crucified with him who asked for remembrance when Jesus returned in triumph, he made a solemn promise: "Truly, I say to you, today you LK. 23:43 will be with me in Paradise." Finally, at the moment of death, Jesus spoke directly to God:

THE CRUELEST PUNISHMENT

Recent archeological discoveries in Israel have clarified our understanding of the exact nature of the horrible practice known as crucifixion. A form of execution employed in Persia and Carthage, it was adopted by the Romans not long before the beginning of the Christian Era. Slaves, robbers, and political criminals were crucified, but rarely was a citizen of the empire thus executed. (Because of this, Paul, a Roman citizen, was martyred by beheading.) These executions were so frightful that writers refrained from describing them and artists rarely depicted them. In Jewish tradition, stoning was the favored method of execution, although the criminal's corpse might be hung from a tree later as a warning to others.

Originally the gibbet was only an upright stake, but later a crossbeam was added to form a T-shape. At Golgotha permanent stakes were probably set up. The victims there, like Jesus, were forced to carry the crossbeam, which was lowered into a groove at the top of the stake. The condemned man's arms were tied or nailed to the beam. Since the palms cannot support the full weight of the body when it is raised, the large, crude iron nails used by Roman carpenters for joints were probably driven through the wrists. The victim straddled a large peg for support. His feet were tied or nailed to the stake.

In 1968 the skeleton of a young man who had died by crucifixion in the first century A.D. was found in Jerusalem. Nails pierced each wrist, but only one was used for both heel bones. The position of the victim is uncertain, but scholars suggest a jackknife configuration, with both legs forced together and bent to one side or possibly with knees apart. Contorted in this manner, hanging as a dead weight, the victim could scarcely breathe. Carbon dioxide would slowly build up in the blood, putting ever greater demands upon the heart. Unable to move and deprived of oxygen, the muscles would begin to contract in wrenching spasms. Weakening from fatigue and hunger, the victim was prey to inclement weather, swarms of biting insects, and the taunts or physical abuse of passersby. Eventually, heart failure or suffocation would result in death. Breaking a victim's legs hastened death, because he could not raise himself up to take air into his lungs.

In 71 B.C. some 6,000 slaves were crucified on the Via Appia in Rome, following their leader, the slave-gladiator Spartacus.

LK. 23:46 "Father, into thy hands I commit my spirit!"
John gives three different last words of Jesus. Looking down on his mother and the beloved disciple who had dared to be present at the crucifixion, Jesus demonstrated his concern for human needs. "Woman, behold, your son!" he said
JN. 19:26 to Mary. "Behold, your mother!" he said to the
JN. 19:27 disciple. Next, Jesus revealed his humanity by
JN. 19:28 calling out, "I thirst." Finally, he uttered a triumphant cry to announce the completion of his
JN. 19:30 mission on earth: "It is finished!"

Where was Jesus buried?

Following his ignominious death, Jesus was given a tender and dignified burial by a dissenting member of the Sanhedrin, Joseph of Arimathea,
JN. 19:38 who "was a disciple of Jesus, but secretly." Boldly, he had gone to Pilate to ask for custody of the body, which he buried in a tomb near Golgotha.
Joined by a Pharisee named Nicodemus, Jo-
JN. 19:40 seph bound Jesus' body "in linen cloths with the spices, as is the burial custom of the Jews." After he placed the body in the tomb, Joseph rolled a stone across the entrance and departed.

The Church of the Holy Sepulchre in Jerusalem marks the traditional site of Jesus' burial, having been identified as such in the fourth century by Helena, the mother of Emperor Constantine the Great. By the time of Helena, Jerusalem's walls had been rebuilt and extended so that the burial place she designated was no longer outside the city. Her son's massive building project to incorporate the tomb in a place of worship completely obliterated whatever vestiges remained of the original last resting place of Jesus.

Who was the first to see Jesus after his resurrection?

According to John, it was Mary Magdalene who was the first to see Jesus after his resurrection. This is confirmed by Mark, who also places her

THE BELIEF IN RESURRECTION

By the time of Jesus, faith in the resurrection of the body was widely accepted among Jews. The most notable dissenters were the Sadducees, who rejected the doctrine apparently because it was not in the Pentateuch.

Though several Old Testament passages express an undefined hope for a blessed life after death, the more dominant view was that "he who goes down to Sheol does not come up [Job 7:9]." Only after the Babylonian exile was a clear doctrine of resurrection expressed. The Book of Daniel envisioned a time when "many of those who sleep in the dust of the earth shall awake [Dan. 12:2]," and Jewish martyrs in the time of the Maccabees defied their tormenters by saying,

Abraham with the souls of the blessed at the Last Judgment; a 13th-century stained glass.

"You dismiss us from this present life, but the King of the universe will raise us up to an everlasting renewal of life [2 Macc. 7:9]."

The doctrine of resurrection embodied a belief that true life required a unity of body and spirit or soul. Without the body the soul may exist but cannot be said to be truly alive, since neither body nor soul can function without the other. This contrasts with the Greek view of the immortal and independent soul. Paul revealed his Jewish roots when he spoke of existence between death and resurrection as being naked and needing to be clothed. He recognized the Greek objections to the belief in resurrection, however, when he asserted that the resurrected body is not a physical body, but a spiritual body that is immortal: "For the trumpet will sound, and the dead will be raised imperishable [1 Cor. 15:52]."

The crucified Jesus is purposely distorted to show his suffering on the Isenheim Altar; this deeply emotional work is by the 16th-century German Gothic painter Matthias Grünewald.

alone at the tomb. Matthew and Luke say she was in the company of other women.

As John recounts the event, Mary Magdalene arrived at the tomb before dawn on Sunday. Seeing that the large stone was gone from the entrance, she ran to tell Peter and an unnamed disciple "whom Jesus loved" that the body had been removed—presumably by Jesus' enemies. The two hastened back to the garden with her to confirm that the tomb was empty, the linens in which his body had been wrapped now lying loosely about. Mystified, the two departed, "for as yet they did not know the scripture, that he must rise from the dead." JN. 20:2 JN. 20:9

Remaining behind to weep outside the tomb, Mary Magdalene gathered courage to look within and was astounded to see "two angels in white, sitting where the body of Jesus had lain." Asked why she was weeping, she told them that it was ✳ JN. 20:12

because she did not know what had been done with the body of Jesus. But as she turned to leave the tomb, she saw another figure—whom she at first mistook for the gardener. Again she explained the cause of her tears and asked where she could find the missing body. The third figure uttered her name and, recognizing the voice, Mary Magdalene cried out, "*Rabboni*" (Hebrew for teacher). Joyously, she went to the disciples to report, "I have seen the Lord." JN. 20:16 JN. 20:18

How many times was the risen Jesus seen and by whom?

In his First Letter to the Corinthians, Paul lists the post-resurrection appearances of Jesus. He names six: to Cephas (that is, Peter); to "the twelve" (though only 11 remained after Judas' 1 COR. 15:5

served the moment that he rose from the tomb.

Matthew, perhaps, comes nearest to describing actual witnesses to the event. When Mary Magdalene and the other Mary went to the sepulcher on Sunday morning, they experienced a powerful earthquake and observed an angel from heaven rolling back the stone and sitting on it. Trembling in fear, the tomb's guards fell to the ground unconscious. The angel told the women not to be afraid or to seek there the body of Jesus, announcing to them, "He is not here; for he MT. 28:6 has risen, as he said. Come, see the place where he lay." It seems that the stone was rolled back, not to allow Jesus to emerge, but rather to permit the women to see that the tomb was empty.

How does the New Testament explain why Jesus had to die?

New Testament writers draw on a variety of images to explain the meaning of Jesus' death. From the worship in the temple came the description of his death as a sacrifice, an expiation that wipes out sin. Paul describes Jesus as the sacrificial victim offered by God himself, and the anonymous author of the Letter to the Hebrews elaborates this image by portraying Jesus as a high priest who offers himself and through his death enters heaven.

Another image used to explain why Jesus had to die is drawn from the practice of redeeming or ransoming slaves and prisoners of war. Jesus' death is seen as the price paid for human freedom from sin. Mark records Jesus' own statement that he "came not to be served but to serve, MK. 10:45 and to give his life as a ransom for many."

Paul makes a connection with Adam's fall. "As ROM. 5:18 one man's trespass led to condemnation for all men," he wrote to the Romans, "so one man's act of righteousness leads to acquittal and life for all men."

The New Testament also stresses that Jesus' death was not simply a miscarriage of justice that occurred by chance but was part of a great plan of God that had to be carried out. "Was it LK. 24:26 not necessary," the risen Jesus asked two disciples, "that the Christ should suffer these things and enter into his glory?" Christians believed that the crucifixion was "according to the definite ACTS 2:23 plan and foreknowledge of God" and had been foretold in Scripture.

THREE. *The number 3 implies completeness—a beginning, a middle, and an end. In the New Testament, it is associated with the life of Jesus several times. Three gifts were given to the infant by the wise men. Satan tempted Jesus three times in the desert. The triad of Jesus, Moses, and Elijah was present at the Transfiguration. Peter denied Jesus three times.*

The figure 3 seems associated with the period Jesus was in the tomb, which included parts of three days. John's Gospel reports that in Jerusalem Jesus said, "Destroy this temple, and in three days I will raise it up [Jn. 2:19]." No one understood him because "he spoke of the temple of his body [Jn. 2:21]." Matthew's Gospel tells that when opponents demanded a miraculous sign from Jesus, he would give them only "the sign of Jonah [Mt. 16:4]." Just as Jonah was in the belly of the whale three days, so Jesus would be three days "in the heart of the earth [Mt. 12:40]."

1 COR. 15:6 betrayal); to "more than five hundred brethren at one time"; to James (whom he elsewhere de-
1 COR. 15:7 scribes as Jesus' brother); to "all the apostles" (whom Paul knew as a different group from "the
1 COR. 15:8 twelve"); and "last of all," he concludes, "he appeared also to me."

The Gospels confirm appearances to the Twelve and add several others: to Mary Magdalene (and another Mary) near the tomb; to two disciples on the road to Emmaus outside Jerusalem; and to seven disciples by the Sea of Galilee. The first verses of the Book of Acts speak of Je-
ACTS 1:3 sus "appearing to them during forty days," thus hinting at many more.

Were there any witnesses to the moment of resurrection?

As described in the New Testament, Jesus' resurrection had no actual witnesses; it has always remained a matter of faith, not proof. Any number of people could have witnessed Jesus being publicly crucified, and many of his disciples bore witness that he had appeared to them alive several days later. But no one claimed to have ob-

What is the meaning of Jesus' ascension?

The accounts of Jesus' ascension in the New Testament dramatically state that God not only raised Jesus from the dead but exalted him to heaven. It is usually assumed that only one of Jesus' resurrection appearances ended with his body rising from the earth as a visual symbol of that exaltation. Luke, however, reports Jesus' ascension twice, once at the end of his Gospel, where it takes place on the same day as his resurrection, and again at the beginning of Acts, where he places it 40 days later. The ascension is also mentioned in Chapter 16 of Mark's Gospel, where Jesus is said to be "taken up into heaven" MK. 16:19 and seated "at the right hand of God." Jesus' as- MK. 16:19 cension was understood to be a fulfillment of Psalm 110: "The Lord says to my lord: 'Sit at PS. 110:1 my right hand, till I make your enemies your footstool.' "

Although the other Gospels do not describe a physical ascension, John reports that Jesus sent word to the disciples by Mary Magdalene that "I JN. 20:17 am ascending to my Father and your Father, to my God and your God." The Gospel of Matthew ends not with a visible ascension but with Jesus' assurance to his disciples of his continued spiritual presence: "Lo, I am with you always, to the MT. 28:20 close of the age."

In "The Ascension" by Rembrandt, Jesus is depicted as being lifted by the power of the Holy Spirit, an interpretation of an event described by Luke and Mark as a visible occurrence.

The Promise Fulfilled

Why was it important that Jesus be a descendant of King David?

By the time of Jesus' ministry, more than five centuries had passed since a king from the dynasty of David had reigned in Jerusalem. Yet many Jews still trusted in God's ancient pledge: PS. 89:3 "I have sworn to David my servant: 'I will establish your descendants for ever, and build your throne for all generations.'" Even before the dynasty had ended in the Babylonian exile, the prophets had watched the moral collapse of the kingdom in Judah and predicted that God would JER. 23:5 one day cause David's family tree to produce "a righteous Branch, and he shall reign as king and deal wisely, and shall execute justice and righteousness in the land." During the exile it was again foretold that the nation would be restored EZEK. 37:24 and that "my servant David shall be king over them; and they shall all have one shepherd."

Their shepherd was slow in coming, however.

King David dreams of the future Messiah's resurrection in this 15th-century illumination from a French manuscript.

Even the Hasmonean kings who ruled Judea after overcoming foreign domination were from the tribe of Levi, not descendants of David, and Herod was descended from non-Israelites. When people saw Jesus' deeds, therefore, and asked, "Can this be the Son of David?" or cried out, MT. 12:23 "Hosanna to the Son of David," the hopes they MT. 21:9 expressed carried the weight of a long history. Both Matthew and Luke show that Jesus was not only descended from David but also recognized by many believers as the long-expected king.

Did Jesus claim to be the Messiah?

The Gospels ringingly proclaim Jesus to be the Christ or Messiah, but they also make it clear that he was reluctant to claim the title for himself. Jesus is never portrayed telling crowds that he is the Messiah; rather, his messianic role often seems to be a secret that gets out despite his efforts to stop it. Luke says that when Jesus cast out demons, he "would not allow them to speak, LK. 4:41 because they knew that he was the Christ." Mark recounts that even when Peter affirmed before the other disciples, "You are the Christ," Jesus MK. 8:29 "charged them to tell no one about him." Matthew tells that the imprisoned John the Baptist had heard that Jesus was performing "the deeds MT. 11:2 of the Christ," but still awaited an explicit answer: "Are you he who is to come, or shall we MT. 11:3 look for another?" Jesus refused to be explicit and only pointed to his deeds. In the Gospel of John people expressed their frustration with Jesus: "How long will you keep us in suspense? If JN. 10:24 you are the Christ, tell us plainly." Jesus again pointed to his deeds: "The works that I do in my JN. 10:25 Father's name, they bear witness to me."

Only in two passages does Jesus directly affirm his role as the Christ or Messiah. The Gospel of John records a private conversation between Jesus and a Samaritan woman. When she asserted, "I know that Messiah is coming (he who is JN. 4:25 called Christ); when he comes, he will show us all things," Jesus responded, "I who speak to you am he." At Jesus' trial as recorded in the Gospel of Mark, when the high priest asked him, "Are you MK. 14:61 the Christ, the Son of the Blessed?" Jesus replied, "I am." This straightforward response appears more ambiguous in the Gospels of Matthew and Luke, where Jesus answered, "You have said so" MT. 26:64 and "If I tell you, you will not believe." LK. 22:67

JESUS IN EARLY HISTORIES

Practically all our detailed knowledge of Jesus is based on the four Gospels. Contemporary references from other sources, however, reveal that there was an awareness of him even among those people who despised Christianity.

The earliest Roman writer to mention Christ was a governor in Asia Minor named Pliny, who wrote to the emperor Trajan in A.D. 112 describing the trials of Christians and remarking that "they had been accustomed to meet before daybreak, and to recite a hymn antiphonally to Christ, as to a god." A few years later the Roman historian Tacitus wrote that the name Christians "derives from Christus, who was condemned by Pontius Pilate during the reign of Tiberius."

The most intriguing nonbiblical reference comes from the Jewish historian Josephus, whose first-century *Jewish Antiquities* includes

A Judean city under Roman attack is depicted in a medieval edition of Josephus' The Jewish War.

the following passage: "About this time there lived Jesus, a wise man, if indeed one ought to call him a man. For he was one who wrought surprising feats and was a teacher of such people as accept the truth gladly. He won

over many Jews and many of the Greeks. He was the Messiah. When Pilate . . . had condemned him to be crucified, those who had in the first place come to love him did not give up their affection for him. On the third day he appeared to them restored to life, for the prophets of God had prophesied these and countless other marvelous things about him. And the tribe of the Christians, so called after him, has still to this day not disappeared."

Opinions about the origin of this passage vary. It is so explicit in calling Jesus the Messiah that many historians consider it the later work of a Christian who inserted it while copying Josephus' text. Other scholars, both Christian and Jewish, conclude that although the passage contains some alterations, it still essentially represents the work of Josephus.

Were others seen as messiahs in ancient times?

Many Jews in the first century were looking for a Messiah. The Gospel of Luke reports that when John the Baptist appeared, "the people were in expectation, and all men questioned in their hearts concerning John, whether perhaps he were the Christ."

LK. 3:15

After the time of Jesus, according to the Jewish historian Josephus, several presented themselves as prophets who would deliver the Jews from oppression. One, named Theudas, emerged some 15 years after Jesus' death and inspired a great number of Jews to "take up their possessions and to follow him to the Jordan river." The Roman governor, however, sent out troops who killed or scattered the followers and ✳ brought Theudas' head back to Jerusalem, probably as a warning to others.

About 10 years later, a Jew from Egypt gained a reputation as the great prophet who would overthrow the Romans. He roused thousands to assemble on the Mount of Olives, promising that God would cause Jerusalem's walls to crumble and allow them to liberate the holy city. They were met by Roman cavalry and infantry, who killed hundreds of the believers and sent their prophet into hiding.

The last significant messianic figure among the Jews in ancient times was Simon ben Kosiba, better known as Bar Kochba, who led the rebellion against Rome that ended in A.D. 135. The revolt ended in disaster and led to the banishment of Judea's remaining Jews from their ancestral homeland.

THE BIBLE THROUGH THE AGES

In Jerusalem there is a museum called the Shrine of the Book where a visitor can study at close hand the most ancient Bible manuscripts in existence. These texts were copied with elegant simplicity by the careful, steady hands of monks who lived their lives at the monastery at Qumran, located in the scorching wilderness west of the Dead Sea.

Approximately two millennia later, in 1947, the work of those dedicated scribes came to light as the Dead Sea Scrolls, which are now known to have been produced over a period starting in the third century B.C. and ending in the first century A.D. Standing before these famous manuscripts at the Shrine of the Book, a visitor senses the profound reverence with which every stroke of writing was done. In some manuscripts, each time the scribe comes upon the name of God, he changes his style of lettering and as a mark of homage writes the four Hebrew letters (usually represented in English as YHWH) of God's name in a distinctive archaic script that stands out from the writing around it. Seeing the original ink on ancient parchment, one almost feels able to reach through the barrier of 2,000 years and touch the hand of the anonymous scribe whose faith in the scriptures joins him spiritually with the believers of today.

Yet even for the monks at Qumran, much of the Scripture was already ancient. In some instances they were making copies of copies whose ancestry reached back at least several hundred years, and beyond that to an oral tradition that told of an omnipotent God who was always present, rewarding his people when they obeyed him and punishing them when they did not. Before they were first written on leather scrolls, many of the words had been repeated countless times, drawn from their safe treasury in the hearts of the Israelite people.

During the last decades of the Qumran monastery, a new movement arose in Judea. Centering around Jesus the Messiah, it came to be called Christianity. It would add new texts to the scriptures, texts with a message almost unimaginable to the monks of Qumran. Early Christians, Qumran monks, and devoted Jews outside the monastery all read the same ancient Scripture. Yet each found different messages. For the monks, the sacred writings confirmed their withdrawal from the life and practices of their compatriots. For Christians, reading the Scripture in the light of Jesus' teaching, the important message lay in the prophecies and promises that heralded their new faith and a new covenant with God. Such is the range and power of the library of books called the Bible that it can give meaning to the lives of all believers, no matter how different.

So far as we know, not a single one of the Bible's authors knew that his words would be part of a great work revered as the Bible. Its writers, whether named or anonymous, transmitted the voice of God, and they eloquently expressed the response of people to God, but it was faith alone that inspired them, not the hope of personal fame or literary posterity.

Out of that selfless faith came a book as strong and enduring as the belief that created it. True, the book has undergone some changes. Through centuries of copying by hand, errors crept into the text. In recent times, the discovery of early Hebrew and Greek manuscripts of the Bible has allowed scholars to recognize and correct many of these mistakes. Translations also pose the risk of errors. All translators—from the Jews who first rendered the Pentateuch into Greek in the third century B.C. to the scores of translators working today on editions yet to be published—must make hundreds of difficult decisions on how to communicate obscure terms and passages, whether in English, Chinese, Swahili, Urdu, or hundreds of other languages. A comparison of several English translations shows how much variety can result even in a language with a long tradition of Bible translation. When the Bible is translated into obscure tribal languages, which may have never had a written literature before, the problems multiply.

Through all this—through all the vagaries of human interpretation and translation—what is most remarkable is that the book preserves its strength. In any version the Bible is vast and deep and varied. It forces introspection and self-criticism. It gives voice to human anguish as well as joy, and sets the reader before both the judgment and love of God. It is no wonder that a book that gives so much to the heart and soul—and at the same time recounts such an intriguing historical saga—remains the world's most widely read book, an object of reverence, study, and fascination.

Top left: Cross, ninth-century German illuminated Gospels.

Origin of the Bible

The New Testament, like the Old, was based on oral tradition—stories about the life of Jesus, retold many times before being written down; above, Paul preaches in Athens in a work by Raphael.

BIBLE. *Commonly understood today to mean the book, this English word comes from an identically spelled word in Old French. The Latin antecedent is* biblia, *from the Greek word meaning books, which in turn derives from the fact that scrolls were written on papyrus, called* byblos *because it was imported from the Phoenician city of Byblos. The transition from the plural "books" in Greek and Latin to the singular "book" in English and other modern languages reflects the theological view that, for all the great variety that marks Scripture, it is bound together by an overlying unity. There is an Old Testament reference to the prophetic writings as "books": "I, Daniel, perceived in the books [Dan. 9:2]. . . ." The first Christian use of the term occurred in the second century in a letter by an early church father named Clement. The passage speaks of the authority of "the books and the Apostles."*

What historical periods does the Bible cover?

Excluding the creation story and the other accounts in the Book of Genesis before the narratives about the patriarchs, the Old and New Testaments together cover a vast time period from approximately 2000 B.C. to the last half of the first century A.D. But because the Bible does not give dates that can be matched precisely to modern systems, it is difficult to determine the years in which events occurred. Much of the chronology of biblical events has therefore been developed from reading contemporary sources and through archeology.

Abraham, the first patriarch, probably lived around the year 2000 B.C. The period of Hebrew enslavement and the Exodus occurred sometime before 1500; the establishment of the Israelite monarchy, about 1020. The monarchy split apart in the second half of the 10th century, the northern kingdom of Israel fell to the Assyrians toward the end of the eighth century, and the Babylonians destroyed the southern kingdom of Judah at the beginning of the sixth century. The Books of Chronicles, Ezra, and Nehemiah trace events up to about 400 B.C.

In the New Testament, the Gospels of Matthew, Mark, Luke, and John record events in the life of Jesus covering the first three decades A.D. The Book of Acts and the Epistles of Paul deal with the foundations of Christianity to about A.D. 60, while the other New Testament writings carry the story to the end of the first century.

When was the Bible written?

Many sections of the Old Testament are believed to have been told and retold—by mothers and fathers as well as by tribal elders and professional storytellers—long before they came to be written down. The art of writing probably began in the Near East during the fourth millennium B.C. among the Sumerians, who had invaded Mesopotamia; but the Hebrews apparently did not use written records to any great extent until the era of the united kingdom, which began under Saul in the 11th century B.C. and continued under David and Solomon. As the united kingdom grew in power and influence, trade and industry prospered, and the demand for written records and information increased. Then as writing and reading became widespread, a literature began to emerge out of the narratives of storytellers.

Probably during the reign of Solomon in the 10th century B.C., some of the ancient Israelite traditions, until then predominantly oral, began to be written down, and this process of turning the spoken word into written texts continued for hundreds of years. After the initial writing down of a part of Scripture—on a scroll that was perishable and grew more so with time and repeated use—scribes painstakingly labored to make exact copies. After them came other scribes who made copies of copies, on down through the centuries. The long chain of copying and recopying makes it difficult to determine exactly when the originals were written, though in general even

the oldest surviving copies of biblical passages were made centuries after they were first composed. Much of the collecting and editing of the writings in the Old Testament was done by the Judean captives in Babylon in the sixth century B.C. Among the captives was Ezra, whom tradition credits with the achievement.

The New Testament was written down mainly in the second half of the first century A.D. Like the Old Testament, it was partly based on stories and reports that had circulated orally. The difference was that no more than about half a century elapsed between these events and the recording of them, while the process took many centuries for much of the Old Testament.

In what language was the Bible written?

Most of the Old Testament was written in Hebrew. Sections not originally written in Hebrew include Ezra 4:8 to 6:18 and 7:12–26 and Daniel 2:4 to 7:28. These were written in Aramaic, a language similar to Hebrew that was the most common language in the Babylonian and Persian empires. It was widely used by the Jewish people after their return from the Babylonian exile, when the Books of Ezra and Daniel were produced. In addition, Genesis uses both the Aramaic name Jegar-sahadutha and the Hebrew Galeed for the heap of stones that was "a witness" of an agreement between Jacob and Laban; and Jeremiah contains a verse in Aramaic about the fate of false gods: "The gods who did not make the

GEN. 31:48

JER. 10:11

A Hebrew papyrus dating from the seventh century B.C. shows signs of being erased and reused, a common practice at a time when writing materials were scarce.

heavens and the earth shall perish from the earth and from under the heavens."

All of the New Testament was originally written in Greek, although some of Jesus' sayings (including his last words on the cross in the Gospels of Matthew and Mark) are quoted in Aramaic, a language he knew along with Hebrew. Paul's letters also quote expressions in Aramaic.

What writing materials were used?

Writing from biblical times has been found on a variety of surfaces—rock, clay tablets, pottery, and metals such as copper and silver. The Bible says the Ten Commandments were inscribed on "tables of stone," and Moses' successor Joshua EX. 24:12

LIBRARIANS OF THE DESERT

The existence of an ancient Jewish sect called the Essenes has long been an established historical fact. In the early first century A.D., the Jewish philosopher Philo described them as living in farming communities, though he did not specify where. According to Philo, the Essenes owned all property in common, practiced celibacy, and stressed prayer and ritual purity. One generation later, the Roman writer Pliny stated that the Essenes lived near the western shore of the Dead Sea.

At the very end of the first century—after the Roman defeat of the Jewish rebels—the Jewish historian Josephus wrote that Essene communes were scattered all over Palestine. He confirmed the previous accounts, including the sect's celibacy, but noted that one Essene group did recognize the institution of marriage.

Several clues point to the Essenes as the ones who accumulated the library that came to be called the Dead Sea Scrolls. First, the scrolls were found around Qumran, just west of the Dead Sea, where Pliny had said Essenes lived. Second, some of the nonbiblical scrolls contained community rules that matched descriptions by Josephus. Third, archeological evidence that both men and women lived at Qumran connects with Josephus' report of a noncelibate Essene group.

Overlooking the Dead Sea, the caves at Qumran yielded dramatic new insights into Bible history.

JOS. 8:32 "wrote upon the stones a copy of the law of Moses." A silver amulet found in a Jerusalem tomb dating from before 500 B.C. is inscribed with the blessing of Aaron in Numbers, NUM. 6:24 which begins, "The Lord bless you and keep you."

The Bible also mentions scrolls but does not specify whether the scrolls were papyrus or leather—both of which were found among the Dead Sea collection. The scroll of Jeremiah that King Jehoiakim JER. 36:23 angrily threw "into the fire in the brazier" was probably made of papyrus because burning animal skin would have created a very bad odor.

By the second century B.C. the technique of making animal skins into parchment (the name is derived from the city of Pergamum in Asia Minor) seems to have been known in much of the Greco-Roman world. Jewish tradition requires that the Torah parchment scrolls still used in synagogues be made of specially prepared skins of animals.

The earliest known New Testament copies are on papyrus, and this is clearly what John means 2 JN. 12 when he refers to "paper and ink" to write letters. Paul mentions parchment, which after the fourth century largely replaced papyrus.

The choice of writing tool depended on what was being written upon. Stone was inscribed with a chisel, and papyrus with a reed pen that was used like a brush. Writing on animal skins required a fine-pointed pen sharpened with a knife. The use of ink, which began in Egypt before 3000 B.C., was apparently a well-known technique to the scribes responsible for the Dead Sea Scrolls, since inkwells have been found in the Qumran caves.

What are the oldest Bible manuscripts so far discovered?

New archeological discoveries keep pushing back the date of the oldest surviving manuscripts of biblical text. At present the most ancient ✳

Using a sharpened stylus, a Roman scribe writes on a clay tablet in this relief.

known manuscript is a fragmentary one of the Books of Samuel dating from about 225 B.C., found among the extensive Dead Sea Scrolls. Manuscripts of parts of Exodus and Jeremiah from the same collection are practically as old.

The most ancient fragment of the New Testament is a tiny piece of papyrus, just over three inches by two inches, found in the dry sands of Egypt early in this century. Containing three verses of the Gospel of John, including Pilate's question to Jesus, "Are you JN. 18:33 the King of the Jews?", it dates from A.D. 125 to 150 and so represents a copy made only about a generation after the Gospel was originally composed. Papyrus manuscripts bearing more substantial portions of the New Testament have also been discovered, dating from about A.D. 200—again preserved by Egypt's dry climate. Among them there is a manuscript containing all but three of Paul's letters and another fragment with most of the text of the Gospel of John.

Until the discovery of the Dead Sea Scrolls in 1947, the oldest known manuscript of any part of the Bible was the Nash papyrus. Written in Egypt around 150 B.C., it is a single sheet on which were copied the Ten Commandments and a few verses from Deuteronomy, including "Hear, O Is- DT. 6:4 rael: The Lord our God is one Lord; and you shall love the Lord your God with all your heart, and with all your soul, and with all your might."

Did the Bible exist in different versions?

Beginning in the late 1940's, analysis of the Old Testament manuscripts found at Qumran and at other sites near the Dead Sea revolutionized scholarly thinking on how the Bible developed. In the 11 caves at Qumran there were about 170 biblical manuscripts, some quite complete and others mere fragments. They date from about 225 B.C. to A.D. 70. In caves south of Qumran, biblical manuscripts were found that have been dated somewhat later—after the destruction of the Jerusalem temple in A.D. 70 to about 135. Taken together, these and other archeological finds seem to indicate that at least some Old Testament books existed in different versions before a standardized text began to emerge toward the end of the first century A.D.

Who are the people of the Book?

"The people of the Book" describes the central place of the Bible in the faith of those who hold it sacred, but the phrase does not appear in the Bible and was not coined by devout Bible readers. Instead, it was first used by Muslims. Early in the history of Islam, the religion founded by Muhammad (A.D. 570–632), its believers referred to Jews and Christians—with great admiration—as the people of the Book. And indeed, both Islam and Christianity, which ultimately stem from Judaism, owe to Judaism their emphasis on a revealed religious text.

DT. 4:2   The Old Testament itself gives evidence that the ancient Israelites understood its laws as the word of God. "You shall not add to the word which I command you," God said, "nor take from it; that you may keep the commandments of the Lord your God which I command you." Furthermore, the very acts of studying the law and teaching it to the next generation were also highly esteemed and considered a religious obligation: "And these words which I command you DT. 6:6 this day shall be upon your heart; and you shall teach them diligently to your children, and shall talk of them when you sit in your house, and when you walk by the way, and when you lie down, and when you rise."

The centrality of the biblical books to Jewish religion goes far to explain why historical catastrophes—even the destruction of the Jerusalem temple—could be overcome: whatever disaster befell the people, the written Bible survived intact. And the Bible could be adapted to fit new social, economic, and political circumstances through a process of interpretation. Jews justified such interpretation on the assumption that, along with the written Torah received at Mount Sinai, Moses also was taught an oral Torah—the methods whereby Scripture could be understood in new ways to answer new problems.

How was the Bible first read?

The earliest books were in the form of scrolls made out of sheets of papyrus, parchment, or leather fastened together end to end to make a long strip. The writing, from right to left in Hebrew, was generally confined to one side of the sheet, though some scrolls had writing on both sides. A scroll was read by holding it in one's left hand and unrolling it slowly with the right hand. Wooden rollers were attached to each end of scrolls considered especially important.

Apparently scrolls were usually read aloud in front of a group. The Book of Nehemiah describes Ezra reading the law of Moses "from ear- NEH. 8:3 ly morning until midday, in the presence of the men and the women and those who could understand; and the ears of all the people were attentive to the book of the law." People usually learned Bible passages by listening, rather than by silent reading. Learning to read written words—and to speak them fluently as one read—was a skill that required much training. Early Hebrew writing had no vowels, word separations, or punctuation.

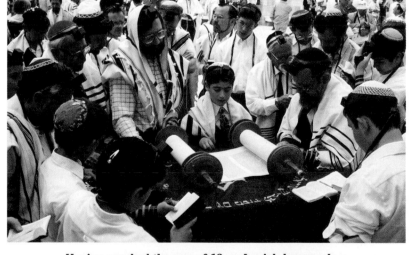

Having reached the age of 13, a Jewish boy reads a passage from the Torah in the traditional ceremony marking his emergence as a bar mitzvah, or son of the law.

THE TREASURES OF QUMRAN

Sometime in early 1947, a Bedouin shepherd, walking near Wadi Qumran in the Judean desert northwest of the Dead Sea, entered one of the numerous caves in the area and found several clay jars containing ancient manuscripts. News of the Bedouin's discovery reached local authorities, and three of the scrolls came into the hands of E. L. Sukenik, an archeologist at the Hebrew University in Jerusalem.

This was not a good time for a calm, dispassionate examination of these materials; for just at this juncture fighting broke out in the area between Jews and Arabs. In the ensuing chaos few could keep track of the scrolls' whereabouts. In 1954, after the end of hostilities, Yigael Yadin, Sukenik's son and an eminent archeologist in his own right, managed to arrange for the government of Israel to purchase several scrolls that had earlier been bought by the Syrian Orthodox archbishop.

Meanwhile, the cave where these manuscripts had been found and other caves around it were being searched, and a great number of antiquities surfaced. Although the 11 caves at Qumran yielded by far the most important group of scrolls and fragments, several other caves west of the Dead Sea were found to contain valuable ancient manuscripts, which came to light in the decade and a half after the initial Qumran discovery.

Many of the texts in the huge amount of material unearthed at Qumran were in such a state of disorder and decay that making sense of them proved a formidable task that continues to this day. (In particular, scholars

anxiously await publication of many of the 15,000 to 40,000 fragmentary texts from what is called Qumran Cave Four.) Taken together, the finds include parts of every book of the Hebrew Bible except Esther, as well as many nonbiblical books—some of which were previously unknown.

Scientific testing of the manuscripts revealed that they were written between the late third century B.C. and A.D. 68— when Roman soldiers brought an end to the Qumran community of Essenes, the sect most scholars believe was responsible for building the magnificent collection of scrolls. The Dead Sea manuscripts remain the oldest and most extensive surviving texts of the Hebrew Bible.

Repositories of ancient wisdom, these earthenware jars and others like them, averaging just over 2 feet high and about 10 inches wide, held the Dead Sea Scrolls.

Around Wadi Qumran, 11 caves (to which archeologists assigned the numbers on the map below) yielded the priceless scrolls.

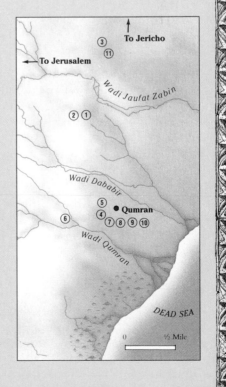

How the Bible Is Organized

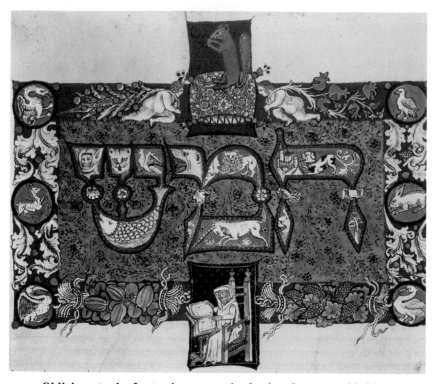

Oblivious to the fantastic menagerie sharing the page with him, a Talmudic scholar ponders a commentary on the Mishnah in this illuminated German manuscript dating from the 1300's.

How are Jewish and Christian Bibles different?

Aside from the fact that Christian Bibles include the New Testament and Jewish Bibles do not, there are major differences of organization between the Old Testaments used by the Christian churches and the Bible of the Jewish synagogues.

The Jewish Bible has three major divisions: the Torah, Prophets, and Writings. The Torah, or the first five books of the Bible, was the earliest part to be considered Scripture and the only part whose order is also the same in the Christian traditions. The second division, the Prophets, covers the so-called former prophets, from Joshua through 2 Kings (excluding Ruth), and the books called the latter prophets, which include the major prophets (Isaiah, Jeremiah, Ezekiel) and the 12 minor prophets (Hosea through Malachi). The third division is the Writings, or Hagiographa, which has three subsections: Psalms, Proverbs, and Job; five diverse books—Song of Solomon, Ruth, Lamentations, Ecclesiastes, Esther—and the historical narra-

tives of Daniel, Ezra, Nehemiah, and Chronicles.

The Christian Old Testament, based on the Greek translations known as the Septuagint, which was begun in the third century B.C., puts the Old Testament books following the Torah in a different order from the Jewish Bible. The Prophets are placed last, so that the final verse of Malachi, which prophesies the return of Elijah as the Messiah's forerunner, immediately precedes the New Testament: "Behold, I will send you Eli- MAL. 4:5 jah the prophet. . . . And he will turn the hearts of fathers to their children and the hearts of children to their fathers."

What is the basic difference between the Catholic and Protestant Bibles?

Following the tradition established in the Septuagint (the early Greek translation of the Old Testament), the Roman Catholic and Eastern Orthodox Bible incorporates many books not found in the Hebrew Bible, such as Tobit, Judith, the Book of Wisdom (or Wisdom of Solomon), Sirach (or

Ecclesiasticus), and the First and Second Books of Maccabees. There are also additions incorporated into the Book of Daniel (the Prayer of Azariah and the Song of the Three Young Men, Susanna, and Bel and the Dragon) and into the Books of Esther and Jeremiah.

In the 16th century Martin Luther and other reformers, challenging the Roman Catholic tradition, decided that the Christian Bible should include only those Old Testament books that were in the Hebrew canon. Though they kept the basic order of books in the Septuagint—that is, their Old Testament ended with the Prophets—they placed the books not found in the Hebrew Bible in another category, often called the Apocrypha ("secondary" or "hidden" works). Roman Catholic scholars refer to the Apocrypha as the deuterocanonical books of Scripture.

Why do Jews avoid using the term Old Testament?

The terms Old Testament and Hebrew Bible refer essentially to the same book, but Old Testament implies that there is also a companion volume, a New Testament, which is a necessary supple-

Practical advice from the wisdom books includes avoiding quarrels, which often spark the kind of violence depicted in this 17th-century painting.

ment to the Old. Old Testament is a term used by Christians. Jews use a variety of other terms, such as Tanakh, an acronym for the three parts of the Jewish Bible—Torah, Nebi'im (Prophets), and Ketubim (Writings). Jews also use the terms Bible or Holy Scriptures to refer to what Christians call the Old Testament.

The term Hebrew Bible is used primarily by modern biblical scholars, indicating the language in which the Old Testament was written (except for some Aramaic passages in the Books of Daniel, Ezra, and Jeremiah).

What is the Talmud?

The word *Talmud* comes from the Hebrew for learning or study and has come to mean specifically the study of traditional Jewish law. The Talmudic tradition in Judaism has two underlying texts: the first is called the Mishnah and the second is the commentaries on the Mishnah, known as the Gemara.

The Mishnah is a collection of laws that were compiled by rabbis about A.D. 200. After the Mishnah was closed to further additions, discussions arose among the rabbis about how to interpret its laws, and the resulting commentaries make up the Gemara.

There are two versions of the Talmud: the smaller Jerusalem Talmud, compiled in Galilee around A.D. 450, and the Babylonian Talmud, collected in the large Jewish community in Babylonia around A.D. 550. Both contain legal discussions and ethical reflections as well as stories about rabbis and biblical heroes and other commentaries on a wide variety of subjects.

In modern times Conservative and Reform Jews view the Talmud as a source of wisdom but do not regard its laws as absolutely authoritative. Orthodox Jews still study the Talmud as an infallible religious guide to Judaism.

Which parts of the Bible were written first?

The earliest parts of the Bible to be composed were the sequence of Old Testament books from Genesis through Kings. By the middle or late sixth century B.C., scribes were writing them down in a form whose content and perspective are recognizable today. Within these books are many passages whose language and poetic forms suggest that they are even older, such as the Song of the Sea in Exodus 15, the Song of Deborah in Judges 5, Jacob's blessing of his sons (Genesis 49), and Moses' blessing of the people of Israel (Deuteronomy 33).

The earliest book of the New Testament is 1 Thessalonians, written about A.D. 50 by the Apostle Paul to the Christian community in the Macedonian city of Thessalonica.

Which are the most recent writings to be included in the Bible?

According to most authorities, the last part of the Old Testament to have been written is the Book of Daniel, which may have been composed as late as 160 B.C. However, stories of Daniel trace back to the sixth century B.C.

The most recent book in the New Testament is difficult to identify. Some scholars believe the Second Letter of Peter was written in honor of

GOSPEL. *The word* gospel *derives from the Old English* godspell, *which was used by early English Bible translators to render the Latin word* evangelium *(from the Greek* euangelion*) into English. The shared meaning was good news, and this is the sense in which* gospel *is used by Matthew and Mark.*

When Mark says, "The beginning of the gospel of Jesus Christ, the Son of God [Mk. 1:1]," he is not using gospel *to describe his own book, but the good news that Jesus is the Messiah and the son of God. Mark also uses* gospel *for the message preached by Jesus: "The kingdom of God is at hand; repent, and believe in the gospel [Mk. 1:14]." Matthew conveys a similar meaning: "And he went about all Galilee . . . preaching the gospel of the kingdom [Mt. 4:23]."*

Not until the middle of the second century was the word gospel *applied specifically to the Books of Matthew, Mark, Luke, and John about the life and ministry of Jesus. In about 150, the Greek Christian philosopher Justin Martyr wrote of "the memoirs composed by [the Apostles], which are called Gospels."*

the Apostle Peter, not by him, and may have been written as late as A.D. 130. This would make 2 Peter the last completed New Testament work.

What are the Synoptic Gospels?

The first three Gospels—Matthew, Mark, and Luke—present the life and death of Jesus in a similar way and use identical wording in many passages. For that reason they are often termed *synoptic*, from a Greek word that means viewing together. The narrative and viewpoint of the fourth Gospel, the Gospel of John, sets it apart from the Synoptic Gospels. For example, John describes only a few of the same events of Jesus' ministry in the other Gospels; and he rarely uses wording similar to the others'.

Most biblical scholars agree that Mark is the earliest Gospel, written about A.D. 70, perhaps for the Christian community in Rome or Syria. Matthew was probably written around A.D. 85, possibly at Antioch in Syria, and the author's principal source may have been Mark. Luke was written around the same time, and the author similarly is thought to have used Mark as one of his main sources. Many scholars think that the authors of Matthew and Luke both consulted one or more additional written sources, from which they took material not found in Mark. One of the additional sources—although an actual manuscript has never been found—is thought to be a collection of Jesus' sayings called "Q," from the German *Quelle*, meaning source.

Not all scholars support this traditional order. Some see Matthew as the earliest Synoptic Gospel and Luke and Mark as the later ones.

What are the wisdom books?

The Books of Job, Proverbs, and Ecclesiastes are related to an ancient Near Eastern tradition of recording thoughts and aphorisms about the ways of divinity and the universe and the proper role of humans. They differ profoundly from that tradition, however, in placing God above all in their universe. They are often called the wisdom books of the Old Testament. In the organization of the Bible, the wisdom books provide a contrasting perspective to the historical narratives and the prophetic writings.

The Roman Catholic Bible, following the prec-

MORE THAN MERE NUMBERS

Many numbers have a symbolic meaning in the Bible.

The number 1 is the symbol of monotheism and unity: "The Lord our God is one Lord [Dt. 6:4]," and "a man . . . cleaves to his wife, and they become one flesh [Gen. 2:24]." In the New Testament, Paul tells the Ephesians, "There is one body and one Spirit . . . one Lord, one faith, one baptism, one God and Father of us all [Eph. 4:4]."

The number 2 suggests pairing, a kind of fulfillment that is not possible if two beings or things remain separated. Humanity requires a female and a male. Two animals of each kind go into the ark. Moses receives two tablets of the law on Mount Sinai. Two witnesses are required for an accusation to be admissible in court.

The figure 3 is a number of totality. The universe consists of heaven, earth, and under the earth. Noah has three sons, who are the ancestors of all people. The tabernacle and the temple have three areas: the courtyard, the "holy place [Lev. 6:16]," and the inner sanctum.

Four is also a number of totality. Earth in its entirety has four quarters and four corners; four winds blow across land and sea. Four rivers flow out of the Garden of Eden to water the world. The Lord's name, Yahweh, has four letters in Hebrew (YHWH), and he has four creatures around his throne. In the Book of Revelation, four horsemen bring destruction and death to the people of the earth.

Significant from the very first chapters of Genesis is 7. God promises sevenfold vengeance if

Two by two, animals of every kind enter Noah's ark in a painting by the French artist J. James Tissot.

anyone murders Cain. Jacob serves seven years for Rachel's hand in marriage, and seven more after he got Leah instead. There are seven years of plenty and seven years of famine in the pharaoh's dream. Many of the visions of Revelation occur in 7's: golden lampstands, stars, seals, angels, trumpets, thunders, plagues, and golden bowls full of wrath. Mark and Luke mention seven demons that went out of Mary Magdalene, one of several women "healed of evil spirits and infirmities [Lk. 8:2]" by Jesus.

The number with a marvelous practical application is 10—counting with the 10 fingers probably led to the decimal system—in addition to sacred and symbolic significance in visionary books such as Revelation. The sum of the sacred numbers 3 and 7, it also represents complete perfection, as in the Ten Commandments.

The figure 12 is not only the number of tribes of Israel and of Jesus' disciples, but also the months of the year and the hours "in the day [Jn. 11:9]." Just as 7 is the sum of 3 and 4, 12 is the product of 3 and 4. The Jewish philosopher Philo called 12 the perfect number.

A central theme linking Old and New Testaments is the importance of caring for others, a virtue celebrated in this Italian fresco.

BIBLE STATISTICS

The following counts are based on English Bibles and may vary depending on the translation.

	Old Testament	New Testament
Books	39	27
Chapters	929	260
Verses	23,214	7,959
Words	592,493	181,253
Longest book	Psalms	Luke
Shortest book	Obadiah	3 John
Longest chapter	Psalm 119	Matthew 26
Shortest chapter	Psalm 117	Revelation 15
Longest verse	Esther 8:9	Revelation 20:4
Shortest verse	1 Chronicles 1:25 ("Eber, Peleg, Reu;")	John 11:35 ("Jesus wept.")
Middle book	Proverbs	2 Thessalonians
Middle chapter	Job 29	Romans 13–14
Middle verse	2 Chronicles 20:13	Acts 7:7

Middle chapter of the Bible	Psalm 117
Middle verse	Psalm 118:8
Most mentioned mortal	David (1,118)
Longest word	Mahershalalhashbaz (Isaiah 8:1) name of Isaiah's son.

edent of the Greek Septuagint translation, includes two additional wisdom books, the Wisdom of Solomon (also known simply as the Book of Wisdom) and Sirach (its full title is the Wisdom of Jesus the Son of Sirach). The Book of Wisdom was not composed by King Solomon, since it probably dates to the first century B.C., although it is clearly linked to more ancient sources. The actual author is unknown.

The author of Sirach—Jesus the son of Sirach, or Joshua ben Sira in Hebrew—was a scribe and teacher of Jewish law in the second century B.C. He probably lived in Jerusalem and instructed young men in religion and moral law. In the Latin Church, Sirach's book came to be called Ecclesiasticus, meaning church book, because of its usefulness in religious instruction. In the tradition stretching back to the ancient sayings in Proverbs, it was the last of the great Hebrew wisdom literature to be written.

Who decided how to break up the text of the Bible into chapters and verses?

The chapter divisions commonly used in today's Bibles were introduced by Stephen Langton, an English theologian and biblical scholar (later

Archbishop of Canterbury), who taught at the University of Paris in the early 1200's. In his time there were a number of different systems of dividing the Bible into chapters, and Langton and his colleagues saw a need for standardization. The earliest surviving Bible with Langton's chapter divisions is an edition of the Latin Bible published in 1231.

The verse divisions are older than the chapter divisions, at least for the Old Testament. The Hebrew text used in ancient synagogues lacked verse divisions, but by the sixth or seventh century the practice of dividing the text into verses began to take hold. Verse breaks were later inserted into Hebrew Bibles used for teaching and were introduced into Christian Bibles in the 16th century by the famous French printers Henri and Robert Estienne. Robert added verse divisions for the New Testament in 1551 and printed a whole Bible in French with verse divisions in 1553.

Which Old Testament passage is the most quoted in the New Testament?

The most popular Old Testament passage in the New Testament is the first verse of Psalm 110: "The Lord says to my lord: 'Sit at my right hand, PS. 110:1 till I make your enemies your footstool.' " It is quoted, or alluded to, 16 times: in Matthew, Mark, Luke, Acts, Romans, 1 Corinthians, Ephesians, Colossians, and Hebrews. This passage was understood to be a prediction of the Messiah's ascent to God's throne and of his victory over his enemies. The second most popular Old Testament verse in the New Testament is God's command in Leviticus 19:18: "You shall love LEV. 19:18 your neighbor as yourself." This verse is referred to 10 times in the New Testament—six times in the Gospels, three times by the Apostle Paul, and once in the Letter of James.

BOOKS THAT HAVE VANISHED

Daniel, whose vision of the four beasts inspired this 12th-century illumination, is thought to have been the hero of many lost stories.

As a very literate culture, Israel produced voluminous writings, but various clues indicate that many books and parts of books have not survived the ravages of time. In addition to portions of existing books that have disappeared, the Bible mentions roughly 30 books that have long been lost.

Two of the lost books, the Book of Jashar and the Book of the Wars of the Lord, appear to have been collections of early Israelite poems or hymns. Jashar is cited as the source for Joshua's poetic address to the sun and the moon, David's lament over Saul and Jonathan, and probably Solomon's poetic dedication of the temple. Wars of the Lord is quoted in Numbers 21:14 as describing where Israelites encamped—"Waheb in Suphah, and the valleys of the Arnon"—

and the same book may have supplied two other poetic fragments in Numbers 21.

The Bible's historical narratives cite a number of vanished books, including the Book of the Acts of Solomon, the Chronicles of King David, the History of Nathan the Prophet, and the Chronicles of Shemaiah the Prophet and Iddo the Seer. Some of these may have been official annals, such as the Book of the Chronicles of the Kings of Israel and the Book of the Chronicles of the Kings of Judah. Historical annals of other nations, now lost, are also mentioned, such as the Book of the Chronicles of the Kings of Media and Persia.

In the New Testament, the Gospel of Luke alludes to lost books about Jesus; and Paul cites letters to the Laodiceans and Corinthians that are lost.

Authors

A solemn Jeremiah dictates his prophecy of Jerusalem's impending destruction to Baruch, his loyal companion and scribe, in a 19th-century American painting.

Did Moses write the Pentateuch?

The codes of laws that the Israelites believed God had given to Moses—and the religious principles that gave Jewish life its unique identity—are embedded in the first five books of the Old Testament. Over the course of time it became firmly established in Jewish tradition that Moses not only received the law but also wrote the books in which that law was recorded.

Since the 17th century, however, scholars have noted that in none of the books of the Pentateuch is there any claim that Moses is the author, and in fact each gives many internal indications that it was composed long after Moses lived. Moses is often referred to in the third person, for example—sometimes in flattering terms that he would hardly have been likely to use himself. ✳

Certain places are identified with names not given them until centuries after Moses' time, and there are numerous differences in writing style and vocabulary that reflect changes in the Hebrew language that must have occurred over many generations. Indeed, when scholars study the text of the five books they find literary characteristics of an era farther removed from Moses than we are today from Shakespeare. Although these factors all argue against Moses' being the author, the scholars do not conclude that someone else should be given the credit. They propose instead that the writings we know as the Pentateuch are a compilation of at least four ancient Israelite literary sources (which in turn may have been preserved for generations by oral tradition before they were ever written down). In one source God was called Yahweh, while in another he was called Elohim; a third gave special emphasis to the role of priests and rituals, and a fourth, the Book of Deuteronomy, marks a transition from an old to a new religious and political order.

Some readers are inclined to dismiss the question of authorship as unimportant. Many of the scholars themselves agree that it is the content that matters, not who wrote it. But they also believe that finding out as much as possible about the authors is one way to get closer to the actual setting in which the scriptures were written and to follow the various ways in which faith in God was expressed.

Who wrote the Psalms?

Nearly half of the 150 psalms in the Bible are introduced by the phrase "A Psalm of David," and readers have long taken that to mean that David wrote the psalm—hardly surprising for one the Bible calls "the sweet psalmist of Israel." None- 2 SAM. 23:1 theless, there are doubts as to whether David actually composed many of the psalms himself. Some of those credited to David, for instance, mention the temple in Jerusalem—which was not built until after his death—or even the Babylonian exile, which occurred more than three centuries later. Most likely, the psalms were collected over a long period and compiled in their final form around the second century B.C. The attributions may have meant the psalms were in the style of David, or they may have been intended to honor the memory of David, rather than to assign him authorship.

Many of the psalms have a quality of worship that suggests they were used in temple services and may have been written by members of the Levitical guild of musicians. In contrast, some psalms are strongly personal in tone, and such striking disparities support the idea that the present Book of Psalms is an anthology of different collections that cannot with confidence be assigned specific authors or dates.

What is known about the authors of the Old Testament narratives?

As with the Pentateuch and the Psalms, biblical scholars have pored over every verse of the Old Testament for clues to the authors' identities. Some believe they can trace the style of a single man in 1 and 2 Chronicles, Ezra, and Nehemiah. His name is unknown—one tradition identifies him with Ezra, but with little factual evidence to support it—so he is referred to simply as the Chronicler. Others have isolated the work of someone they call the priestly writer, because of his concern with the rituals of formal worship. And there is yet another author, known as the Deuteronomist, whose concept of Israel's sins against God is expressed in the sequence of text from Deuteronomy through 2 Kings.

In each of these cases, however, the evidence is so complex that scholars are uncertain whether they see the work of a single writer or a school of like-minded contributors. Several basic methods have been brought to bear on this continuing study of the scriptures. One is linguistic analysis, which looks for patterns of language and favored words and phrases. Another focuses on similarities in political or religious positions expressed in the text. A third is historical comparison, which involves establishing a date for a piece of writing and then seeing if it matches the dates of the author to whom it has been attributed. Only in rare cases, such as Jeremiah, can a writer be identified as a well-known historical figure—but this search for an individual hand, whatever its outcome, seldom if ever alters the importance of the message itself.

BARUCH AND JEREMIAH

Baruch was the scribe and steadfast friend of the prophet Jeremiah in the last turbulent quarter-century of the kingdom of Judah. Barred from reading his prophecies in the Jerusalem temple, Jeremiah asked Baruch to do so from a scroll the scribe had made of the prophet's oracles. Baruch consented, though he knew that its contents would be unwelcome because Jeremiah predicted that "the king of Babylon will certainly come and destroy this land [Jer. 36:29]."

When news of Jeremiah's prophecies reached Judah's King Jehoiakim, the king ordered his court officials to read him the scroll—and he was infuriated. As each three or four columns were read, "the king would cut them off with a penknife and throw them into the fire in the brazier, until the entire scroll was consumed [Jer. 36:23]." Jehoiakim then ordered the arrest of Baruch and Jeremiah, but, forewarned, the pair escaped and promptly produced an expanded version of the burned scroll.

As Jerusalem lay under siege, the prophet bought a field and entrusted the deed to Baruch with the words: "Houses and fields and vineyards shall again be bought in this land [Jer. 32:15]." The transaction symbolized the two men's trust in each other and their faith in the ultimate triumph of their nation.

After Jerusalem's fall, Baruch and Jeremiah somehow managed to avoid exile to Babylon. Eventually, caught up in bloody power struggles among pro- and anti-Babylon factions, they were taken to Egypt, where they probably died. An alternative tradition holds that they ended their days in Babylon, where Baruch served as the tutor of Ezra.

EVANGELIST. *An evangelist is one who brings good news. The word is related to the Greek* euangelion, *translated as* gospel; *the evangelist was one who preached the Gospel to those who had never heard it. Such a preacher was a trailblazer, distinct from the "pastors and teachers" [Eph. 4:11] who came after to instruct and guide committed Christians. The "work of an evangelist" [2 Tim. 4:5] required special endurance and force of character.*

In time, the Gospels' authors became known as the four evangelists, and they have been represented symbolically as a man, a lion, an ox, and an eagle—the "four living creatures [Rev. 4:6]" that surround God's throne. The images were allegorically linked to each Gospel: the man to Matthew because he gives a genealogy of Christ, the lion to Mark, who begins with a voice "crying in the wilderness [Mk. 1:3]," the ox to Luke because he describes a sacrifice, and the eagle to John for his soaring prologue.

Famous for his musical gifts, David plays the lyre in this 15th-century Dutch miniature.

What special problems faced the authors of the New Testament?

In view of the trying conditions under which some of the 27 books and epistles of the New Testament were written, it is remarkable that they survived. Many of them are letters composed under the pressure of travel, at a time when writing materials were expensive and frequently scarce. Often they were delivered by messengers over land and sea, sometimes across great distances, and they could be reproduced only by laborious hand-copying, one copy at a time. The authors, moreover, wrote them in the firm expectation that the world would soon end. They were not concerned with a remote future in which every word and phrase would be scrutinized, but with the immediate needs of scattered churches confronted by false prophets and, later, by the persecution of Roman authorities and the hostility of neighbors. The New Testament was produced not as a record for the future but as a voice urgently spreading its sacred message to followers often faced with imminent death.

Given such turbulent conditions, it is surprising that so much is known today about the New Testament authors. There is little doubt that the author of the Gospel of Luke was also the author of Acts, for example, or that the author of the fourth Gospel is the same person who wrote the three letters that also bear the name of John. In a few cases, however, the attribution of authorship continues to be debated by scholars. Among the ideas put forth are that the Second Epistle of Peter may have been written 75 years after the Apostle Peter's martyrdom in Rome; and that the letter of James was not written by Jesus' brother but by another early Christian named James. Scholars also express uncertainty about the authorship of three epistles (1 and 2 Timothy and Titus) attributed to Paul.

Attributing works to respected persons may have occurred because the authors wished to show a link between their writings and the authority of a venerated figure. This was a common practice in ancient times. The people who actually wrote down the New Testament were seeking to preserve and transmit Jesus' message, and each of the documents exists as a source of instruction and inspiration to believers, whatever the name of its author.

Who were "the writing prophets"?

The Hebrew prophets were first and foremost preachers, not writers. They called down the judgment of God, they predicted doom and conflagration, and they preached hope and tender care for the unfortunate—all by word of mouth and often with great eloquence. The written words of a select few of these holy men have been preserved for posterity, and thus they came to be known as "the writing prophets." Some of them did in fact write their books, or parts of them, but more often a prophet spoke and his disciples transcribed the words.

Sometimes the process of preserving those words stretched over generations. Isaiah, for example, preached between 742 and 687 B.C.; yet some parts of the book bearing his name were not completed until late in the sixth century B.C. In the case of Jeremiah the process was compressed, scholars believe, probably into two generations. Much of the book was written or dictated by Jeremiah, transcribed and edited by his friend, disciple, and secretary Baruch, and then refined in the next generation by later disciples. Eventually, with the passage of time a prophet's words took on enough authority to be considered untouchable, and the book at that point reached its final form.

The evangelists of the Gospels (Mark and Matthew above, John and Luke below) are portrayed with traditional symbolism in the Book of Kells, *dating from about A.D. 800.*

How much of the Bible is poetry?

Most readers would say that poetry is found everywhere in the Bible, but poetry in the sense of words arranged in metrical verses covers about a third of the Old Testament and a much smaller fraction of the New Testament. From Genesis through the writings of the prophets, almost every book of the Old Testament contains some passages in verse. For example, about half of Ecclesiastes and almost all of Job are in poetic form, as are all of Psalms, Proverbs, Song of Solomon, and Lamentations. Most of the prophetic oracles in Isaiah, Jeremiah, and the minor prophets are also in verse.

In the New Testament, beautiful poetry can be found in the opening chapters of Luke, which recount the births of John and Jesus. Revelation contains more than a dozen verse passages, such as the song of the four living creatures around God's throne that begins, "Holy, holy, REV. 4:8 holy, is the Lord God Almighty, who was and is and is to come!" And some of Jesus' most memorable teachings—the Beatitudes and the Lord's Prayer among them—are unmistakably poetic. In form and technique, most biblical verse reflects ancient traditions of Hebrew poetry, which has no rhyme or exact rhythm but makes use of figurative language and parallel phrasing. Happily, these characteristics help translators preserve the structure and essence of the original, as in the Revised Standard Version rendering of Amos 5:24: "Let justice roll down like waters, and righteousness like an ever-flowing stream."

The Bible in History

Can biblical events be dated?

The Bible and other ancient documents indicate when events happened by a variety of local and often inexact systems, such as a year in the reign of a king. By comparing the numerous systems, scholars have often been able to work out the modern equivalents of ancient dates, though in many cases a wide margin of error remains. For example, Jeremiah dates Jerusalem's surrender JER. 52:28 to Babylon as "the seventh year" of King Nebuchadnezzar, which can be identified as 597 B.C. An ancient Babylonian chronicle—first brought to light in the 1950's—agrees and adds the precise day: the second of the month of Addaru, or March 16. When such benchmark dates are applied to the chronology of events and royal reigns reported in the Old Testament histories, additional probable dates can be figured. Clues also exist within the biblical accounts, such as in the description of village life in Judges, which has details that archeologists know to be typical of the period from about 1200 to 1000 B.C.

A similar approach is used for the New Testament. For example, Paul's letters can be approximately dated by using information in the Book of Acts and the known dates of events given in other sources.

Recently found in Israel, this 3,500-year-old bronze calf dates to the time of the Canaanites and may be a prototype of the golden calf in Exodus.

Today, archeologists continue to find clues to when biblical events occurred by studying pottery styles, coins, items of trade, inscriptions, and household goods.

What do B.C.E. and C.E. signify?

The chronological tags B.C.E. (Before the Common Era) and C.E. (Common Era) are considered religiously neutral, whereas B.C. (Before Christ) and A.D. (Anno Domini, or in the Year of the Lord) reflect Christian belief. B.C.E. and C.E. dates are the same as B.C. and A.D., but do not imply a confession of Jesus as Lord and so can be readily used by non-Christians.

Why is the Rosetta Stone important to Bible history?

In August 1799, one of Napoleon's officers discovered a partly broken tablet of black basalt half buried in mud near the Egyptian village of Rosetta. Only 3 feet 9 inches long and 2 feet 4½ inches wide, the 11-inch-thick slab was inscribed with three different kinds of writing: ancient Greek, the hieroglyphs of Old Egypt, and Egyptian demotic (the cursive writing that replaced hieroglyphics in ordinary documents).

At the time, scholars could not decipher hieroglyphics but surmised that the three inscriptions referred to the same event, a celebration in 196 B.C. of Egypt's King Ptolemy V. The English scholar Thomas Young showed that the king's name appeared six times in each text. Matching the different scripts, the French Egyptologist Jean-François Champollion found Greek equivalents for all known hieroglyphic signs. He saw that individual images in the mysterious picture writing sometimes stood for a whole idea, sometimes for a syllable, and sometimes for a single letter. Translations made possible by this achievement opened up a wealth of information to scholars on the historical background of biblical events.

What do tells hide?

In Arabic, a *tall* (tell in English) is simply a hill, but archeologists use the word to mean a mound built up from several successive communities at one site. In ancient Palestine, a place might have continued to attract settlers over many centuries

As Sir Percival and Sir Bors look on, the young Galahad, whose virtue earned him the privilege of claiming the Holy Grail for all Christendom, kneels before the chalice in this Victorian tapestry.

THE QUEST FOR THE GRAIL

More than 1,000 years after the last word of Scripture was written, one of the holiest events for Christians, the Last Supper, took on a new life in the adventure-filled world of the Knights of the Round Table.

Knights went forth in pursuit of the Holy Grail—the cup that Jesus filled with wine and over which he spoke the words, "This is my blood of the covenant, which is poured out for many [Mk. 14:24]." To the medieval imagination, a cup with traces of the actual blood of God offered unimaginable powers to its owner. The Middle Ages were a time of pilgrimages to venerate holy relics and crusades to rescue sacred objects from heathen hands. The quest for the Holy Grail emerged as the ultimate in pilgrimages, the final goal of any crusade.

The Holy Grail was sometimes believed to be the plate that contained the bread over which Jesus said, "Take; this is my body [Mk. 14:22]." In another tradition the vessel belonged to Joseph of Arimathea, who used it to collect the blood that flowed from the wounds of Jesus on the cross.

In some versions of the grail story, monks replace the knights. The quest becomes a quest for Christian virtues, especially those of chastity and charity.

Scholars have detected echoes from a variety of sources, including ancient rituals, Christian legends and Celtic lore, Irish sagas and Welsh tales. In each version, some set of Christian ideals is exemplified. And with all the allusions to crusades, worship, castles, monks, pilgrimages, wars, wanderings of the young, redemption of sinners, and so much more, the story of the Holy Grail has created a momentum of its own, ever able to renew itself for generation after generation while maintaining a unique blend of reverence and romance, exciting adventure, and the deep and mysterious power of faith.

because it had a reliable water supply, stood close to major trade routes or had desirable natural resources, and could be well defended. If all or part of the settlement's buildings were destroyed in some natural or man-made disaster, it was likely that new structures would sooner or later be built atop the debris of the old, and the site would gradually rise higher. The Book of Joshua refers to "cities that stood on mounds." JOS. 11:13 Today, thousands of tells, some of them 50 to 75 feet high, can still be seen in biblical lands. Within them they hold, layer beneath layer, a physical record of generations stretching far back in biblical times.

Canon

The Council of Trent, depicted by a 16th-century artist, was called by the Roman Catholic Church to review its canon of Old and New Testament books and address other basic issues raised by the Protestant Reformation.

When were the books of the Hebrew Bible established?

Beginning with the attempt to preserve the Ten Commandments by carrying the stone tablets on which they were inscribed in the Ark of the Covenant, the people of Israel believed themselves to be the guardians of divinely inspired texts. However, there are no firm dates for when the Hebrew canon—those writings now accepted as authoritative that are included in the Bible—was clearly and unambiguously determined. Instead, time and tradition imparted religious authority to certain texts.

Two historical events reported in the Hebrew Bible are regarded as significant milestones in the development of the canon. First, in about 621 B.C. during King Josiah's reign, a law scroll believed to be a portion of Deuteronomy was discovered in the temple, and Josiah decreed that these writings be considered law for his society. His action was a step in establishing the overriding importance of written Scripture. Second, scholars suggest that Ezra's public reading and enforcement of the book of the law after the return from Babylonia in the late sixth century B.C. marks the point when the first five books of the Bible, the Torah, became officially canonical.

The canon of the Hebrew Bible recognized today was not completely established until about the end of the first century A.D. There has never been a dictate that the Hebrew canon is closed; however, the Hebrew Bible has remained as it is today for almost 2,000 years.

What books in the Bible do not mention God?

Neither the Song of Solomon nor the Book of Esther mentions the word *God*. In the Apocrypha, the same is true of 1 Maccabees.

288

The Song of Solomon contains love poems describing the passions felt by a bride and groom. Its lack of religious language made it problematic as an authoritative text until allegorical interpretation enabled teachers to use the book to describe God's love for his people.

Though the theme of the church as a bride and Christ as a groom appears in both Ephesians and Revelation, the Song of Solomon is not mentioned or quoted in these passages, or anywhere else in the New Testament—perhaps an indication that the book posed difficulties for early Christians too. During the second and third centuries A.D. some church authorities interpreted the Song of Solomon as an allegory of Christ and the church, while others viewed it as symbolizing the soul's love for God.

As for the Book of Esther, traditional religious authorities have been less troubled by its failure to mention the name of God than by its command to observe a feast (Purim) not specified in the law of Moses. Although God's name is absent, there are memorable heroes of faith in the dramatic victory of the Jewish people.

1 MACC. 2:27 — Similarly, 1 Maccabees recounts the exploits of heroes who are "zealous for the law" but, unlike its companion 2 Maccabees, it does not describe miraculous interventions by God. Like Esther, it is up to the reader whether the providence of God is seen in the story.

Tobias and his bride sleep blissfully after exorcising a vengeful demon.

TOBIT, TOBIAS, AND THE ANGEL

Tobit—part of the Apocrypha in Protestant Bibles—is the story of a devout Jewish man, his wife Anna (or Hannah), and their son Tobias. As the Assyrians completed the conquest of the northern kingdom of Israel (721 B.C.), the family was deported to Nineveh, the Assyrian capital.

In an alien land, Tobit held fast to his beliefs. He boldly refused to stop arranging for the proper burial of his fellow Jews, who were persecuted by King Sennacherib (reigned 705–681 B.C.) and his successor Esarhaddon.

Though each burial rendered Tobit ritually unclean according to the laws of Moses, he faithfully observed the required cleanliness rituals. One night, however, when he fell asleep before performing the rites, sparrow droppings fell into his eyes and blinded him. For eight years he prayed to have his sight restored.

His prayers were answered in a roundabout way—mainly through the adventures of his son Tobias, aided at every turn by the archangel Raphael. One night when they camped by the Tigris River, a fish leapt from the water. Tobias caught and ate it, but on Raphael's advice kept the heart, liver, and gall of the fish.

Raphael led Tobias to the beautiful Sarah, unmarried because the demon Asmodeus had killed each of her seven husbands. Marrying Sarah, Tobias drove away Asmodeus by burning the fish's heart and liver on an incense fire in the bridal chamber.

At last Tobias returned home with Sarah and Raphael. Tobias took out the fish gall and placed it upon his father's eyes, restoring Tobit's sight.

After a long prayer of praise and rejoicing, the story ends with Tobit telling Tobias to leave Nineveh before the city's predicted destruction.

Judith, the Apocrypha's supreme heroine, returns with her maid to Bethulia bearing the head of Assyria's general Holofernes, in a work by Botticelli.

SCRIPTURE and CANON. *Derived from the Latin for writing,* Scripture *refers generally to writings esteemed as authoritative by any religious community. For Jews and Christians, the term, often capitalized, denotes those writings accepted as canonical, or authoritative, by their religious leaders.*

Almost all of the approximately 50 New Testament references to "the scriptures [Mt. 21:42]" mean the Old Testament. In 2 Peter, Paul's letters are compared with "the other scriptures [2 Pet. 3:16]," and gradually the term came to be used for Christian writings.

Canon, traceable to a Sumerian word meaning reed, comes directly from the Greek kanon—*something used as a measure or standard. Beginning in the fourth century,* canon *came to signify those books considered authoritative in matters of religious belief and practice.*

Who decided what should be in the New Testament?

The earliest Christians found confirmation of their faith in the Hebrew Bible, which they cited to prove that Jesus was the Messiah. Subsequently, however, Christians came to recognize another kind of authority, stemming from the testimony of Paul and the other Apostles and from the oral tradition of Jesus' teachings.

As the Christian message spread far and wide, letters became an increasingly important form of communication between church groups, and many believers felt a need to preserve the oral tradition by writing it down. Luke attests to this new emphasis on the written word when he refers in his Gospel to the many who "have undertaken to compile a narrative of the things which have been accomplished among us." LK. 1:1

Of the great amount of material (much of it now lost and forgotten) written about Jesus and his followers during this period, it is the books and letters of the New Testament that have stood the test of time. Composed in the latter half of the first century, these were the writings that achieved wide circulation and were most often read during church services. Within a century they had been deemed authoritative by general consent in the Christian community. Then in A.D. 367 Athanasius, bishop of Alexandria, listed the 27 books of the New Testament, called them "the sources of salvation," and asserted that "in these alone is the doctrine of piety recorded." By the end of the fourth century, the church had declared these books canonical.

How different are the canons of the various Christian faiths?

The major difference is that the Old Testament in Protestant Bibles follows the Hebrew canon, while the Roman Catholic and Eastern Orthodox churches include more than a dozen additional books and parts of books as authoritative Scripture in their Bibles. These additional books are called the Apocrypha by Protestants. Despite the absence of the Apocrypha from their canons, Protestants and Jews recommend the material for its religious and ethical teaching.

Differences also exist between the Roman

Catholic and Eastern Orthodox canons. For example, the Greek Orthodox and Russian Orthodox churches both recognize the First and Second Books of Esdras and the Third Book of Maccabees as authoritative.

How did early Christians regard the Hebrew scriptures?

Most of the earliest Christians were devout Jews who considered the Old Testament their only scriptures. They believed their religious duty was to become knowledgeable, in Jesus' words, about "the law of Moses and the prophets and the psalms [or writings]," a common way of referring to all the Hebrew scriptures at the time.

LK. 24:44

Acceptance of Jesus as the Messiah caused early believers to search their scriptures for confirmation that he was the long-expected Anointed One. All four Gospels cite Old Testament prophecies to underscore Jesus' authority as the Messiah, and Paul's letters constantly refer to the Old Testament in support of his views. The Gospel of Matthew directly quotes or clearly alludes to more than 60 Old Testament passages to show how Jesus fulfilled messianic prophecies.

Early Christians also turned to the Old Testament to explain Jesus' crucifixion and resurrection. The crucifixion is interpreted in light of the laments in Psalm 22; and the resurrection is understood in the context of passages such as Psalm 16:10, which speaks of deliverance from Sheol, the Hebrew abode of the dead.

EXTRABIBLICAL RELIGIOUS TEXTS

Many Jewish and Christian texts that were not accepted as canonical books of the Bible are assiduously studied today for their insights into religious ferment in the period between the time when the last books of the Old Testament were written and the point when the exact contents of the New Testament were determined. Ethics and the precepts of ancient wisdom, including the ideas of neighboring cultures, are fundamental to this noncanonical intertestamental literature, of which one important segment is a collection of 65 books known as the Pseudepigrapha. Many of the books develop concepts of individualism and strongly emphasize obedience to the Torah. One of the most significant of the Pseudepigrapha is the Book of Enoch, whose description of future judgment inspired William Blake and Lord Byron. Many New Testament authors may have been familiar with the pseudepigraphic literature, and indeed the Letter of Jude quotes a passage from the Book of Enoch that begins, "Behold, the Lord came with his holy myriads, to execute judgment on all, and to convict all the ungodly [Jude 14]."

Another collection of texts, buried near Nag Hammadi in Upper Egypt in the fourth century, was discovered in 1945. Coptic translations from ancient Greek, these 52 separate works were preserved on 13 papyrus codices, or books. They illuminate several different schools of Christian Gnostic thought in the first centuries after Jesus. The

Enoch, top right, records his visions in this Ethiopian manuscript painting.

collection also contains writing called Sethian because Adam's son Seth is given a prominent role as a revealer of wisdom. Among the Nag Hammadi texts is a work called the Gospel of Thomas, which provides new perspectives on the sayings of Jesus recorded in the Bible.

Ancient Versions

What are the earliest complete copies of the Bible?

The oldest complete Hebrew Bible is the Leningrad Codex (A.D. 1008). The Aleppo Codex (A.D. 900–950) is older, but portions of this formerly complete manuscript were destroyed in 1947 during Arab-Israeli hostilities. Until the Dead Sea Scrolls, these two codices and a number of earlier but incomplete manuscripts represented the oldest available sources for studying the text of the Old Testament.

Manuscripts like the Leningrad and Aleppo codices reflect the work of the Masoretes, early medieval Jewish scribes who carefully pored over biblical manuscripts and produced a standardized text. The traditional Bible used by Jews today is called the Masoretic text.

As scholars compared the Masoretic text with the Dead Sea Scrolls (some of which date from about 200 B.C.), it became apparent that three different versions of the Old Testament probably circulated in Jesus' time. Of these, one was the primary source of later copies and the other two survived only in hidden manuscripts such as

Two pages from the Codex Sinaiticus, the oldest complete New Testament known to exist.

the Dead Sea Scrolls or in translations like the Septuagint.

The oldest complete copy of the New Testament is a large parchment manuscript from the fourth century discovered in 1844 at the monastery of St. Catherine at Mount Sinai and thus known as Codex Sinaiticus. A nearly complete and equally ancient copy of the New Testament and Old Testament in Greek is the Codex Vaticanus,

A scholar of rare brilliance, St. Jerome (portrayed here in a Renaissance painting) translated singlehanded the Bible's original Hebrew and Greek text into a Latin version, the Vulgate, which dominated church history for a thousand years.

THE SEPTUAGINT: THE FIRST TRANSLATED BIBLE

Ptolemy II, the driving force behind Alexandria's fabled library.

One of the greatest literary enterprises of the ancient world was the translation of the Hebrew Bible into Greek, the most widely spoken language in the Mediterranean area after the fourth century B.C. The work evidently began with a rendering of the Pentateuch by Jews in Alexandria, Egypt, in the third century B.C. Within a century an elaborate tapestry of legend and fact had been woven around the translation. It was said that Ptolemy II, king of Egypt from 285 to 246 B.C., desired a copy of the great law of the Jews for his splendid new library in Alexandria. Ptolemy sent to the high priest in Jerusalem and requested that 72 outstanding scholars be dispatched to Egypt to begin the translation. Their number gave the work its traditional name: Septuagint, Latin for 70.

Legend told that the scholars spent a week at banquets with King Ptolemy engaged in long philosophical discussions, and then were given lodgings on an island off the coast of Alexandria. Working together, they produced, it was said, a translation so excellent and sacred that it should never be altered. By the first century A.D. the legend had grown even more elaborate. The Jewish philosopher Philo of Alexandria asserted that as the translators worked individually, "they became as it were possessed, and, under inspiration, wrote . . . the same word for word, as though dictated to each by an invisible prompter."

The translation of the Pentateuch was gradually supplemented with translations of the remainder of the Hebrew scriptures, as well as some other works that are now in the Apocrypha. The Septuagint served as the Bible for the vast numbers of Jews of the Diaspora whose native tongue was Greek. It was also this translation that the Christians used in their preaching and study. Most of the quotations from the Old Testament appearing in the New Testament are drawn from the Septuagint. As Christianity and Judaism came increasingly into conflict, however, the Christian use of the Septuagint led Greek-speaking Jews to reject the Septuagint in favor of new and more literal translations.

which has been in the Vatican Library since before the library was first catalogued in 1475. It is possible that both of these manuscripts were commissioned by the emperor Constantine soon after Christianity began to receive imperial support in the fourth century.

Why did Christians reject the scroll?

Libraries in the Greco-Roman world held nothing that looked like a book. Their walls were lined with boxlike niches containing stacks of scrolls. ✳

A complete copy of the Old Testament required a great many scrolls, and comparing a passage in Genesis with one in Isaiah, for example, required a great deal of rolling and unrolling. Moreover, scrolls were unwieldy to use, and the constant rolling could damage them.

The writings of the New Testament were evidently composed on scrolls as well. But by the second century A.D., Christian scribes began copying their texts in a new format called the codex, made of several sheets of papyrus or parchment, folded in the middle and stitched or otherwise bound together along the fold, producing

Matthew records his words in a codex in this Armenian Bible miniature.

pages that could be read like a modern book. There was no need for rolling and, compared to the scroll, passages could be located quickly. The codex was also more economical because both sides of the papyrus or parchment could more readily be used. Still another advantage was that more writings could be bound in a single unit. Even the small early papyrus codices could hold all four Gospels, for example, or all the letters of Paul. Later parchment codices like Codex Sinaiticus could contain all of the Old and New Testaments. The codex made it easier to study the scriptures and facilitated the transmission of knowledge and ideas of all kinds.

Every New Testament manuscript or fragment known today is from a codex rather than a scroll. Early Christians in fact may have invented the codex format for their scriptures. These manuscripts provide the oldest examples of codices; non-Christian works, in contrast, continued for centuries to be copied on traditional scrolls.

What Bible did Jesus use?

Jesus and his disciples probably knew the Bible—that is, the Old Testament—in two forms. First, they would have heard the original Hebrew scrolls read in synagogues on the Sabbath. It was most likely from such a scroll in the synagogue of Nazareth that Jesus, as reported by Luke, read the first lines of Isaiah 61: "The Spirit of the Lord is upon me." The synagogue service typically involved readings from both the Torah, or Pentateuch, and the Prophets. Such scrolls were both expensive and sacred, and they were kept in a chest called an ark. Few individuals owned personal copies of the scriptures. As Luke records, Jesus was handed the text to read, and after finishing, he "gave it back to the attendant," who would have returned it to the chest for safekeeping.

Jesus and his first disciples would also probably have known the scriptures in Ara-

LK. 4:18

LK. 4:20

Scholars in the library at Alexandria, the greatest of the ancient world, study some of its thousands of scrolls in a 19th-century engraving.

maic translation. Persia's long rule had made Aramaic the everyday language of most people in the Middle East. Jews who were not scholars normally knew little Hebrew, and it had been traditional since as early as Ezra's time to accompany the reading of the Bible with an oral Aramaic translation. Even though the Aramaic translations, called Targums, were relatively fixed, they were handed down for centuries only in oral form. In his teaching, Jesus probably quoted the Bible in the Aramaic most people understood.

Why was the Latin Vulgate important?

As early as the second century A.D. Christians in North Africa and elsewhere began to use several different Latin translations made from the Greek New Testament and the Septuagint. The church in Rome, surprisingly, continued to use Greek. In 382, however, Pope Damasus commissioned Jerome, the greatest Latin-speaking Christian scholar of his time, to make a new translation to replace all the divergent Old Latin versions.

Jerome, who knew Greek but not much Hebrew, began well enough by working on the Gospels; but when he turned next to the Psalms, he could provide only a translation of the Septuagint translation, just as the Old Latin versions had. Determined to use the original source, he settled in a monastery in Bethlehem to study Hebrew with Jewish scholars. By 391 he began again to translate the Old Testament, working directly from the Hebrew text, and over the next 15 years produced the translation known as the Vulgate, meaning a translation in the common language.

At first, Jerome's work met stiff resistance from partisans of the Old Latin translations. But ultimately it won its place as the dominant Bible of western Christianity. The first printed book, the Gutenberg Bible (about 1455), was a copy of the Vulgate. When the Vulgate's authority was challenged by Protestant reformers, the Roman Catholic Council of Trent (1545–63) proclaimed the Vulgate the authentic edition of the Bible.

What were other early translations of the Bible?

As Christianity spread through the various populations of the Roman Empire and beyond, its scriptures were rendered into many languages. ✳

Though the New Testament was originally written in Greek, the missionaries made little effort to teach their converts Greek. Rather they translated the Bible into the vernacular, sometimes inventing an alphabet for languages that had no written literature.

Very early translations were made into several dialects of Coptic, a language descended from Egypt's ancient hieroglyphics and used by the native people of Egypt. Like the Old Latin versions, these translations are as old as the oldest manuscripts of the New Testament and the Septuagint and often help scholars in reconstructing the original text. Similarly, early translations were made from Greek into Syriac, a dialect of Aramaic used in Palestine and eastern Syria. Syriac New Testaments show evidence that the four Gospels were replaced by a single text that wove them together into a harmonized narrative.

In the fourth century, a missionary named Ulfilas went to preach among the barbarian Visigoths along the Danube River. He invented an alphabet for them and translated the Bible into their Gothic language—making this Gothic Bible the oldest known literature in any Teutonic tongue. When the Visigoth king Alaric conquered Rome in 410, therefore, he was already a Christian (although he, like Ulfilas, held a number of beliefs that had been declared heretical). As Christianity spread, meanwhile, other ancient translations were made into the languages of Ethiopia, Arabia, and Armenia.

Two saints hold a cross in this limestone relief from a third-century Coptic community in Egypt.

Spreading the Word

When were Bibles first illustrated?

The earliest known illustrated manuscript of any kind is the Egyptian Book of the Dead, a religious scroll written on papyrus that dates from the 20th century B.C. The practice of illustrating religious writings appeared much later in the Judeo-Christian tradition, with its Old Testament warning against "a graven image." By the third century A.D., however, Jews were decorating their synagogue at Dura-Europos, in what is now Syria, with scenes from the Bible, and Christians also adorned some of their early churches with religious pictures. By the sixth century, Christians had begun adding illustrations to their Bibles. The earliest illustrated Bible was compiled in an English monastery shortly before 716 as a gift from the abbot to the pope. It is now in the Laurentian Library in Florence, Italy. Complete illustrated Bibles were rare until the 11th and 12th centuries; much more common were individual books or groups of books, such as the Pentateuch or the four Gospels.

The early biblical illustrations—such as miniature portraits, decorated initial letters and titles, and ornamental borders—are collectively called illuminations. The artists, or illuminators, were not necessarily monks; lay artists appear to have often worked in the monasteries.

As a scribe wrote down the words, he would leave spaces for illustrations. Then an artist would take up the manuscript, first sketching in light ink and later embellishing his illustration with colors, including gold and silver. The result was work of high artistic merit. Most of the painting that survives from the Middle Ages is in illuminated manuscripts. What has not survived are the names of many of the artists who produced these beautiful works.

The life of Jesus was popular with manuscript illuminators, but many artists of the period also found inspiration in the people

EX. 20:4

A miniature from a 12th-century French manuscript shows the copying of the Bible onto parchment; the knife kept the pen sharp.

and events of the Old Testament and in the lives of the saints. The most popular biblical book in the Middle Ages—apart from the Gospels—was Psalms, and illustrations were commissioned for psalters to be used both in church and at home.

The art of illumination gradually died out following the invention of the printing press late in the 15th century. By the 16th century, biblical texts were being illustrated with woodcuts that could be used again and again.

What are the masterpieces of illuminated texts?

Among the most beautiful examples of illuminated texts of the Bible are three Anglo-Irish manuscripts of the seventh and ninth centuries: the *Book of Durrow*, produced about 675 and celebrated for its intricate patterns and depictions of animals; the *Lindisfarne Gospels* of the same period, which survived intact and whose single artist, Eadfrith, is the first illuminator known by name in the British Isles; and the *Book of Kells*, compiled about a century later and drawing on the earlier works for inspiration but displaying greater sophistication with complex designs and extraordinary ornamented initials. *Durrow* and *Kells* are at Trinity College in Dublin; the *Lindisfarne Gospels*, at the British Museum in London.

Byzantine artists of the Eastern church adapted the techniques of Greek artists who had illustrated such classics as the works of Homer. Among the most celebrated of their works is a Menologion (a book of the lives of saints) prepared in the reign of the Byzantine emperor Basil II (976–1025). It contains 430 miniature paintings.

The illumination of manuscripts reached a peak with the so-called books of hours, a type of devotional work of prayers and meditations appropriate to different days and seasons. Intended for the use of a wealthy cleric or nobleman, such books featured

The monks at the monastery of St. Catherine on Mount Sinai were long active in copying and preserving the scriptures—a fact dramatized in 1975 when workmen found some 3,000 manuscripts hidden there.

realistic figures in recognizable settings and elegant border designs. The recognized masterpiece of this type of illuminated manuscript is *Les tres riches heures du Duc de Berry*, which is at the Musée Condé in Chantilly, France.

How did monks help ensure the survival of Scripture?

Beginning in about 500 and lasting until the dawn of the Renaissance in the 14th century, virtually all intellectual and artistic accomplishments in Western Europe took place under the auspices of the church. The monks who faithfully copied and recopied biblical manuscripts ensured that the written record of Christianity would be handed down to future generations.

The monasteries were the centers of these activities, and most of them had a special room, the scriptorium, where manuscripts were copied. This scholarly workroom had windows through which daylight fell on the tables at

which the monks labored. It was usually situated next to the monastery library, where existing texts could be examined. Each scriptorium was headed by a monk who directed the work and distributed the materials needed. Surviving manuscripts reveal that some were the work of a single copyist, while others were a collaborative effort, with different monks working on separate sections of the text.

Complete Bibles and other biblical texts, such as psalters—books of psalms—were produced for use mainly in the monasteries. Texts were exchanged between monasteries, copied, and the original returned. Thus comparisons could be made and errors corrected.

How was the Bible taught to people who couldn't read?

Late in the 13th century, churchmen in southern Germany came up with an ingenious method of teaching the Gospels to nonreaders. The clerics

*The master of a monastic workshop reads
to his brethren around the table in a miniature
almost engulfed by the other decorations
on this ornate 15th-century French manuscript.*

used picture books known as *Bibliae pauperum*, or Bibles of the poor, to explain how events in Jesus' life were foretold in the Old Testament.

A typical page in one of these Bibles of the poor had a large central depiction of a significant New Testament event, such as the Annunciation or the baptism of Jesus, flanked by pictures of related or corresponding events from the Old Testament. Above and below such illustrations were pictures of individual prophets from which flowed scrolls bearing the words of their prophecies—much like the balloons that carry the words of modern cartoon characters. Additional text, from which the teacher could read aloud, contained explanations of the links between the events. Such books were valuable teaching tools ✳

for poor clergy who could not afford complete Bibles and yet had to fulfill their mission of reaching the unenlightened and illiterate.

Although *Bibliae pauperum* did not come into widespread use until about the year 1300 (70 manuscripts survive from this period), they represented an ancient Christian teaching method called typological representation—a doctrine expressed by the Latin saying, *Novum Testamentum in Vetere latet, Vetus in Novo patet* (The New Testament lies hidden in the Old, the Old lies open in the New). The use of such religious picture books spread from Germany to France and the Low Countries (today's Belgium and the Netherlands) and were extremely popular through the late Middle Ages.

Closely related to the Bible of the poor, and more popular in France, was the *Bible moralisée*, in which the text attempted to draw a moralizing lesson from the illustrations it accompanied. In some surviving manuscripts the link from the life of Jesus is not to the Old Testament but rather to events in ancient history or even to nature.

What were the first modern-language translations?

Before printed texts proliferated in the 16th century, the Bible had been translated—in whole or in part—into 33 different languages. There was a German translation of a biblical text as early as the 11th century. Books of the Bible appeared in Dutch, French, Icelandic, Italian, and Spanish during the 12th and 13th centuries; in English, Norwegian, and Polish in the 14th century; and in Hungarian and Swedish in the 15th century. All of them, of course, were copied by hand.

The second printed Bible (after Gutenberg's edition of the Latin Vulgate, 1456) was a German one, published by Johann Mentelin in Strassburg in 1466. A third printed Bible, an Italian translation of the Vulgate, came out in 1471; a Catalan Bible of 1478 was the fourth printed text; the fifth Bible was printed in Czech in 1488.

By 1534, when Martin Luther completed the first modern-language Bible translated from the original Hebrew and Greek, there were already 14 different translations of the Vulgate in High German (from which modern German and Yiddish are derived) and four in Low German (from which Dutch, English, and Afrikaans are derived. In the wake of the Protestant Reformation, modern-language Bibles were published in French by Lefèvre in 1534 and by Olivetan in 1535; in Spanish and Czech in 1602; and in Italian by Diodati in 1607. Bibles translated into English appeared as early as 1535.

How did Martin Luther renew interest in the Bible?

In the fourth century, Jerome's translation of the Bible into Latin (the so-called Vulgate, or common-language version) made Scripture accessible to the Latin-speaking peoples of the Roman Empire. A millennium later Martin Luther's translation into German made the Bible available to all German speaking peoples of the 16th century.

Following his ordination as a priest in 1507, Luther studied theology at Erfurt and later at the new university in Wittenberg, to which the Augustinian order of monks had transferred him. After a return to Erfurt and a journey to Rome, he completed his doctorate at Wittenberg and started teaching the Bible there in 1513. Breaking with the Roman Catholic Church, he retreated to secluded Wartburg Castle, where he spent part

Images of the great fish Leviathan and the raging bull Behemoth adorn a Hebrew text of the early 1300's.

Scribes at work in the garden of a Benedictine monastery are glimpsed in this 14th-century illumination.

of the year 1522 working on his translation of the New Testament from Greek into German. Twelve years later he had completed translating both the Old and the New Testaments.

The western church had stressed the authority of the Latin Vulgate and made little use of the original Hebrew or Greek texts. Luther's fresh translation based on the original languages sparked new interest in the entire Bible, and the availability of Scripture in the ordinary language of the German people gave strength to the burgeoning Protestant Reformation.

How important is the Bible in missionary work?

Ever since the sayings of Jesus and the accounts of the Apostles were written down, Scripture has been at the center of the work of the Christian missionary. Missionaries receive their first understanding of Christian teaching from the study of the Bible, and their faith in its message sends them out into the world to proclaim the word, recalling Jesus' command to "make disciples of all nations." As the written record of the Chris- MT. 28:19

tian faith, the Bible explains the basic principles that a convert is expected to live by and is the only source for the teachings of Jesus.

The Bible alone has been known to convert nonbelievers simply by the force of its message. For example, western missionaries were not allowed in Korea until the 1880's, but copies of Gospels translated into Korean had been smuggled across the Manchurian border some years before. When missionaries were finally admitted, they found converts ready to be baptized because they had read the Gospels and accepted their message.

In modern times, a primary focus of missionary activity has been on making the Bible available and accessible to people everywhere through translations into the languages of groups that lack vernacular Bibles. By the 18th century, Christian missionaries had learned through experience that the success of their work was heavily dependent on the availability of a Bible in the native tongue. Faced with this reality, many misssionaries became linguists and translators as well, and their efforts led to dozens of new

*Martin Luther, whose German translation
of the Bible had far-reaching effects,
in a portrait by his friend Lucas Cranach.*

translations in the 19th century. Generally, the release of a new translation was not held back until the whole project was completed. Books were released one or a few at a time, with one of the Gospels being a customary starting point. Often, by the time the entire Bible was translated, many of its books had been circulating for years, and Christianity had taken hold in the region.

Into how many languages has the Bible been translated?

The Bible—in whole or in part—has been translated into everything from Afrikaans to Zulu and more than 1,900 languages in between. By 1989, according to the American Bible Society, there were complete Bible translations in 314 languages (including all of the world's major tongues), New Testament translations in 715, and translations of at least one book of the Bible in 890. The most widely translated book is the Gospel of Mark, available in 800 different languages and dialects.

During the 19th century, several Bible societies were founded to oversee the translation efforts; a coordinating agency, the United Bible Societies, was established after World War II. Today, the largest such group is the Wycliffe Bible Translators International and its sister organization, the Summer Institute of Linguistics, which began when missionaries recognized the need for translations in smaller language groups.

Every year, between 16 and 20 new languages or dialects receive their own Bible translations. Linguists will no doubt be busy with this task for years to come. In Africa, for example, there are still a great many spoken languages for which no translations of the Bible have been made.

The hazards of translating a work as large and complex as the Bible are legion: grammatical structures usually do not match, and often biblical references are totally foreign to other cultures. In one Indonesian-language version, wolf "in sheep's clothing" had to be translated as MT. 7:15 "crocodile in human form," a much more graphic image in a culture that lacked wolves but had an abundance of crocodiles. A too literal early translation of the 23rd Psalm into the language of the Tlingit Indians in Alaska created the misunderstanding that "The Lord is my shepherd" PS. 23:1 meant that God is a goatherd.

Left: Johannes Gutenberg inspects the first proof of his printed Bible at Mainz about 1455, a historic moment re-created in this 19th-century engraving.

Below: a page from one of Gutenberg's Bibles is embellished with hand-drawn designs and a portrait of King Solomon.

THE MAKING OF THE GUTENBERG BIBLE

Perhaps more than any event since the invention of the wheel, the invention of the printing press with its movable type revolutionized civilization. There is some controversy over who was the first to come up with the ingenious idea and where it was first employed (there is evidence that movable type was in use in Korea at least 50 years before Johannes Gutenberg made the same advance), but there is no doubt that it was Gutenberg's utilization of the press that made possible the spread of the written word.

Gutenberg, who was born in Mainz (in what is now Germany) sometime around 1397, was a goldsmith who used his skills to cast individual pieces of metal type in molds. He began his experimentation with the press as early as 1439. The earliest known examples of his printing work are a poem, a Latin grammar, and a calendar, all dating from the years 1444 to 1447.

In order to finance the printing of a large Latin Bible, his first complete book, Gutenberg went into partnership with and borrowed heavily from Johann Fust, a Mainz lawyer. The planning for this project began in 1450, but the Bible was not finished until 1455 or 1456. By this time, Gutenberg was bankrupt and had to give Fust the press to repay his debt. The printing job was completed by Fust's partner, calligrapher Peter Schoeffer.

The type used, known as black letter or Gothic, came from a popular handwriting style of the time. A roller was covered with an ink made from linseed oil, which was then rolled over the metal letters held in place within a form. This inked form was then pressed onto a sheet of paper. Decorations of the borders and margins of the Bible were done by hand, although shortly thereafter woodcuts were used to illustrate printed works. The Gutenberg Bible was printed with two columns of 42 lines of type on each of 1,282 pages. For this reason, the Gutenberg Bible is sometimes called the 42-Line Bible.

Although Gutenberg died a blind pensioner of the archbishop of Mainz in 1468, his name will forever be associated with the invention that put the Bible in the hands of the many. There are 47 existing copies of the Gutenberg Bible, the most admired of which is in the Library of Congress in Washington, D.C.

The Bible in English

St. John (top), from the seventh-century **Lindisfarne Gospels;** *the arrest of Christ, from the* **Book of Kells** *(about 800); Alfred the Great, from a ninth-century treaty.*

When was Scripture first translated into English?

Christianity reached the Celt-inhabited British Isles while they were part of the Roman Empire, but the fall of Rome and repeated invasions by the Anglo-Saxons all but wiped out the church in England. A new mission, arriving in 597 to evangelize these barbarian settlers, met with surprising success. Within 75 years, portions of the Latin Bible were being rendered into Anglo-Saxon.

A seventh-century herdsman named Caedmon, inspired by a vision, began singing a song of the creation of the world. He was taken into the abbey at Whitby, where he put into Anglo-Saxon verse parts of the Pentateuch and some New Testament stories the monks told him. In the ninth century Cynewulf composed a poetic version of Jesus' story; the psalms were rendered by Bishop Aldhelm; and the Venerable Bede, historian of the early English church, was at work on a translation of John at his death in 735.

King Alfred, who died in 901, incorporated Anglo-Saxon versions of the Commandments, parts of Exodus, and some of Acts into his legal code. And as the Norman Conquest of 1066 approached, glosses, or commentaries, on Scripture became known throughout the land.

By the time the Normans invaded and began imposing the French language on England's former ruling class, a considerable beginning had been made on the great project of bringing Scripture to the ears of simple men and women in the former Roman province of Britannia.

Who produced the first English translation of the complete Bible?

More than 200 years before the publication of the famous King James Version of the Bible, an Oxford scholar named John Wycliffe (or Wyclif) had an idea that seems harmless and commendable today but was viewed in 14th-century England as revolutionary and even heretical. He thought that the English people should have a Bible in their own language. Undaunted by the likelihood of severe repercussions, Wycliffe went ahead with the project, which resulted in the first manuscript in the English language of the complete Bible. For this monumental task, he enlisted the aid of fellow scholars John Purvey and Nicholas of Hereford, who are thought to have done much of the actual translating. The language into which they rendered the Bible was Middle English, the transitional form (1100–1500) between Old English and the modern tongue. The source they used was itself a translation: the fourth-century Vulgate of St. Jerome.

Wycliffe and his followers completed the New Testament in 1380, followed over the next several years by the Old Testament. The demand for their English translation was evidently brisk, for between 150 and 200 partial or complete copies of the manuscript survive to this day. After Wycliffe's death his collaborators were hounded and imprisoned for breaking the ban on vernacular translations, and many followers, called Lollards, were burned at the stake for heresy.

How many English versions preceded the King James?

The Wycliffe Bible had been illegally circulating in manuscript for almost 150 years before the first printed English Bible appeared. In 1526, about 70 years after the invention of printing, William Tyndale produced a printed edition of the New Testament in English. He followed this with the Pentateuch a few years later, but did not complete publication of the Old Testament.

Between Tyndale's efforts and the King James Bible in 1611, six major English Bibles were produced. Three appeared in the 1530's: the Coverdale (1535), the first complete printed edition in English; the Matthew (1537), which relied heavily on the Tyndale and Coverdale versions; and the Great Bible (1539), named for its large size and mandated for church use throughout England. These were eclipsed in popularity, at least outside the established church, by the Geneva Bible (1560), whose small size made it easy to use and which introduced enduring phrases like "I shall not want" in the 23rd Psalm (in place of the Great Bible's "Therefore can I lack nothing"). However, the bishops of the Church of England under Elizabeth I never officially approved the Geneva Bible and authorized a new version, which was published in 1568 and came to be called the Bishops' Bible. Confronted by so many Protestant Bibles in English, the Roman Catholics produced one of their own from the Vul- ✳

Implicated in a 1586 plot to kill Protestant queen Elizabeth I and return England to Catholicism, Mary Queen of Scots swears innocence on her Bible.

gate. The translation was called the Douay (or Douai) Bible, for the town in Flanders where English scholars fled to do the work. The first Catholic Bible in English, it appeared in 1610, the year before the King James Bible.

What is the Geneva Bible?

During her brief reign (1553–58), the Roman Catholic queen Mary sought to curb the Reformation, thus driving from England many Protestant scholars and churchmen. Some of them fled to Geneva, where the exiles produced the Geneva Bible. Published in 1560, it helped shape the course of English history.

The Geneva Bible was the one carried by Oliver Cromwell and the Puritan army in the English civil war. It was the Bible taken to Massachusetts Bay by the stern men and women who founded the New England colonies; and it was the Bible that spread Puritan doctrines throughout the realm of Mary's successor, Elizabeth. The Geneva Bible passed through 140 editions, influenc-

THE PATIENCE OF JOB. *"There was a man in the land of Uz, whose name was Job; and that man was blameless and upright [Job 1:1]." So begins the Book of Job, in which God tests Job's faith by allowing Satan to afflict him, even to the loss of all his 10 children. In the initial portions of the book, Job bears the suffering and holds to his faith, saying: "Naked I came from my mother's womb, and naked shall I return; the Lord gave, and the Lord has taken away; blessed be the name of the Lord [Job 1:21]." Thus he became a model of patience and faith amid the afflictions of this life.*

"Job's comforters" refers to the friends of Job who came to offer consolation but instead insisted that Job must have sinned; otherwise the Lord would not be punishing him. To them an exasperated Job cried: "Miserable comforters are you all. Shall windy words have an end [Job 16:2]?"

ing English and American religious thought over several generations.

The main force behind the Geneva Bible was William Whittingham, a colleague of John Calvin. In the spirit of the Protestantism of that era, Whittingham intended the translation and notes to reach not only the learned but also simple folk. He believed that the Bible was the source of the help all men and women needed.

Why was the Douay Bible significant?

Facing increasing hostility under Elizabeth I, some English Catholics fled across the Channel and in 1568 established an English college at Douay in Flanders. Led by Gregory Martin, they translated the Vulgate into English, publishing the New Testament in 1582 and the Old Testament in 1609–10. The translation is sometimes known as the Douay-Rheims Bible because the college moved to Rheims in France and back to Douay as the work proceeded.

The translators' aim was to strengthen Catholic doctrine on the meaning of the Bible against what they saw as heretical interpretations. As the English cardinal William Allen wrote in 1578, ✳

"Perhaps indeed it would have been more desirable that the scriptures had never been translated into barbarous tongues; nevertheless at the present day, when either from heresy or other causes, the curiosity of man, even of those who are not bad, is so great, and there is often such need of reading the scriptures in order to confute our opponents, it is better that there should be a faithful and catholic translation, than that men should use a corrupt version to their peril or destruction."

Why has the King James Version proved so enduring?

The new edition of the Bible presented to King James I of England in 1611 remained the principal Bible of English-speaking Protestants for over 250 years. Known as the King James Version in America and the Authorized Version in Britain, it was not revised until late in the 19th century.

The King James Version was the work of 54 university scholars (47 of whose names are known) appointed by King James in 1604. These learned men formed six committees of nine men each. Two committees labored at Oxford, two at Cambridge, and two at Westminster. The group had both Anglican (Church of England) and Puritan members.

That so large and diverse a group had differences of opinion is hardly surprising—some passages are said to have been reworked as many as 17 times—but what is astonishing is that out of the committees came a unified masterpiece of translation. No doubt certain individuals were leaders and shapers of the project, but little is known about who they were and the extent of their contribution. What is known is that they did not attempt a completely new translation and almost unerringly recognized the best of their predecessors' work. About one-third of their New Testament, for example, was carried over from William Tyndale's translation; and overall some 60 percent of their Bible was derived from earlier editions.

More than 300 years after its publication, the work was hailed by Harvard English professor John Livingston Lowes as "the noblest monument of English prose." It has been praised for its musical cadences, for its simplicity, dignity, and power. Today any English-speaking person who

SHAKESPEARE AND THE SCRIPTURES

According to a boys' school headmaster of Shakespeare's time (1564–1616), the education of the young (young males, at least) was designed "to furnish thy mind, and that in thy tender years, with good opinions and true religion." Shakespeare's mind was so furnished, and his plays are immeasurably enriched by his knowledge of the "true religion" of the Bible and of the Anglican Book of Common Prayer. So pervasive is the biblical influence in his work that it is difficult to imagine a William Shakespeare who did not know the Bible and whose pen was not prompted on many occasions by biblical events. His *King Lear*, for example, echoes with similarities to the story of Saul told in the First Book of Samuel.

All together Shakespeare quotes or refers to 42 books of the Bible. His favorites are Genesis, Job, and the Apocryphal Sirach. Among New Testament books he relies most heavily on Matthew.

Falstaff (*1 Henry IV*) cites the fall of Adam to excuse his own villainy. Jacques (*As You Like It*) snidely remarks, "There is sure another flood toward, and these couples are coming to the Ark. Here comes a pair of very strange beasts." A murderer in *Richard III* wishes he could "like Pilate . . . wash my hands of this most grievous guilty murder." Claudius (*Hamlet*) alludes to Jesus' temptation: "The devil can cite Scripture for his own purpose."

And when in *Hamlet* Claudius murders his brother, he is acutely aware of the parallel with Cain and Abel. There are at least 25 references to this story in Shakespeare's work, including Bolingbroke's harsh words to the king's murderer in *Richard II:* "With Cain go wander through the shade of night, and never show thy head by day nor light."

Even when he seems to be using no allusions, he may have a biblical phrase in mind. He speaks in five plays of the "pangs of death." The idea is translated "snares of death [Ps. 18:5]" and "pains of death [Acts 2:24]" in the King James Version and "snares of death [Ps. 18:5]" in the Revised Standard Version, but it was "pangs" in Psalm 18 of the Bishops' Bible, which Shakespeare used along with the Geneva Bible.

Hamlet looks on as his uncle, the king, asks forgiveness for "the primal eldest curse . . . a brother's murder" in a modern depiction of the scene by Jean Leon Huens.

William Tyndale, translator of the first New Testament printed in English, was executed for heresy in 1536.

can read Shakespeare can enter this book with ease. It is not just a noble monument but a book that continues to inspire and move people as few others can.

Who is known as the father of the English Bible?

Although there are many heroes and martyrs in the story of bringing the Bible to the English people in their own language, one name stands out. Educated at Cambridge and Oxford, William Tyndale chose the life of a clergyman. As he got to know his congregation, he "perceived by experience" that it was difficult to teach the truths of religion if people could not read the Bible because they knew no Latin.

Tyndale was well aware that the established church was set against the idea of a vernacular Bible. As one opponent of translation put it, "The New Testament translated into the vulgar tongue is in truth the food of death, the fuel of sin, the veil of malice, the pretext of false liberty." Tyndale passionately disagreed. "If God spare my life," he told his opponents, "ere many years I will cause a boy that drives the plow shall know more of the scripture than you." God spared Tyndale just long enough for him to make good this vow.

Finding the church hostile to him at home, he went to Hamburg in 1524 and then to Wittenberg, where he became an associate of Martin Luther, whose doctrines deeply influenced Tyndale's subsequent work. In 1525 he began printing his translated New Testament in Cologne but was discovered by enemies of Luther. He escaped to Worms, where he printed his New Testament with notes and shipped the books to England hidden in crates of goods. The English authorities burned as many copies as they could find and in some instances killed the booksellers.

Persevering, though continually harassed by agents of the English king, Tyndale produced new editions of his New Testament and began translating the Old Testament. In 1535, while staying in Antwerp, he was betrayed to the authorities and thrown into prison. After a year of confinement he was strangled and burned as a heretic. His dying prayer: "Lord, open the king of England's eyes."

It could be said that this prayer too was granted, for even as Tyndale was being executed as an enemy of the king and the church, his battle was all but won. Two years after his death, there appeared in English an edition of the Coverdale Bible carrying the legend: "Set forth with the King's most gracious license."

What are the oddest English editions of the Bible?

Some printings of the Bible picked up unofficial nicknames as a result of a typographical error or a curious translation of a word or phrase.

Among these was "the Wicked Bible," also called "the Adulterer's Bible." By forgetting an all-important "not," the printer produced a commandment that said, "Thou shalt commit adultery." This was in 1632, when the authorities in England, embroiled in religious and political controversies, were not inclined to dismiss such an error lightly, and the printer was fined £300, a very hefty penalty to pay at the time.

"The Bug Bible" tells its readers not to be afraid of "bugs by night" as a result of a peculiar translation of the line, "You will not fear the terror of the night [Ps. 91:5]." In "the Placemakers'

306

Bible," Jesus' words are mistakenly given as "Blessed are the placemakers" instead of peacemakers [Mt. 5:9]. And the psalmist of "the Printer's Bible" laments erroneously: "Printers [not princes, the correct word] have persecuted me without a cause [Ps. 119:161]."

Translators have introduced numerous euphemisms into the Bible, always with good inten-

tions but with mixed effect. For example, the Geneva Bible published in 1560 came to be called "the Breeches Bible" because Adam and Eve, after discovering their nakedness, go off and sew together fig leaves to make "breeches." The word must have seemed as quaint then as it does now in order for it to be used ironically to describe the whole book.

The blind lead the blind in this painting by the 16th-century Flemish master Brueghel.

EVERYDAY BIBLE TALK

Whether in allusions, paraphrases, or direct quotations, the Bible turns up frequently in everyday speech. Many Jews and Christians are often not fully aware of their debt to the language of the Bible. In the simple narrative that follows, for example, there are no fewer than 18 biblical references.

There once was a man unwilling to go the second mile [Mt. 5:41], but he still hoped to kill the fatted calf [Lk. 15:23] and thought it was all right to eat the forbidden fruit [Gen. 3:3]. Obviously he did not believe in

following the straight and narrow [Mt. 7:14]. This miserable person could not see the handwriting on the wall [Dan. 5:5]. He thought he was a law unto himself [Rom. 2:14] and would probably end up inheriting the wind [Pr. 11:29].

He expected manna to fall from heaven [Ex. 16:4], probably because he was the kind who thought he could walk on water [Mt. 14:25]. Maybe his trouble began when his parents spared the rod and spoiled the child [Pr. 13:24]. In any case, he seems never to have learned that the love of money is the root of all

evil [1 Tim. 6:10], and he must have believed that the lazy, not the meek, would inherit the earth [Mt. 5:5]. Someone may have told him that man does not live by bread alone [Mt. 4:4], but it was casting pearls before swine [Mt. 7:6] because, like the leopard, he could not change his spots [Jer. 13:23]. Undoubtedly, he will go on trying to be all things to all men [1 Cor. 9:22] because all he remembers from the Bible is something to the effect that one should eat, drink, and be merry [Ec. 2:24]. Oh well, let him go. Are we our brother's keeper [Gen. 4:9]?

The Scripture Today

Why are there so many versions of the Bible?

Scholarly research continually expands our knowledge of the meaning of biblical words and our understanding of customs and ideas in the Bible. Each new translation, therefore, offers an opportunity to get closer to the original meaning. There is moreover constant change in our own language. New words are added; old words take on new meanings—often in a very short time. Consequently, fresh translations speak with power and relevance to each new generation.

Personal preference and theological outlook also encourage new versions. Some readers prefer conversational English; others like a formal style. Finally, some editions are prepared exclusively by Roman Catholic, Protestant, or Jewish scholars, for instance, whereas others draw from many religious perspectives.

Which Bibles are most used in America?

With millions of copies in circulation representing scores of editions, precise figures on Bible use are virtually impossible to obtain. Many versions are noteworthy, including the following:

King James Version (KJV), 1611. Commissioned by King James I of England, this beautiful translation supplanted earlier English versions. Over the centuries, however, discoveries of early Hebrew and Greek manuscripts called for changing hundreds of words and phrases, resulting in new translations.

Revised Standard Version (RSV), 1952. Created for ecumenical use by the National Council of the Churches of Christ and considered accurate by Roman Catholic, Protestant, and Eastern Orthodox churches, the RSV, a revision of the KJV, succeeded the 1901 *American Standard Version.*

ECHOES OF THE BIBLE

The debt of the creative arts to the Bible is so great that simply to list the works either wholly or partially inspired by Scripture would take a sizable volume. Paintings, poems, novels, plays, films, songs, operas—every form of creative expression would be poorer without the Bible. Outside the arts, the Bible underlies much of the best political oratory. It is difficult to imagine a speech by Abraham Lincoln or Winston Churchill, for example, that would be as strong had its author grown up lacking knowledge of the Bible.

Western literature would simply not be the same. In 20th-century America alone, titles chosen by three famous authors illustrate the fact: *Absalom, Absalom* [2 Sam. 19:4] by William

Gregory Peck starred in the 1944 film **Keys of the Kingdom** *[Mt. 16:19], about a Scottish priest in 19th-century China.*

Faulkner; *East of Eden* [Gen. 3:24] by John Steinbeck; *The Sun Also Rises* [Ec. 1:5] by Ernest Hemingway. And in the American theater, Lillian Hellman took from the Bible the title *The Little Foxes* [S. of S. 2:15]; Thornton Wilder, *The Skin of Our Teeth* [Job 19:20]; Marc Connelly, *The Green Pastures* [Ps. 23:2]; John van Druten, *The Voice of the Turtle* [S. of S. 2:12]. Musicals, too, like Richard Rodgers's *Two by Two* [Gen. 7:9], owe their titles to the Bible, as do a number of films, such as *Chariots of Fire* [2 Kg. 6:17], *Inherit the Wind* [Pr. 11:29], and *Lilies of the Field* [Mt. 6:28].

Resting one hand on a Bible held by his wife Nancy, President Ronald Reagan takes the oath of office for his second term in January 1985.

New American Standard Bible (NASB), 1963. Seeking to make the *English Revised Version* of 1885 less British, American scholars produced the *American Standard Version* in 1901. Used widely in the United States for over half a century, it was then revised to make the NASB.

Jerusalem Bible, 1966. Scholars at the Roman Catholic School of Biblical Studies in Jerusalem produced this version, admired for its careful use of newly discovered ancient manuscripts.

New American Bible, 1970. Catholic scholars compiled this major translation, which was published under the auspices of the Bishops' Committee on the Confraternity of Christian Doctrine.

The Living Bible, 1971. Not a new translation but a paraphrase, this popular work (also titled *The Book*) by Kenneth Taylor grew out of the author's retelling of Bible stories for his children.

New International Version (NIV), 1973. Prepared by an international team of evangelical scholars, the NIV quickly became a favored translation among American Protestants.

Today's Bible, 1976. Sponsored by the American Bible Society and also called the *Good News Bible*, this work aimed at blending freshness and simplicity of language with scholarly accuracy.

New King James Version, 1982. The purpose of this edition was to modernize antiquated English while preserving the beauty of the original.

New Revised Standard Version (NRSV), 1990. Produced by Protestant, Catholic, Eastern Orthodox, and Jewish scholars, the NRSV avoids "male-centered" expressions. References to God ✳

and to Jesus remain masculine, but neutral language is used wherever possible ("Man shall not LK. 4:4 live by bread alone," for example, becomes "One does not live by bread alone").

How did swearing on the Bible begin?

Calling on God to bear witness to one's truthfulness is an ancient custom, as seen in such Old Testament phrases as "God is witness between GEN. 31:50 you and me." Jews also swore oaths by touching a sacred object or putting a hand on the Torah. Apparently by Jesus' time, oath taking was being abused, and he discouraged swearing by heaven or earth: "Let what you say be simply 'Yes' or MT. 5:37 'No'; anything more than this comes from evil."

In the Middle Ages it became customary to swear by a cross, a prayer book, a relic, or a copy of Scripture. One kissed the sacred object or placed a hand on it. But over the centuries, it was mainly the Bible that was used in oath taking.

Two young Sunday-school members dressed as Mary and Joseph retell the Nativity story in a Christmas pageant at their church in Arkansas.

Index of Questions

HEROES OF FAITH

KINGS AND CONQUERORS

THE MIRACULOUS AND THE UNSEEN

THE MESSIAH

THE BIBLE
THROUGH THE AGES

ABBREVIATIONS OF THE BOOKS OF THE BIBLE

Acts	The Acts	Jude	Jude
Am.	Amos	1 Kg.	1 Kings
1 Chr.	1 Chronicles	2 Kg.	2 Kings
2 Chr.	2 Chronicles	Lam.	Lamentations
Col.	Colossians	Lev.	Leviticus
1 Cor.	1 Corinthians	Lk.	Luke
2 Cor.	2 Corinthians	Mal.	Malachi
Dan.	Daniel	Mic.	Micah
Dt.	Deuteronomy	Mk.	Mark
Ec.	Ecclesiastes	Mt.	Matthew
Eph.	Ephesians	Nah.	Nahum
Est.	Esther	Neh.	Nehemiah
Ex.	Exodus	Num.	Numbers
Ezek.	Ezekiel	Ob.	Obadiah
Ezra	Ezra	1 Pet.	1 Peter
Gal.	Galatians	2 Pet.	2 Peter
Gen.	Genesis	Phil.	Philippians
Hab.	Habakkuk	Philem.	Philemon
Hag.	Haggai	Pr.	Proverbs
Heb.	Hebrews	Ps.	Psalms
Hos.	Hosea	Rev.	Revelation
Is.	Isaiah	Rom.	Romans
Jas.	James	Ru.	Ruth
Jer.	Jeremiah	1 Sam.	1 Samuel
Jg.	Judges	2 Sam.	2 Samuel
Jl.	Joel	S. of S.	Song of Solomon
Jn.	John	1 Th.	1 Thessalonians
1 Jn.	1 John	2 Th.	2 Thessalonians
2 Jn.	2 John	1 Tim.	1 Timothy
3 Jn.	3 John	2 Tim.	2 Timothy
Job	Job	Tit.	Titus
Jon.	Jonah	Zech.	Zechariah
Jos.	Joshua	Zeph.	Zephaniah

ABBREVIATIONS OF THE BOOKS OF THE APOCRYPHA

Ad. Est.	The Additions to Esther
Bar.	Baruch
Bel	Bel and the Dragon
1 Esd.	The First Book of Esdras
2 Esd.	The Second Book of Esdras
Jdt.	Judith
Let. Jer.	The Letter of Jeremiah
1 Macc.	The First Book of the Maccabees
2 Macc.	The Second Book of the Maccabees
3 Macc.	The Third Book of the Maccabees
4 Macc.	The Fourth Book of the Maccabees
Man.	The Prayer of Manasseh
Ps. 151	Psalm 151
Sir.	Ecclesiasticus, or the Wisdom of Jesus the Son of Sirach
S. of 3 Y.	The Prayer of Azariah and the Song of the Three Young Men
Sus.	Susanna
Tob.	Tobit
Wis.	The Wisdom of Solomon

Bibliography

Achtemeier, Paul J., ed. *Harper's Bible Dictionary*. San Francisco: Harper & Row, Publishers, 1985.

Ackroyd, P.R., ed. *Cambridge History of the Bible*, Vol. 1. Cambridge: Cambridge University Press, 1970.

Aharoni, Yohanan. *The Land of the Bible*. Philadelphia: Westminster Press, 1979.

Aharoni, Yohanan, and Michael Avi-Yonah. *The Macmillan Bible Atlas*. New York: Macmillan Publishing Co., 1977.

Aland, Kurt. *Synopsis of the Four Gospels*. United Bible Societies, 1982.

Albright, William Foxwell. *Archaeology and the Religion of Ancient Israel*. Baltimore: The Johns Hopkins Press, 1968.

Albright, William Foxwell. *From the Stone Age to Christianity*. Garden City, N.Y.: Doubleday & Co., Inc., 1957.

Albright, William Foxwell, ed. *The Anchor Bible: The Acts of the Apostles, The Gospels According to Luke, John and Matthew*. Garden City, N.Y.: Doubleday & Co., Inc., 1966.

Alexander, David, and Pat Alexander, eds. *Eerdmans' Handbook to the Bible*. Grand Rapids: William B. Eerdmans Publishing Co., 1973.

Anderson, Bernhard W., ed. *Creation in the Old Testament*. Philadelphia: Fortress Press, 1984.

Avi-Yonah, Michael, ed. *A History of the Holy Land*. New York: The Macmillan Co., 1969.

Avi-Yonah, Michael, ed. *World History of the Jewish People*, Vol. 7. New Brunswick, N.J.: Rutgers University Press, 1975.

Baly, Denis, and A.D. Tushingham, eds. *Atlas of the Biblical World*. New York: The World Publishing Co., 1971.

Barthel, Manfred. *What the Bible Really Says*. New York: Quill, 1983.

Barton, John. *Oracles of God*. Oxford: Oxford University Press, 1986.

Bauman, Edward W. *The Life and Teaching of Jesus*. Philadelphia: The Westminster Press, 1960.

Ben-Dov, Meir. *In the Shadow of the Temple*. New York: Harper & Row, Publishers, 1985.

Blair, Edward P. *Abingdon Bible Handbook*. Nashville: Abingdon Press, 1981.

Bouquet, A.C. *Everyday Life in New Testament Times*. New York: Charles Scribner's Sons, 1953.

Brandon S.G.F. *The Trial of Jesus of Nazareth*. New York: Stein & Day, Publishers, 1968.

Bright, John. *A History of Israel*. Philadelphia: The Westminster Press, 1981.

Bromiley, Geoffrey W., ed. *The International Standard Bible Encyclopedia*, 4 vols. Grand Rapids: William B. Eerdmans Publishers, 1979.

Brown, Raymond E. *The Birth of the Messiah*. Garden City, N.Y.: Doubleday & Co., Inc., 1979.

Brown, Raymond E., ed. *The Jerome Bible Commentary*. Englewood Cliffs, N.J.: Prentice-Hall, Inc., 1968.

Brown, Raymond E., ed. *The New Jerome Bible Commentary*. Englewood Cliffs, N.J.: Prentice-Hall, Inc., 1990.

Bruce, F.F. *Jesus and Paul: Places They Knew*. Nashville: Thomas Nelson Publishers, Inc., 1983.

Bruce, F.F. *New Testament History*. Garden City, N.Y.: Doubleday & Co., Inc., 1971.

Bury, J.B., ed. *The Cambridge Ancient History*, Vols. 3–4, 7–10. Cambridge: Cambridge University Press, 1965.

Buttrick, George A., ed. *The Interpreter's Dictionary of the Bible*, 4 vols. Nashville: Abingdon Press, 1962.

Buttrick, George A., ed. *The Interpreter's Bible*, 12 vols. Nashville: Abingdon Press, 1952.

Chadwick, Henry. *The Early Church*. New York: Viking Penguin, 1987.

Coleman, William L. *Today's Handbook of Bible Times and Customs*. Minneapolis: Bethany House Publishers, 1984.

Corcos, Georgette, ed. *The Glory of the New Testament*. New York: Villard Books, 1984.

Cornfeld, Gaalyah. *Archaeology of the Bible: Book by Book*. New York: Harper & Row, Publishers, 1976.

Crim, Keith, ed. *The Interpreter's Dictionary of the Bible*, Supplementary Volume. Nashville: Abingdon Press, 1976.

Cross, F.L., ed. *The Oxford Dictionary of the Christian Church*, 2nd ed. Oxford: Oxford University Press, 1983.

Daniel-Rops, Henry. *Daily Life in the Time of Jesus*. New York: Hawthorn Books, Publishers, 1962.

Daniel-Rops, Henry. *Jesus and His Times*. New York: E.P. Dutton Co., Inc., 1956.

DeVaux, Roland. *Ancient Israel: Its Life and Institutions*. New York: McGraw-Hill Book Company, Inc., 1961.

Davies, W.D., ed. *Cambridge History of Judaism*, Vol. 1. Cambridge: Cambridge University Press, 1984.

Douglas, J.D. *The Illustrated Bible Dictionary*, 3 vols. Wheaton, Ill.: Tyndale House Publishers, 1980.

Drane, John. *Early Christians*. New York: Harper & Row, Publishers, 1982.

Durant, Will. *Caesar and Christ*. New York: Simon & Schuster, 1972.

Eliade, Mircea, ed. *The Encyclopedia of Religion*, 16 vols. New York: Macmillan Publishing Co., 1987.

Eusebius. *The History of the Church from Christ to Constantine*. New York: Dorset Press, 1984.

Friedman, Richard Elliott. *Who Wrote the Bible?* New York: Harper & Row, Publishers, 1989.

Gehman, Henry Snyder. *The New Westminster Dictionary of the Bible*. Philadephia: The Westminster Press, 1970.

Gentz, William H., ed. *The Dictionary of Bible and Religion*. Nashville: Abingdon Press, 1986.

Ginzberg, Louis. *Legends of the Bible*. Philadelphia: Jewish Publication Society of America, 1956.

Ginzberg, Louis. *On Jewish Law and Lore*. New York: Atheneum, 1981.

Goergen, Donald. *A Theology of Jesus*, 2 vols. Wilmington, Del.: Michael Glazier, 1987.

Goodspeed, Edgar J. *A History of Early Christian Literature*. Chicago: University of Chicago Press, 1966.

Gower, Ralph. *The New Manners and Customs of Bible Times*. Chicago: Moody Press, 1987.

Grant, Michael, and Rachel Kitzinger, eds. *Civilization of the Ancient Mediterranean*, Vol. 2. New York: Charles Scribner's Sons, 1988.

Grant, Michael. *Herod the Great*. New York: American Heritage Press, 1971.

Grant, Michael. *Jesus, An Historian's Review of the Gospels*. New York: Charles Scribner's Sons, 1977.

Greenslade, S.L., ed. *Cambridge History of the Bible*, Vol. 3. Cambridge: Cambridge University Press, 1963.

Guignebert, Charles. *Jesus*. New Hyde Park, N.Y.: University Books, 1966.

Guthrie, D., ed. *The Eerdmans' Bible Commentary*. Grand Rapids: William B. Eerdmans Publishing Co., 1970.

Hammond, N.G.L., and H.H. Scullard, eds. *The Oxford Classical Dictionary*. Oxford: Clarendon Press, 1970.

Harrelson, Walter. *From Fertility Cult to Worship*. Garden City, N.Y.: Doubleday & Co., Inc., 1970.

Harris, J.R., ed. *The Legacy of Egypt*. New York: Oxford University Press, 1988.

Heaton, Eric William. *Everyday Life in Old Testament Times*. New York: Charles Scribner's Sons, 1956.

Hendin, David. *Guide to Biblical Coins*. New York: Amphora Books, 1987.

Hindley, Geoffrey. *A History of Roads*. Secaucus, N.J.: The Citadel Press, 1972.

Hoehner, Harold W. *Herod Antipas*. Cambridge: Cambridge University Press, 1972.

Hoffman, R. Joseph, and Gerald A. LaRue. *Jesus in History and Myth*. Buffalo: Prometheus Books, 1986.

Hull, John M. *Hellenistic Magic and the Synoptic Tradition*. London: SCM Press, Ltd., 1974.

James, Montague Rhodes, trans. *The Apocryphal New Testament*. Oxford: Clarendon Press, 1985.

Jeremias, Joachim. *Jerusalem in the Time of Jesus*. Philadelphia: Fortress Press, 1969.

Johnson, Paul. *A History of the Jews*. New York: Harper & Row, Publishers, 1987.

Josephus, Flavius. *Jewish Antiquities*, Loeb Classical Library,

Josephus, Flavius. *The Jewish War*, Loeb Classical Library, 9 vols. Cambridge, Mass.: Harvard University Press, 1976. 9 vols. Cambridge, Mass.: Harvard University Press, 1978.

Kee, Howard Clark, Franklin W. Young, and Karlfried Froelich. *Understanding the New Testament*. Englewood Cliffs, N.J.: Prentice-Hall, Inc., 1965.

✳ Kee, Howard Clark. *Miracle in the Early Christian World*. New

Haven, Conn.: Yale University Press, 1983.

Keller, Ernst, and Marie-Luise Keller. *Miracles in Dispute*. London: SCM Press, Ltd., 1969.

Kelsey, Morton. *Afterlife*. New York: Paulist Press, 1979.

Kelsey, Morton T. *God, Dreams and Revelation*. Minneapolis: Augsburg Publishing House, 1974.

Kelsey, Morton T. *Psychology, Medicine and Christian Healing*. San Francisco: Harper & Row, Publishers, 1988.

Kenyon, Kathleen. *Jerusalem: Excavating 3,000 Years of History*. New York: McGraw-Hill Book Co., 1967.

Kingfield, Irving, ed. *The Family Bible Encyclopedia*. 22 vols. New York: Copylab Publishing Counsel, Inc., 1972.

Kitchen, K.A. *The Bible in Its World*. Downers Grove, Ill.: InterVarsity Press, 1979.

Koenig, John. *Jews and Christians in Dialog*. Philadelphia: The Westminster Press, 1979.

Koester, Helmut. *Introduction to the New Testament*, 2 vols. Philadelphia: Fortress Press, 1982.

Kraeling, Emil G. *Rand McNally Bible Atlas*. New York: Rand McNally & Co., 1966.

Lampe, G.W.H., ed. *Cambridge History of the Bible*, Vol. 2. Cambridge: Cambridge University Press, 1969.

Landay, Jerry M. *The House of David*. New York: E. P. Dutton & Co., 1973.

Laymon, Charles M., ed. *The Interpreter's One-Volume Commentary on the Bible*. Nashville: Abingdon Press, 1971.

Louth, Andrew, ed. *Early Christian Writings*. New York: Viking Penguin Inc., 1987.

Malamat, Abraham, ed. *World History of the Jewish People*, Vol. 4. Jerusalem: Masada Press Ltd., 1979.

Manson, T.W., and H.H. Rowley, eds. *A Companion to the Bible*, 2nd ed. Edinburgh: T. & T. Clark, 1963.

May, Herbert G., and Bruce M. Metzger, eds. *The New Oxford Annotated Bible With the Apocrypha* (Revised Standard Version). New York: Oxford University Press, 1977.

May, Herbert G. *Oxford Bible Atlas*, 2nd ed. London: Oxford University Press, 1974.

Mays, James L., ed. *Harper's Bible Commentary*. San Francisco: Harper & Row, Publishers, 1988.

Mazar, Benjamin, ed. *World History of the Jewish People*, Vols. 2–3. New Brunswick, N.J.: Rutgers University Press, 1970.

Mazar, Benjamin. *The Mountain of the Lord*. Garden City, N.Y.: Doubleday & Co., Inc., 1975.

McDonald, William J., ed. *New Catholic Encyclopedia*, 17 vols. New York: McGraw-Hill Book Co., 1967.

Miller, Madeleine S., and J. Lane. *Harper's Bible Dictionary*. New York: Harper & Row, Publishers, 1973.

Miller, Madeleine S., and J. Lane. *Harper's Encyclopedia of Bible Life*. New York: Harper & Row, Publishers, 1971.

Miller, J. Maxwell, and John H. Hayes. *A History of Ancient Israel and Judah*. Philadelphia: The Westminster Press, 1986.

Murphey, Cecil B. *The Dictionary of Biblical Literacy*. Nashville: Thomas Nelson, Publishers, 1989.

Murphy-O'Connor, Jerome. *The Holy Land*. Oxford: Oxford University Press, 1980.

Nickelsburg, George W.E., and Michael E. Stone. *Faith and Piety in Early Judaism*. Philadelphia: Fortress Press, 1983.

Nickelsburg, George W.E. *Jewish Literature Between the Bible and the Mishnah*. Philadelphia: Fortress Press, 1981.

Nolan, Albert. *Jesus Before Christianity*. Maryknoll, N.Y.: Orbis Books, 1978.

Noll, Mark A., ed. *Eerdmans' Handbook to Christianity in America*. Grand Rapids: William B. Eerdmans Publishing Co., 1983.

Osborne, Charles, ed. *The Israelites*. New York: Time-Life Books, 1975.

Packer, James I, ed. *All the People and Places of the Bible*. Nashville: Thomas Nelson Publishers, 1982.

Packer, James I., ed. *The Bible Almanac*. Nashville: Thomas Nelson Publishers, 1980.

Packer, James I., ed. *The World of the Old Testament*. Nashville: Thomas Nelson Publishers, 1982.

Parrot, Andre. *Abraham and His Times*. Philadelphia: Fortress Press, 1968.

Pelikan, Jaroslav. *Jesus Through the Centuries*. New York: Harper & Row, Publishers, 1985.

Perowne, Stewart. *The Life and Times of Herod the Great*. London: Hodder and Stoughton, 1956.

Pfeiffer, Robert H. *History of New Testament Times*. New York: Harper & Brothers, Publishers, 1949.

Pritchard, James B. *The Ancient Near East in Pictures*. Princeton, N.J.: Princeton University Press, 1969.

Pritchard, James B. *The Harper Atlas of the Bible*. New York: Harper & Row, Publishers, 1987.

Reicke, Bo. *The New Testament Era*. Philadelphia: Fortress Press, 1968.

Rest, Friedrich. *Our Christian Symbols*. Philadelphia: The Christian Education Press, 1959.

Riedel, Eunice, et al. *The Book of the Bible*. New York: William Morrow & Co., Inc., 1979.

Rogerson, John. *Atlas of the Bible*. New York: Facts on File Publications, 1985.

Roth, Cecil, ed. *Encyclopedia Judaica*, 16 vols. Jerusalem: Keter Publishing House Jerusalem Ltd., 1972.

Sandmel, Samuel. *The Genius of Paul*. New York: Schocken Books, 1970.

Sandmel, Samuel. *The Hebrew Scriptures*. New York: Oxford University Press, 1978.

Sarna, Nahum M. *Exploring Exodus*. New York: Schocken Books, 1986.

Sarna, Nahum M., ed. *The JPS Torah Commentary: Genesis*. Philadelphia: The Jewish Publication Society, 1989.

Sarna, Nahum M. *Understanding Genesis*. New York: Schocken Books, 1970.

Schalit, Abraham, ed. *World History of the Jewish People*, Vol. 6. New Brunswick, N.J.: Rutgers University Press, 1972.

Schultz, Hans Jurgen, ed. *Jesus in His Times*. Philadephia: Fortress Press, 1976.

Schurer, Emil. *The History of the Jewish People in the Age of Jesus Christ*, 2 vols. Edinburgh: T. & T. Clark, Ltd., 1973.

Sherwin-White, A.N. *Roman Society and Roman Law in the New Testament*. Oxford: Clarendon Press, 1963.

Singer, Isidore, ed. *The Jewish Encyclopedia*, 12 vols. New York: Ktav Publishing House, Inc.

Sparks, H.F.D., ed. *The Apocryphal Old Testament*. Oxford: Clarendon Press, 1984.

Speiser, E.A., ed. *World History of the Jewish People*, Vol. 1. New Brunswick, N.J.: Rutgers University Press, 1964.

Stephens, William H. *The New Testament World in Pictures*. Nashville: Broadman Press, 1987.

Suetonius, Gaius. *The Twelve Caesars*, trans. Robert Graves. Hammondsworth, England: Penguin Books Ltd., 1957.

Tacitus, Cornelius. *The Annals of Imperial Rome*, trans. Michael Grant. Hammondsworth, England: Penguin Books Ltd., 1956.

Tuckett, Christopher. *The Messianic Secret*. Philadelphia: Fortress Press, 1983.

Unger, Merrill F. *The New Unger's Bible Handbook*. Chicago: Moody Press, 1966.

Van Der Woude, A.S., ed. *The World of the Bible*. Grand Rapids: William B. Eerdmans Publishing Co., 1986.

Walsh, Michael. *The Triumph of the Meek*. San Francisco: Harper & Row, Publishers, 1986.

Ward, James A. *The Prophets*. Nashville: Abingdon Press, 1982.

Whitaker, Richard E. *The Eerdmans Analytical Concordance to the Revised Standard Version of the Bible*. Grand Rapids: William B. Eerdmans Publishing Co., 1988.

Wigoder, Geoffrey, ed. *Illustrated Dictionary and Concordance of the Bible*. New York: Macmillan Publishing Co., 1986.

Wigoder, Geoffrey, ed. *The Encyclopedia of Judaism*. New York: Macmillan Publishing Co., 1989.

Wilken, Robert. *The Myth of Christian Beginnings*. Notre Dame, Ind.: University of Notre Dame Press, 1980.

William, Ian. *Jesus, the Evidence*. New York: Harper & Row, Publishers, 1988.

Winter, Paul. *On the Trial of Jesus*. Berlin: Walter de Gruyter & Co., 1961.

Wright, G. Ernest, and David Noel Freedman, eds. *The Biblical Archaeologist Reader*. Garden City, N.Y.: Anchor Books, 1961.

Wright, G. Ernest, and Reginald H. Fuller. *The Book of the Acts of God*. Garden City, N.Y.: Doubleday & Co., Inc., 1957.

Wright, G. Ernest, ed. *Westminster Historical Atlas*. Philadelphia: Westminster Press, 1956.

Yadin, Yigael. *The Art of Warfare in Biblical Lands*, 2 vols. New York: McGraw-Hill Book Co., Inc., 1963.

Credits and Acknowledgments

The editors would like to give particular thanks to the following artists: Howard Friedman, for the illustrations on pages 203 and 251; Victor Lazzaro, for the reconstructions on pages 34 and 70; Joe Le Monnier, for the maps on pages 10, 11, 104, 161, 174, 223, 275; Vladimir Remington, for the borders first appearing on page 21; Steven Schindler, for the decorative borders first appearing on page 10.

2 Laura Lushington/Sonia Halliday Photographs. **5** The Granger Collection, New York. **7** The Pierpont Morgan Library. **9** Paul L. Garber.

THE BEGINNINGS

12 The Pierpont Morgan Library. **14 & 15** David Harris. **16** The Granger Collection, New York. **17** Hessisches Landesmuseum Darmstadt. **18** The Pierpont Morgan Library. **19** Shelburne Museum, Shelburne, Vermont. **20** Marburg/Art Resource, N.Y. **21** *left* The Pierpont Morgan Library; *right* Zev Radovan. **23** The Metropolitan Museum of Art, Robert Lehman Collection, 1975 (1975.1.31). **24** Scala/Art Resource, N.Y. **26** The National Trust/ Art Resource, N.Y. **27** Hamburger Kunsthalle. **28** Erich Lessing/ Magnum. **29** Scala/Art Resource, N.Y. **30** Laura Lushington/ Sonia Halliday Photographs. **31** C.M. Dixon. **32** Scala/Art Resource, N.Y. **33** *top* Erich Lessing/Magnum; *bottom* R. Brandl/ Zev Radovan. **34** *left* SuperStock International. **35** Scala/Art Resource, N.Y.

THE WORSHIP OF GOD

36 Zev Radovan. **38** Scala/Art Resource, N.Y. **39** *top* David Harris; *bottom* The Ancient Art & Architecture Collection. **40** The Pierpont Morgan Library. **41** Zev Radovan. **42** Scala/Art Resource, N.Y. **44** Scala/Art Resource, N.Y. **45** Sonia Halliday Photographs. **46** Scala/Art Resource, N.Y. **47** Österreichische Nationalbibliothek. **48** *top* Scala/Art Resource, N.Y.; *bottom* The Ancient Art & Architecture Collection. **50** Giraudon/Art Resource, N.Y. **51** Israel Museum, Jerusalem/The Shrine of the Book/D. Samuel & Jeane H. Gottesman Center for Biblical Manuscripts. **52** Lee Boltin. **53** The Pierpont Morgan Library. **54** Erich Lessing/Magnum. **55** Kupferstichkabinett Staatliche Museen Preussischer Kulturbesitz, Berlin/Photography by Jörg P. Anders. **56** SEF/Art Resource, N.Y. **57** *top* Marburg/Art Resource, N.Y.; *bottom* The Pierpont Morgan Library. **58** Zev Radovan. **60** Richard T. Nowitz. **61** Scala/Art Resource, N.Y. **62** *top* Jewish National & University Library, Jerusalem; *bottom* Karl-Marx-Universität, Leipzig. **63** Jacques Mesguich. **64** Historical Pictures Service, Chicago. **65** *left* Gianni Giansanti/Sygma; *middle* J. Langevin/Sygma; *right* Eve Arnold/Magnum. **66** Mary Evans Picture Library. **67** Zev Radovan. **68** *left* Courtesy of the Biblical Archaeology Society, Washington, D.C. **68–69** Lloyd K. Townsend. **69** *right* Paul L. Garber. **70** *top right* Zev Radovan. **71** Zev Radovan. **72** Mary Evans Picture Library. **73** *top* Zev Radovan; *bottom* Scala/Art Resource, N.Y. **74** Scala/Art Resource, N.Y. **76** Erich Hartmann/Magnum. **77** Scala/Art Resource, N.Y. **78** The Brooklyn Museum, purchased by public subscription. **79** Reproduced by courtesy of the trustees, The National Gallery, London. **80 & 81** Zev Radovan. **83** The Jewish Museum/Art Resource, N.Y. **84** Marburg/Art Resource, N.Y. **85** Erich Lessing/Magnum. **86** Andre Held, Ecublens. **87** Zev Radovan. **89** *top* Zev Radovan; *bottom* Leonard Freed/Magnum. **91** Scala/Art Resource, N.Y. **92** Michael Holford. **93** Richard T. Nowitz.

HEROES OF FAITH

94 Walters Art Gallery, Baltimore. **96 97** Hermitage Museum, Leningrad. **98** The Metropolitan Museum of Art, Rogers Fund, 1938. **100** The Ancient Art & Architecture Collection. **101** Jean-Loup Charmet. **102** Syndication International Ltd. **103** Jon L. Abbott. **105** The New York Public Library, Oriental Division. **106** The Brooklyn Museum, 58.28.8/Photography by Scott Hyde. **107** Blauel/Gnamm: Artothek. **108** Reproduced from *The Doré Bible Illustrations*, published by Dover Publications, Inc., in 1974. **109** Robert Harding Picture Library. **110** Jean-Loup Charmet. **111** Boston Public Library. **112** Robert Harding Picture Library. **113** Marburg/Art Resource, N.Y. **114** The New York Public Library Picture Collection. **116** Art Resource, N.Y. **117** Andre Held, Ecublens. **118, 119, & 120** Scala/Art Resource, N.Y. **121** Culver Pictures. **123** The Granger Collection, New York. **124** Bibliothèque Nationale, Paris. **125** Michael Holford. **126** Bibliothèque Nationale, Paris. **127** The Mansell Collection Ltd.

EVERYDAY LIFE

128 By permission of the British Library. **131** The Ancient Art & Architecture Collection. **132** Zev Radovan. **133** *left* The Pierpont Morgan Library; *right* The Ancient Art & Architecture Collection. **134** David Harris. **135** Scala/Art Resource, N.Y. **136** Laura Lushington/Sonia Halliday Photographs. **137** The Jewish Museum/ Art Resource, N.Y. **138** Giraudon/Art Resource, N.Y. **139** Ara Güler, Istanbul. **140** Werner Forman Archive/Byzantine Museum, Athens. **141** *top* Richard T. Nowitz; *bottom* Giraudon/Art Resource, N.Y. **142** Scala/Art Resource, N.Y. **143** The Jewish Museum/Art Resource, N.Y. **144** *top* Österreichische Nationalbibliothek; *bottom* Israel Museum, Jerusalem/Photography by David Harris. **145** *left* Richard T. Nowitz; *right* © Arlene Gottfried 1987/Contact Press Images/Woodfin Camp & Associates. **146** The Pierpont Morgan Library. **147** Andre Held, Ecublens. **148** Guildhall Art Gallery, London/The Bridgeman Art Library. **149** Robert Harding Picture Library. **150** The New York Public Library Picture Collection. **151** *top* Zev Radovan; *bottom* Marburg/ Art Resource, N.Y. **153** Illustration by Gino d'Achille, reproduced by permission of Wm. Collins Sons & Co. Ltd. **154** Art Resource, N.Y. **156** Fabbrica del Vaticano/Madeline Grimoldi Archives. **157** The Granger Collection, New York. **158** Scala/Art Resource, N.Y. **159** The Ancient Art & Architecture Collection. **160** Württembergische Landesbibliothek. **162** Reproduced from *The Doré Bible Illustrations*, published by Dover Publications, Inc., in 1974. **163** Andre Held, Ecublens. **164** Sonia Halliday Photographs. **165** *top* Scala/Art Resource, N.Y.; *bottom* Borromeo/Art Resource, N.Y. **166** The Granger Collection, New York. **167** Robert Harding Picture Library. **168** Scala/Art Resource, N.Y. **169** The Granger Collection, New York. **170** *top* Michael Holford; *middle* Zev Radovan; *bottom* Scala/Art Resource, N.Y. **171** The Granger Collection, New York. **172** *top* Richard T. Nowitz; *bottom* SEF/Art Resource, N.Y. **173** *top* The Bridgeman Art Library; *bottom* The Granger Collection, New York. **174** The Granger Collection, New York. **175** *top* © 1975 Larry Mulvehill/Photo Researchers. **176** The Granger Collection, New York. **177** *left* Zev Radovan.

KINGS AND CONQUERORS

178 Jean-Loup Charmet. **180** Sonia Halliday Photographs. **181** Scala/Art Resource, N.Y. **182** The New York Public Library Picture Collection. **185** The New York Public Library Picture Collection. **186** The Metropolitan Museum of Art, gift of J. Pierpont Morgan, 1917. **187** Israel Museum, Jerusalem/Photography by David Harris. **188–189** The Bridgeman Art Library. **189** *top* The Cleveland Museum of Art, purchase from the J.H. Wade Fund. **190** Giraudon/Art Resource, N.Y. **191** Zev Radovan. **192** Sonia Halliday Photographs. **193** By permission of the British Library. **194** Michael Holford. **195** Laura Lushington/Sonia Halliday Photographs. **196** The Ancient Art & Architecture Collection. **197** St. Godehard Kirche, Hildesheim. **198** Scala/Art Resource, N.Y. **199** Zev Radovan. **200** Holman Bible Publishers. **201** *top* Bibliothèque Nationale, Paris; *middle* Peter A. Clayton. **202** Erich Lessing/Magnum. **204** Blauel/Gnamm: Artothek.

THE MIRACULOUS AND THE UNSEEN

206 The Pierpont Morgan Library. **209** *top* The Ancient Art & Architecture Collection; *bottom* Photographie Bulloz, Paris. **210** *top* The Granger Collection, New York; *bottom* Bodleian Library, Oxford. **211** Scala/Art Resource, N.Y. **212** The Granger Collection, New York. **215** Piccolomini Library, Siena/Madeline Grimoldi Archives, Photography by Lensini. **217** Parke-Davis Division of Warner-Lambert Company, Morris Plains, New Jersey. **219** Beniaminson/Art Resource, N.Y. **220** *top* Andre Held, Ecublens; *bottom* Giraudon/Art Resource, N.Y. **221** Bibliothèque Nationale, Paris. **222** Jean-Loup Charmet. **223** Sonia Halliday Photographs. **224 & 226** Scala/Art Resource, N.Y. **227** By permission of the British Library. **228** Agnew & Sons/The Bridgeman Art Library. **229** The Metropolitan Museum of Art, Rogers Fund, 1915 (15.106.2)/Photography by Geoffrey Clements. **230** The Ancient Art & Architecture Collection. **231** Staatsbibliothek Bamberg. **232** The Metropolitan Museum of Art, The Cloisters Collection, 1968 (68.174). **233** *left* National Gallery, London/The Bridgeman Art Library. **234** Scala/Art Resource, N.Y. **235** The Louvre, Paris/The Bridgeman Art Library.

THE MESSIAH

236 City of York Art Gallery/The Bridgeman Art Library. **238** Scala/Art Resource, N.Y. **239** Laura Lushington/Sonia Halliday Photographs. **240** The Ancient Art & Architecture Collection. **241** Birmingham City Museums and Art Gallery/The Bridgeman Art Library. **242** Copyright The Frick Collection, New York. **244** Erich Lessing/Magnum. **245** Collection of Mr. and Mrs. Owen N. Elliott. **247** *top* Galerie George, London/The Bridgeman Art Library; *bottom* Laura Lushington/Sonia Halliday Photographs. **248 & 250** Scala/Art Resource, N.Y. **251** *middle* Andre Held, Ecublens; *bottom* Sonia Halliday Photographs. **253** Musée des Beaux-Arts, Marseilles/The Bridgeman Art Library. **254** Erich Lessing/Magnum. **255** Scala/Art Resource, N.Y. **256** Giraudon/Art Resource, N.Y. **258 & 259** The Bridgeman Art Library. **260** Pierpont Morgan Library. **261** Painting by Louis S. Glanzman © National Geographic Society. **262** Laura Lushington/Sonia Halliday Photographs. **263** The Bridgeman Art Library. **265** Scala/Art Resource, N.Y. **266 & 267** Giraudon/Art Resource, N.Y.

THE BIBLE THROUGH THE AGES

268 The Pierpont Morgan Library. **270** Victoria & Albert Museum, London/Art Resource, N.Y. **271** From the Collections of the Israel Department of Antiquities/Photography by Erich Lessing. **272** Richard Nowitz. **273** The New York Public Library Picture Collection. **274** Zev Radovan. **275** From the Collections of the Israel Department of Antiquities/Photography by David Harris. **276** Bibliothèque Nationale, Paris. **277** Alte Pinakothek München/Joachim Blauel/Artothek. **279** The Jewish Museum/Art Resource, N.Y. **280** Scala/Art Resource, N.Y. **281** The British Museum, London/The Bridgeman Art Library. **282** Yale University Art Gallery, Gift of Samuel F.B. Morse, B.A. 1810. **284** The Pierpont Morgan Library. **285** The Granger Collection, New York. **286** David Rubinger/*Time* Magazine. **287** Birmingham City Museum and Art Gallery/The Bridgeman Art Library. **288** Scala/Art Resource, N.Y. **289** The Bridgeman Art Library/Art Resource, N.Y. **290** Scala/Art Resource, N.Y. **291** Courtesy of the Monastery of Gunda Gundie, Ethiopia. **292** *top* The Ancient Art & Architecture Collection; *bottom* The Granger Collection, New York. **293** The Granger Collection, New York. **294** *top* Ara Gülar; *bottom* Jean-Loup Charmet. **295** Coptic Museum, Cairo/Werner Forman Archive. **296** The Granger Collection, New York. **297** Micha Bar-Am/Magnum. **298** Bibliothèque Nationale, Paris/The Bridgeman Art Library. **299** The Granger Collection, New York. **300** Courtesy of the Bristol Museum & Art Gallery/The Bridgeman Art Library. **301** The Granger Collection, New York. **302** The Granger Collection, New York. **303** Culver Pictures. **305** Jean Leon Huens. **306** The Granger Collection, New York. **307** Scala/Art Resource, N.Y. **308** Photofest/Jagarts. **309** *top* AP/Wide World Photos; *bottom* Jim Veneman/Baptist Sunday School Board.

Efforts have been made to contact the holder of the copyright for each picture. In several cases these have been untraceable, for which we offer our apologies.

Index

A

Aaron, 38, 43, 80, 104, 170, 210
  descendants of, 62, 65, 130
  golden calf made by, 50
  miracles of, 102–103, 208
  priesthood of, 62, 64, 65, 213
  Promised Land denied to, 180
  rod of, 21, 103
Abba, 256
Abbreviations
  books of the Bible, 317
  books of the Apocrypha, 317
Abel, 23, 24, 25, 26, 61, 165
  Cain's murder of, 23, 24, 25, **27**
  offering to God by, 23, **24**
Abimelech, King, 47, 108, 226
Abner, 186
Abraham, 31, 32, 62, 138, 139, 165,
    220, 224, 240, **262,** 270
  Canaan journey of, **96,** 174
  conflict between God and, 43
  descendants of, 35, 54, 96, 98,
    130, 134, 136
  as first patriarch, 96, 97
  and God's command to sacrifice
    Isaac, **58,** 59, 61, 67,
    96, **97**
  God's communications with, 54,
    96, 98, 174, 226
  God's covenant with, 47, 96, 100,
    135, 215
  hospitality of, **154,** 155
  Lot and, 96–97
  as prophet, 108
  renaming of, 136
  Sarah buried by, 138, 176
  sons of, 98, **98,** 133, 134, 136, 137,
    142, 145
  visions of, 227
Absalom, 188–189
Achan, 158, **162**
Acts of the Apostles, 60, 76, 113,
    123, 124, 156, 255, 284, 286
  first Gentile conversion in, 125
A.D. *(Anno Domini),* 286
Adam, **19,** 26, 96, 130, 264, 307
  children of, 23, 24–25
  creation entrusted to, 16, 19
  creation of, 16, 17, **17,** 18
  eternal life given to, **139, 219**
  in expulsion from Garden of
    Eden, 19, 22–23, **23**
  name of, 18, 23

Adam *(contd.)*
  punishment of, 21–22
  sin of, 20–21
Adonai, 16, 39
Adonijah, 189
Adoption, 135
Adoram, 190
"Adulterer's Bible," 306
Adultery, 146, 147, 158, 162, 247
Agabus, 113
Agriculture. *See* Farming.
Ahab, King, 71, 109, 112, 133, 160,
    192, 211, 221
Ahasuerus, King, 88, 169
Ahaz, King, 58, 113, **176,** 177
Ahaziah, King, 110, 133, 192
Ai, 215
Alaric, King, 295
Alchemist, The (Jonson), 252
Aldhelm, Bishop, 302
Aleppo Codex, 292
Alexander Janneus, King, 200
Alexander the Great, 201, 243
Alexandria, 195
  library in, 293, **293, 294**
Alfred the Great, King, 302, **302**
Allen, William Cardinal, 304
Altars, 55, 61, **61,** 64, **72,** 81
  origin of, 60
  Succoth and, 88
  types of, 60, 61
Amalekites, 151
Ammonites, 97, 151, 187
Amnon, 188
Amorites, 151, 215
Amos, Book of, 59, 108, 122, 165
Ananias, **124**
Anath, 71
Andrew, 118, **118,** 121, 122, **164**
Angelico, Fra, **119, 135, 220, 240**
Angels, 42, 43, **154,** 155, 221,
    222, 230
Animals
  clean vs. unclean, 29
  eating of, 16, 29, 41
  man as caretaker of, 16, 18, 19
  on Noah's ark, 28–29, **32**
  sacrifice of, 29, 41, 56, 57, **57,**
    60, 61, 64, 65, 70, 74, 88, 255
  talking, 215
Anna (Hannah), 289
Anna (prophetess), 239
Annas, 255
Antichrist, 234, **234**
Antigonus II, King, 153
Antiochus III, King, 201
Antiochus IV Epiphanes, 200, **200,**
    201, **201**

Antipater the Idumean, 202, 203
Apocalypse, 225
  See also Revelation, Book of.
Apocrypha (Deuterocanonical
    books), 277, 288, 289, 290,
    290, 293, 317
Apollonius, 200
Apostles, 87, 118–123, 231, 257
  derivation of, 121
  Gamaliel's saving of, 163
  Jesus' resurrection and, 122
  as possible revolutionaries,
    119–120
  temple attended by, 60
  transfiguration and, 250, **250**
  See also specific Apostles.
Appian Way, **175**
Aquila, 76
Arab conquest of Jerusalem, 71
Aramaean tribes, 187–188
Aramaic language, 242–243, 256,
    271–272, 277, 294–295
Ararat, mountains of, 30, 33
Archelaus, 205
Arch of Titus, **91**
Aristobulus I, King, 200
Aristobulus II, King, 202
Ark, 28, 294
Ark, Noah's. *See* Noah's ark.
Ark of the covenant, 28, 46, 52–53,
    52, 53, 288
  in battle, 150
  chamber for, 66, 72
  cherubim of, 72
  fate of, 53
  in Jerusalem, 52, 53, 67, **173,** 187,
    188
  in Jordan crossing, 181–182
  mercy seat of, 52, 89
Army. *See* War and military.
Art, 296, 308
Artaxerxes I, 198, 199
Asa, King, 217
"Ascension, The" (Rembrandt), **265**
Asclepius, 217, **217**
Asher, 101
Assyria, 42, 101, 193, 197
  Aramaeans and, 187, 188
  Israel conquered by, 43, 188, 193,
    194, 270, 289
Athanasius, 290
Athens, 55
Athletics, 172–173
Augustus, Emperor (Octavian),
    203–204, 238
Awan, 25
Azura, 25

*Page numbers in **bold** type refer to illustrations and captions.*

B

Baal, 71, **71, 108,** 109, 111, 192, 208, 211
Babel, 34
  tower of, 34–35, **34, 35,** 38
Babies, 132
  buried in city walls, 134–135
  naming of, 136
  See also Children.
Babylon, 231
Babylonia, 72, 193, 270–271
  creation story of, 14
  flood story of, 31, **31**
  Solomon's temple destroyed by, 70
Babylonian exile, 65, 68, 71, 75, 80, 101, 123, 124, 130, 177, 194–197, **197,** 199, 208, 266, 271, 282
  history altered by, 196
  of Judah vs. that of northern Israel, 194
  return to Judah after, 230
  Satan and, 222
  scribes in, 149
Balaam, **109,** 215, 226
Baptism, 73, 116, 117, 125, 225
Barabbas, 162, 257
Bar Kochba revolt, **70,** 197, 267
Bar Mitzvah, **274**
Barnabas, Joseph, 76, 121
Barrenness. *See* Childlessness.
Barsabbas Justus, 124
Bartholomew, 121
Bartimaeus, 250
Baruch, **282,** 283, 285
Baths, ritual, 73
Bathsheba, 173, 186, 189
B.C. (Before Christ), 286
B.C.E. (Before the Common Era), 286
Beatitudes, 248, 249
Bede, the Venerable, 302
Behemoth, **299**
Belshazzar, King, 227
Benjamin, 100, 101, 132, 230
Berosus, 33
Bestiality, 162
Beth Alpha, synagogue at, **80**
Bethel, 54, **55,** 188, 190
Bethlehem, Star of, **239,** 240
Beth-shemesh, 53
Bethuel, 142
Beth Zur, 85
Betrothal, 145–146

Bible
  abbreviations of books of, 317
  ancient versions of, 292–295
  Authorized Version of, 304
  authors of, 282–285
  books without mention of God in, 288–289
  canon of, 288–291
  Catholic, 276–277, 278–280, 290–291, 303
  chapters and verses of, 280–281
  Christian, 276, 281
  Christian vs. Jewish, 277
  conversational expressions from, 307
  creative works inspired by, 308
  dating of events in, 286
  Dead Sea Scrolls and, 275
  earliest complete copies of, 292–293
  earliest written parts of, 277–278
  early translations of, 295
  Eastern Orthodox, 276, 290–291
  English, 302–307
  first English translation of, 302–303
  first forms of, 274
  first modern-language translations of, 298–299
  Gutenberg, 295, 301, **301**
  Hebrew, 276, 277, 281, 288, 290, 292
  historical periods covered by, 270–271
  history of, 268–309
  for the illiterate, 297–298
  illustrated, 296–297
  Jesus' use of, 294
  King James Version of, 303, 304–306, 308
  Latin Vulgate translation of, **292,** 295, 298, 299, 303, 304
  lost books of, 281
  Luther and, 299
  in missionary work, 299–300
  modern versions of, 308–309
  monks and, 297
  most recent writings in, 278
  most used version of, 308–309
  oldest English editions of, 306–307
  oldest manuscripts of, 273
  organization of, 276–281
  original language of, 271–272

Bible *(contd.)*
  origins of, 270–275
  "people of the Book" and, 274
  poetry in, 285
  Protestant, 276–277, 289, 290–291, 303
  Rosetta Stone and, 286
  Shakespeare and, 305
  spreading the Word through, 296–301
  swearing on, 309
  Synoptic Gospels in, 278
  Talmud and, 277
  translations of, 295, 298–299, 300
  versions of, 273–274, 308
  wisdom books in, 278–280
  writing of, 271
  See also New Testament; Old Testament.
Bible moralisée, 298
Bible societies, 300
Bilhah, 101, 135
Birth, 132–137
  agony of, 132
  miraculous, 132–134
Bishops' Bible, 303
Bitter herbs, **169**
Blake, William, **26,** 291
Blasphemy, 45–46, 158, 161
  Jesus charged with, 46, 162, 246, 256–257
Blessings, 249
Blood vengeance, custom of, 161
Boaz, 143–144, **144,** 166
Book of Durrow, 296
Book of hours, **260,** 296–297
Book of Kells, **285,** 296, **302**
Books of Moses, 154
Booths, Feast of. *See* Succoth.
Botticelli, Sandro, **256, 290**
Bread, 168
  at Last Supper, 254–255
  unleavened, 86
Breastpiece of judgment, 63, **63, 64, 64**
"Breeches Bible," 307
Brides, **145**
Brown, Ford Madox, **112**
Bubonic plague, 52, 140
"Bug Bible," 306
Burial, 134, 138, 139, 141
Burning, death by, 162
Burning bush, **38,** 39, 42, 73, 182, 212–13
Burnt offerings (holocausts), 56, 57, 58, 65, 70, 106, 132, 213, 252
Byron, George Gordon, Lord, 291

C

*Page numbers in **bold** type refer to illustrations and captions.*

D

Dagon, 52, 115
Damasus, Pope, 295
Dan, 101, 190
Daniel, 68
  dreams interpreted by, 227, 228–229
  visions of, 226, 228, **228, 281**
Daniel, Book of, 277, 278
  God described in, 40
Darius I, King, 198
Dates, calendar, 176, 286
David, King, 63, 72, 106, 122, 137, 140, 141, 144, 145, 150, 155, 165, **173,** 186, 189, 199, **266**
  ark of the covenant and, 52, **53, 173**
  as author of Psalms, 282–283
  Bathsheba and, 173, 186
  empire built by, 187–188, 189
  God's covenant with, 47, 188
  Goliath and, 136, 152, **153,** 216
  Jerusalem taken by, 187
  Jesus descended from, 130, **131,** 266
  Jonathan and, 47
  Levite choirs organized by, 74
  lyre played by, 172, **172,** 184, **284**
  as "man after God's own heart," 186
  priests appointed by, 62
  Samuel and, **186**
  Saul and, 184, **185,** 186, 281
  sins of, 186
  Solomon's succession of, 188–189
  Solomon's temple and, 67
  wives of, 143
Davidic dynasty, 188, 189, 190, 194, 266
Day of Atonement (Yom Kippur), 52, 66, 72, 81, 88, 91
  scapegoat ritual and, 89–90
Day of judgment, 224, 232, 233
Day of Lights, 93
Day of the Lord, 232
Dead body, touching of, 140
Dead Sea Scrolls, 79, 272, **272,** 273, 275, **275,** 292
Death, 138–141, 219, 232
  life after, 262
  mourning rituals and, 138
  principal causes of, 139–140
  Sheol and, 139, 221, 262, 291

Death *(contd.)*
  sin as responsible for, 225
Death penalty. *See* Execution.
Deborah, 114, **114,** 136
Debts, 160
Decalogue, 49
Decapolis, 205, 244
Delilah, 115
Demons, 222–223, 225, **234**
  Jesus' casting out of, 223, 244, 266, 279
Deportation, 197. *See also* Babylonian exile; Diaspora.
Deuterocanonical books. *See* Apocrypha.
Deuteronomy, Book of, 62, 84, 101, 108–109, 112, 154, 176, 183, 273, 278, 288
Diaspora, 123, 124, 195, 196, 197
Diet, 168–169
  Jewish laws on, 16, 76, 127, 157, 169, 201
Dillon, Frederick, **102**
Dinah, 99
Diodorus Siculus, 105
Disciples, 43, 77, 118 123, 257, 265, 279
  derivation of, 121
  faith of, 249
  gathering of, 118
  hospitality toward, 155
  importance of, 118
  Jesus' farewell to, 45
  Jesus' resurrection witnessed by, 122
  at Last Supper, **255**
  of Paul, 127
  ritual purity and, 79
  Second Coming announced to, 234
  secrecy of ministry and, 245
  See also specific disciples.
Disease, 139, 216, 217
Divination, 63, 226, 230, **230**
Divorce, 146–147
Dome of the Rock, 71
Donkey, talking, 215
Dorcas, 219
Doré, Gustave, **108, 162, 259**
Douay Bible, 303
Douay-Rheims Bible, 304
Dove, 30–31
  great flood and, 30, **30**
  as Holy Spirit, 31, **45**
Dragon, 17, 21
Dreams and visions, 42, 226–229, 230
  difference between, 226

Dreams and visions *(contd.)*
  interpretation of, 227–228, 239
  recipients of, 226
Duccio di Buoninsegna, **242**
Dulac, Edmund, **182**
Dyeing of fabric, 170

E

Earth, man's relationship to, 18
Easter, 90, 92
Eastern Orthodox Bible, 276, 290–291
Eber, 32
Ecclesiastes, Book of, 29, 46, 139, 278
Ecclesiasticus (Sirach), 276, 280
Eden. *See* Garden of Eden.
Edomites, 151, 187
Education, 148–149
Egypt, **107,** 187, 201, 240
  Exodus from. *See* Exodus.
  Holy Family's flight to, **174, 175,** 229, 240
  Israelites enslaved in, 103–104, 105, 109, 270
Egyptian Book of the Dead, 296
Egyptian monuments, **105**
El, 39, 71
Eleazar, 53, 62
Eli, 45, 132, **133,** 136
Elijah, 26, 42, 51, 61, 71, 77, 109, **110,** 111, **112,** 136, **210,** 213
  Elisha's succession to, 110
  miracles of, 110, 208, 210–211, 219
  in transfiguration, 250, **250, 264**
Elimelech, 144
Elisha, 109, **110,** 160, **210**
  Elijah succeeded by, 110
  miracles of, 110, 112, 208, 210–211, 212, 213, 216, 219
Elizabeth, 134, 242
Elizabeth I, Queen of England, 303, **303,** 304
Elkanah, 132
Embalming, 138–139
Emmanuel, 113
England, 302, 303
Enoch, 25–26, 28, **291**
Enoch, Book of, 291
Enosh, 44
Enuma elish, 14
Ephesians, Paul's Letter to, 32, 75, 279, 289

*Page numbers in **bold** type refer to illustrations and captions.*

*Page numbers in **bold** type refer to illustrations and captions.*

K

*Page numbers in **bold** type refer to illustrations and captions.*

Q

R

*Page numbers in **bold** type refer to illustrations and captions.*

*Page numbers in **bold** type refer to illustrations and captions.*